Capital Budgeting

This book explains the financial appraisal of capital budgeting projects. The coverage extends from the development of basic concepts, principles and techniques to the application of them in increasingly complex and real-world situations. Identification and estimation (including forecasting) of cash flows, project appraisal formulae and the application of net present value (NPV), internal rate of return (IRR) and other project evaluation criteria are illustrated with a variety of calculation examples. Risk analysis is extensively covered by the use of the risk-adjusted discount rate, the certainty equivalent, sensitivity analysis, simulation and Monte Carlo analysis.

The NPV and IRR models are further applied to forestry, property and international investments. Resource constraints are introduced in capital budgeting decisions with a variety of worked examples using the linear programming technique.

All calculations are extensively supported by Excel workbooks on the Web, and each chapter is well reviewed by end-of-chapter questions.

DON DAYANANDA is Senior Lecturer in the School of Commerce at Central Queensland University.

RICHARD IRONS is Lecturer in the School of Commerce at Central Queensland University.

STEVE HARRISON is Associate Professor in the School of Economics at the University of Queensland.

JOHN HERBOHN is Senior Lecturer in the School of Natural and Rural Systems Management at the University of Queensland.

PATRICK ROWLAND is Senior Lecturer in the Department of Property Studies at Curtin University of Technology.

Capital Budgeting

Financial Appraisal of Investment Projects

Don Dayananda,

Richard Irons, Steve Harrison,

John Herbohn and Patrick Rowland

CAMBRIDGE
UNIVERSITY PRESS

CAMBRIDGE UNIVERSITY PRESS
Cambridge, New York, Melbourne, Madrid, Cape Town, Singapore, São Paulo

Cambridge University Press
The Edinburgh Building, Cambridge CB2 8RU, UK

Published in the United States of America by Cambridge University Press, New York

www.cambridge.org
Information on this title: www.cambridge.org/9780521817820

First published 2002

A catalogue record for this publication is available from the British Library

Library of Congress Cataloguing in Publication data

Capital budgeting: financial appraisal of investment projects / Don Dayananda ... [et al.].
    p.   cm.
Includes bibliographical references and index.
ISBN 0 521 81782 X (hb) – ISBN 0 521 52098 3 (pb)
1. Capital budget. 2. Capital investments. I. Dayananda, Don.
HG4028.C4 C346 2002
658.15′242 – dc21   2002019249

ISBN 978-0-521-81782-0 hardback
ISBN 978-0-521-52098-0 paperback

Transferred to digital printing 2008

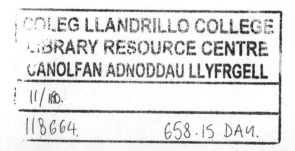

Contents

Figures

Tables

Preface

Capital budgeting is primarily concerned with how a firm makes decisions on *sizable* investments in *long-lived* projects to achieve the firm's overall goal. This is the decision area of financial management that establishes criteria for investing resources in *long-term* real assets.

Investment decisions (on *sizable long-term* projects) today will determine the firm's strategic position many years hence, and fix the future course of the firm. These investments will have a considerable impact on the firm's future cash flows and the risk associated with those cash flows. Capital budgeting decisions have a long-range impact on the firm's performance and they are critical to the firm's success or failure.

One of the most crucial and complex stages in the capital budgeting decision process is the financial or economic evaluation of the investment proposals. This 'project analysis' is the focus of this book. Project analysis usually involves the identification of relevant cash flows, their forecasting, risk analysis, and the application of project evaluation concepts, techniques and criteria to assess whether the proposed projects are likely to add value to the firm. When the project choice is subject to resource constraints, mathematical programming techniques such as linear programming are employed to select the feasible optimal combination of projects.

Motivation for the book

The writing of this book was motivated by the lack of a suitable capital budgeting textbook with the following desirable features and coverage:

- Analysis and applications based on sound conceptual and theoretical foundations with pedagogical tools appropriate for capital budgeting
- Cash flow forecasting
- Project choice under resource constraints
- Comprehensive illustrations of concepts, methods and approaches for project analysis under uncertainty (or risk), with applications to different industries
- Preparing the reader for actual project analysis in the real world which involves voluminous, tedious, complex and repetitive computations and relies heavily on computer packages.

The book bridges this gap in the market by including these features and areas of coverage.

Distinctive features and areas of coverage

Distinctive features include:

- Practical approach with applications based on sound and appropriate concepts and theory
- Concepts, techniques and applications are illustrated by worked examples, tables and charts
- Worked examples are extensively supported with live Excel workbooks easily accessible on the Web
- Use of pedagogical tools – such as Excel spreadsheet calculations accessible on the World Wide Web – to help the users of the book grasp important and difficult concepts and calculations, and make them clear, useful, attractive and sometimes fun by the use of technology (computer packages)
- Complex and difficult topics are explained intuitively with tableaux rather than in terms of algebra.

Areas of coverage include:

- Quantitative and qualitative techniques for cash flow forecasting
- Application of mathematical programming techniques such as linear programming for decision support when the project choice is subject to resource constraints
- Sensitivity and break-even analysis and simulation – with applications to various industries such as the computer, airline, forestry and property industries, each of which has its unique characteristics
- As well as the standard industrial investment examples, the exotic and environmentally sensitive area of forestry investment and the increasingly demanding area of property investment are analysed with examples and case studies. The intricacies of investment across international borders are also discussed.

All of this material is reinforced with some challenging end-of-chapter review questions. Solutions to all the calculation questions are fully worked on Excel spreadsheets and are available on the Web.

Organization of the book

This book follows a natural progression from the development of basic concepts, principles and techniques to the application of them in increasingly complex and real-world situations. Identification and estimation of cash flows are important initial steps in project analysis and are dealt with in Chapters 2 to 4. Once the cash flows have been estimated, investment proposals are subjected to project evaluation techniques. The application of these techniques involves financial mathematics (Chapter 5). Chapter 6 uses the cash flow concepts and the formulae (from Chapters 2 and 5) to evaluate case study projects using several project evaluation criteria such as net present value (NPV), internal rate of return (IRR) and payback period, and demonstrates the versatility of the NPV criterion. This basic model is then expanded to deal with risk (or uncertainty of cash flows) through the use of the risk-adjusted discount rate and certainty equivalent methods (Chapter 7), sensitivity and break-even analyses (Chapter 8) and risk simulation methods (Chapter 9). These concepts and methods are then applied in a case study involving the evaluation of a forestry investment in Chapter 10. Resource constraints on the capital budgeting decision are considered in Chapters 11 and 12 by introducing the basics of linear programming (LP), applying the LP technique for selection of the optimal project portfolios and presenting extensions to the LP technique which make the approach more versatile. A number of special topics in capital budgeting are covered towards the end of the book. They include forestry investment analysis (Chapter 13), property investment analysis (Chapters 14 and 15) and evaluation of international investments (Chapter 16).

Joint authorship

The positive side of joint authorship has been the rich interplay of ideas and lively debate on both conceptual and applied matters. The book has certainly benefited from this spirited interplay of ideas. Keeping five academics working, and working towards a common goal, an integrated exposition, has been a challenging management task. We have all benefited from the discipline of a common goal and pressing deadlines.

Intended audience

We have endeavoured in this text to make the capital budgeting concepts, theory, techniques and applications accessible to the interested reader, and trust that the reader will garner a better understanding of this important topic from our treatment. This book should suit both advanced undergraduate and postgraduate students, investment practitioners, financial modellers and practising managers. Although the book relies on material that is covered in corporate finance, economics, accounting and statistics courses, it is self-contained in that prior knowledge of those areas, while useful, is not essential.

Teaching and learning aids

Excel workbooks referred to in the text are accessible on the Web (at http://publishing. cambridge.org/resources/052181782x/). They provide details relating to calculations and the student can use the examples provided to practise various computations. Estimating regression equations, performing sensitivity and break-even analyses, conducting simulation experiments and solving linear programming problems are all done using Excel and they are all provided on the Web for the readers of this book to experiment with.

An *Instructor's Manual* includes answers to end-of-chapter review questions.

Acknowledgements

We have benefited from the encouragement and support of colleagues, family and friends. We particularly acknowledge the support given by Kathy Ramm, Head of the School of Commerce, Central Queensland University. We are also grateful to the talented staff at Cambridge University Press, especially Ashwin Rattan (Commissioning Editor, Economics and Finance), Chris Harrison (Publishing Director, Humanities and Social Sciences), Robert Whitelock (Senior Copy-Editorial Controller, Humanities and Social Sciences), Chris Doubleday (commissioned copy-editor for this book), Karl Howe (Production Controller) and Deirdre Gyenes (Design Controller).

A final word

We have significant combined research, teaching and industry experience behind us, and trust that this understanding of the learning process shines through in the text. Corporate financial management is not a process to be lightly embarked upon, but we hope your journey can be made more rewarding by the way in which this book has been presented.

1 Capital budgeting: an overview

Financial management is largely concerned with *financing*, *dividend* and *investment* decisions of the firm with some overall goal in mind. Corporate finance theory has developed around a goal of maximizing the market value of the firm to its shareholders. This is also known as shareholder wealth maximization. Although various objectives or goals are possible in the field of finance, the most widely accepted objective for the firm is to maximize the value of the firm to its owners.

Financing decisions deal with the firm's optimal capital structure in terms of debt and equity. Dividend decisions relate to the form in which returns generated by the firm are passed on to equity-holders. Investment decisions deal with the way funds raised in financial markets are employed in productive activities to achieve the firm's overall goal; in other words, how much should be invested and what assets should be invested in. Throughout this book it is assumed that the objective of the investment or capital budgeting decision is to maximize the market value of the firm to its shareholders. The relationship between the firm's overall goal, financial management and capital budgeting is depicted in Figure 1.1. This self-explanatory chart helps the reader to easily visualize and retain a picture of the capital budgeting function within the broader perspective of corporate finance.

Funds are invested in both short-term and long-term assets. Capital budgeting is primarily concerned with *sizable* investments in *long-term* assets. These assets may be tangible items such as property, plant or equipment or intangible ones such as new technology, patents or trademarks. Investments in processes such as research, design, development and testing – through which new technology and new products are created – may also be viewed as investments in intangible assets.

Irrespective of whether the investments are in tangible or intangible assets, a capital investment project can be distinguished from recurrent expenditures by two features. One is that such projects are significantly *large*. The other is that they are generally *long-lived* projects with their benefits or cash flows spreading over many years.

Sizable, long-term investments in tangible or intangible assets have long-term consequences. An investment today will determine the firm's strategic position many years hence. These investments also have a considerable impact on the organization's future cash flows and the risk associated with those cash flows. Capital budgeting decisions thus have a long-range impact on the firm's performance and they are critical to the firm's success or failure.

1

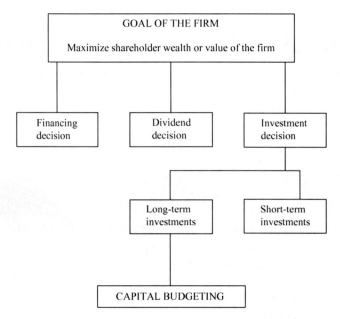

Figure 1.1.   Corporate goal, financial management and capital budgeting.

As such, capital budgeting decisions have a major effect on the value of the firm and its shareholder wealth. This book deals with capital budgeting decisions.

This chapter defines the shareholder wealth maximization goal, defines and distinguishes three types of investment project on the basis of how they influence the investment decision process, discusses the capital budgeting process and identifies one of the most crucial and complex stages in the process, namely, the financial appraisal of proposed investment projects. This is also known as economic or financial analysis of the project or simply as 'project analysis'. This financial analysis is the focus of this book.

Actual project analysis in the real world involves voluminous, tedious, complex and repetitive calculations and relies heavily on computer spreadsheet packages to handle these evaluations. Throughout this book, Excel spreadsheets are used to facilitate and supplement various calculation examples cited. These calculations are provided in workbooks on the Cambridge University Press website. Those workbooks are identified at the relevant places in the text.

Study objectives

After studying this chapter the reader should be able to:

* define the capital budgeting decision within the broader perspective of financial management
* describe how the net present value contributes to increasing shareholder wealth
* classify investment projects on the basis of how they influence the investment decision process

- sketch out a broad overview of the capital budgeting process
- identify the financial appraisal of projects as one of the critically important and complex stages in the capital budgeting process
- appreciate the importance of using computer spreadsheet packages such as Excel for capital budgeting computations
- gain a broad overview of how the material in this book is organized.

Shareholder wealth maximization and net present value

The efficiency of financial management is judged by the success in achieving the firm's goal. The shareholder wealth maximization goal states that management should endeavour to maximize the net present (or current) value of the expected future cash flows to the shareholders of the firm. *Net present value* refers to the discounted *sum* of the expected net cash flows. Some of the cash flows, such as capital outlays, are cash outflows, while some, such as cash proceeds from sales, are cash inflows. Net cash flows are obtained by subtracting a given period's cash outflows from that period's cash inflows. The *discount rate* takes into account the *timing* and *risk* of the future cash flows that are available from an investment. The longer it takes to receive a cash flow, the lower the value investors place on that cash flow now. The greater the risk associated with receiving a future cash flow, the lower the value investors place on that cash flow.

The shareholder wealth maximization goal, thus, reflects the *magnitude, timing* and *risk* associated with the cash flows expected to be received in the future by shareholders. In terms of the firm's objective, shareholder wealth maximization has been emphasized because this book has a corporate focus.

For a simplified case where there is only one capital outlay which occurs at the beginning of the first year of the project, the net present value (NPV) is calculated by subtracting this capital outlay from the present value of the annual net operating cash flows (and the net terminal cash flows). If the capital outlay occurs only at the beginning of the first year of the project then it is already a present value and it is not necessary to discount it any further. The formula for the NPV in such a simplified situation is:

$$NPV = \sum_{t=1}^{n} \frac{C_t}{(1+r)^t} - CO$$

where CO is the capital outlay at the beginning of year one (or where $t = 0$), r is the discount rate and C_t is the net cash flow at end of year t.

For example, suppose project Alpha requires an initial capital outlay of \$900 and will have net cash inflows of \$300, \$400 and \$600 at the end of years 1, 2 and 3, respectively. The discount rate is 8% per annum. The net present value is:

$$NPV = \frac{300}{(1.08)} + \frac{400}{(1.08)^2} + \frac{600}{(1.08)^3} - 900 = 197.01$$

Project Alpha will add \$197.01 to the firm's value.

Classification of investment projects

Investment projects can be classified into three categories on the basis of how they influence the investment decision process: independent projects, mutually exclusive projects and contingent projects.

An *independent project* is one the acceptance or rejection of which does not directly eliminate other projects from consideration or affect the likelihood of their selection. For example, management may want to introduce a new product line and at the same time may want to replace a machine which is currently producing a different product. These two projects can be considered independently of each other if there are sufficient resources to adopt both, provided they meet the firm's investment criteria. These projects can be evaluated independently and a decision made to accept or reject them depending upon whether they add value to the firm.

Two or more projects that cannot be pursued simultaneously are called *mutually exclusive projects* – the acceptance of one prevents the acceptance of the alternative proposal. Therefore, mutually exclusive projects involve 'either-or' decisions – alternative proposals cannot be pursued simultaneously. For example, a firm may own a block of land which is large enough to establish a shoe manufacturing business or a steel fabrication plant. If shoe manufacturing is chosen the alternative of steel fabrication is eliminated. A car manufacturing company can locate its manufacturing complex in Sydney, Brisbane or Adelaide. If it chooses Adelaide, the alternatives of Sydney and Brisbane are precluded.

Mutually exclusive projects can be evaluated separately to select the one which yields the highest net present value to the firm. The early identification of mutually exclusive alternatives is crucial for a logical screening of investments. Otherwise, a lot of hard work and resources can be wasted if two divisions independently investigate, develop and initiate projects which are later recognized to be mutually exclusive.

A *contingent project* is one the acceptance or rejection of which is dependent on the decision to accept or reject one or more other projects. Contingent projects may be complementary or substitutes. For example, the decision to start a pharmacy may be contingent upon a decision to establish a doctors' surgery in an adjacent building. In this case the projects are complementary to each other. The cash flows of the pharmacy will be enhanced by the existence of a nearby surgery and conversely the cash flows of the surgery will be enhanced by the existence of a nearby pharmacy.

In contrast, substitute projects are ones where the degree of success (or even the success or failure) of one project is increased by the decision to reject the other project. For example, market research indicates demand sufficient to justify two restaurants in a shopping complex and the firm is considering one Chinese and one Thai restaurant. Customers visiting this shopping complex seem to treat Chinese and Thai food as close substitutes and have a slight preference for Thai food over Chinese. Consequently, if the firm establishes both restaurants, the Chinese restaurant's cash flows are likely to be adversely affected. This may result in negative net present value for the Chinese restaurant. In this situation, the success of the Chinese restaurant project will depend on the decision to reject the Thai restaurant proposal. Since they are close substitutes, the rejection of one will definitely boost the cash flows of the other. Contingent

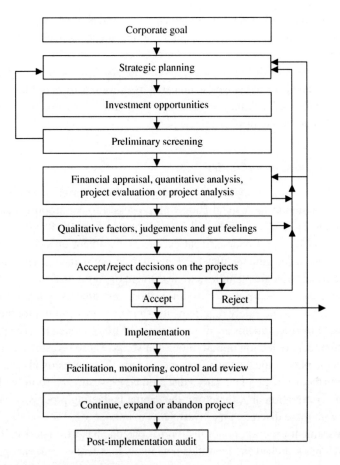

Figure 1.2. The capital budgeting process.

projects should be analysed by taking into account the cash flow interactions of all the projects.

The capital budgeting process

Capital budgeting is a multi-faceted activity. There are several sequential stages in the process. For typical investment proposals of a large corporation, the distinctive stages in the capital budgeting process are depicted, in the form of a highly simplified flow chart, in Figure 1.2.

Strategic planning

A strategic plan is the grand design of the firm and clearly identifies the business the firm is in and where it intends to position itself in the future. Strategic planning translates the firm's corporate goal into specific policies and directions, sets priorities, specifies the structural, strategic and tactical areas of business development, and guides the planning process in the pursuit of solid objectives. A firm's vision and mission is encapsulated in its strategic planning framework.

There are feedback loops at different stages, and the feedback to 'strategic planning' at the project evaluation and decision stages – indicated by upward arrows in Figure 1.2 – is critically important. This feedback may suggest changes to the future direction of the firm which may cause changes to the firm's strategic plan.

Identification of investment opportunities

The identification of investment opportunities and generation of investment project proposals is an important step in the capital budgeting process. Project proposals cannot be generated in isolation. They have to fit in with a firm's corporate goals, its vision, mission and long-term strategic plan. Of course, if an excellent investment opportunity presents itself the corporate vision and strategy may be changed to accommodate it. Thus, there is a two-way traffic between strategic planning and investment opportunities.

Some investments are mandatory – for instance, those investments required to satisfy particular regulatory, health and safety requirements – and they are essential for the firm to remain in business. Other investments are discretionary and are generated by growth opportunities, competition, cost reduction opportunities and so on. These investments normally represent the strategic plan of the business firm and, in turn, these investments can set new directions for the firm's strategic plan. These discretionary investments form the basis of the business of the corporation and, therefore, the capital budgeting process is viewed in this book mainly with these discretionary investments in mind.

A profitable investment proposal is not just born; someone has to suggest it. The firm should ensure that it has searched and identified potentially lucrative investment opportunities and proposals, because the remainder of the capital budgeting process can only assure that the best of the proposed investments are evaluated, selected and implemented. There should be a mechanism such that investment suggestions coming from inside the firm, such as from its employees, or from outside the firm, such as from advisors to the firm, are 'listened to' by management.

Some firms have research and development (R&D) divisions constantly searching for and researching into new products, services and processes and identifying attractive investment opportunities. Sometimes, excellent investment suggestions come through informal processes such as employee chats in a staff room or corridor.

Preliminary screening of projects

Generally, in any organization, there will be many potential investment proposals generated. Obviously, they cannot all go through the rigorous project analysis process. Therefore, the identified investment opportunities have to be subjected to a preliminary screening process by management to isolate the marginal and unsound proposals, because it is not worth spending resources to thoroughly evaluate such proposals. The preliminary screening may involve some preliminary quantitative analysis and judgements based on intuitive feelings and experience.

Financial appraisal of projects

Projects which pass through the preliminary screening phase become candidates for rigorous financial appraisal to ascertain if they would add value to the firm. This stage is also called quantitative analysis, economic and financial appraisal, project evaluation, or simply project analysis.

This project analysis may predict the expected future cash flows of the project, analyse the risk associated with those cash flows, develop alternative cash flow forecasts, examine the sensitivity of the results to possible changes in the predicted cash flows, subject the cash flows to simulation and prepare alternative estimates of the project's net present value.

Thus, the project analysis can involve the application of forecasting techniques, project evaluation techniques, risk analysis and mathematical programming techniques such as linear programming. While the basic concepts, principles and techniques of project evaluation are the same for different projects, their application to particular types of projects requires special knowledge and expertise. For example, asset expansion projects, asset replacement projects, forestry investments, property investments and international investments have their own special features and peculiarities.

Financial appraisal will provide the estimated addition to the firm's value in terms of the projects' net present values. If the projects identified within the current strategic framework of the firm repeatedly produce negative NPVs in the analysis stage, these results send a message to the management to review its strategic plan. Thus, the feedback from project analysis to strategic planning plays an important role in the overall capital budgeting process.

The results of the quantitative project analyses heavily influence the project selection or investment decisions. These decisions clearly affect the success or failure of the firm and its future direction. Therefore, project analysis is critically important for the firm. This book focuses on this complex analytical stage of the capital budgeting process, that is, financial appraisal of projects (or simply, project analysis).

Qualitative factors in project evaluation

When a project passes through the quantitative analysis test, it has to be further evaluated taking into consideration qualitative factors. Qualitative factors are those which will have an impact on the project, but which are virtually impossible to evaluate accurately in monetary terms. They are factors such as:

• the societal impact of an increase or decrease in employee numbers
• the environmental impact of the project
• possible positive or negative governmental political attitudes towards the project
• the strategic consequences of consumption of scarce raw materials
• positive or negative relationships with labour unions about the project

- possible legal difficulties with respect to the use of patents, copyrights and trade or brand names
- impact on the firm's image if the project is socially questionable.

Some of the items in the above list affect the value of the firm, and some not. The firm can address these issues during project analysis, by means of discussion and consultation with the various parties, but these processes will be lengthy, and their outcomes often unpredictable. It will require considerable management experience and judgemental skill to incorporate the outcomes of these processes into the project analysis.

Management may be able to obtain a feel for the impact of some of these issues, by estimating notional monetary costs or benefits to the project, and incorporating those values into the appropriate cash flows. Only some of the items will affect the project benefits; most are externalities. In some cases, however, those qualitative factors which affect the project benefits may have such a negative bearing on the project that an otherwise viable project will have to be abandoned.

The accept/reject decision

NPV results from the quantitative analysis combined with qualitative factors form the basis of the decision support information. The analyst relays this information to management with appropriate recommendations. Management considers this information and other relevant prior knowledge using their routine information sources, experience, expertise, 'gut feeling' and, of course, judgement to make a major decision – to accept or reject the proposed investment project.

Project implementation and monitoring

Once investment projects have passed through the decision stage they then must be implemented by management. During this implementation phase various divisions of the firm are likely to be involved. An integral part of project implementation is the constant monitoring of project progress with a view to identifying potential bottlenecks thus allowing early intervention. Deviations from the estimated cash flows need to be monitored on a regular basis with a view to taking corrective actions when needed.

Post-implementation audit

Post-implementation audit does not relate to the current decision support process of the project; it deals with a post-mortem of the performance of already implemented projects. An evaluation of the performance of past decisions, however, can contribute greatly to the improvement of current investment decision-making by analysing the past 'rights' and 'wrongs'.

The post-implementation audit can provide useful feedback to project appraisal or strategy formulation. For example, *ex post* assessment of the strengths (or accuracies) and weaknesses (or inaccuracies) of cash flow forecasting of past projects can indicate the level of confidence (or otherwise) that can be attached to cash flow forecasting of current invest-ment projects. If projects undertaken in the past within the framework of the firm's current strategic plan do not prove to be as lucrative as predicted, such information can prompt management to consider a thorough review of the firm's current strategic plan.

Organization of the book

This book follows a natural progression from the development of basic concepts, principles and techniques to the application of them in increasingly complex and real-world situations.

An important and initial step in project analysis is the estimation of cash flows. Chapter 2 commences with the basic concepts and principles for the identification of *relevant cash flows* followed by illustrative cash flow calculation examples for both asset expansion and asset replacement projects. All the cash flows for project evaluation are expected future cash flows. Estimation of cash flows, therefore, involves forecasting. Quantitative and qual-itative (judgemental) methods useful for forecasting project cash flows are discussed, with examples, in Chapters 3 and 4.

Once the cash flows are estimated, projects are subjected to project evaluation techniques. The application of these techniques involves financial mathematics. Frequently encountered formulae in capital budgeting are illustrated with simple examples in Chapter 5. A thorough understanding of the application of these formulae provides a springboard for the project analysis material in the remainder of the book.

Chapter 6 uses the cash flow concepts and the formulae (from Chapters 2 and 5) to evaluate the projects using several criteria, such as net present value, internal rate of return and payback period, and demonstrates the versatility of the net present value criterion. Project appraisal is carried out in Chapter 6 under the following assumptions:

• a single goal of wealth maximization for the firm
• capital expenditures and cash flows known with certainty
• no resource constraints (all the profitable projects can be accepted).

This basic model is then expanded to deal with risk (or uncertainty of cash flows) in Chapters 7 to 10. Chapter 7 discusses, with illustrative examples, the risk-adjusted dis-count rate and certainty equivalent methods for incorporating risk. Chapter 8 illustrates the use of sensitivity and break-even analyses as tools for aiding the decision-makers to make investment decisions under uncertainty. Project risk analysis is further extended by intro-ducing simulation concepts and methods in Chapter 9 and then applying those concepts and methods to a case study in evaluation of a forestry investment in Chapter 10.

Resource constraints on the capital budgeting decision are considered in Chapter 11 by introducing the basics of linear programming (LP) and applying the LP technique for selec-tion of the optimal project portfolios. Chapter 12 presents extensions to the LP technique which make the approach more versatile.

A number of special topics in capital budgeting are covered towards the end of the book. They include property investment analysis (Chapters 14 and 15), and evaluation of inter-national investments (Chapter 16). Capital budgeting decisions under resource constraints analysed in the two linear programming chapters (11 and 12) also provide a number of special cases in project analysis. Simulation and financial modelling in forestry project evaluation as discussed in Chapters 10 and 13 may also be viewed as special topics in capital budgeting because they apply to specific type of investments, namely investments in forestry.

Using Excel for computations

As mentioned earlier, actual project analysis in the real world involves voluminous, tedious, complex and repetitive calculations and relies heavily on computer packages. Capital budgeting concepts, processes, principles and techniques can be made clear by words, graphs and numerical examples. Numerical examples – particularly those which involve repeated, complex, tedious or large calculations – are made simple, clear, useful, attractive and sometimes fun by the use of such computer packages.

In this book, the Excel spreadsheet package is used, wherever appropriate, for calculations in examples. Excel workbooks are held on the Cambridge University Press website (http://publishing.cambridge.org/resources/052181782x/). For convenience, the relevant Excel workbook is indicated with a marker at the appropriate places in the text.

This book is written in such a way that the materials can be studied independently of the Excel workbooks or computer access. However, Excel workbooks will help in understanding the computations and may facilitate the clarification of any computational queries for which answers cannot be found in the text. The many Excel workbooks may be viewed as supplementary or complementary to the discussion in the text. These workbooks will aid in working through problems and will provide templates that may be applied in this work.

Concluding comments

This introductory chapter has set the capital budgeting decision within the broader perspective of the finance discipline and its financial management context. A broad overview of the capital budgeting process was presented in Figure 1.2. The financial appraisal of projects, which is the focus of this book, was identified as one of the critically important and complex stages in the capital budgeting process. The financial appraisal is often known in simple and general terms as 'project analysis'.

Emphasis has been placed on shareholder wealth maximization as the firm's goal (i.e. the book has a corporate focus).

The use of Excel as a teaching and learning aid in this book and then as a practical tool for real-world project analysis has been emphasized.

The flow of materials in this book follows a natural progression from the development of basic concepts, principles and techniques to the application of them in increasingly complex and real-world situations. With this background, the main areas covered in the various chapters have been outlined, together with their relationships to one another.

Review questions

1.1 In finance theory, what is the most widely accepted goal of the firm? How does the net present value of a project relate to this goal?

1.2 Discuss the relationships between the firm's goal, financial management and capital budgeting.

1.3 Present two examples for each of the following types of investment projects:
(a) independent projects
(b) mutually exclusive projects
(c) contingent projects.

1.4 Should relatively small capital expenditures be subjected to thorough financial appraisal and the other key stages of a typical capital budgeting process?

1.5 Briefly discuss the main stages of a typical, well-organized capital budgeting process in a large corporation.

2   Project cash flows

An important part of the capital budgeting process is the estimation of the cash flows associated with the proposed project. Any new project will cause a change in the firm's cash flows. In evaluating an investment proposal, we must consider these expected changes in the firm's cash flows and decide whether or not they add value to the firm. Successful investment decisions will increase the shareholders' wealth through increased cash flows.

Valuing projects by estimating their net present values (NPV) of future cash flows is a means of gaining an idea of their expected addition to shareholder wealth. Correct identification of the *relevant* cash flows associated with an investment project is one of the most important steps in the calculation of NPV or in the project appraisal. *Cash flow* is a very simple concept, although it is easily confused with accounting profit or income. Cash flows are simply the dollars received and dollars paid out by the firm at particular points in time.

The focus of project analysis is on cash flows because they easily measure the impact upon the firm's wealth. Profit and loss in financial statements do not always represent the net increase or decrease in cash flows. Cash flows occur at different times and these times are easily identifiable. The timing of flows is particularly important in project analysis. Some of the figures in standard financial statements, such as income statements or profit and loss accounts, may not have a corresponding cash flow effect for the same period; some of their actual cash flows may occur in the future or might already have occurred in the past. For example, a sale on credit is recorded as occurring on the day the transaction takes place while the actual cash inflow may occur many weeks or months later.

In order to evaluate a project, the cash flows *relevant* to the project have to be identified. In simple terms, a *relevant cash flow* is one which will change (decrease or increase) the firm's overall cash flow as a direct result of the decision to accept the project. Relevant cash flows thus deal with *changes* or *increments* to the firm's existing cash flows. These flows are also known as *incremental* or *marginal* cash flows.

Project evaluation rests upon *incremental cash flows*. Incremental cash flows are the cash inflows and outflows traceable to a given project, which would disappear if the project disappeared. The incremental cash flows can be measured by comparing the cash flows of the firm 'with' the project and the cash flows of the firm 'without' the project. It is a marginal, or incremental, analysis comparing two situations. Erroneous comparisons such as 'before versus after' should be avoided.

For example, suppose a new manufacturing plant uses land that could otherwise be sold for $500,000. The firm owns the land 'before' the project and the firm still owns the land 'after' the project. Therefore, if a 'before versus after' comparison is used, the cash flow attributed to the manufacturing project will be zero. However, the land is a valuable resource and it is not free. It has an opportunity cost which is the cash it could generate for the firm if the project were rejected and the land sold or put to some other productive use. Therefore, 'without' the project, the firm could generate $500,000 cash if the land is sold (and some other amount if the land is put to some other use). 'With' the project, the firm would not be able to generate this cash inflow. Therefore, $500,000 is assigned to the proposed manufacturing project as a cash outflow.

For analytical purposes project cash flows may be separated into two categories: capital cash flows and operating cash flows. Capital cash flows may be disaggregated into three groups: (1) the initial investment (2) additional 'middle-way' investments such as upgrades and increases in working capital investments, and (3) terminal flows. These are all cash flows and the distinctions among them are only to facilitate the convenient identification of the different categories.

The largest single capital flow is traditionally the initial investment. This is also called the 'initial capital outlay' or just 'capital expenditure'. Initial capital outlay generally involves the cash outflows required to start a project by purchasing or creating assets and putting them into working order. As such, the necessary expenditures to establish sufficient working capital for the project and the installation costs of the machines purchased are included in the initial capital outlay. The word 'initial' is quite important. It denotes both the amount to 'initiate' or 'start' the project, and the time at which this outlay occurs.

Once the initial investment is made and the project is in operation, the project is expected to generate cash flows over its economic life. These flows are called operating cash flows and include: cash inflows from sales, cash outflows for advertising and marketing, payments for wages, heating and lighting bills, and purchases of raw materials.

At the end of the project's economic life there will be another set of capital flows. These are generally known as terminal cash flows. For example, the terminal cash inflows could be the sale of the project as a going concern, the salvage value of the asset net of tax, and recovery of any remaining working capital. Terminal cash outflows could be, for example, the cost of asset disposal or demolition, the cost of environmental rehabilitation, and redundancy payments to employees.

It is important to classify the investment decision correctly as this will help with cash flow identification. Investment projects are generally of two types: asset *expansion* projects and asset *replacement* projects. Asset expansion projects are those that propose to invest in additional assets in order to expand an existing product or service line, enter a new line of business, increase sales or reduce costs etc. Asset replacement decisions involve retiring one asset and replacing it with a more efficient asset. This category of decision also encompasses asset retirement, asset abandonment and asset replication over the longer term.

In projects generally, the relevant cash flows will be easy to identify. These will be the straightforward amounts for the initial outlay, ongoing receipts of cash from sales, ongoing cash expenditures on production costs and individual asset termination flows. However, there are some cash flows that are not so straightforward, and are sometimes difficult to identify. These include synergistic effects and opportunity costs.

This chapter will provide guidelines for identifying a project's incremental cash flows, with illustrative examples. The discussion includes the stand-alone project principle, indirect or synergistic effects, the opportunity cost principle, the sunk cost concept, overhead cost allocation, the treatment of working capital, taxation, depreciation, investment allowances, financing (debt and interest) flows and inflation and timing of cash flows. Cash flow estimation of *asset expansion* projects and *asset replacement* projects will be illustrated by calculated examples.

Study objectives

After studying this chapter the reader should be able to:

- identify a project's *incremental* cash flows
- calculate initial investment outlay, operating cash flows, and terminal cash flows for *asset expansion* and *asset replacement* projects
- determine the effects of depreciation on after-tax cash flows
- separate the investment decision from the financing decision and distinguish between project flows and financing flows
- calculate after-tax cash flows to be used in project valuation
- gain an insight into the differences between accounting income and cash flows

Essentials in cash flow identification

In estimating the relevant cash flows, a number of principles and concepts are employed.

Principle of the stand-alone project

A project's *incremental cash flows* can be calculated by comparing the total future cash flows of the firm 'with' and 'without' the project. In practice, this would be very cumbersome, particularly for large firms with many different product lines. Fortunately, it is not generally necessary to do this because once the effect of undertaking the proposed project on the firm's cash flows has been identified, only that project's incremental cash flows need to be considered.

This marginal form of analysis suggests that we can view the proposed project as a kind of 'mini-firm' with its own future capital expenditures and operating cash flows. Thus, what the stand-alone principle says is that we will be evaluating the proposed project purely on its own merits, in isolation from any other activities or projects of the firm, but including its incidental or synergistic effects.

Indirect or synergistic effects

All the indirect or synergistic effects of a project should be included in the cash flow calculation. Synergistic effects can be negative or positive. For example, if a car manufacturing company considers introducing a new model called, say, Mako, which is a close substitute for an existing model called Raptor, then there could be a fall in sales of Raptors due to the new model Mako. Let us suppose that the Raptor sales are expected to decrease by $25 million over the project's life from this effect. This negative effect would then have to be counted as an incremental cost of the proposed Mako project. The rationale is that 'without' the Mako project, the firm's future cash flows would have been higher by $25 million. In other words, 'with' the Mako project, the firm's Raptor cash flow would be reduced by $25 million. The $25 million reduction is calculated into the Mako project by reducing its future net cash flows by this amount.

As another example, assume that a proposed project introduces a new product or service which is complementary to an existing product or service of the firm and consequently will enhance the sales of the existing product. Establishing a pharmacy adjacent to an existing doctor's surgery is likely to have a favourable impact on the surgery's cash flows. Patient numbers may increase at the surgery because of the convenience of a pharmacy next door. This positive flow-on effect should be included in the proposed pharmacy project's cash inflow.

The rationale for the incorporation of these indirect effects has its base in the opportunity cost principle.

Opportunity cost principle

When a firm undertakes a project, various resources will be used and not be available for other projects. The cost to the firm of not being able to use these resources for other projects is referred to as an 'opportunity cost'. The value of these resources should be measured in terms of their opportunity cost. The opportunity cost, in the context of capital budgeting, is the value of the most valuable alternative that is given up if the proposed investment project is undertaken. This opportunity cost should be included in the project's cash flows. Let us consider two examples.

Example 2.1

A proposed project involves the establishment of a production facility. This facility will be located within a factory the firm already owns. The estimated rental value of the space that the production facility will occupy is $29,000 per year. The space has not been rented in the past, but the firm expects to rent it in the future. Then, the firm will lose $29,000 'with' the project because that space will be used for the project. Therefore, the opportunity cost is $29,000 per year in rent forgone and it should be included as a cash outflow. This example also illustrates that even when no cash changes hands, there could be an opportunity cost. Why does this not contradict the principle that we should only consider cash flows?

The reason is that opportunity cost of the space measures an extra cash flow that would be generated (for the firm) 'without' the project.

Suppose that this space has not been rented in the past and there is no intention to rent, sell or use for any other purpose in the future. In this case, there is no opportunity cost if the resource is used for the proposed project. Therefore, in this situation, the $29,000 will not be included as a cash outflow.

Example 2.2

A project under consideration involves the use of an existing building to set up a factory to produce shoes. The market value of this building is $200,000. If the project is undertaken, there will be no direct cash outflow associated with purchasing the building since the firm already owns it. In evaluating the proposed shoe-manufacturing project, should we then assume zero cost for the building? Certainly not. The building is not a 'free' resource for the project because if the building was not used for this project it could be used for some other purpose; for example, it could be sold to generate cash. Using the existing building for the proposed shoe project thus has an opportunity cost of $200,000.

Sunk costs

Another key concept used in identifying relevant cash flows is the notion of sunk costs. A sunk cost is an amount spent in the past in relation to the project, but which cannot now be recovered or offset by the current decision. Sunk costs are past and irreversible. They are not contingent upon the decision to accept (or reject) a proposed project. Therefore, they should not be included in the cash flows. To illustrate the concept, two excellent real-world examples are reproduced in the following paragraphs from Brealey, Myers, Partington and Robinson (2000, p. 133) and Moyer, McGuigan and Kretlow (2001, p. 307) respectively.

In 1971 Lockheed sought a United States federal government guarantee for a bank loan to continue development of the TriStar aeroplane. Lockheed and its supporters argued that it would be silly and imprudent to abandon a project on which nearly $1 billion had already been spent. Some of the opponents argued that it would be equally silly and imprudent to continue with a project that offered no prospect of a satisfactory return on that $1 billion. Both groups were wrong. The $1 billion was spent in the past and it was a sunk cost, irrelevant to the investment analysis. The TriStar project has been analysed by Reinhardt (1973) and that analysis does not include $1 billion as an opportunity cost.

In 1999, the Chemtron Corporation was considering a project to construct a new chemical disposal facility. Two years earlier, the corporation had hired the R.O.E. Consulting Group to make an environmental impact study of the proposed site at a cost of $500,000. This money cannot be recovered whether the proposed project (being considered in 1999) is undertaken or not. Therefore, it should not be included in the project's cash flows.

Overhead costs

Two examples of overhead costs are utilities (such as electricity, gas and water) and executive salaries. Cost accounting is in part concerned with the appropriate allocation of various overhead costs to particular production units. In the project evaluation, however, the issue is not the allocation of overheads to production units, but the identification of *incremental* overhead costs. Very often, overhead expenses would occur 'with' or 'without' the proposed project; they occur whether or not a given project is accepted or rejected. There is often not a single specific project to which the overhead costs can be allocated. Thus, the question is not whether or not the proposed project would benefit from the overhead facilities, but whether or not the overhead expenses are *incremental* cash flows associated with the proposed project.

In project appraisal, the decision as to what overheads should be allocated to a proposed project's cash flows can be guided by the opportunity cost and sunk cost principles. Only the incremental cash flows resulting from changes in overhead expenses should be included in evaluating a project proposal. If the expenses are already being incurred, a proportion should not be allocated to the new project.

For example, Cedar Ltd currently incurs utility overheads of $500,000 from the operation of its main office complex, which it allocates to the production departments on the basis of floor space. Suppose Cedar Ltd is considering extending its factory in order to manufacture a new product. In doing so, a new production department will be created which will take up 20% of the available floor space of the factory. The new project is not expected to affect main office utility overheads. The firm's management accountant, employing accepted cost accounting principles, would allocate $100,000 (being 20% of a $500,000 utilities cost incurred in the last year) as an expense associated with the new project. While it would be tempting to include this overhead expense in the evaluation of the proposed project, it would be incorrect to do so. From a project evaluation perspective, this utilities overhead would not be included in the project analysis, because this cost is not an incremental cost to the project; 'with' or 'without' the project, this utilities cost is incurred.

Continuing with the previous example, Cedar Ltd also allocates executive salaries to the production department, based on the floor space. The firm's management accountant, using the same cost accounting principles, would allocate $160,000 (being 20% of the $800,000 chief executive's salary) as an expense associated with the new project. Again, while it would be tempting to include this overhead expense in the evaluation of the proposed project, it would be incorrect to do so, because this cost is not an incremental cost to the project; 'with' or 'without' the project, this salary is paid. If, however, 25% of the chief executive's time is spent on the project causing a decrease in the productivity of the firm's other activities then this would be considered an opportunity cost of the proposed project and included in the analysis.

Alternatively, if additional staff (costing $200,000) were recruited to look after the firm's existing business (thus preventing possible adverse effects on the productivity of the firm's other activities), then the $200,000 would be an increment to the project and should be included in its evaluation.

Treatment of working capital

More often than not, new projects will involve additional investments in working capital. Working capital is equal to a firm's current assets minus its current liabilities. Cash, inventories of raw materials and finished goods, and accounts receivable (customers' unpaid bills) are examples of current assets. Current liabilities include accounts payable (the firm's unpaid bills) and wages payable.

When a new project starts, it may be necessary to increase the amount of cash held as a float to accommodate more transactions. Further inventories of raw materials may be required to run the new production lines smoothly. Additional investment in finished goods inventories may be necessary to handle increased sales. When the finished product is sold, customers may be slow to pay, thus causing an increase in accounts receivable. All of these changes require increased working capital investment.

Increases in working capital requirements are considered cash outflows even though they do not leave the firm. For example, an increase in inventory is considered a cash outflow even though the goods are still in store, because the firm does not have access to the cash value of that inventory. Consequently, the firm cannot use that money for other investments. That is, an increase in working capital represents an *opportunity cost* to the firm. Production and sales fluctuate during the project's progress and accordingly cash may flow into or out of working capital. When the project terminates, any working capital recovered is treated as a cash inflow.

The flows of working capital must be treated as capital flows and not operational flows. Because working capital is allied to sales, you might be tempted to consider such flows as income or expense flows. This is not the case: working capital represents a pool of funds committed to the project in the same manner as is fixed capital. The fixed capital cost is accounted for as an opportunity cost in the NPV discounting process, and so too is the working capital pool.

After-tax cash flows

Tax is a cash payment to a government authority. If the project generates tax liabilities, then the tax payable is relevant to the project, and must be accounted for as a cash outflow.

Corporate tax is a cash outflow. If the tax were levied on net cash inflow and paid at the same time as cash was received, then the after-tax net cash flow would be easily calculated. However, tax is not based on net cash flow, but on taxable income.

Taxable income is defined by the relevant taxation legislation and does not necessarily mean the same thing as net cash flow or even accounting income or accounting profit. Taxable income is generally calculated by subtracting allowable deductions from assessable income. These terms are specific to particular tax acts, and are not easily dealt with in a general context. However, project evaluation needs to be able to accord some treatment to this calculation to determine after-tax cash flows. In this book, a simple flat rate (e.g. 30%) of tax is applied to illustrate the after-tax cash flow calculations in examples.

The tax definition of 'deductions' treats some non-cash items as allowable expenses. One such item frequently encountered in project analysis is asset depreciation.

Treatment of depreciation

Depreciation is not a cash flow. It is an allocation of the initial cost of an asset over a number of accounting periods. Asset costs are allocated within accrual accounting systems so that they are matched over time against the income generated by the assets. That is, the initial cost of an asset is expected to benefit the firm over several years, hence the total initial cost is spread over those future benefit years.

The actual per annum dollar amount of depreciation is only a notional amount. It does not represent the annual decline in value of the asset, it does not measure the value of the asset used up, and it does not measure the actual unit costs of the asset's services.

In preparing the financial statements of the firm, accounting depreciation may be calculated in several different ways, for example:

- The 'life' or 'straight-line' method allocates an equal amount of the initial cost to each year of the asset's life.
- The 'reducing balance' method allocates a fixed percentage of the asset's written down value in each year.
- The 'sum of the year's digits' method allocates a reducing proportion of the asset's cost in each year.
- The 'units of production' method allocates an amount on the basis of a ratio of the asset's expected productive capacity to each year of measured production.

All these methods attempt to allocate the initial cost of an asset over a number of accounting periods.

In project evaluation, what is relevant is not the accounting depreciation but the tax-allowable depreciation. The methods of calculating tax-allowable depreciation are prescribed by the tax act. Sometimes the firm will have a choice among these prescribed methods, and in those cases the firm usually selects the method which will reduce the overall tax bill. The tax bill will be reduced if higher depreciation is claimed in the earlier years, thus delaying the payment of tax. The reducing balance method has this effect. Many national tax acts permit *accelerated depreciation* of equipment by allowing depreciation methods (defined in the tax act) which allow higher tax deductions in early years and lower deductions later. The Modified Accelerated Cost Recovery System (MACRS) in the United States is an example.

To keep focused on project analysis (without being distracted by depreciation methods), the straight-line method is used in the illustrations. This is not necessarily the most advantageous method, but a project with a positive NPV under this method will only be enhanced using the additional tax benefits from any accelerated depreciation methods such as reducing balance and sum of the year's digits.

It is important to understand that our interest in depreciation lies only in its tax effect, i.e. the depreciation tax shield, or the reduction in taxes attributable to the depreciation allowance. If it were not a tax deduction we would not consider it within an NPV evaluation. Three ways of calculating the tax shield of allowable depreciation are presented in a later section of this chapter.

Tax payable

Tax payable is a cash outflow. The form of tax encountered in project analysis is corporate tax. It is calculated as a percentage of taxable income. The rate of corporate tax is usually a fixed rate for every dollar of taxable income.

Taxation is a very volatile area, and tax rules are constantly changing. In any situation where a project may be subject to particular and special tax laws or rulings, expert tax advice must be sought. Even this help may not afford sufficient protection, as tax laws can be changed retrospectively or they can change from time to time after the project has commenced. The best course to follow in this situation is to ensure that the project is not dependent upon tax savings or tax shields for its success.

Investment allowance

Governments often provide special temporary incentives to the private sector to encourage investments in selected industries. These incentives normally take the form of a tax benefit where a given percentage of the cost of investment is assigned as an allowable deduction for arriving at taxable income. This kind of investment allowance normally does not affect the allowable depreciation of the asset, which is based on the full cost of the investment before the investment allowance.

The tax rules attached to these sorts of schemes are quite complex, so when using these schemes clarifications must be sought from appropriate tax experts. These incentives do enhance the NPVs of projects and should be incorporated into the analysis where necessary.

Financing flows

Treatment of financing flows is an area of confusion and sometimes a source of error in project analysis. It is important to distinguish between *project cash flows* and *financing cash flows*. For the purpose of identifying the relevant cash flows for project evaluation, the investment decision (project) must be separated from its financing decision. The financing decision concerns the relative proportions of the project's capital expenditures to be provided by debt-holders and equity-holders respectively. The decision about the particular mixture of debt and equity used in financing the project is a management decision concerning the trade-off between financial risk and the cost of capital. This debt–equity mixture determines how the resultant project cash flows are divided between debt-holders and equity-owners. By contrast the investment evaluation decision determines whether the project's discounted cash flows exceed the initial capital outlay (investment), and so adds (net present) value to the firm.

Generally, interest charges or any other financing costs such as dividends or loan repayments are not deducted in arriving at cash flows, because we are interested in the cash flow generated by the assets of the project. Interest is a return to providers of debt capital. It is an expense against the income generated to equity-holders, and as such is deducted in the determination of accounting profit. However, it is not included in project cash flow analysis, as the discount rate employed in the NPV analysis accommodates the required returns to both equity and debt providers. Therefore, inclusion of interest charges in cash flow calculations would result in a double counting of the interest cost.

Interest is tax deductible, and therefore provides a tax shield for any investment. This benefit is also accounted for in the discount rate, as the rate employed in project analysis is an 'after-tax' rate. Accordingly, tax savings on interest expenses are not included in project cash flow analysis.

Almost always there are exceptions to general rules or practices and this is the case for the general rule for the treatment of financing flows. There are situations where interest charges are explicitly incorporated into the cash flows. The question here is not whether it is right or wrong to incorporate financing flows into the cash flow analysis, but whether that incorporation is done correctly or incorrectly. If it is necessary to show the financing flows explicitly in the cash flows, as is often preferred by non-financial managers and chief executives, it is quite possible to do this in a correct and consistent manner without distorting the final results.

In property investment analysis, 'property' cash flows are distinguished from 'equity' cash flows. Property cash flows are the equivalent of 'project' cash flows discussed in this chapter. Property cash flow calculations do not include loan repayments and interest charges as deductions. This approach is consistent with the general cash flow definition in this chapter. 'Equity' cash flow calculations, in contrast, deduct loan repayments and interest expenses.

One of the objectives of property investment analysis is to evaluate the return to the investor under different debt and tax situations. A mortgage is for one particular property, rather than being an unidentified part of the capital structure of a corporation. Some investment in property is to gain tax advantages from interest deductions associated with debt financing. For these reasons, in property investment analysis, equity cash flows are calculated after deducting loan repayments (principal plus interest) from other cash inflows to enable the effects of borrowing and taxation to be evaluated. This is explained fully when real estate investments are described and analysed in Chapter 14.

Within-year timing of cash flows

Normally, cash flows occur at various points of time within a year. The standard practice in capital budgeting is to assume that capital expenditures occur at the beginning of the year and all other cash flows occur at the end of the year. This assumption simplifies cash flow timing and to some degree imitates reality. The yearly time frame is assumed because large capital projects have very long lives, and the loss of within-year cash flow timing detail is not material.

To maintain consistency for calculation purposes, the points in cash flow timing are set at the *end* of each year. Flows which would normally occur at the start of any year will be timed as occurring at the end of the immediately preceding year. For example, an initial capital outlay of $200 at the start of year 1 will be timed as occurring at the end of year 0. The idea of a year 0 should not introduce any confusion. Year 0 simply means that there has been some notional historical time which has now elapsed, and we now stand 'at the end of year 0'. The end of year 0 is in fact the start of year 1. The notion of a year 0 is used so that we can maintain a consistent set of acronyms: the points in time are often tallied as EOY 0, EOY 1, EOY 2 and so on. Equivalently, we may use Y0, Y1, Y2 and so on. Capital expenditure at the start of the project is timed as occurring at EOY 0. Operating cash flows in the first year are timed as occurring at EOY 1. Subsequent operating cash flows are timed at EOY 2, EOY 3 and so on.

The standard practice in capital budgeting assumes that capital expenditures occur at the beginning of a year and all other cash flows occur at the end of a year. The capital expenditure occurring at the 'start of year 3', for example, would be netted out against the other cash flows as occurring at the 'end of year 2 (EOY 2)' since we have no timing position called 'start of year 3', and in any case, the 'end of year 2' and the 'start of year 3' are the same point in time.

The timing of tax payments may vary. In some tax jurisdictions, tax payable is assessed at the end of a year, and actually paid in the subsequent year. If this is the case, then the tax outflow will have to be shown as a delayed payment in the following year. In other tax jurisdictions, tax is paid progressively on quarterly or half-yearly earnings, or on estimated yearly earnings. In these cases, the tax is paid within the current year. The treatment of tax will thus depend upon the tax situation in a particular country. So that we can concentrate on the analytical side of project appraisal, we assume tax payments are made in the same year in which taxable income is generated, unless specifically noted otherwise.

Inflation and consistent treatment of cash flows and discount rates

Inflation will have an effect on the expected cash flows of a project. Both cash inflows and outflows could be affected by inflation. Market rates, such as interest rates and equity returns, in general will also rise when the expected inflation rate is high. As the market rates rise, the required rate of return by investors will also rise. To deal with inflation appropriately, the project analysis must recognize expected inflation in the forecast of future cash flows and use a discount rate that reflects investors' expectations of future inflation.

If all cash flows as well as the discount rate are equally affected by expected inflation, the net present value is the same whether inflation is included or excluded. However, most projects consist of a multitude of cash flows over a number of years and it would be erroneous to assume that all of these cash flows will increase by exactly the same rate each year, or to assume the same effect on the discount rate. Some cash flows are unaffected by inflation while other cash flows are affected to varying degrees by inflation.

An outstanding example of the differential impact of inflation on a project's cash flow is the 'depreciation tax shield' (or the tax saving from the tax-allowable depreciation). Tax-allowable depreciation is totally unaffected by inflation. Depreciation tax shields are calculated on the basis of the historical costs of the assets at the time of their acquisition. Similarly, a long-term raw-material contract or the purchase of a commodity in the *forward* or *futures* markets may lock in the present prices, thereby insulating the cash flow from inflationary effects.

Given the differential impact of inflation on various cash flow components, cash flow forecasts in *nominal* terms, i.e., incorporating the inflationary effect, have an advantage over cash flow forecasts in *real* terms, i.e., excluding the inflationary effects. That is, nominal cash flow forecasts can incorporate potentially different inflationary trends in selling prices, labour costs, material costs and so on, into cash flow estimates by applying different inflation rates for different components of the cash flow.

The required rate of return used for discounting cash flows is normally derived from observed market rates such as interest rates and returns on equity. These observed market rates usually have the expected annual inflation rates built in and are usually quoted in *nominal* terms (as opposed to *real* terms). Observed market rates expressed in nominal terms can, if necessary, be converted into real terms using the algebraic relationship expressed in the Fisher effect. The Fisher equation is:

$$(1 + n) = (1 + r)^*(1 + p)$$

where:

$n =$ the annual nominal interest rate (expressed as a decimal value)
$r =$ the annual real interest rate (expressed as a decimal value)
$p =$ the expected annual inflation rate

From the above equation the real interest rate can be easily derived:

$$r = \frac{(1 + n)}{(1 + p)} - 1$$

Consistency in the discounted cash flow analysis requires that if a project's cash flows are in nominal terms, they should be discounted by nominal discount rates, and if a project's cash flows are in real terms they must be discounted by real discount rates. Real and nominal quantities should not be mixed.

As we see later in Chapters 6 and 7, the interest rate used for discounting cash flows is normally derived from observed market rates. In an efficient financial market, investors' required rate of return will include a component, $(1 + p)$, to compensate for expected inflation. The use of observed market-required rates then implies that we should incorporate inflation into cash flows to be consistent. On rare occasions (such as the computer project example in Chapter 9), real cash flows are appropriate in the analysis. In such situations, the real discount rate can be calculated from market (nominal) rates using the Fisher equation presented above.

Asset expansion project cash flows

Principles, concepts and the treatments relating to cash flow calculation were discussed in the preceding section. This section presents suitable formats for calculating the three main components of cash flows: initial investment, net operating cash flows and terminal cash flows. Brief discussions or illustrations are provided where necessary.

The basic formats for determining initial investment, operating cash flows, and terminal cash flows of an asset expansion project are outlined below.

Initial investment

The initial net investment in an asset expansion project is defined as the project's initial cash outflow, that is, the capital outlay (or capital expenditure or capital outflow) at the beginning of the project. It is calculated using the following typical format:

> Cost of new asset(s)
> + Installation and shipping costs
> + Initial investment in working capital
> _____
> = Initial investment

It is worth noting here that for the purpose of tax-allowable depreciation, working capital is not an allowable item. The asset cost plus installation and shipping costs form the basis upon which depreciation is computed. The typical wording of a tax act covering the value of depreciable items says: 'the cost of plant and equipment installed ready for use'. This definition does not include working capital.

Net operating cash flows

A project's after-tax net operating cash flows for any given year during the economic life of the project may be calculated using the following typical format. To focus on the format without being distracted by the details of the timing of cash flows for sales and cost of goods sold, it is assumed that they are all cash flows received or paid during the year. More explicitly, it is assumed that all sales are for cash and that opening and closing inventories remain unchanged (hence, the cost of goods sold equals purchases) and that all purchases are in cash. In fact, the forecasts of sales revenues and costs of goods sold are generally done on a cash basis and the distinction between cash and non-cash values for a given year is not an issue.

> Cash inflow from sales
> − Cost of goods sold
> − Selling, general, administrative and other expenses
> − Depreciation
> _____
> = Taxable income
> − Tax payable
> _____
> = Net income (after tax)
> + Depreciation
> _____
> = After-tax net operating cash flow

This method 'adds back' the amount of depreciation. This is quite common, and is correct. An alternative approach which isolates the cash flows from the non-cash flows is shown below.

> Cash inflow from sales
> − Cost of goods sold
> − Selling, general, administrative and other expenses
> _____
> = Net cash income

$$\underline{- \text{Depreciation}}$$
$$= \text{Taxable income}$$

Net cash income
$$\underline{- \text{Tax payable}}$$
$$= \text{After-tax net operating cash flow}$$

Another format which identifies the 'tax shield of allowable depreciation' explicitly is:

Cash inflow from sales
$- $ Cost of goods sold
$\underline{- \text{Selling, general, administrative and other expenses}}$
$= $ Net cash income
$\underline{- \text{Tax on net cash income}}$
$= $ Net after-tax cash income
$\underline{+ \text{Tax shield of allowable depreciation}}$
$= $ After-tax net operating cash flow

where tax shield of depreciation = (depreciation × tax rate).

Any of these formats can be used depending upon the circumstances.

If there are net 'losses' (as opposed to net income), their tax treatment may vary under different tax rules for different industries in different countries. Two possible general treatments of losses may be:

- Carry forward the losses to future years of the project until there is sufficient income to offset the losses, or
- Deduct the losses from the firm's other business activities (which include projects other than the project being considered) thus realizing tax benefits for the firm 'with' the project.

In the latter case, such tax benefits may be treated as a cash inflow of the proposed project, because 'without' the proposed project the firm's cash flows would be reduced by that amount.

Terminal cash flow

In the final year of a project's economic life, there is another cash flow on top of the normal annual operating cash flows. This is termed the terminal cash flow. Typically, it has two components: the recovery of the working capital and the recovery of the after-tax salvage value of the assets.

The typical format for calculating the terminal cash flow is:

Proceeds from sale of assets
$\underline{- \text{Taxes on sale of assets}}$
$= $ After-tax salvage value
$\underline{+ \text{Recovery of working capital}}$
$= $ Terminal cash flow

Taxes on the sale of an asset

Whenever an asset is sold, there are tax consequences which will affect the net proceeds from the sale. These tax rules vary not only among different countries but also over time within a single country. Therefore, expert tax advice ought to be sought at the time of evaluating the project. However, for analytical purposes, as well as to become familiar with the different possible tax situations, the tax treatment on 'sale of assets' may be categorized into four cases.

Case 1: Sale of an asset for its *tax book-value*. Normally if an asset is sold for an amount exactly equal to its tax book-value, there will be no tax consequences as there will be no gain or loss on the sale. Tax book-value is equal to the installed cost of the asset minus accumulated tax depreciation.

Case 2: Sale of an asset for less than its tax book-value. In this case there will be a loss, which is equal to sale proceeds minus tax book-value. This loss may be treated as an operating loss, thus reducing the total tax payment.

Case 3: Sale of an asset for more than its tax book-value but less than its original cost. In this case the amount equal to the book-value may be treated as a tax-free cash flow while the remainder which is in excess of the book-value may be taxed at the same rate as that applied to the operating income.

Case 4: Sale of an asset for more than its original cost. In this case part of the gain may be treated as ordinary income and part may be treated as capital gain. The part treated as ordinary income may be equal to the difference between the original cost and the current tax book-value. The capital gain portion may be the amount in excess of the original asset cost. The tax rates for the two components may be different.

In all four cases the tax book-value will be equal to the 'written down book-value', a more commonly used accounting term. Since we are using tax-allowable rates and methods of depreciation for our analyses, these amounts will be the same.

To concentrate on the analytical side of project evaluation, we adopt only the simplest tax treatment. We assume that a single flat corporate tax rate applies, and that it applies both to taxable income from operations and to any gain (or loss) from the sale of assets. Gain (or loss) from the sale of assets is defined, for simplicity, as being equivalent to the sale proceeds minus tax book-value.

Recovery of working capital

Normally the total value of the pool of working capital is assumed to be recovered at the termination of the project. This is a capital cash inflow and has no taxation implications.

Table 2.1. *Delta Corporation's historical sales*

Year	Sales (units)
1990	500,000
1991	550,000
1992	540,000
1993	560,000
1994	565,000
1995	590,000
1996	600,000
1997	610,000
1998	615,559
1999	669,000
2000	700,000

Example 2.3. The Delta Project

This example illustrates the calculation of after-tax cash flows for an asset expansion project. It will be used again in later chapters with appropriate modifications. The after-tax cash flows obtained here are used in Chapter 6 to illustrate the application of capital budgeting techniques to project appraisal under the assumption of certainty. An extended version of the same example is used in Chapter 7 to illustrate the incorporation of risk into project appraisal. This extended version is used again in Chapter 8 to illustrate sensitivity and break-even analysis for decision support under risk.

The proposal

Delta Corporation is considering an investment proposal (the Delta Project), to expand one of its product lines. The project is planned to start at the beginning of the year 2001 (denoted EOY 0, which in this case is the end of 2000). Capital outlay in the first year is $1 million. At the end of year 3, another capital expenditure of $0.5 million is required for an upgrade. The economic life of the project is estimated to be eight years. The *level* of working capital for the project is tabulated below.

Year	0	1	2	3	4	5	6	7	8
Working Capital ($)	2,000	2,500	3,100	3,600	4,000	4,300	4,500	3,000	0

The salvage value of the total capital expenditure ($1.5 million) at the end of the eighth year is estimated as $16,000. The depreciation rate for the initial investment, for tax purposes, is 12.5% per annum. The upgrade depreciates at $100,000 per year for years 4 to 8.

The forecast sales for the project are to be based on a time-trend regression on the company's last eleven years of sales, shown in Table 2.1.

Table 2.2. Delta Project: cash flow analysis ($)

Calendar year	2000	2001	2002	2003	2004	2005	2006	2007	2008
End of notional year	0	1	2	3	4	5	6	7	8
Capital flows									
1. Capital outlay	−1000000								
2. Upgrade				−500000					
3. After-tax salvage value									11,200
4. Working capital	−2000	−500	−600	−500	−400	−300	−200	1500	3,000
5. Cash flow: capital	−1,002,000	−500	−600	−500,500	−400	−300	−200	1,500	14,200
Operating flows									
6. Forecast sales units		691,106	707,812	724,518	741,224	757,931	774,637	791,343	808,049
7. Extra sales units					500,000	500,000	500,000	500,000	500,000
8. Total sales units		691,106	707,812	724,518	1,241,224	1,257,931	1,274,637	1,291,343	1,308,049
9. Unit selling price		0.50	0.50	0.50	0.50	0.50	0.75	0.75	0.75
10. Sales income		345,553	353,906	362,259	620,612	628,965	955,978	968,507	981,037
11. Unit cost		0.10	0.10	0.10	0.10	0.10	0.10	0.10	0.10
12. Production cost		69,111	70,781	72,452	124,122	125,793	127,464	129,134	130,805
13. Other cost		50,000	50,000	50,000	50,000	50,000	55,000	55,000	55,000
14. Total cost		119,111	120,781	122,452	174,122	175,793	182,464	184,134	185,805
15. Depreciation initial		125,000	125,000	125,000	125,000	125,000	125,000	125,000	125,000
16. Depreciation upgrade					100,000	100,000	100,000	100,000	100,000
17. Taxable income		101,442	108,125	114,807	221,490	228,172	548,514	559,373	570,232
18. Tax payable		30,433	32,437	34,442	66,447	68,452	164,554	167,812	171,070
19. Net income		71,010	75,687	80,365	155,043	159,721	383,960	391,561	399,162
20. Cash flow: operations		196,010	200,687	205,365	380,043	384,721	608,960	616,561	624,162
21. Net cash flow	−1,002,000	195,510	200,087	−295,135	379,643	384,421	608,760	618,061	638,362

Forecast sales obtained from the time-trend regression are to be adjusted from year 4 onwards to account for the increased sales resulting from the upgrade, which are estimated as 500,000 units per year.

The selling price of the product is expected to be 50 cents per unit for the first five years, and 75 cents thereafter. The production cost is estimated to be 10 cents per unit. Other operating costs (which do not include depreciation) are $50,000 per year for the first five years and $55,000 per year for the rest of the project life. The corporate tax rate is 30%.

Delta Project: cash flow analysis

Workbook
2.1

A detailed cash flow analysis which distinguishes between capital flows and operating flows is shown in Table 2.2. Definitions of some of the items in the table are provided below.

Calendar year and *notional year* are recorded in the table for illustrative purposes. The initiation of the project is denoted as end of notional year 0, and the end of the first year is denoted as end of notional year 1. These will correspond to the end of calendar year 2000 (or the beginning of 2001) and the end of 2001, respectively.

The *capital outlay* row records $1 million initial capital expenditure under year 0, as the capital outlays are normally assumed to occur at the beginning of the relevant year. This has occurred in year 1 and to place it at the beginning of year 1, we insert it in the column 'end of notional year 0'.

The *working capital* row records the change in working capital (or the incremental working capital) calculated from the *level* of working capital given in the example. Investments in working capital, just like investment in plant and equipment, require a cash outflow. Disinvestments in working capital produce a cash inflow. The investment in working capital at the beginning of the project is $2,000. This capital outflow is placed under year 0. The amount of working capital required increases by $500 from year 0 to year 1 (i.e. from $2,000 to $2,500). This is shown under year 1. Up to year 6, working capital requirements increase annually, thus tying more cash into working capital. In years 7 and 8, working capital is recovered. In year 7, working capital requirements decrease by $1,500 from $4,500 to $3,000, thus releasing cash tied up in the working capital. At the end of the project's life, the remaining $3,000 in the pool of working capital is recovered and generates a positive cash inflow.

Initial investment in the Delta Project example is equal to initial capital outlay ($1 million) plus the investment in working capital at the beginning of the project ($2,000). Thus it is $1,002,000.

Upgrade of equipment is to occur at the end of year 3. Since it is specifically stated that it is to occur at the end of year 3 (as opposed to during year 3), it is timed as at the end of year 3. If we were told, however, that the upgrade is to occur in year 3, then following the standard practice that capital expenditures are assumed to occur at the beginning of the year, we would have timed it as at the end of year 2 so that it is treated as a capital expenditure at the beginning of year 3. Recall the general principle for timing of the capital expenditures stated in a previous subsection titled 'Within-year timing of cash flows'.

After-tax salvage value is calculated following the typical format for calculating the terminal cash flow described earlier. It is equal to 'proceeds from sale of assets' ($16,000) minus 'taxes on sale of assets' ($4,800): $11,200.

'Taxes on sale of assets' is equal to:

$$(\text{Sale proceeds} - \text{Tax book-value}) \times \text{Tax rate} = (16{,}000 - 0) \times 0.3 = \$4{,}800$$

$$\text{Tax book-value} = \text{Cost} - \text{Tax-allowable accumulated depreciation}$$

$$= 1{,}000{,}000 - (1{,}000{,}000 \times 0.125 \times 8) = 0$$

Forecast sales units are obtained by running a regression on the historical sales units of the company for the past eleven years. The annual sales figure is the dependent variable and the year number is the independent variable. For the independent variable, time, the numbers 1 to 11 are used to represent the years 1990 to 2000. The estimated regression equation is then used to forecast sales for the next eight years.

Forecasting using regression analysis is discussed in Chapter 3, where quantitative forecasting techniques are presented. An example of a time-trend regression is given in Workbook 3.3. You will become familiar with time-trend regression forecasting in Chapter 3. Until then, you may take the figures for 'forecast sales units' in Table 2.2 as given.

Total sales units are obtained by adding the extra sales units (expected to be generated from the equipment upgrade) to forecast sales units.

Sales income is obtained by multiplying the total sales units by the unit selling price.

Production cost is obtained by multiplying total sales units by the unit cost.

Total cost is equal to production cost plus other costs.

Depreciation initial is the 12.5% per annum depreciation of the $1 million initial investment.

Depreciation upgrade is the additional $100,000 depreciation allowable per annum for the final five years beginning in year 4. Year 4 is the first full year of production after the installation of the upgrade at the end of year 3. Under some tax jurisdictions, the first full $100,000 of depreciation may be claimable on the last day of year 3, if the equipment was 'installed ready for use' at the close of business that day. This point highlights the fact that taxation is a complex area, and the need to seek expert help in any detailed tax analysis.

Taxable income is equal to sales income less total cost and total depreciation.

Tax payable is calculated by applying the 30% tax rate to taxable income. In computerized calculations it is important to set up the logic in such a way that tax is not paid on negative income.

Net income is equal to taxable income minus tax payable.

Net operating cash flow is calculated by adding back total depreciation to net income. In the table this amount is called 'cash flow: operations' to distinguish between capital flows and operating flows while at the same time highlighting the fact that they both are cash flows. Net operating cash flow can also be calculated by netting out the cash flows, rather than by adding back total depreciation. Three ways to incorporate the tax effect of allowable depreciation were described in an earlier subsection.

Net cash flow is the overall annual total flow, capital plus operating, and is the figure used in project evaluation. These net cash flows will be used in Chapter 6 to illustrate the application of four project evaluation criteria for decision support.

Asset replacement project cash flows

The previous example (the Delta Project) took the life of the plant and equipment (included in the project's capital expenditure) as fixed. In many cases, the point at which equipment is replaced reflects economics, not physical collapse. The decision-makers decide when to replace the machines; the machines will rarely decide for the decision-maker.

The basic principles and procedures involved in determining initial investment, incremental operating cash flows and terminal cash flow of an asset replacement project are outlined below by presenting the appropriate formats for their computation.

Initial investment

> Cost of new asset
> + Installation costs
> − Proceeds from sale of old asset
> + Taxes on sale of old asset
> + Initial investment in working capital
> = Initial investment

Incremental operating cash flows

> Operating cash flow new asset
> − Operating cash flow old asset
> = Incremental cash flow of the proposed replacement project

Terminal cash flow

> Proceeds from sale of new asset
> − Proceeds from sale of old asset
> − Taxes on sale of new asset
> + Taxes on sale of old asset
> + Recovery of working capital
> = Terminal cash flow

The application of these formats is illustrated in the following Repco Corporation example.

Example 2.4. The Repco Replacement Investment Project

Repco Corporation is considering a replacement investment. The machine currently in use was purchased two years ago (in 1999) for $49,000. Depreciation for tax purposes is $9,800 per year for five years. The market value of this machine today (at the beginning of year 2001) is $35,000. The new machine will cost $123,000 and requires $3,000 for installation. Its economic life is estimated to be three years and tax-allowable depreciation is $42,000 per year for three years. If the new machine is acquired, the investment in accounts receivable is expected to rise by $8,000, the inventory by $25,000 and accounts payable by $13,000. The annual income before depreciation and taxes is expected to be $65,000 for the next three years (2001, 2002 and 2003) with the old machine, and $122,000, $135,000 and $130,000 for the 1st, 2nd and 3rd years, respectively, with the new machine. The salvage values of the old and new machines three years from today (end of 2003) is expected to be $3,500 and $4,000, respectively. The income tax rate is 25%. This income tax applies to operating income as well as to the book gains or losses on the machinery. Book gain or loss is defined as the difference between market value and the tax book-value of the machine. Book-value for taxation purposes is the original cost minus accumulated depreciation.

Tables 2.3 to 2.6 provide the calculation of initial investment, incremental operating cash flows, terminal cash flows and overall cash flows for the proposed Repco Replacement Investment Project.

For replacement projects, we need to include proceeds from both the new asset and the old asset. The rationale for each of these flows is:

· At the termination of the project the new machine will be sold for its salvage value and a cash inflow will occur.
· The proceeds from the sale of the old machine are subtracted in arriving at the terminal cash flow of the proposed replacement investment, because if the replacement project commenced (at the beginning of year 2001), the old asset would have been sold at that time. The proceeds from the sale of the old machine at that time were $35,000. This was treated as a capital outflow in calculating the initial investment value of the proposed replacement investment project. The $3,500 salvage value of the old machine

Table 2.3. *Repco Replacement Investment Project: initial investment*

Cost of new machine	123,000	(depreciable outlay)
+ Installation	3,000	(depreciable outlay)
− Proceeds from sale of old machine	35,000	
+ Taxes on sale of old machine	1,400	
+ Change in net working capital		
(8,000 + 25,000 −13,000)	20,000	
Initial investment	$112,400	

$$\text{Taxes on sale of old machine} = (\text{Sale proceeds} - \text{Book-value}) \times \text{Tax rate}$$
$$= (35{,}000 - 29{,}400) \times 0.25$$
$$= \$1{,}400$$

$$\text{Book-value} \quad = \text{Cost} - \text{Tax-allowable accumulated depreciation}$$
$$= 49{,}000 - (9{,}800 \times 2)$$
$$= \$29{,}400$$

Table 2.4. *Repco Replacement Investment Project: incremental operating cash flows ($)*

	EOY 1	EOY 2	EOY 3
New machine			
1. Operating income	122,000	135,000	130,000
2. Depreciation	42,000	42,000	42,000
3. Income before tax ((1) − (2))	80,000	93,000	88,000
4. Tax @ 25%	20,000	23,250	22,000
5. Income after tax ((3) − (4))	60,000	69,750	66,000
6. Operating cash inflows ((5) + (2))	102,000	111,750	108,000
Old machine			
1. Operating income	65,000	65,000	65,000
2. Depreciation	9,800	9,800	9,800
3. Income before tax ((1) − (2))	55,200	55,200	55,200
4. Tax @ 25%	13,800	13,800	13,800
5. Income after tax ((3) − (4))	41,400	41,400	41,400
6. Operating cash inflows ((5) + (2))	51,200	51,200	51,200
Incremental			
1. New machine	102,000	111,750	108,000
2. Old machine	51,200	51,200	51,200
3. Proposal's incremental cash inflows ((1) − (2))	50,800	60,550	56,800

at the end of 2003 is included as a terminal cash outflow as it represents an opportunity cost. That is, the old machine's sale proceeds of $3,500 (which would have been a terminal cash inflow 'without' the proposed project) are now lost 'with' the proposed project. Therefore, that amount is attributed as a cash outflow for the proposed replacement project.

Table 2.5. *Repco Replacement Investment Project: terminal cash flow*

Proceeds from sale of new machine	4,000
− Proceeds from sale of old machine	3,500
− Taxes on sale of new machine	1,000
+ Taxes on sale of old machine	875
+ Recovery of working capital	20,000
	$20,375

Taxes on sale of new machine = (Sale proceeds − Book-value) × Tax rate
$$= (4,000 - 0) \times 0.25$$
$$= \$1,000$$
Book-value = Cost − Tax-allowable accumulated depreciation
$$= 126,000 - (42,000 \times 3) = 0$$
Taxes on sale of old machine = (Sale proceeds − Book-value) × tax rate
$$= (3,500 - 0) \times 0.25$$
$$= \$875$$
Tax book-value = Cost − Tax-allowable accumulated depreciation
$$= 49,000 - (9,800 \times 5) = 0$$

Table 2.6. *Repco Replacement Investment Project: overall cash flow ($)*

	EOY 0	EOY 1	EOY 2	EOY 3
Initial investment	−112,400			
Terminal cash flow				20,375
Operating cash flows		50,800	60,550	56,800
Total cash flow	−112,400	50,800	60,550	77,175

The two capital flow components – the initial investment and the terminal cash flow – and the operating cash flow component represent a project's overall cash flows. These are summarized in Table 2.6.

Concluding comments

Cash flow estimation is a complex task. The question to be asked when defining these cash flows is: what will the firm's cash flows be like 'with the project' and 'without the project'? Each individual case will have idiosyncratic flows, and only persistent application of the principle of comparing the situations 'with' and 'without' the project will help to define the relevant cash flows. All relevant cash flows are *future* cash flows – sunk costs are not relevant in capital budgeting. Estimation of cash flows, therefore, involves forecasting. The next two chapters discuss selected quantitative and qualitative forecasting methods. Chapter 6 shows how to evaluate projects by applying the NPV and other project valuation criteria to cash flows to facilitate decision-making on proposed projects.

Review questions

2.1 A simplified hypothetical accounting income statement for XYZ Company is given below.

Income Statement for XYZ Company, year ending 31 December 2002

	$ millions
Sales	45,000
Cost of goods sold	14,000
Other expenses	350
Selling, general and administrative expenses	12,455
Depreciation	2,500
Earnings before interest and taxes (EBIT)	15,695
Interest expense	495
Taxable income	15,200
Tax payable @ 30%	4,560
Net income (after tax)	10,640

Further information:

Sales: It is reasonable to assume that approximately 50% of sales are on credit. The credit terms are 90 days. For simplicity, assume all credit customers take the full 90 days to pay.

Cost of goods sold: In addition to the cost of goods sold given in the table, inventories increased $60 million in this year.

Selling, general, administrative and other expenses: The XYZ Company has 90 days to pay on all accounts and the company takes full advantage of this facility.

(a) What is the difference between the 'sales' in this financial statement and in what would be recorded as a project's cash flow? What is the cash inflow from sales for XYZ?

(b) How is the 'cost of goods sold' recorded in financial statements? Can the cost of goods sold and its cash flow be easily reconciled? Is it really necessary to reconcile these two in order to arrive at cash outflow related to cost of goods sold for project cash flow analysis?

(c) What is the cash flow related to the 'selling, general, administrative and other expenses' of XYZ?

(d) Distinguish between 'accounting depreciation' and 'tax-allowable depreciation' and explain why only tax-allowable depreciation has implications for project cash flows.

(e) What is 'EBIT' and why is it not used in project cash flows?

(f) Why is 'interest expense' and its tax savings not included in project cash flow analysis?

(g) In the context of project cash flow analysis, define 'taxable income'.

(h) Define 'tax payable' in the context of project cash flow analysis.

(i) Define 'net income'.

(j) Derive the year's cash flow from the XYZ Income Statement after considering the points discussed in the answers to previous parts.

2.2 Kajukotuwa Corporation is considering the purchase of a new item of equipment to replace the current one. The new equipment will cost $100,000 and requires $7,000 in installation costs. It will be depreciated using the straight line method over a five-year period. The old equipment was purchased for $40,000 five years ago. It was being depreciated using the straight line method over a five-year economic life. The old machine's market value today is $45,000. As a result of the proposed replacement the corporation's investment in working capital is expected to increase by $12,000. The tax rate is 30%.

(a) Calculate the book-value of the old machine.

(b) Calculate the taxes, if any, attributable to the sale of the old machine.

(c) Determine the initial investment associated with the proposed equipment replacement.

3   Forecasting cash flows: quantitative techniques and routes

Forecasting is important in all facets of business. A supermarket needs to forecast the demand for different types of cleaning agents, soft drinks and meat products. A car manufacturer has to forecast the demand for the different types of cars it produces. A farmer must forecast the demand for a variety of crops when deciding what to plant next spring. A government must forecast its tax revenue in order to design its budget each year. A business corporation needs to forecast the future requirement of different types of labour inputs, raw materials, machines and buildings as an integral part of its business processes. All business firms have to plan for the future. The success of a business firm is closely related to how well management is able to anticipate the future and develop suitable strategies. No business organization can function effectively without forecasts for the goods and services it provides and the inputs it purchases.

In project evaluation, the 'cash flows' of a proposed project refer to expected future cash flows of that project. The reference is not to past or historical data, but to future data expected from the proposed project. Perhaps the most critically important task in project appraisal is the forecasting of expected cash flows. The cash flows form the basis of project appraisal. If the cash flow estimates are not reliable, the detailed investment analyses can easily lead, regardless of the sophisticated project appraisal techniques used, to poor business decisions. Therefore, reliable estimates of cash flows by careful and diligent forecasting are critically important.

The estimation of cash flows for project appraisal may be viewed as having four main stages:

- forecasting the capital outlays and operating cash inflows (e.g. cash proceeds from product sales) and outflows (e.g. expenses) of the proposed project;
- adjusting these estimates for tax factors, and calculating the after-tax cashflows;
- determining the variables which have the greatest impact on the project's net present value (sensitivity analysis); and
- allocating further resources, if necessary, to improve the reliability of the critical variables identified in the preceding stage.

Capital outlays of the project may be relatively easy to estimate. In many cases, they are made during the first year or the first few years of the project in its establishment stages.

Sales and operating expenses normally occur throughout the planning period for the project analysis. From the sales and operating expenses, net operating cash flows can be derived. By adjusting these estimates for tax factors, the after-tax cash flows can be calculated.

It is also important to identify all the variables that determine the cash flows and to assess which of those variables have the greatest influence on cash flows. These variables (which have the greatest influence on cash flows and hence on the project's net present value) are usually called *critical variables*, because the values of these variables are critical to the project's success or failure. An unexpected change in values of these variables can considerably affect the project's expected NPV, turning a viable project into a non-viable one. *Sensitivity analysis*, which will be discussed in Chapter 8, is used to determine which variables have a pronounced effect on the project's NPV.

Once these critical variables are identified, further resources may, if warranted, be allocated to obtaining more reliable forecasts of their future values. These variables require close monitoring both during the data acquisition process and after the project's implementation, with a view to early intervention if necessary.

Managers can use sound judgement, intuition and awareness of the state of the economy to obtain an idea or a 'gut feeling' of what is likely to happen in the future. However, translating this feeling into numbers which can be used to represent the next five years' sales, the next years' raw material requirements, or the next ten years' cash flows is often difficult. Knowledge of suitable forecasting methods and the ability to apply them can help managers to estimate future values now. Since the interest in capital budgeting is in medium- to long-term investment projects, the focus is on annual cash flow forecasts (and not on weekly, monthly or quarterly forecasts).

Forecasting is a highly complex and detailed subject. Some forecasting techniques involve a rigorous, formal methodology while some are more informal and subjective. Entire books have been written about forecasting, and a large number of forecasting techniques are available.

An analyst, who will use a selected technique or combination of techniques, may (depending upon the nature of the project) use different *routes* (or paths or procedures) to arrive at a set of forecasts. Selected techniques and routes which are widely used in capital budgeting forecasts are sketched in Figure 3.1.

Selected techniques (or methods) have been classified into two main groups, namely, quantitative and qualitative. As the ways of thinking for forecasting, two *routes* have been identified, i.e. top-down and bottom-up. This chapter will discuss the *quantitative techniques* and *routes* listed in Figure 3.1. Chapter 4 will discuss *qualitative* (or judgemental) *techniques*, examples of which are again listed in Figure 3.1. Given the special features associated with forestry projects and property investments, cash flow forecasts will be revisited in the specific contexts of forestry project evaluation, in Chapters 10 and 13, and property investment analysis, in Chapter 15.

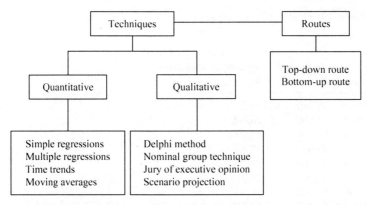

Figure 3.1.   Forecasting techniques and routes

Study objectives

After studying this chapter the reader should be able to:

- evaluate the suitability of several quantitative forecasting techniques for a given project
- employ a selected technique or combination of techniques to forecast cash flows for a given project
- identify a suitable forecasting route for estimating cash flows for a given project.

Quantitative techniques

Quantitative techniques can be used when (1) past information about the variable being forecast is available, and (2) information can be quantified. These techniques use quantitative data and quantitative methods to estimate relationships between variables or to identify the behaviour of a single variable over a period of time. These relationships or behaviours are then used for making forecasts.

Forecasting with regression analysis

Regression equations attempt to explain the behaviour of a selected dependent variable by the behaviour of one or more independent (or explanatory) variables. For example, the behaviour of sales (units) of a particular brand of car may be dependent on four explanatory variables – personal income, the price and advertising expenditure of that brand and the price of its closest substitute brand.

In order to forecast the future values using an estimated regression equation, it is first necessary to identify the variables which explain the historical behaviour of the dependent variable. If the historical values for the relevant variables can be collected, an appropriate regression equation can be estimated using, for example, the ordinary least squares (OLS) technique. If the future values of the explanatory (or independent) variables of

Table 3.1. *Desk sales and number*
of households

Year	Desks sold Y	Number of households X
1992	50,010	26,500
1993	47,500	26,600
1994	53,410	27,000
1995	56,005	27,800
1996	52,605	28,300
1997	58,015	29,010
1998	61,900	31,500
1999	66,005	32,300
2000	72,200	32,900
2001	68,000	33,100

this regression equation can be predicted, those values can then be used to forecast the future values of the dependent variable. For example, car sales can be forecast by substituting the future values of the explanatory variables into the estimated car sales regression equation.

When the dependent variable being forecast is largely influenced by a single explanatory variable, the two-variable regression model – one explanatory variable explaining the behaviour of the dependent variable – is used. When the variable being forecast is influenced by two or more explanatory variables, the multiple regression model – two or more variables explaining the behaviour of the dependent variable – is used.

The two-variable regression model

Two-variable (or simple) regression analysis is best explained using an example. A desk-manufacturing company, Top Desk Inc., has experienced, over the last decade or so, a gradual increase in demand for its desks. The company finds that this increase is caused by the gradual increase in the number of households in the region over time. Desk sales and number of households for the period 1992–2001 are presented in Table 3.1. Top Desk's research and development department has access to a set of reliable population projections for the next five years and believes that the past pattern of increase in the number of households in the region will continue over the next five years. Research also suggests that no (desk-manufacturing) competitor is expected to enter this particular market for at least the next five years provided Top Desk continues to satisfy the market. The company is considering expanding its capacity to meet the increasing demand by investing a considerable sum of capital. This is the proposed project for which cash flow forecasts are being sought. As a first step, Top Desk wants to forecast the demand for its desks for the next five years.

Since the past trend is expected to continue in the future and one single variable (the number of households) seems to influence the desk sales, the project analyst would use simple regression analysis. In this case, the form of the regression equation is:

$$Y = \alpha + \beta X + U$$

where:

$Y =$ the dependent variable, which is Top Desk's annual desk sales
$X =$ the independent (or explanatory) variable, which is the number of households in the region.
$\alpha =$ a parameter of the regression equation called the regression intercept
$\beta =$ a parameter of the regression equation called the regression slope or
regression coefficient
$U =$ stochastic disturbance, or error term.

The error term U is also called the random (or stochastic) disturbance since it disturbs an otherwise deterministic relation. This error term is a surrogate for all those variables which may have negative and positive influences on Y. The expected (or average) value of these influences is assumed to be zero.

The values of the two parameters in the above regression equation can be estimated using the ordinary least squares (OLS) regression technique, which is widely used in statistical estimation and forecasting. The data set in Table 3.1 is used for illustration.

> Workbook
> 3.1

The regression function in Excel is used for estimating the regression equation with the data in Table 3.1. This function is found in Excel under the Tools, Data Analysis menu. Following the insertion of appropriate data for input Y and input X, regression analysis can be performed. The Excel regression output is held in Workbook 3.1. Using selected data from the Excel output, the regression equation (along with relevant test statistics) can be written as:

$$\hat{Y} = -28,326 + 2.945\,X \qquad R^2 = 0.92$$

$$(-3.2) \quad (9.9)$$

The values in parentheses are t values, which are used to test whether the coefficient estimates are statistically significant. R^2 is a measure of overall 'goodness of fit' of the regression equation.

The estimated value of α, the regression intercept, is $-28,326$, and β, the regression slope is 2.945.

The details pertaining to various statistical significance tests of regression models are found in most statistics and econometric textbooks. Two examples are Kmenta (1990) and Gujarati (1995). In this capital budgeting textbook, it is not intended to go into the details of statistics. As a rule of thumb, for samples of more than ten observations, it is quite safe to assume that if the t value is greater than two, the coefficient is statistically significant, and if it is less than two, the relevant coefficient is not statistically significant (meaning it cannot be declared different from zero).[1] For example, the t value for the coefficient estimate 2.945 is 9.9, suggesting the estimate is strongly (statistically) significant.

The t value for the intercept estimate $-28,326$ is -3.2, indicating that the estimate is statistically significant. The value of the intercept indicates the average level of desk sales when the number of households is zero. However, this is a mechanical interpretation of the intercept term and, in regression analysis, such literal interpretation of the intercept term may not always be meaningful. Very often we cannot attach any physical meaning to the intercept (Gujarati, 1995, pp. 82–4). Except in cases where the regression analysis is deliberately set up to emphasize the intercept value, statistical significance tests on the intercept or interpretation of its value are not generally important or relevant. In our example, it does not make much sense to interpret the intercept value. The sample range of the explanatory variable (number of households) does not include zero as one of the observed values.

For the purpose of forecasting, the statistical significance of individual coefficients is not as important as the regression equation as a whole. To test the statistical significance of the regression equation as a whole, we can look at the value of R^2, the coefficient of determination. A regression with an R^2 value close to 1 is preferred. As a rough guide, regressions with R^2 greater than 0.6 are accepted as reasonable for forecasting purposes in industrial research.

The (adjusted) R^2 value of 0.92 says that 92% of the variation in the dependent (or explained) variable Y is explained by the independent (or explanatory) variable X, number of households.

The estimated equation (presented above) can be used to forecast sales of desks. This will be illustrated later in this section.

The multiple regression model

In the two-variable regression model, there was only one independent (or explanatory) variable. In many situations, the behaviour of a given variable is explained not by a single independent variable but by a number of variables. An example is the sales of a particular brand of car, mentioned earlier. Also in the Top Desk example, the desk sales may be influenced not only by the number of households but also by household income.

Here we consider the multiple regression model which enables the incorporation of more than one explanatory variable in the regression. A multiple regression equation has one dependent variable (Y) and two or more explanatory variables. For example, a multiple regression equation with two explanatory variables may be written in the form:

$$Y = \alpha + \beta_1 X_1 + \beta_2 X_2 + U$$

A multiple regression equation with three explanatory variables may be written in the form:

$$Y = \alpha + \beta_1 X_1 + \beta_2 X_2 + \beta_3 X_3 + U$$

---

[1] More precisely, the critical value of the t-statistic for rejecting the null hypothesis that a parameter differs from zero (in a two-tailed test) approaches 1.96 as the sample size approaches infinity. If the null hypothesis is rejected, it may be concluded (though some uncertainty still remains) that the coefficient in the underlying time series 'population' is not zero.

Table 3.2. *Desk sales, number of households and average household income*

Year	Desks sold Y	Number of households X_1	Income ($) X_2
1992	50,010	26,500	39,300
1993	47,500	26,600	36,600
1994	53,410	27,000	40,000
1995	56,005	27,800	40,500
1996	52,605	28,300	41,450
1997	58,015	29,010	43,500
1998	61,900	31,500	42,500
1999	66,005	32,300	47,200
2000	72,200	32,900	51,400
2001	68,000	33,100	49,000

Let us now estimate a three-variable multiple regression (which has one dependent variable and two explanatory variables). To illustrate a multiple regression and, at the same time, to show how the regression coefficient values change when another variable is added, another variable, household income, is added as X_2 to the data in Table 3.1. The new data set is presented in Table 3.2.

> Workbook
>   3.2

Again, Excel's regression function is used to estimate the regression. The full Excel regression output can be viewed in Workbook 3.2.

Using selected Excel output, the regression equation (along with the relevant test statistics) can be written as:

$$\hat{Y} = -24,237 + 1.426\,X_1 + 0.944\,X_2 \qquad R^2 = 0.96$$

$$(-3.86) \quad (2.67) \qquad (3.09)$$

Notice the change in the X_1 slope coefficient (from 2.945 to 1.426). Compared to the two-variable regression estimate, the multiple regression seems to improve slightly the R^2 (from 0.92 to 0.96) as a result of the addition of another explanatory variable. Both regression estimates are highly statistically significant. In this case, either of the two equations can be used for forecasting purposes. The assumption, of course, is that population and income projections are available.

Forecasting using regression results

Assume that the company wants to forecast desk sales for the next five years, 2002–2006, and the relevant household and income projections are available. These data are presented in Table 3.3.

Table 3.3. *Household and income projections, 2002–2006*

	Number of households	Income ($)
Year	X_1	X_2
2002	35,000	52,000
2003	35,990	54,100
2004	37,000	55,000
2005	38,500	56,970
2006	39,800	58,000

Table 3.4. *Desk sales forecasts using two-variable and multiple regressions*

	Sales forecasts using	
	Household projections	Household and income projections
Year	X_1	X_1 and X_2
2002	74,749	74,761
2003	77,665	78,155
2004	80,639	80,445
2005	85,057	84,444
2006	88,885	87,270

Using either the two-variable or the multiple regression analysis, the expected number of desk sales can be forecast. The results from Workbook 3.2 are reproduced in Table 3.4. As an illustration of the mechanics of producing these forecasts, the estimation of the first figure using both one-variable and multiple regressions is shown below:

Workbook
3.2

Forecast for year 2002 using two-variable regression:

$$\hat{Y} = -28{,}326 + 2.945\,(35{,}000) = 74{,}749$$

Forecast for year 2002 using multiple regression:

$$\hat{Y} = -24{,}237 + 1.426\,(35{,}000) + 0.944\,(52{,}000) = 74{,}761$$

The two forecasting models provide similar estimates in this particular case and, therefore, either set of forecasts can be chosen. In reality, however, forecasts produced from two models can vary considerably. In such situations, the two sets of forecasts can be used in two alternative scenarios of the project when a project is analysed under different scenarios.

The reliability of the forecast values depends on the reliability of the predicted values for the explanatory variables. Often, the values for the predictors are readily available. For example, population and household income projections as well as other leading statistical indicators of the economy or industrial performance are readily available from reliable sources for most of the countries in the world.

If the past pattern is expected to continue into the future, regression models can provide reasonable forecasts for the key cash flow variables. It is also worth noting here that if turning points in the predictors can be foreseen, then turning points in cash flow variables can also be predicted.

Forecasting with time-trend projections

One basic requirement when using regression analysis for forecasting is the availability of predictions for the explanatory variable or variables. In the preceding example, predictions were available for both the number of households and income. When such predictions are not available and when the time series exhibits a long-term trend, time-trend projections can be used for forecasting. Time-trend projections are flexible and may be used both for short-term or long-term forecasts. Time-trend forecasts are particularly suitable for time series which exhibit a consistent increase or decrease over time and where the past pattern is expected to continue in the future.

The time-trend method may be viewed as a special case of simple regression analysis where the independent variable is 'time'. Since the desk sales for Top Desk seem to have an overall upward trend, that time series (from Table 3.1) can be used to estimate a time-trend regression equation. This equation can then be used to forecast desk sales for the next five years (2002–2006).

```
Workbook
  3.3
```

Again, the Excel regression function is used. To represent time (years 1992–2001), the values 1 to 10 are used. Time is the explanatory variable; the number of desks sold is the explained (or dependent) variable. The full Excel output can be viewed in Workbook 3.3. Using selected Excel output, the estimated regression equation can be written as:

$$\hat{Y} = 44{,}535.67 + 2{,}550.788\,T \qquad R^2 = 0.87$$

where T is the explanatory variable, time.

Desk sales forecasts for the five years 2002–2006 can be obtained by substituting values of 11 to 15 for T. These calculations are shown in Workbook 3.3. The final results are reproduced in Table 3.5.

Forecasting using smoothing models

The earlier discussion of regression and time-trend models applies to situations where the historical time series exhibits a trend. However, there are situations where the historical time series does not exhibit a significant trend.

Table 3.5. *Desk sales forecasts using time-trend regression*

Values for time-trend variable (T) (corresponding to years 2002–2006)	Forecast desk sales
11	72,594
12	75,145
13	77,696
14	80,247
15	82,797

In such cases, smoothing models can be used for forecasting because these models adapt well to changes in the level of the time series. These models are particularly suitable for situations where the more recent observations are more indicative of future values. This is because these techniques can assign greater weight to the most recent observations of the time series in making forecasts. In some smoothing models, such as 'simple moving average', the average of the last three or four observations is used as the forecast for the next period. This may result in loss of information. However, if the historical data series does not exhibit a trend and if the decision-makers believe that only the most recent data are relevant, the loss of information pertaining to past periods, which are many years before the current period, is irrelevant.

Smoothing models are easy to use and generally provide reasonable forecasts for the short- to medium-term forecasting periods, for example, the next two to three years. A disadvantage of smoothing models is that they will not catch turning points since the basis of the forecast is nothing but a weighted average of the historical data. Smoothing models are also not suitable for a project concerned with a new product, as the moving averages are based on historical data for an existing product.

This subsection will illustrate the application of three smoothing-based forecasting methods: simple moving average, weighted moving average and exponential smoothing.

Simple moving average

Consider the hypothetical sales data for the past twelve years in Table 3.6, column 2. There is no trend apparent in these data. The data are used to demonstrate the calculation of the simple moving average (SMA) and its associated test statistic, the mean standard error (MSE). This test statistic is also called the root mean square error, because the square root is taken in calculating the mean standard error from the mean squared errors.

> Workbook
> 3.4

The simple moving average (SMA) uses the average of the n most recent values in the time series as the forecast for the next period. Choosing $n = 3$, three-year moving averages have been calculated using Excel and are shown in Table 3.6. Column 3 presents the simple

Table 3.6. *Hypothetical sales data and calculation of simple moving average*

Year (1)	Sales units (2)	Three-year SMA (3)	Errors = (2) − (3) (4)	Squared errors (5)
1	39,000			
2	30,500			
3	45,000	38,167	6,833	46,694,444
4	50,000	41,833	8,167	66,694,444
5	59,000	51,333	7,667	58,777,778
6	40,000	49,667	−9,667	93,444,444
7	38,000	45,667	−7,667	58,777,778
8	35,000	37,667	−2,667	7,111,111
9	45,000	39,333	5,667	32,111,111
10	50,000	43,333	6,667	44,444,444
11	41,000	45,333	−4,333	18,777,778
12	49,000	46,667	2,333	5,444,444
			Sum of squared errors =	432,277,778
			Mean standard error =	6,575

moving average values, column 4 the difference between the actual sales and the SMA values, and column 5 the squared errors which are used to calculate the mean standard error (MSE). The data in Table 3.6 along with the formulae to calculate the MSE can be viewed in Workbook 3.4. The MSE is calculated by taking the square root of the mean of the squared errors.

The first three-year moving average is calculated as:

$$SMA = \frac{39,000 + 30,500 + 45,000}{3} = 38,167$$

The next moving average is calculated by dropping year 1 and adding year 4, as follows:

$$SMA = \frac{30,500 + 45,000 + 50,000}{3} = 41,833$$

As the term *moving* suggests, the average keeps on moving by dropping the oldest observation and adding the next new observation for each new calculation. Proceeding this way, the last three-year moving average is calculated as:

$$SMA = \frac{50,000 + 41,000 + 49,000}{3} = 46,667$$

In terms of forecasting for future periods, the last moving average value (46,667 from Table 3.6, column 3) can be taken as the forecast for the next period (i.e. for year 13). A forecast for year 14 may be arrived at by obtaining the three-year moving average of the year 11 and 12 actuals (from Table 3.6, column 2) and year 13 forecast (46,667). It is 45,555. A forecast for year 15 may be arrived at by obtaining the three-year moving average of year 12 actual (49,000) and year 13 and 14 forecasts (46,667 and 45,555). It is 47,074. These forecasts can be viewed in Workbook 3.4. The moving average method may not be suitable for any forecasts beyond two to three future periods.

How to choose the value of n? If four-year moving averages are used, different forecasts will be obtained. In practice, values of n in the range three to five are often used. The Excel spreadsheet facility makes it easy to obtain sets of moving averages using different values for n. Then, the n which yields the minimum MSE can be selected for calculating the moving averages.

Weighted moving average

In SMA, each observation in the calculation receives equal weight. For example, in the three-year SMA example, all three selected observations have equal weights of one-third. In the *weighted moving average* (WMA), different weights are assigned to the values in the time series. For example, if the decision-maker believes that recent values are more important than less recent ones in arriving at forecasts, greater weight can be given to these. The weights must add up to 1.

For example, using the sales data set in Table 3.6, the sales for year 13 could be forecast by taking the three-year WMA. The allocation of weights is as follows: a weight of 0.6 for the most recent observation (which is 49,000), 0.3 for the next older observation (which is 41,000) and 0.1 for the oldest observation (which is 50,000). Then the three-year WMA for the period of years 10–12 is:

$$WMA = 50,000\,(0.1) + 41,000\,(0.3) + 49,000\,(0.6) = 46,700.$$

This forecast is different from the three-year SMA forecast which was 46,667. Depending upon the weights, this difference can be smaller or greater. Allocation of weights is largely a matter of judgement. If decision-makers believe that the recent past is a better predictor of the future than the distant past, then larger weights can be allocated to more recent observations.

Forecasting for future periods can be done following the same procedure as for SMA. To determine whether one particular combination of n and a set of weights is better than another combination, a number of combinations may be tested on an Excel spreadsheet; the combination which produces the smallest MSE may be chosen for forecasting purposes.

Exponential smoothing

This may be viewed as a special case of the weighted moving average method in which only one weight – the weight for the most recent observation – is selected. The weight assigned to this most recent observation is called the *smoothing constant*, α. The weights for the past data are computed according to a formula which assigns smaller and smaller weights as the observations move farther into the past. In other words, the weight assigned to past observations declines exponentially. The basic exponential smoothing model is:

$$F_{t+1} = \alpha Y_t + (1 - \alpha)F_t$$

Table 3.7. *Forecasts using exponential smoothing model*

Year	Calculation	Forecast
13	Reproduced from Workbook 3.5	43,995
14	$0.2 \times 49{,}000 + (1 - 0.2) \times 43{,}995 =$	44,996
15	$0.2 \times 49{,}000 + (1 - 0.2) \times 44{,}996 =$	45,797

where:

$$F_{t+1} = \text{forecast value for period } t + 1$$
$$F_t = \text{forecast value for period } t$$
$$Y_t = \text{actual value for period } t$$
$$\alpha = \text{the smoothing constant } (0 < \alpha < 1)$$

The calculations are demonstrated in Workbook 3.5. The sales data set is repeated from Table 3.6. The chosen value for α is 0.2.

> Workbook
> 3.5

The formula for exponential smoothing shows that a forecast can be constructed for only one period ahead of the final actual value. Using the above formula, the forecast for year 13 is calculated as 43,995 units. Calculation details can be viewed in Workbook 3.5. An *ad hoc* method for forecasting values for years 14 and 15 is illustrated in Table 3.7. A forecast for year 14 can be made using the actual value in year 12 (49,000), for Y_t and the year 13 forecast for F_t. The forecast for year 15 is made using the same actual value in year 12 (49,000) for Y_t and the year 14 forecast for F_t. In the absence of a technically and conceptually correct approach, this *ad hoc* method may provide an acceptable forecast for years 14 and 15.

There is no hard and fast rule for determining the value for α. It could be anywhere between 0 and 1. In practice the values between 0.1 and 0.3 are more frequently used. The closer α is to 0, the less influence the current observation has on the forecast. When α is near 1, the current observation has the greatest impact on the forecast.

In general, if the time series contains substantial random variability, a small value of the smoothing constant is favoured. If there is substantial variability, much of the forecast error emanates from that random variability. In such situations, it is not appropriate to overreact and adjust the forecasts too much. Hence, a smaller value for the smoothing constant is favoured. On the other hand, if the time series has relatively little variability, larger values of the smoothing constant lead to greater adjustments in the forecasts, thus allowing the forecast to react faster to changing conditions.

More complex time series forecasting methods

This chapter so far has illustrated the application of ordinary least squares regression (OLS) analysis – simple regressions, including time-trend projections, and multiple regressions – and three types of moving average (or smoothing) model for forecasting cash flows. These methods combined with the qualitative methods discussed in Chapter 4 may be adequate for forecasting cash flows in most cases. It is worth noting, however, that a variety of statistical techniques for forecasting using time series methodologies are available. The classical time series approach is to separate an observed series for a variable into the components of trend, cyclical variation, seasonal movements and random variation. Various forms of relationship can be assumed among these components, e.g. the additive and multiplicative models, represented respectively by $Y = T + C + S + I$ and $Y = T \times C \times S \times I$, where T is trend (which could be linear or non-linear), C is cycle, S is season and I is irregular movement. These models can be estimated by least squares regression, including use of dummy or 0–1 variables for seasonal components of the additive model and logarithms of components in the multiplicative model.

The classical method may be extended to determine causal relationships between time series variables by adding further explanatory variables (in addition to time). For example, quarterly housing starts may be explained by the four components above, and also by household formation (e.g. number of marriages), average household income, mortgage interest rate and other variables.

Various more modern time series analysis techniques are available, some of which adopt a rather mechanical (as distinct from causal) approach to forecasting. These techniques, and the statistical tests that accompany them, are referred to by a collection of acronyms, e.g. ARCH, GARCH, ARIMA, VAL and ADL. These stand for autoregressive conditional heteroscedasticity, generalized autoregressive conditional heteroscedasticity, autoregressive integrated moving average, vector autoregression and autoregressive distributed lag models, respectively. They often involve differencing a series to remove trend, and calculating a range of autocorrelation coefficients to determine lag structures. These can be powerful methods for detecting statistically significant patterns in time series data that may not be apparent from visual inspection of a graphed series. Techniques are also available to examine the relationship between two time series (referred to as cointegration techniques), which may assist in forecasting one variable when information is available about another variable.

In the context of forecasting variables determining cash flows for projects with moderate to long planning horizons, more advanced time series forecasting methods suffer from a number of limitations:

- they normally require a large number of observations of the variable or variables
- they tend to be more suitable for explaining the behaviour of, and relationship between, time series in the past than for predicting their future behaviour
- accuracy can be high for short-term forecasts (e.g. the next two quarters), but forecasts tend to fluctuate wildly when extrapolated over a number of years into the future
- future patterns in the behaviour of time series variables may differ from those observed in the past
- where a mechanical, as distinct from causal, model is used, which lacks economic logic, it can be difficult to convince a decision-maker of the reliability of the forecasts

• a time series analysis specialist is generally required to use these techniques, or at least to check that they have been applied, and the findings interpreted, in a valid manner.

This is not to say that sophisticated time series forecasting techniques should be ignored. Various excellent books are available on these techniques (e.g. Mills, 1993; Hamilton, 1994), and they will not be discussed further here.

Forecasting routes

There are various paths that an analyst can follow to obtain a set of cash flow forecasts for a proposed project. These are different ways of thinking about the forecasting process; they are not the ways in which the forecast will be expressed or modelled. The kind of path an analyst will take is determined by the nature of the project. For example, for a project dealing with an internationally traded commodity, it may be better to start from the global macro level, say by reviewing international economic conditions, in order to arrive at a set of forecasts for the individual firm's proposed project at the micro level. This is called a *top-down* route. On the other hand, for a relatively small project aimed at a local or regional market, it may be better to start at the micro level with the individual firm and then refine the forecasts to take into account possible national and international influences, if any. This is known as a *bottom-up* route. In both routes, one can use a single technique, or more often a combination of techniques, to obtain suitable cash flow forecasts.

Forecasting by the top-down route

Consider the example of a new investment in a copper-mining project. Copper is an internationally traded commodity. International economic conditions strongly influence the demand for copper and world copper prices. Therefore, the first step in forecasting copper prices may be to form a view about likely international economic conditions. *World Economic Outlook*, normally published twice a year by the International Monetary Fund, is a good source of international economic and financial forecasts. Such information may help the formation of a view about the international economic outlook and its impact on world copper demand and prices. Within the broader context of the world economic outlook, this publication provides, among other things, details on commodity price developments, including those for copper. These details may provide a basis for the proposed copper project's price forecasts. These data may be combined with the project analyst's own trend projections (obtained from moving averages or regression analysis) and qualitative (expert) judgement to arrive at a final set of copper price forecasts. On the other hand, the analyst may choose to use more sophisticated econometric models of the world copper market to forecast world copper demand and prices.

Once the copper price (P) forecasts have been prepared, the next step may be to estimate the quantities (Q) of copper that the proposed project is going to produce over the planning horizon. These estimates may be obtained from geological engineers and other experts working on the project. Sales revenue can then be obtained by multiplying P by Q. This is just a simple example to give an idea of how to obtain forecasts of sales revenues in a particular case.

The sales forecasts have to be followed by operational expenditure forecasts for the project, for example of wages, raw materials and travel expenses. By deducting these expenditures from the sales revenues, the net operating cash flows can be obtained. After making appropriate adjustments for tax factors, the net after-tax operating cash flows can be estimated.

If a firm acts without an appreciation of macro events, it will become reactive rather than proactive, and will be at the mercy of wider market forces which it has not recognized and for which it is not equipped to deal.

Forecasting by the bottom-up route

It is not necessary for all projects to start with an examination of international economic and financial developments. For example, consider a relatively small project to expand an existing local business by undertaking an additional investment. In such a case, the trend in the past sales of the existing business may be used to forecast the expected sales of the proposed investment.

Instead of starting from the international economic and financial outlook, this process begins by examining the firm's existing business trends and then adjusting these trends to suit the changing conditions in the industry and the economy, if necessary. This approach is suitable for a project which is an expansion of existing business activities and is relatively small such that the project will not have a great impact on the aggregate industry supply and price. The Top Desk project introduced previously in this chapter is a good example.

Time-trend projections estimated from the historical data of the existing business can produce an initial set of forecasts for selected variables such as unit price, unit sales, production labour cost and sales expenses. These values can then be adjusted, if necessary, to suit the changing conditions in the industry and the economy by using qualitative judgement. For example, the firm's historical data on production labour cost, sales expenses and other variable costs may suggest that they are gradually increasing over time. The trends in these variables can be estimated by fitting simple time-trend regressions to each of these historical data sets. They can then be extrapolated for future periods to obtain an initial set of forecasts. These forecasted values can then be modified to suit the expected changes in industrial relations (which may change wages and salaries), raw material prices, fuel prices, industry and general economic prospects. The more the future is expected to differ from the past, the more judgement should be incorporated into the forecasted values.

Concluding comments

This chapter has illustrated regression models (two-variable and multiple regressions and time-trend projections) and smoothing models as quantitative techniques for forecasting cash flows. In regression and time-trend models, the trend line for forecasting is computed using all the available data in the time series with equal weight given to all the past observations. Regression and time-trend models are suitable for forecasting project cash flows provided that the historical relationship among the variables will continue into the future and forecasts for the predictors are available. In smoothing models, greater weight is assigned to more recent periods. Smoothing models are suitable for forecasting cash flows of short-term projects, when the historical time series do not exhibit trends and the decision-makers believe that greater weight should be assigned to more recent years' data values.

Given the detailed and complex nature of quantitative forecasting techniques, the discussion of such techniques in this chapter is not complete. Entire books can be written on the subject and still not do it justice. The objective in this chapter has been to provide insight into some of the techniques more frequently used in capital budgeting cash flow forecasts. Regardless of which technique is considered, their success is determined by two critical factors: (1) how well the model fits the historical time series, and (2) how much the future time series looks like the past.

Two paths (or routes) that analysts frequently adopt in approaching a forecasting task, but which are not normally documented in the literature, have been identified as top-down and bottom-up routes.

Decision-makers generally combine various forecasting techniques (quantitative and qualitative) and use suitable forecasting routes to arrive at a final forecast. In the large majority of cases, some form of quantitative technique is used to arrive at a base forecast, which is then adjusted through a qualitative judgement process. The next chapter will extend the discussion of forecasting techniques to a number of qualitative (or judgemental) methods such as the Delphi method, the nominal group technique and the jury of executive opinion.

Review questions

3.1 What role does forecasting play in capital budgeting?

3.2 Explain the terms: quantitative techniques, qualitative techniques, top-down route, bottom-up route.

3.3 Two calculation methods are included within 'quantitative techniques'. These are 'regression analysis' and 'smoothing models'. Explain the processes of each, and their separate applications.

3.4 Silver Screen Inc. is a movie distribution company. It has kept records of total annual movie ticket sales for one community over ten years. These data have been related to other publicly available data as shown in Table 3.8.

For these data:

(a) Plot the data so that you can advise Silver Screen's management on a predictive model for movie ticket sales for the next few years.

(b) Discuss the relative merits of various regression and smoothing models with reference to the available data.

(c) Calculate both simple and multiple regressions.

Table 3.8. *Ticket sales, households and household income*

Year	Ticket sales	Households	Average household income ($/year)
1992	75,000	20,000	32,250
1993	82,000	20,850	34,825
1994	81,100	22,000	37,580
1995	85,250	21,800	42,015
1996	94,350	21,450	41,870
1997	92,700	22,100	44,280
1998	95,280	23,750	47,850
1999	96,480	24,100	49,250
2000	94,300	24,800	51,380
2001	97,800	25,370	54,890

(d) Calculate moving average, weighted moving average and exponential smoothing models.

(e) Establish three-year forecasts under each of the above models.

(f) Advise management as to the suitability and reliability of forecasts established under each model.

3.5 Should Silver Screen Inc. be concerned with the world-wide or country-wide economic situation when it is making predictions of movie ticket sales for the given community?

4 Forecasting cash flows: qualitative or judgemental techniques

In a perfect world, all cash flows associated with a project would be known with certainty. However, this obviously is not the case, and it is common for estimates of parameters determining cash flows to be derived by a number of techniques. In Chapter 3, the importance of forecasting cash flows was discussed and a number of quantitative means of estimating cash flows were outlined.

Quantitative forecasting techniques can be used when (1) past information about the values being forecast is available, and (2) this information can be quantified. Past information is not, however, always available or relevant. For example, for a new product, there are no data on sales on which to base estimates of future sales. Similarly, past sales of a product might not be relevant if a competitor launches a new product with superior features or performance. In other situations, there is insufficient time to obtain data or use quantitative techniques, or circumstances are changing so rapidly that a statistically based forecast would be of little guidance. Even when statistical techniques are available there is strong evidence that human judgement is the overwhelming choice of managers for forecasting. Further, managers appear to be more comfortable dealing with their own judgements or with those of a colleague, than with forecasts generated via a computer package and lacking transparency. Even when quantitative techniques are used, estimates may be combined with qualitative judgements, or supplemented, reviewed or screened by subjecting them to qualitative judgements.

It has been suggested that the widespread use of human judgement in making business forecasts can be rationalized in two ways. The first is that, in comparison with statistical models, people might be better able to detect changing patterns in time series which exhibit considerable random variation. The second rationale for the use of human judgement is that people might be able to integrate external (i.e. non-time series) information into the forecasting process. A number of qualitative forecasting techniques have been developed to provide estimates of key parameters for use in financial analysis in such situations. Qualitative forecasts can be obtained from individuals (usually experts) or by groups of people combining their judgements. In some situations, such as sales estimates, stated preferences of consumers undertaken as part of market research may be used to provide estimates.

This chapter extends the discussion of the techniques available to estimate cash flows to a number of qualitative (or judgemental) methods used either by individuals or through group processes. The use of surveys and interviewing to gather expert judgement or the opinions of individuals is first examined. A number of group techniques – including the Delphi method, the nominal group technique and the jury of executive opinion – are then explained. Two applications of the Delphi method to forecasting parameters in forestry projects are then presented.

Study objectives

After studying this chapter the reader should be able to:

- evaluate the suitability of several qualitative techniques for forecasting cash flows in a given project
- employ a selected technique or combination of techniques to forecast cash flows in a given project
- recognize the limitations of qualitative forecasting techniques.

Obtaining information from individuals

Once it has been decided that qualitative estimates are required, the analyst is faced with a number of options. For instance, the analyst must decide whether to seek estimates from individuals or from groups, and once this is decided, how to go about collecting the information. This section will discuss how qualitative estimates can be obtained from individuals, while the following section will deal with the collection of information from groups.

Information or estimates from individuals can be obtained in a number of ways. If the information requirements are simple, such as an estimate of the fuel efficiency of a particular vehicle under a particular circumstance, then a simple telephone call or email to someone with the appropriate expertise will suffice. This type of informal information gathering is undertaken on a routine basis and warrants little further discussion. There are, however, cases where the information requirements are more complex and require careful elicitation of professional or expert judgement. In such cases, more formal techniques for data collection are warranted, the most common of which is the sample survey. Hence it is appropriate here to review some aspects of the application of sample surveys in obtaining information for forecasting purposes.

Conducting a survey

The survey process for generating forecasts may be thought of as both the development and administration of a questionnaire or survey instrument, and the analysis of the survey data. That is, a survey is a process with a series of steps linked with one another. The major steps involved in the survey process are set out in Figure 4.1. The decisions made in the early stages will affect the choices at the later stages – thus the forward links in Figure 4.1. For instance, the information needs specified at the start will affect the choice of sampling design, the way in which the questionnaire is structured and the selection of data analysis

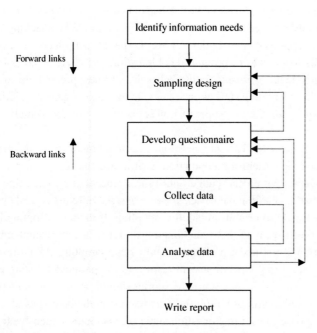

Figure 4.1. Major steps in the survey and data analysis process. (*Source:* Based on Alreck and Settle, 1995, p. 26.)

techniques. If there were only forward links in the process then a survey could be developed one step at a time, completing each step before considering the next. Implicit in this 'single direction' approach is the assumption that there are no limiting factors in later steps. This is seldom, if ever, the case. For instance there are often limitations on data collection or data processing resources, i.e. a budget. These limitations restrict the alternatives available at earlier steps; these backward linkages are indicated in Figure 4.1 by dotted lines running upwards. Backward links run from the 'Collect data' and 'Analyse data' boxes back to the 'Develop questionnaire' and 'Sampling design' boxes. This illustrates that major decisions concerning data collection and analysis should always be considered before selecting a sample and designing a questionnaire.

The amount of information that can be collected about a project is almost unlimited. However, because time and resources are limiting, it is necessary to prioritize the information needs. *Information needs* can be categorized into three levels of importance: (1) *absolutely essential*, constituting the reason for the survey (in the case of project appraisals, these data are required for the appraisal to be undertaken), (2) *highly valuable* for making important decisions, and (3) *supporting data* which clarifies the picture but is not essential. Care must be taken to group questions logically, and to identify the most important questions to be put to respondents, and to place these appropriately within the questionnaire, e.g. at a point where rapport has been established with the respondent. More intrusive or personal questions are often placed near the end of the questionnaire.

A crucial part of any survey is deciding what group of people or objects is to be surveyed; this group is commonly referred to as the *reference population*. When seeking estimates for input into project appraisals it is critical to ask the people who have the experience, knowledge and skills to be able to provide reliable estimates. There is no point asking people in production to make estimates about likely sales of a new product; this question is best addressed to either marketing staff or customers. In the case of gathering judgemental estimates used in project appraisals, the population is likely to comprise a small number of experts or semi-experts.

In such cases, it is feasible to distribute questionnaires to all members of the population, i.e. to carry out a census. Where the population is of a size that does not permit every member to be contacted, within the budget and time frame of the forecasting effort, a choice needs to be made regarding the basic *sampling design*. Here the typical choices are between probability (random) or non-probability sampling. If random sampling is chosen then further choices need to be made between sampling designs, the typical contenders being simple random sampling, stratified sampling and multi-stage sampling. As a rule of thumb, the less expert or focused the population with respect to the parameters being estimated (often corresponding to a large population), the shorter should be the questionnaire. Long questionnaires distributed to groups with little or no interest in the outcomes of the survey will result in low response rates. Long questionnaires are also more expensive to produce and analyse and are thus highly costly when large numbers are distributed.

Questionnaire development usually proceeds through a number of drafts. As part of this process the instrument may be tested on a small sub-sample in a pilot survey; this usually leads to some revision of questions. It is also critical to ensure the questionnaire is designed to elicit all the information required and that no redundant information is sought. This is best done by reference back to the previously identified information needs.

Implementation of the survey may be through personal interview, telephone interview, drop-off-and-collect or by post. Personal interviews are generally expensive and time-consuming and are suited to the situation where the target or reference population is small and not widely dispersed. Non-response bias is generally not a problem because of high participation rates generally associated with this method. This is especially so if respondents are being interviewed as part of their employment duties, which is sometimes the case when information is being collected as input into project appraisal. Telephone interviewing can be effective, especially where the information required is straightforward, but is not suitable for the collection of information that is complex and requires detailed thought or calculations. Postal surveys are usually undertaken when large sample numbers are required with a modest survey budget. Non-response bias is an issue that needs to be considered no matter what method is used; however, it is especially a concern with postal surveys.

Data analysis is the process through which the survey responses are summarized into descriptive statistics and graphs, and perhaps subjected to inferential statistical methods such as multivariate analysis and significance tests. In a highly structured questionnaire, highly specific information is sought. Respondents are required to provide specific estimates, such as estimates of sales quantity of a new product or the date that an event is likely to occur. Alternatively, respondents may be required to choose one option from a discrete set of options or to rank a particular statement on a predetermined scale. In such cases, descriptive statistics such as means, medians and standard errors can be easily calculated and used in project appraisal. Open-ended questions within a questionnaire allow respondents the opportunity to answer the question in their own words, and relay their particular perceptions, which can provide insights into specific issues and problems, but also poses challenges when analysing the responses.

Report generation produces a permanent record of the data collection process and findings. When the information is being collected for internal use – often the case in project appraisal – the report, if prepared at all, may be rudimentary and involve simple summary tables and only brief discussion of the data.

The preceding material is a brief outline of some of the major elements of undertaking a survey. A number of texts are available which provide more detail on the survey process. An excellent survey research resource is *The Survey Research Handbook* (Alreck and Settle, 1995).

Surveys and market-research-based assessments

Consumer surveys, which seek to identify the purchasing intentions of consumers, are common and may provide useful data for forecasting. Forecasters may rely on data from surveys undertaken by research-based organizations that publish indices relating to consumer sentiment and consumer buying plans. From these, some indication may be gained about likely increases or decreases in the sales of a company's products, and this may be useful in the forecasting process. An alternative to these published surveys is for the company or forecaster to conduct their own survey.

The sales force composite method

This method is commonly used in the manufacturing and retailing sector to forecast sales. The method involves seeking the views of individual salespersons and sales management as to the sales outlook. The technique can be divided into three general categories, namely the 'grass-roots approach', the 'sales management technique' and the 'distributor approach'.

The *grass-roots approach* is based around the collection of estimates of sales by each salesperson for a company, either on forms submitted to the central office or given to the regional or district sales manager who then forwards them to the central office. These estimates are often collected at an annual budgeting exercise using a bottom-up budgeting approach. The only real quality control over this process is the judgement and assessment by top management of the reasonableness of estimates by local sales people. Sometimes corporate staff may make independent estimates which are then used to check the figures obtained by aggregating the estimates provided by local salespeople. Proponents of the grass-roots approach maintain that its main strengths are (1) the use of the specialist knowledge of those closest to the market-place (2) the placing of responsibility on those who can most affect the actual results, and (3) that it lends itself to the easy breakdown of forecasts into categories, such as by salesperson, region and product line. The major criticism of the technique is that salespeople are actually often unaware of the broader economic factors that drive demand and are thus poor forecasters of future sales activity.

The *sales management technique* and the *wholesaler or distributor approach* are alternatives to the grass-roots approach that also rely on forecasts by people involved in the sales process. With the sales management approach, the sales executives rather than individual salespersons make forecasts. The rationale for this is that sales executives have a greater appreciation of the broader economic factors that affect the demand for particular products, as well as having almost the same level of appreciation of on-ground sales patterns as individual sales staff. This method reduces the number of people involved in providing forecasts but has the disadvantage of sales staff not being committed to achieving the sales forecast because they were not involved in its development. The wholesaler, or distributor, approach is based on obtaining forecasts from distributors of products. This is usually done when a manufacturing company uses independent distribution channels rather than direct sales to end-users of their products.

Using groups to make forecasts

Evidence suggests that forecasts produced by groups offer greater forecasting accuracy than those derived from an individual. Groups also provide more information, although the marginal increase in information content decreases as group size increases. The use of groups also provides an opportunity to gain more information about the range of possible outcome values, hence giving an insight into the risk associated with the estimates. From a behavioural perspective, it is also likely that a group responsible for implementing a project will have greater commitment to it if they are also involved in providing estimates of variables used in the financial analysis leading up to a decision to proceed.

When group members are allowed to interact, this may be in a structured or unstructured manner. Group processes, particularly those that are unstructured (also referred to as 'interacting groups'), also have a number of shortcomings (Janis and Mann, 1977; Lock, 1987), namely:

(1) *Group think*: In meetings, one idea is often pursued for a considerable period of time and thinking consequently becomes narrow or confined. This often reflects a common information base of group members and a desire for and encouragement of conformity.
(2) *Inhibition of contributors*: Within groups there are often power differentials and members of a group may be unwilling to contradict a superior, or even express an opinion. Also, dominant personalities may reduce the willingness of others to contribute.
(3) *Premature closure*: There often is a tendency for the group to adopt the first satisfactory option or estimate without fully exploring other options or possibilities.

A number of structured group techniques have been developed which aim to minimize these social and psychological difficulties. Some of these structured techniques will now be examined.

The jury of executive opinion

This technique is one of the simplest and most widely used forecasting approaches. In its most basic form it simply involves executives meeting and deciding on the best estimate for the item being forecast. As a precursor to the meeting, it is common to provide background information to executives.

A major drawback of this approach is that it places those making the forecasts in direct contact with each other thus allowing *ad hoc* and uncontrolled interaction. The potential exists for problems of group interactions (e.g. dominance of individuals and group think) to arise. In particular, the weight attached to the opinion of a particular individual is likely to be determined by the position of that individual in the organization and their personality. The views of executives with the best information or in the best position to make an accurate forecast are not necessarily given sufficient weight.

One variation of this approach involves the jury periodically submitting estimates in writing, which are then reviewed by the president or some other senior member. The person reviewing the individual forecasts will sometimes make a final assessment based on the opinions expressed. In doing so, this person will often call on past experience to take into account which executives are biased, and in which direction, and then weight each individual's estimate accordingly. Alternatively, the individual estimates can be averaged to derive a forecast which is considered to be a forecast representative of the group. The latter approach could almost be considered an informal variant of the Delphi method discussed below.

The Delphi method

The Delphi method was originally developed by the Rand Corporation in the 1950s to obtain consensus among experts. Since that time it has been refined further and applied to gain information in a wide range of fields. These fields are as diverse as regional economic development, health care policy, sociology, environmental risks, prediction of fruit prices, tourism and recreation, forestry and advanced manufacturing techniques. The Delphi technique may be particularly useful in situations where strictly objective data are scarce.

The Delphi method is designed to elicit estimates from experts within a group or panel without allowing interaction between individuals on the panel, thus avoiding problems with dominant members. Experts do, however, have the ability to revise their estimates on the basis of group views. Such an option is not available using the traditional survey method. This technique proceeds through a series of data collection rounds. In a classic Delphi survey, the first round is unstructured, allowing panellists to identify freely and elaborate on the issues that they consider important. These are consolidated into a single set by the monitors, who then produce a structured questionnaire designed to elicit the views, opinions and judgements of the panellists in a quantitative form. The consolidated list of scenarios is presented to the panellists in the second round, at which time they place estimates on key variables, such as the time an event will occur. These responses are then summarized and the summary information is presented to the panellists, who are invited to reassess their original opinions in the light of anonymous individual responses. In addition, if panellists' assessments fall outside the upper or lower quartiles, they may be asked to provide justification of why they consider their estimates are more accurate than the median values. Further rounds of collection of estimates, compiling summary information and inviting revisions continue until there is no further convergence of expert opinion. Experience reveals this usually occurs after two rounds, or at the most four rounds (Janssen, 1978).

There are a number of variants on the classic Delphi method. When the issues are well defined, a clearly specified scenario can be developed by the monitoring team. In such circumstances, it is common to replace the unstructured first round with a highly structured set of questions through which specific estimates of parameters are obtained. A statistical summary of all responses is then provided to the panel for the second round, rather than the third. In such cases, it is common for the Delphi method to include only one or two iterations.

The classic Delphi method is conducted through a combination of a polling procedure and a conference. However, communication between conference panellists is restricted and undertaken through the monitoring team. Even though panellists are at the same physical location, there is no face-to-face contact. A variant is the 'paper' Delphi (sometimes also known as a 'paper-and-pencil Delphi poll') that is conducted entirely by mail. Another variant is the 'real time' Delphi in which feedback is provided by computer and final results are usually available at the end of the session.

The quality of forecasts provided by the Delphi method (and other forecasting techniques) very much depends on how the technique is applied. The following list of suggestions on how best to apply the Delphi method are primarily those of Parente, Anderson, Myers and O'Brien (1984) with a few additions from other sources:

(1) The criteria for the selection of panellists (education, experience) should be carefully determined and clearly communicated.
(2) A minimum of ten panellists after dropout is recommended, although it is sometimes suggested that five is sufficient.
(3) Commitment to serve on the panel should be secured before the first round of forecasts is requested. This will improve motivation and ensure a balanced sample if dropout is likely. Time should be taken to explain the Delphi technique and the information provided.
(4) A range of forecast problems may be presented, although these should be less than twenty-five in number. Where appropriate, the main forecast should be broken down into sub-problems. Alternatively, different outcomes might be presented and their likelihood requested. Either way, the forecast will be useless unless the right problems are presented, hence effort needs to be put into framing the problem. Some pretesting may be appropriate, especially if the Delphi survey is being undertaken through the post.
(5) Problem statements should not be longer than twenty words and should use quantitative data (e.g. '50% increase') rather than fuzzy language (e.g. 'considerable increase').
(6) Guidelines for good questionnaire design should be applied to the presentation of problems. These include avoiding compound sentences.
(7) If the purpose of the Delphi process is to generate forecast problems then it is suggested that examples of attractive and undesirable scenarios be presented.

(8) Whatever the means of administering the Delphi technique – mail, a networked computer or a face-to-face meeting – the same steps are involved in the process. Factors such as cost, the need for timely information or the availability of experts to attend a face-to-face meeting may determine the appropriate method.

(9) The principle of anonymity should be ensured. The organiser's opinions on the forecast should not be communicated to the panellists.

(10) The amount and form of the feedback will need to be carefully managed. The number of rounds will depend on the panellists and the manner in which the Delphi survey is conducted (e.g. the choice of stage at which to distribute a highly structured questionnaire). The general advice is that more rather than fewer rounds, as well as descriptive feedback, are preferable. Medians should be provided.

(11) Extreme responses should be screened for the panellist's expertise. If the expert has relatively low expertise, then the response might be discounted.

(12) If the Delphi survey is directed to research applications, a detailed report of the process should be published to allow replication by other researchers at a later time. The range of responses should be published to demonstrate the degree of consensus.

The nominal group technique

The nominal group technique (NGT) uses the basic Delphi structure but in face-to-face meetings which allow discussion among participants. A meeting with NGT starts without any interaction, with individuals initially writing down ideas or estimates related to the problem or scenario. Each individual then presents their ideas or estimates, with no discussion until all participants have spoken. Then each idea or estimate is discussed. The process is then repeated. For this reason, NGT is sometimes known as the 'estimate–talk–estimate' procedure. In practical terms, like Delphi, the framing of the questions or the scenario is crucial for the success of the process. Also, ideally, the leader or moderator of the discussion should come from outside the group.

Other group techniques

A number of other group techniques are available. The *Devil's advocate* and *dialectical inquiry* involve individuals or small groups taking a 'devil's advocate' role or using the dialectic approach (presenting multiple views) to explore alternative options. Both methods are considered to be ways of overcoming the problem of 'group think' discussed earlier.

Lock (1987) has also outlined a further approach to group judgemental forecasting which draws upon elements of the nominal group technique and inquiry systems. Inquiry systems, according to Lock, are simply philosophical systems that underlie different approaches to analysing or investigating particular phenomena. This approach consists of seven phases:

(1) problem/task definition
(2) pre-collection of estimates of the variable of interest and the reasoning behind the estimates

(3) sharing of the estimates and clarification of the reasoning behind them
(4) discussion of underlying reasoning
(5) encouragement of multiple advocacy (dialectical inquiry)
(6) individual revision of estimates
(7) synthesis of estimates

This approach recognizes the benefits of communication among group members.

The Delphi technique applied to appraising forestry projects

In this section, the Delphi technique is illustrated in the context of collecting information for a financial analysis of forestry projects. The illustration is based on two real-life Delphi surveys undertaken in northern Australia.

A simple model for appraising forestry investment

A simple model for appraising investment in forestry projects is illustrated in Figure 4.2. This diagram illustrates the key parameters which need to be estimated in evaluating forestry projects, namely harvest volumes and stumpage prices for the various types of timber harvested, and input costs. It is also critical to have estimates of the timing of these items throughout the plantation life, or 'rotation length'. The estimates made at the time of planting become *forecasts* for deriving cash flows for the various years throughout the plantation's life. This information can then be entered onto a spreadsheet in which annual net cash flows

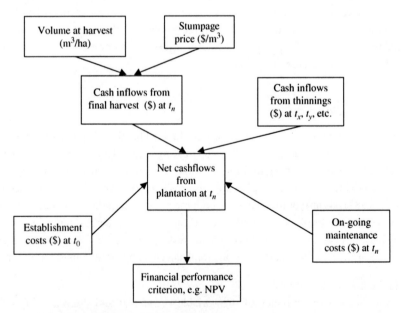

Figure 4.2.   A simple model for appraising investment in forestry projects.

and financial performance criteria are derived. Performance estimates are typically made on a one-hectare basis, and then aggregated to the plantation size.

For a traditional exotic conifer plantation such as radiata or Caribbean pine, it is relatively easy to obtain estimates of the various parameters of the model. For example, costs of establishment, ongoing maintenance and non-commercial thinning are easily obtained, for example from contractors. Yield estimates, along with final harvest price, are the two key parameters in determining final harvest revenue. For pine plantations there are well-developed stand growth models, based on many years of past growth data, that can provide accurate projections of likely yield. The following two examples, on the other hand, apply to situations where non-traditional species are grown, and hence little stand growth data are available.

Example 4.1. Appraising forestry projects involving new species

In recent years there has been a move away from traditional silviculture systems involving monocultures of a small number of mostly softwood species. In Australia, for example, plantations of native hardwoods, including many rainforest species, have been established. In the case of native timber species for which little is known about their cultivation, it is extremely difficult to obtain estimates of growth rates that can be accepted with a high degree of confidence. The Delphi technique is a convenient way of obtaining estimates of the expected growth and the harvest age of native species for which there exist no growth models based on past performance or physiological characteristics. This was the case recently in tropical Australia, where it was necessary to obtain estimates of growth rates and harvest ages for thirty-one species (Herbohn, Harrison and Emtage, 1999). In this case, the Delphi method proved to be an effective method of collecting the plantation productivity data necessary for the financial appraisal.

This project used the Delphi method to provide estimates of (1) mean annual increment or MAI (m^3/ha/yr) and (2) time to harvest (years) of thirty-one species. Harvest age and MAI are the key biological parameters needed to estimate yield and harvest scheduling for use in financial models. In this case the species for which information was sought, were ones that had been either widely planted in the area or included in a previous Delphi survey.

Opinions were sought from thirteen individuals with extensive experience in the growing of Australian tropical and sub-tropical rainforest species for either timber production or reforestation. Individuals generally either had extensive field experience or had undertaken research involving native rainforest and tropical eucalypt species.

Panellists were provided with a table listing the thirty-one selected species and asked to provide their 'best guess' of the optimal rotation period (in years) for each species, along with estimates of 'shortest time to harvest' and 'longest time to harvest'. Also requested was their 'best guess' for expected yield (in m^3/ha/yr) based on the 'best guess' rotation period, along with estimates of 'highest expected yield' and 'lowest expected yield'. In this section, participants were asked to assume that the trees would be planted on relatively fertile basaltic soils, that average annual rainfall would be in the range 1500–2000 mm, that initial planting density would be around 660 stems per hectare and suitable thinning regimes would be applied.

Species	Common name	Optimal rotation period (years)			Yield based on 'best guess' rotation period (m³/ha/yr)		
		Best guess (years)	Shortest time to harvest (years)	Longest time to harvest (years)	Best guess	Highest expected yield	Lowest expected yield
Acacia mangium	Wattle						
Acacia melanoxylon	Black-wood						
Agathis robusta	Kauri pine						
Araucaria cunninghamii	Hoop pine						
Beilschmieda bancroftii	Yellow walnut						
Blepharocarya involucrigera	Rose butternut						
Cardwellia sublimis	Northern silky oak						
Castano-spermum australe	Black bean						
Flindersia brayleana	Maple						
Eucalyptus cloeziana	Messmate						

Figure 4.3.   Modified extract of survey form used in stage 1 of Delphi survey in Example 4.1.

Questionnaires were distributed to participants and a visit was later made by one of the research team. Responses for the estimates of growth rates and harvest ages of the thirty-one selected species were then collated and averages calculated. A summary table including the group averages was prepared and distributed to participants along with their original estimates. In this second round of the Delphi survey, participants were given the opportunity to review their original estimates of growth rates and harvest ages in the light of the group averages and to provide any appropriate revisions or comments. Few revisions were received in this second round and the Delphi process was terminated. An extract of the survey form used in the first round of the Delphi survey is provided in Figure 4.3. In the second round, a similar table was compiled with the averages of estimates provided by all panellists, along with the estimates from that particular panellist.

The outcome of this Delphi survey was a table of harvest ages and yields, where for each variable the group mean and highest and lowest estimates were recorded.

Example 4.2. Collecting data for forestry projects involving new planting systems

In north Queensland it has become a common practice to plant *Flindersia brayleana* (maple) with *Eucalyptus cloeziana* (messmate) and many potential investors are interested in the

Table 4.1. *Planting and harvesting scenario for a maple and messmate mixed plantation*

Stage and activity	Density after treatment (stems/ha)	Estimates requested from participants in Delphi survey of reforestation experts
1. Plant alternating rows of maple and messmate at 3m × 5m spacing.	660 (330 maple, 330 messmate)	
2. Thin to waste every second tree when maple reaches 18 cm dbh.	340 (170 maple, 170 messmate)	Age at which maple expected to reach 18 cm dbh.
3. Thin every second messmate to waste or for strainer posts. Thin when maple reaches 32 cm dbh.	255 (170 maple, 85 messmate)	Age at which maple expected to reach 32 cm dbh. Bole dbh, small-end diameter, bole length of messmate at this age.
4. Remove every second maple for strainer posts or small diameter logs.	170 (85 maple, 85 messmate)	
5. Remove remaining messmate for poles.	85 maple	Ages at which messmate expected to reach five specified pole dimensions
6. Harvest every second maple when crowns touch (50 cm dbh).	43 maple	Age at which maple expected to reach 50 cm dbh. Small-end diameter and bole length at this time.
7. Harvest remaining maple (81 cm dbh).	Nil	Age at which maple expected to reach 81 cm dbh. Small-end diameter and bole length at this time.

Note: dbh = diameter breast height.

possible financial returns from such a plantation. There is, however, a lack of growth models for this mixture. Maple exhibits marked crown shyness (i.e. it stops growing when the leaves in its crown touch the leaves in the crown of another tree). There is also a simple relationship between crown diameter and the diameter of the stem. These two characteristics make it very easy to develop a well-structured plantation scenario involving the two species. A Delphi survey was carried out to obtain information for the development of a financial model for the two-species mixture (Herbohn and Harrison, 2001).

A planting and harvesting scenario was developed for a 50:50 mixture of maple and messmate (Table 4.1). Thinning and harvesting regimes are timed to occur just as maple crowns touch, at which time lock-up of growth would be expected to occur.

Personal interviews were conducted with five north Queensland forestry experts chosen for their familiarity with the species being modelled. At the commencement of interviews

Table 4.2. *Estimates of model parameters for a maple and messmate mixed plantation*

Stage	Parameter	Parameter estimate from Delphi survey	
		average	range
2	Age at which maple expected to reach 18 cm dbh	8.6 years	7–10 years
3	Age at which maple expected to reach 32 cm dbh	17.6 years	15–20 years
4	At this age, the following are expected for messmate		
	bole dbh	41.4 cm	35–50 cm
	small-end diameter	26.2 cm	15–35 cm
	bole length	16.4 m	12–20 m
5	Age at which messmate expected to reach specified dimensions for:		
	pole 1	17.4	10–25 years
	pole 2	17.6	11–25 years
	pole 3	21.0	12–30 years
	pole 4	24.2	14–35 years
	pole 5	25.6	15–35 years
6	Age at which maple expected to reach 50 cm dbh	34 years	25–40 years
	Expected small-end diam. at this age	33 cm	30–40 cm
	Expected bole length at this age	14.8 m	6–20 m
7	Age when maple expected to reach 81 cm dbh	60 years	50–65 years
	expected small-end diam. at this age	57 cm	45–60 cm
	expected bole length at this age	16.6 m	10–20 m

Note: dbh = diameter breast height.

the plantation system was outlined and the requirements for information stated. Panellists were provided with a table, similar to Table 4.2 but with the data columns blank, in which to record their estimates. After collation of estimates, outliers were identified and clarification was sought from participants. The final estimates of the parameters that were used as inputs to the financial analysis are shown in Table 4.2. In this instance, the Delphi method proved to be a timely and cost-effective means through which to collect the information and forecasts necessary to construct the financial model.

While it is difficult to judge the accuracy and quality of the forecast information obtained in Examples 4.1 and 4.2, the Delphi surveys provided information without which the construction of a financial model would have been impossible. The stimulus for choosing to undertake a Delphi survey was the fact that forecasts of tree growth and harvest age from models based on quantitative growth data will not be available until recent plantings using this species mix reach harvest age, and efforts to develop suitable quantitative models based on physiological and environmental parameters had been unsuccessful.

Scenario projection

What will the transport infrastructure requirements in a major city like London be in twenty-five years? What will electricity demand be within a region in ten years and how much electricity will be generated from renewable resources such as the sun and the wind? What demands will the increasing number of retired persons place on health services in a city in twenty years' time? What are the long-term market prospects of a new product requiring large-scale research and development expenditure? All of these questions are important for capital budgeting purposes.

For instance, infrastructure for transport, electricity and health services requires long lead times to develop. In deciding whether to build a new hospital, expand electricity generation capacity or build a new freeway, it is first necessary to estimate demand for those services some time in the future. Scenario projection provides a convenient technique to do this.

Scenarios have been described as 'descriptions of alternative hypothetical futures'. Scenarios can be used to describe what potential futures we might expect, depending on whether or not major events come to pass. Generating scenarios can be a useful tool in capital budgeting.

While the term 'scenario' is used with various meanings, there are several features which characterize scenarios:

- A scenario is hypothetical – it describes some possible future.
- A scenario is selective – it represents one possible state of some complex future.
- A scenario is bound – it consists of a limited number of states, events, actions and consequences.
- A scenario is connected – its elements are related, that is each element is conditional on or caused by other elements.
- A scenario is assessable – it can be judged with respect to its probability or desirability.

Ducot and Lubben (1980) suggest that scenarios can be classified in a number of different ways:

- *Exploratory vs anticipatory*: Exploratory scenarios start with some known or assumed states or events and explore what might result i.e. they are forward-looking. Anticipatory scenarios start with some assumed final state of affairs and look at what preconditions (events or actions) could produce this state of affairs i.e. they are backward-looking.

- *Descriptive vs normative*: Descriptive scenarios present a possible future irrespective of its desirability or otherwise. Normative scenarios take values and goals explicitly into account.
- *Trend vs peripheral*: A trend scenario extrapolates the normal, surprise-free course of events that might be expected if nothing out of the ordinary was to happen or no particular course of action taken. A peripheral scenario depicts radical, trend-breaking or improbable developments.

Based on practical experience, Schoemaker (1991) provides some guidelines for dealing with scenarios:

(1) Develop an understanding of any issues thought important, especially in terms of their history, to get a feel for the degrees of uncertainty.
(2) Identify the major stakeholders who would be interested in these issues. Both those with power and those influenced should be noted to clarify their roles, interests and exact power.
(3) Make a list of current trends that might affect the issues. Explain how these trends might impact on the issues.
(4) Identify key uncertainties and explain how they matter.
(5) Construct two 'forced' scenarios by placing all the positive outcomes in one scenario and all the negative outcomes in the other.
(6) Assess the plausibility of these 'forced' scenarios.
(7) Eliminate impossible combinations. These revised 'forced' scenarios might be called 'learning-only' scenarios.
(8) Reassess the stakeholders in the learning scenarios. Identify and study topics for further consideration.
(9) Develop outline plans based on what has been learned so far. Communicate desired scenarios to responsible managers.

Example 4.3. Using scenario projection to forecast demand

As an example of scenario projection, suppose the planning department of a company in the electricity generation and wholesale sector wishes to forecast electricity demand in ten years' time to assist in deciding whether to construct a new coal-fired power station. The first seven steps in scenario development might proceed as follows:

(1) *Understanding of issues and history.* Develop an understanding of any issues thought important, especially in terms of their history, to get a feel for the degrees of uncertainty. These demands have been growing, but there have been some unrealistically high demand forecasts in the past which have led to excessive capital outlays, and to criticism by environmentalists.
(2) *Identify major stakeholder groups.* The major stakeholders are other electricity generators, electricity consumers (industrial, commercial and domestic) and consumer

advocates (sensitive to price increases), and environmental groups (concerned about increasing greenhouse-gas emissions).

(3) *Identify current trends.* Electricity demand is increasing steadily on account of increased population through natural increase and interstate migration, and increasing adoption of air conditioning. A campaign has been undertaken by government to encourage adoption of more energy-efficient household appliances, including solar hot-water systems. The net impact is likely to be increased electricity demand until air conditioning reaches saturation, then a decline as energy efficiency is pursued.

(4) *Identify key uncertainties.* On the supply side, other generators may install new plant. On the demand side, it is possible that an alumina smelter will be constructed and major rail electrification projects will proceed, but the boom in construction of office blocks could come to an end. These events could lead to major changes in overall generation capacity, and in industrial and commercial demand.

(5) *Identify two 'forced' scenarios.* The most favourable scenario for the generator would be where there is little increase in generation capacity, but a large increase in demand. The most negative outcome would be where other generators rush to build new plant, but the expected increase in demand does not occur. Demand and supply quantities in megawatt hours would need to be placed on these scenarios, and price impacts inferred. Experience indicates that both extremes are possibilities, although installation of competing new plant, a moderate increase in industrial demand and little increase in commercial demand over the forecast period appear more probable.

(6) *Reassessment of the stakeholders in the learning scenarios.* Identify and study topics for further consideration. Here, further investigation might be undertaken into how research developments in the field of renewable energy might affect household consumption and how the capacity for export of energy from co-generation of small electricity producers such as cane mills might change with developing technology.

(7) *Develop outline plans, and communicate scenarios to management.* The 'most probable' forecast and some comments on alternative outcomes would form the core information.

Further information on scenario projections, including scenario projections in the energy industry, can be found in Jungermann and Thüring (1987) and Vlek and Otten (1987).

Concluding comments: which technique is best?

In this chapter a number of techniques useful for estimating future values of key variables as input to financial appraisals have been outlined. Let us now look critically at the reliability of each of the techniques, and the circumstances which favour the choice of one method over another.

Which method provides the most reliable estimates?

A few studies have been conducted which have compared forecasting techniques. Of particular interest is a recent study by Rowe and Wright (1999) in which they critically reviewed the Delphi technique as a forecasting tool. They also compared the accuracy of the Delphi method with the other main techniques available, namely staticized groups (aggregation of estimates from individuals), interacting groups and other procedures, such as NGT. These authors found that the accuracy of Delphi forecasts tends to increase with the number of rounds of revision undertaken. Also, the Delphi method proved more accurate than staticized groups (aggregation of individual estimates) which only have one round of estimates.

The Delphi method is a structured process for collecting information (e.g. using a questionnaire). Estimates generated by Delphi panels were found to be more accurate than those of unstructured interacting groups (i.e. groups that simply meet and talk without any structure to their interactions). The nominal group technique (NGT), like Delphi, is a structured method, but differs from Delphi in that it involves face-to-face meetings that allow discussion between rounds. There is some evidence to suggest that the discussion in these face-to-face meetings improves the accuracy of forecasts. NGT groups thus tend to make more accurate judgements than Delphi groups, although the evidence is somewhat mixed. In comparisons of other structured techniques (e.g. the dialectic procedure) with the Delphi method, there have been few studies that have found any substantial differences in accuracy.

Which method to choose?

From the preceding subsection, the overall impression gained from the critical assessment of the accuracy of the Delphi technique is that it is better than techniques that involve staticized or unstructured groups. In most situations Delphi is at least as accurate as most of the alternative structured techniques that are available, with the exception of NGT.

So why not always use NGT? Why worry about Delphi or these other techniques at all? The answer to this question lies in the old adage 'horses for courses'. Some techniques are better suited to certain circumstances. For instance, if accuracy is of paramount importance and cost not a major consideration, then NGT would probably be the favoured technique. However, bringing a group of experts together for a face-to-face meeting, as is required for NGT or classic Delphi, may be both difficult and expensive. In such cases, a postal Delphi may be the most appropriate technique to use. Staticized group techniques are often even simpler and less costly to apply and may be considered if the trade-off with slightly reduced accuracy is thought appropriate. Staticized group estimates can also be compiled quickly and may be considered when time is short. Furthermore, when there is the potential for major or discrete changes, the use of scenarios is a technique that provides a convenient framework for assessing the potential impact of these.

No matter what technique is selected, it is important to recognize the limitations of the technique, as these will impact on how the technique is applied and the quality of the forecasts obtained. Furthermore, with any technique that involves the collection of data it is essential to proceed in an orderly and considered manner. Sometimes there is a tendency to collect information first and then worry about how it is to be used. The starting point, however, should be to clearly identify what information is needed, decide on the most appropriate technique to collect the data (in the context of the resources, time and other limitations) and *only then* commence collection.

Review questions

4.1 Under what circumstances is the use of qualitative forecasting techniques appropriate?

4.2 Outline the steps involved in undertaking a survey to collect forecast estimates from individuals. Outline the advantages and disadvantages of using groups, as opposed to individuals, to provide forecasts.

4.3 What are the steps normally applied when undertaking a Delphi survey? What are some of the variants of this method?

4.4 How is the nominal group technique (NGT) different from the Delphi method?

4.5 Outline the 'jury of expert opinion' method. How does this differ from the Delphi method?

4.6 A company offering eco-tourism adventures wishes to forecast the numbers of annual tourists of various types coming to a region five years from now, and chooses the Delphi method to develop its forecasts.

(a) Explain how a panel of appropriate experts could be selected.

(b) Suggest how the information given to the panel and the questions could be framed.

(c) How many rounds of data collection would you expect to undertake? Discuss how these would proceed.

4.7 The management of a coal-fired electricity generation station is concerned that new technology to reduce carbon dioxide emissions will be required to offset emissions, and measures such as purchase of carbon credits will be required if the national government signs up to the Kyoto Protocol. The severity of adjustment for the company will depend on the extent of reduction in greenhouse-gas emissions agreed to by the national government. Explain how scenario forecasting could be used to aid decision-making by the company.

4.8 A company engaged in sugar refining and export wishes to make medium-term projections of international sugar prices. Suggest a method that could be used to make these forecasts.

5 Essential formulae in project appraisal

One of the most important principles of finance is that money has a time value. In the most general sense this refers to the fact that a dollar today is worth more than a dollar in one year's time. One reason for this is that a dollar today can earn interest while waiting for one year. This means that a given sum of money (say a cash flow of $5,500) should be valued differently, depending on *when* the cash flow is to occur. If the interest rate is 10% per annum, the present value of $5,500 received at the end of the first year is $5,000. This is because, $5,000 today can be invested at 10% to earn $500 interest at the end of the year. If the $5,500 is received at the end of two years from today, its present value is smaller than $5,000; it is approximately $4,546.

Capital budgeting decisions deal with *sizable* investments in *long-lived* projects. As discussed in Chapter 2, the cash flows of a project are spread over many years. In many cases, large sums of money are invested in the first year and net operating cash flows are received over a number of years. At the termination of the project, terminal cash flows are realized. In addition to the initial investment in the first year of the project, capital expenditures may occur at later stages of the project, for example, upgrades to the plant and equipment. The cash flows occurring at different times have to be converted to a common denominator to assess if the cash inflows exceed the cash outflows.

This can be done by translating all the cash flows into either their *present* or *future* values using a suitable 'rate' to represent the time value of money. A suitable proxy for the time value of money can be obtained from risk-free asset returns such as government bond yields or insured banks' term deposit rates. These rates of return are generally termed 'risk-free rates'. Using a risk-free rate, the cash flows occurring at different points of time can be converted into their *present values* at the beginning of the current year or *future values* at the end of the final year of the project's planning horizon. The commonly used method in finance is to convert all the values into their *present values* using an appropriate discount rate (or interest rate) to represent the time value. The other method is to convert all the values into their future values, again using an appropriate interest rate to represent the time value of money. Whilst the present-value approach is the norm in project appraisal, the future-value approach may be useful at times.

In property investment analysis, discussed in Chapter 14, loan calculation formulae are used in the process of arriving at equity cash flows for the investment. These calculations also involve present- and future-value concepts.

This chapter briefly presents the essential formulae involved in project appraisal and mortgage loan calculations, with examples. It is not intended to be a detailed coverage of standard financial mathematics, but rather a quick illustration of the application of essential project appraisal and loan calculation formulae to facilitate the understanding of the project appraisal content of this book. The underlying philosophy of this chapter is to learn by doing. The emphasis is on problem-solving. Readers are urged to make full use of writing pads, pens, calculators and computers (in particular, the Excel workbooks provided on the Web).

Study objectives

After studying this chapter the reader should be able to:

- apply a discounting rate to cash flows occurring at different points in time to translate them into a common measure of value
- calculate present value, net present value (NPV) and internal rate of return (IRR) from a given cash flow series
- calculate monthly loan (mortgage) repayments, their interest and principal components and the loan balance of a mortgage loan
- understand the financial mathematics involved in the discounted cash flow techniques (such as NPV and IRR) and mortgage loans
- apply the relevant annuity formulae for project appraisal

Symbols used

t	time period
r	discount rate
C	cash flow
C_t	cash flow at end of period t
CO_t	capital outlays at the beginning of period t
A_{nr}	present value of an annuity (of \$1 per period) with the payments being made at the end of each period. The number of periods is n and the discount rate is r.
$(1+r)^{-t}$	present value of a dollar to be received at the end of period t using a discount rate of r.
PV	present value of a cash flow stream where:

$$PV = \sum_{t=1}^{n} (1+r)^{-t} C_t$$

FV	future value of a cash flow stream at the end of period n where:

$$FV = \sum_{t=1}^{n} (1+r)^{n-t} C_t, \quad \text{or } FV = PV(1+r)^n$$

| NPV | net present value |
| IRR | internal rate of return |

Rate of return

The rate of return (ROR) is a basic concept in finance. If there are only two cash flows, a cash outlay or an investment at the beginning of the year and a cash inflow or the realization of the investment at the end of the year, the rate of return is usually measured by:

$$r = \frac{C_1 - C_0}{C_0}$$

The symbol, r, used for the discount rate is also employed for the rate of return to alert the reader that the discount rate is a rate of return.

> Workbook
> 5.1

Example 5.1

Suppose you invest $1,000 at the beginning of the year and receive a total of $1,100 at the end of the year. The rate of return is:

$$r = \frac{1,100 - 1,000}{1,000} = 0.1 \qquad \text{or 10\% per annum.}$$

Note on timing and timing symbols

In Example 5.1, the initial cash outlay occurs at the start of the year, and the cash inflow occurs at the end of the year. This structure reflects the standard timing assumptions within financial analysis. These are that cash flows occur at particular points of time, rather than within time periods, and that the initial investment (or capital outlay) occurs at the *beginning* of the period and subsequent cash flows occur at the *end* of the relevant time periods.

The length of the time period adopted is related to the analysis in hand. In a capital budgeting analysis, cash flows are assumed to occur yearly, as the project will usually extend over many years. In a short-term financial analysis, such as that of liquid cash management, the timing period may be shortened to a day or a week.

In stating when a particular flow is to occur, the convention is to use EOY as an acronym for 'end of year', although the symbol Y is also commonly used. Similarly EOM or M is used to denote 'end of month'. The symbol used will be appropriate to the context. Each of these acronyms has a trailing digit which identifies the period. For example, EOY 1, or Y1, is 'end of year 1', and EOY 2, or Y2, is 'end of year 2'.

It is important to note that cash flows occurring at the start of a project are denoted by EOY 0, or Y0. This timing structure allows *all* cash flows, including the present one, to be expressed as 'end of year' flows. The EOY 0 concept is that year 0 has just come to an end today, and that year 1 will start tomorrow. Thus EOY 0 may be interpreted as the beginning of year 1.

In project analysis it is particularly important to identify and assign the cash flows to their relevant periods accurately. This means that the analyst must become adept at using the appropriate timing symbols. Correct nomenclature is vitally important in setting the analysis up for computer calculation, because the various computational routines, as in Excel for example, require particular classification of the cash flows. The workbooks accompanying the examples in this chapter demonstrate how to do this.

Future value of a *single* sum

The future value is the amount to which a present sum (such as a fixed term deposit placed with a bank) will grow at a future date, through the operation (or the add-on effect) of interest. Suppose you invest $1,000 today (EOY 0) for a period of two years at an interest rate of 10% per annum, with interest paid at the end of each year. At the end of the first year (EOY 1), you would have accumulated $1,100 (i.e. the original sum of $1,000 plus $100 (1,000 × 10%) interest). Assume that this interest is reinvested, thus increasing the level of investment to $1,100 at EOY 1. At EOY 2, the $1,100 would have increased to $1,210 (i.e. $1,100 plus $110 (1,100 × 10%) interest). The $1,210 is the *future value* of $1,000 invested at 10% per annum for two years.

The interest has been *compounded* annually. Compound interest simply means 'interest earned on interest'. In the example above, $100 interest has been received at EOY 1. This $100 has been reinvested to receive $10 (100 × 10%) interest at EOY 2 thus bringing the interest for year 2 to $110 (1,000 × 10% + 100 × 10%). Compound interest is the norm in financial calculations and compound interest is assumed throughout this book, unless otherwise stated.

Future value is calculated using the following formula:

$$FV = PV(1+r)^n$$

Here, *PV* may be interpreted as the principal (or initial amount) invested in, for example, a term deposit. For simplicity, *r* may be viewed as the interest rate. For example, if the interest rate is 10% per annum, *r* is equal to 0.10.

Example 5.2

You place $1 in a term deposit at the beginning of year 1 for a period of six years at a compound interest rate of 10% per annum. How much will you get at the end of six years?

> Workbook
> 5.2

The same question can be stated in the context of capital budgeting as follows. The capital outlay of a project incurred at the beginning of year 1 (that is, at EOY 0), is $1. The economic life of the project is six years. Assuming an annual return of 10%, what is the future value of this $1 investment at the end of year 6? The answer is:

$$FV = 1.00 \times (1.10)^6 = \$1.771561 \approx \$1.77$$

Example 5.3

Instead of $1, suppose you deposited $2,000 (or incurred a capital expenditure of $2,000). Then, the future value of this investment is:

> Workbook
> 5.3

$$FV = 2,000 \times (1.10)^6 = 2,000 \times (1.771561) = \$3,543.12$$

Present value of a *single* sum

Present value is the opposite of future value. The formula for the future value presented previously can be rearranged to calculate the present value of a future cash flow:

$$PV = \frac{FV}{(1+r)^n}$$

If we use symbol C_n (instead of FV) to denote the cash flows at the end of period n, then:

$$PV = \frac{C_n}{(1+r)^n}$$

Recall that:

$$\frac{1}{(1+r)^n} = (1+r)^{-n}$$

Then:

$$PV = C_n(1+r)^{-n}$$

$\frac{1}{(1+r)^n}$ or $(1+r)^{-n}$ is called the 'present value factor'.

Example 5.4

In Example 5.2, the future value of $1 in six years' time, at an interest rate of 10%, was approximately $1.77. Now, let us ask the question the other way round: what is the present value of $1.771561 ($\approx$$1.77) to be received in six years' time, if the time value of money (or the appropriate discount rate) is 10% per annum?

> Workbook
> 5.4

$$PV = \$1.771561 \times (1+0.10)^{-6} = \$1.771561 \times (0.56447393) = \$1.00$$

We now end up with $1.00. Note that rounding errors can make a small difference.
The present value factor in this example is $\frac{1}{(1+r)^6} = \frac{1}{(1.1)^6} = \frac{1}{1.771561} = 0.56447393$

Example 5.5

The future-value question in Example 5.3 can be turned around to convert it to a question of present value.

Workbook
5.5

What is the present value of $3,543.12 to be received at the end of a six year period, if the time value of money is 10% per annum?

$$PV = 3{,}543.12 \times (1.1)^{-6} = \frac{3{,}543.12}{(1.1)^6} = \$1{,}999.999 = \$2{,}000$$

This $2,000 was the initial investment in Example 5.3, which grew to a future value of $3,543.12 in six years.

Future value of a *series* of cash flows

So far, the calculations have involved a *single* sum. Project analysis normally involves a *series* of cash flows occurring at different points in time. Therefore, an understanding of the calculation of future and present values of a *series* of cash flows is desirable. The future value of a series of cash flows is calculated using the formula:

$$FV = \sum_{t=1}^{n} C_t (1 + r)^{n-t}$$

Example 5.6

It is estimated that an investment project will receive net cash inflows at the end of each of the first five years. They are $10,000, $20,000, $30,000, $45,000 and $60,000. What is the future value of these cash flows at the end of year 5, if the time value of money is 20% per annum?

Workbook
5.6

$$FV = 10{,}000 \times (1.2)^{5-1} + 20{,}000 \times (1.2)^{5-2} + 30{,}000 \times (1.2)^{5-3}$$
$$+ 45{,}000 \times (1.2)^{5-4} + 60{,}000 \times (1.2)^{5-5}$$
$$= 10{,}000(1.2)^4 + 20{,}000(1.2)^3 + 30{,}000(1.2)^2$$
$$+ 45{,}000(1.2)^1 + 60{,}000(1.2)^0$$
$$= 20{,}736 + 34{,}560 + 43{,}200 + 54{,}000 + 60{,}000$$
$$= \$212{,}496$$

Note that a number raised to power 0 is equal to 1. So $(1.2)^0$ equals 1. The timing of the cash flows is important in setting up the correct powers in this example. The first cash flow occurs at EOY 1. It has then only four years to run until the end of the project. The power value is thus 4. The power value of 4 for the first cash flow is shown in the calculation as $(5-1)$ to demonstrate that, even though the project is for five years overall, the cash flow occurs when the project has only four years to run.

Present value of a *series* of cash flows

Project analysis normally estimates the present value of a series of future cash flows in the process of computing the project's net present value. The present value of a series of future cash flows is calculated using the formula:

$$PV = \sum_{t=1}^{n} \frac{C_t}{(1+r)^t} = \sum_{t=1}^{n} C_t (1+r)^{-t}$$

Example 5.7

What is the present value of the three cash flows $100, $200 and $600, to be received at EOY 1, EOY 2 and EOY 3, respectively, if the time value of money (or discount rate) is 10% per annum?

Workbook
5.7

$$PV = \frac{100}{(1.1)} + \frac{200}{(1.1)^2} + \frac{600}{(1.1)^3}$$
$$= 90.91 + 165.29 + 450.79 = \$706.99$$

Example 5.8

What is the present value of three cash flows $100, $200 and $600, to be received at EOY 1, EOY 3 and EOY 6, respectively, if the time value of money is 10% per annum?

Workbook
5.8

$$PV = \frac{100}{(1.1)} + \frac{200}{(1.1)^3} + \frac{600}{(1.1)^6}$$
$$= 90.91 + 150.26 + 338.68 = \$579.85$$

In these examples, the first cash flow occurs at EOY 1. As its present value is being calculated, it must be discounted for one full year. Its power value is 1. The other power values are applied accordingly.

Present value when the discount rate varies

Generally, the cash flows of future years are converted to present values by applying a single discount rate to all the cash flows. There are circumstances, however, where the use of different rates for different periods is justified. For example, when the discount rate is adjusted to incorporate a risk premium and if the degree of uncertainty of annual cash flows varies from year to year, the use of different discount rates for different periods may be warranted. It must be noted that when the discount rate includes a risk premium for the uncertainty of the cash flows, that discount rate is greater than the interest rate used to represent just the time value of money. These distinctions are considered in detail in Chapter 7. In this chapter, the focus is on illustrating computation formulae.

Example 5.9

Assume cash flows at the end of years 1, 2, 3, 4 and 5 are $100, $300, $400, $500 and $10, respectively.

The relevant interest rates (or discount rates) for different periods are:

Year 1:   10%
Year 2:   5%
Year 3:   10%
Year 4:   12%
Year 5:   11%

Then the present value is calculated as follows:

Workbook
5.9

$$PV = \left[\frac{100}{(1.1)}\right] + \left[\frac{300}{(1.1)(1.05)}\right] + \left[\frac{400}{(1.1)(1.05)(1.1)}\right]$$

$$+ \left[\frac{500}{(1.1)(1.05)(1.1)(1.12)}\right] + \left[\frac{10}{(1.1)(1.05)(1.1)(1.12)(1.11)}\right]$$

$$= \$1,023.20$$

Present value of an ordinary annuity

Annuity formulae are useful in NPV calculations in which the value of the cash flows is the same for a number of years.

To use the ordinary annuity formula, the following conditions should be satisfied:

• the *value* of the cash flows in each period is the same; for example,
  $500 at end of year 1
  $500 at end of year 2
  $500 at end of year 3, etc.

- the *period* or the *interval* for the cash flows remains unchanged; for example, if they are annual, they have to remain annual; if they are six-monthly, then they have to remain as six-monthly periods; if they are monthly, then they have to remain as monthly etc.
- the receipt/payment of the cash flows should occur at the *end* of each regular period; for example, end of each year or end of each month, as the case may be.

The present value of a $1 annuity is:

$$A_{nr} = \frac{1-(1+r)^{-n}}{r}$$

The present value of an annuity of C dollars thus becomes:

$$PV = C \times A_{nr} = C\left[\frac{1-(1+r)^{-n}}{r}\right]$$

This can also be written as:

$$PV = \frac{C}{r}\left[1-\frac{1}{(1+r)^n}\right]$$

Example 5.10

A project is expected to have an economic life of five years. The value of this project's net cash inflows is estimated to be $2,000 for each year and this is to be received at the end of each year. The appropriate discount rate is 15% per annum. What is the present value of this project's cash inflows?

> Workbook
> 5.10

$$PV = 2,000 \times \left[\frac{1-(1.15)^{-5}}{0.15}\right]$$

$$= 2,000 \times \left[\frac{1-\dfrac{1}{(1.15)^5}}{0.15}\right]$$

$$= 2,000 \times \left[\frac{1-0.49717}{0.15}\right]$$

$$= 2,000 \times [3.3522]$$

$$= \$6,704.40$$

A note on financial tables

Many corporate finance textbooks produce tables giving the present values of ordinary annuities, along with present values and future values of $1 at different interest rates for different time periods. These tables are useful quick references for common interest rates and common time periods. The ranges that they present are, however, limited. These financial tables are artefacts of past times when electronic calculators and spreadsheets, which allow rapid and easy calculation of these factors, were not available. In this text, such tables are not included.

Present value of a deferred annuity

This is also useful in reducing the number of steps in calculating the NPV in project evaluations.

Deferred annuity means that the annuity starts not from the end of the first year (or period) but from a few years (or periods) later. The present value of such an annuity can be found by a two-stage process. First, the present-value concept is applied to find the value of the annuity at the beginning of the first annuity period. Then this single sum is discounted to the present, using the formula introduced in the earlier section, titled 'Present value of a single sum'.

$$PV = C \times \left[\frac{1 - (1+r)^{-n}}{r} \right] \times (1+r)^{-t}$$

Example 5.11

There is an annuity payment of $60 per year for twenty years, but the first payment is at the end of year 10. The interest rate is 10% per annum. What is the present value of these twenty payments?

Workbook
5.11

$$PV = 60 \times \frac{1 - (1.1)^{-20}}{0.1} \times 1.1^{-9}$$

The index t has the value 9 because the normal present-value annuity formula has already calculated the present value *to the beginning* of the tenth year, that is, to the end of the ninth year.

$$PV = 60 \times 8.5136 \times 0.4241 = \$216.64$$

Next, we will give another example, repeating some of these figures, but applying them to a case of project evaluation where the wording differs so as to give a different meaning. Compare and contrast the previous example with the next example to understand more clearly the meanings and applications of a deferred annuity in NPV calculations.

Example 5.12

A project's annual net cash inflows (to be received at the end of each year) are estimated as follows. For the first nine years the project does not generate any cash inflow. For the next eleven years (i.e. from the tenth to the twentieth years inclusive), it generates $60 per year. The discount rate is 10% per annum. What is the present value of this project's cash inflows?

> Workbook
> 5.12

$$PV = 60 \times \frac{1 - (1.1)^{-11}}{0.1} \times 1.1^{-9}$$

$$= 60 \times 6.4951 \times 0.4241$$

$$= \$165.27$$

To understand this properly, recalculate this using the formula for the present value of a series of individual future cash flows:

$$PV = \frac{0}{(1.1)} + \frac{0}{(1.1)^2} + \frac{0}{(1.1)^3} + \frac{0}{(1.1)^4} + \frac{0}{(1.1)^5} + \frac{0}{(1.1)^6} + \frac{0}{(1.1)^7} + \frac{0}{(1.1)^8}$$

$$+ \frac{0}{(1.1)^9} + \frac{60}{(1.1)^{10}} + \frac{60}{(1.1)^{11}} + \frac{60}{(1.1)^{12}} + \frac{60}{(1.1)^{13}} + \frac{60}{(1.1)^{14}} + \frac{60}{(1.1)^{15}}$$

$$+ \frac{60}{(1.1)^{16}} + \frac{60}{(1.1)^{17}} + \frac{60}{(1.1)^{18}} + \frac{60}{(1.1)^{19}} + \frac{60}{(1.1)^{20}}$$

$$= 0 + 0 + \cdots + 0 + 23.13 + 21.03 + 19.11 + 17.38 + 15.80 + 14.36$$

$$+ 13.06 + 11.87 + 10.79 + 9.81 + 8.92$$

$$= \$165.26$$

This is the same answer as obtained by using the deferred annuity formula.

Perpetuity

A perpetuity is a special case of an annuity in which the number of equal cash flows is infinite. Because the cash flows go on forever, we cannot calculate the future value of a perpetuity; a perpetuity does not have an end of life. Hence, a future value cannot be calculated. The formula for the present value of a perpetuity is:

$$PV = \frac{C_t}{r}$$

This formula is adapted from the annuity formula used in Example 5.10, which is repeated here:

$$PV = \frac{C}{r}\left[1 - \frac{1}{(1+r)^n}\right]$$

In a perpetuity, n is infinite. In the limit, as n approaches infinity, $\left[\frac{1}{(1+r)^n}\right]$ approaches zero, so the overall equation becomes $PV = \frac{C}{r}$.

The application of this formula is straightforward and does not require an example.

Net present value

The net present value (NPV) of a project is calculated by subtracting the present value of the capital outlays from the present value of the cash inflows. If the capital outlay occurs only at the beginning of year 1, that is, at EOY 0, then it is already at a present value and it is not necessary to discount it any further. The formula for the NPV in such situations is:

$$NPV = \sum_{t=1}^{n} \frac{C_t}{(1+r)^t} - CO$$

CO is the capital outlay at the beginning of year 1, where $t = 0$.

If capital outlays occur in different years, the relevant formula is:

$$NPV = \sum_{t=1}^{n} \frac{C_t}{(1+r)^t} - \sum_{t=0}^{n} \frac{CO_t}{(1+r)^t}$$

Example 5.13

Net cash inflows of a project are estimated as: EOY 1 $3,000; EOY 2 $4,000; and EOY 3 $8,000. Capital outlays for the project will occur during the first and second years and they are estimated as $2,000 and $1,500, respectively. They are assumed to occur at the beginning of each period. The timing notation for the correct discounting of these will be: EOY 0 $2,000; and EOY 1 $1,500. The discount rate is 10% per annum.

> Workbook
> 5.13

$$NPV = \frac{3,000}{(1.1)} + \frac{4,000}{(1.1)^2} + \frac{8,000}{(1.1)^3} - \frac{2,000}{(1.1)^0} - \frac{1,500}{(1.1)^1}$$

$$= 2,727.27 + 3,305.79 + 6,010.52 - 2,000 - 1,363.64$$

$$= 12,043.58 - 3,363.64 = \$8,679.94$$

Net present value of an infinite chain

When mutually exclusive projects have unequal lives, net present value cannot be used directly to compare the projects. In such cases it is appropriate to calculate NPV_p, which is simply the net present value of an infinite series of identical projects. The formula applied in each case is that for a 'perpetuity due', that is, the formula for the present value of an ordinary perpetuity, with the addition of the initial NPV as at today:

$$NPV_p = NPV_r + \frac{NPV_n}{\left[(1+r)^n - 1\right]}$$

where,

NPV_p = NPV at the present time of all the NPVs in the replicating stream to perpetuity

NPV_r = NPV of the initial replication

NPV_n = NPV of each replication at year n

$[(1+r)^n - 1]$ = periodic interest rate for each replication length

This formula is used in Chapter 6 where the 'replacement chain' method is applied to compare projects with unequal lives. NPV_p is particularly useful for comparing forestry projects of different durations, and will be used in the forestry case study in Chapter 10. NPV_p when applied to forestry is often referred to as the land expectation value (LEV), which is the net present value of an infinite sequence of identical timber rotations. LEV is simply a special case of NPV_p which is used when comparing projects of unequal duration. For short rotations, the LEV will be considerably higher than the NPV, but for long rotations will differ little from the NPV.

Internal rate of return

The internal rate of return is an alternative measure for evaluating projects. It is the calculated rate of return (or discount rate) r at which the NPV will be equal to zero. In project evaluation this rate has to be equal to or greater than the required rate of return for the project to be acceptable. It is calculated manually by trial and error, or by a special routine in computerized spreadsheets. In our example, it would be set up as:

Example 5.14

Workbook
5.14

$$0 = \frac{3,000}{(1+r)} + \frac{4,000}{(1+r)^2} + \frac{8,000}{(1+r)^3} - \frac{2,000}{(1+r)^0} - \frac{1,500}{(1+r)}$$

Net cash flows are represented as occurring at the end of each year. The second outlay of cash, $1,500, as capital, occurs at the start of year 2. For timing purposes, as explained above, this is discounted as occurring at EOY 1. Hence, after collecting up like-timed values the equation becomes:

$$0 = \frac{1,500}{(1+r)} + \frac{4,000}{(1+r)^2} + \frac{8,000}{(1+r)^3} - \frac{2,000}{(1+r)^0}$$

Solving by trial and error, or electronically, r (as the IRR) = 133.76%. At this rate the project's NPV will be equal to zero. Arriving at the IRR solution will involve a number of iterations, so where there are more than two cash flows, a computer package (such as Excel) or a financial calculator (with an IRR function) is recommended.

Note on the calculation of IRR

There are several points that are worth noting in IRR calculations:

- There are as many possible solutions for the IRR as there are changes of sign. In our example there is one change of sign. This means there can be either no solution or just one solution. With more changes of sign there can be more solutions.
- A particular structure of cash flows may have no IRR solution.
- When using hand-held calculators it is important to ensure that the correct cash flow signs are entered.
- Some hand-held calculators require a 'seed' rate of return to be entered to start the calculation.
- The Excel calculation of IRR has specific rules. A perusal of the workbook example provided on the Web will help in setting up an IRR problem on an Excel spreadsheet. The use of the Excel Help facility can ensure the correct setting up of the problem for an IRR calculation.

Loan calculations

Monthly or annual loan instalments (or repayments), interest and principal components of a loan instalment, loan balances at different points in a series of repayments, and so on, are involved in the real estate property investment analysis in Chapter 14. Present-value and annuity formulae form the basis of the financial mathematics of loan calculations. It is important to understand how the present-value and annuity formulae are manipulated to do various loan calculations. This is now illustrated using an example which assumes equal loan payments.

Example 5.15

- A loan of $150,000 is amortized monthly over ten years at an interest rate of 11% per annum. What is the monthly repayment?
- If the loan is fully paid off prior to the completion of the ten-year term, a prepayment fee of three months' interest is charged. Assume that the loan is fully repaid after six years. What is the principal outstanding after six years? What is the early redemption fee? What is the total charge to redeem the loan?

In terms of present-value formulae, the amount borrowed under the loan is the present value. This relationship between the present value and the set of repayments is constant throughout the life of the loan, and the general expression of this rule is 'The balance of the loan outstanding at any time is the present value of the remaining payments.' The loan amount may be denoted as PV or L.

The equal periodic payments (monthly loan instalments) are the equal cash flows in the ordinary annuity formula. We used the symbol C in our present-value and annuity formulae. In loan calculations, the abbreviation PMT (payment) is commonly used for this; either C or PMT may be used. The symbol r, interest rate per compounding period, has the same meaning as used in present-value and annuity calculations. The symbol n is used to denote the number of periods over which the loan is amortized.

> Workbook
> 5.15

$$PV = L = \$150,000$$

$$n = 120 \ (12 \text{ months} \times 10 \text{ years})$$

$$r = \frac{0.11}{12} = 0.009166667$$

$$C = PMT = ?$$

By algebraic manipulation of the formula for the present values of an annuity:

$$C = PV \times \left[\frac{r}{1-(1+r)^{-n}} \right] \quad \text{or} \quad PMT = L \times \left[\frac{r}{(1-(1+r)^{-n}} \right]$$

$$PMT = 150,000 \times \frac{0.009166667}{1-(1.009166667)^{-120}}$$

$$PMT = 150,000 \times \left[\frac{0.009166667}{1-(1/2.989149721)} \right] = 150,000 \times \left[\frac{0.009166667}{1-0.334543296} \right]$$

$$= 150,000 \times \left[\frac{0.009166667}{0.665456704} \right]$$

$$PMT = 150,000 \times 0.013775001$$

$$= \$2,066.25$$

This is the monthly loan repayment.

What is the amount of the loan outstanding (OL) at the end of six years? It will be the present value of the remaining four years of payments. This amount is equal to the present value of an annuity of 48 (4 × 12) monthly payments of $2,066.25.

$$OL = PMT \times \left[\frac{1-(1+r)^{-m}}{r} \right]$$

where $m =$ number of periods outstanding $(120 - 72 = 48)$

$$OL = 2,066.25 \times \left[\frac{1-(1+0.009166667)^{-(120-72)}}{0.009166667} \right]$$

$$= 2,066.25 \times 38.69142085$$

$$= \$79,946.15$$

This is the loan amount outstanding after six years of repayments.

The early redemption fee is equal to three months' interest. The three months' interest defined in this loan contract is the sum of the interest components of each of the three

Table 5.1. *First three months of a loan amortization schedule ($)*

Repayment number	Repayment amount	Interest component	Principal component	Balance outstanding
0				150,000.00
1	2,066.25	1,375.00	691.25	149,308.75
2	2,066.25	1,368.66	697.59	148,611.16
3	2,066.25	1,362.27	703.98	147,907.18

repayments that would have followed the payment due at the early redemption date. The amount of interest in each of these three months is calculated as follows:

Loan balance outstanding after 72 payments	79,946.15
Interest due in PMT 73: 79,946.15 × 0.009166667	732.84
Principal paid in PMT 73: 2,066.25 − 732.84 = 1,333.41	−1,333.41
Loan balance outstanding after 73 payments	78,612.74
Interest due in PMT 74: 78,612.74 × 0.009166667	720.61
Principal paid in PMT 74: 2,066.25 − 720.61 = 1,345.63	−1,345.63
Loan balance outstanding after 74 payments:	77,267.11
Interest due in PMT 75: 77,267.11 × 0.009166667	708.28

Therefore, the total three months' penalty interest is 732.84 + 720.61 + 708.28 = $2,161.73

The total amount required to redeem the loan after six years is:

Loan balance + early redemption fee = 79,946.15 + 2,161.73 = $82,107.88.

Loan amortization schedule

In analysing annuity-type loans, it is useful to lay out fully the interest, principal and principal reduction in each of the repayments over the life of the loan. This layout is known as a loan amortization schedule. These are tedious to do by hand, but are easily automated in Excel. The first few lines of a schedule for Example 5.15 is given in Table 5.1. The full schedule is held in the Excel workbook.

> Workbook
> 5.16

Concluding comments

In this chapter, we illustrated the application of frequently encountered formulae in capital budgeting with simple calculated examples. Understanding them provides a good spring-board for the project analysis material in the remainder of the book.

Review questions

5.1 What is the basic principle underlying the conversion of cash flows into their present values using a suitable discount rate? Give two aspects of the rationale for this principle.

5.2 Explain the difference between *present value* and *future value*.

5.3 A company invests $400,000 at the beginning of the year and receives $450,000 at the end of the year. What is the rate of return?

5.4 What are the basic conditions that should be satisfied to enable the use of the ordinary annuity formula?

5.5 An investment costs $2,000 and pays $200 per annum in perpetuity. If the interest rate is 8% per annum, what is the NPV?

5.6 If you invest $500 at the end of each of the next five years at an interest rate of 12% per annum, how much will you have at the end?

5.7 An investment of $250 will produce $350 in two years. What is the annual interest rate?

5.8 If the present value of $145 is $125, what is the discount factor over one year?

5.9 A project's capital outlay is $2,500. It produces net cash inflows of $450, $3,000, $2,500 and $300 in years 1, 2, 3 and 4 respectively. The discount rate is 8% per annum. What is the NPV? What is the IRR?

5.10 Recalculate the NPV of the project in Question 5.9 with the discount rates now varying between years: Y1, 9.2%; Y2, 10.5%; Y3, 11.7%; Y4, 8.62%.

5.11 Refer to the information in Example 5.15. What is the amount of the loan outstanding after seven years of repayments?

5.12 Refer to Example 5.15. Demonstrate that you can arrive at the same answer for the three months' penalty interest (early redemption fee) by an alternative calculation procedure. Go through the following steps:
   (a) Calculate the principal outstanding after six years.
   (b) Calculate the principal outstanding after six years and three months.
   (c) Subtract (b) from (a).
   (d) Calculate the amount equal to three monthly payments.
   (e) Take away the answer to (c) from (d).

6   Project analysis under certainty

In the previous chapters, we have discussed the identification and estimation of project cash flows and illustrated the mathematical formulae essential for project evaluation. This chapter now uses these elements for investment analysis. There are two groups of project evaluation techniques: discounted cash flow (DCF) analysis and non-discounted cash flow (NDCF) analysis. The first group includes the net present value (NPV) and the internal rate of return (IRR). The second group includes the payback period (PP) and the accounting rate of return (ARR).

Generally, DCF analysis is preferred to NDCF analysis. Within DCF analysis, the theoretical and practical strengths of NPV and IRR differ. Theoretically, the NPV approach to project evaluation is superior to that of IRR. The NPV technique discounts all future project cash flows to the present day to see whether there is a net benefit or loss to the firm from investing in the project. If the NPV is positive, then the project will increase the wealth of the firm. If it is zero, then the project will return only the required rate of return, and will not increase the firm's wealth. If the NPV is negative, then the project will decrease the value of the firm and should be avoided.

In spite of the theoretical superiority of the NPV technique, project analysts and decision-makers sometimes prefer to use the IRR criterion. The preference for IRR is attributable to the general familiarity of managers and other business people with *rates of return* rather than with actual dollar returns (values). Since interest rates, profitability, investment income and so on are normally expressed as annual rates of return, the use of IRR makes sense to financial decision-makers. They find it easy to understand, and useful for comparing the profitability of alternative investments. Decision-makers and other business people tend to find NPV more difficult to use because it does not really measure benefits *relative to the amount invested* in terms of *a rate of return* that they are familiar with.

The computational method for IRR can be modified so that particular algebraic pitfalls within the IRR analysis can be avoided. In these cases the IRR technique is safe to use, so the widespread use of IRR should not be viewed as reflecting a lack of sophistication on the part of project analysts and financial decision-makers.

This chapter illustrates the application of the four project evaluation criteria using the cash flow estimates of the Delta Project example introduced in Chapter 2. The chapter content assesses the suitability of the four criteria, explains why the DCF techniques are better than the NDCF techniques and shows that within the DCF techniques NPV is superior to IRR.

Project ranking and choice is discussed for mutually exclusive projects using both NPV and IRR. The versatility of the NPV criterion is also demonstrated within this discussion. For example, it is demonstrated that the NPV model can be used to aid project ranking in the context where projects have size disparities, time (or cash flow pattern) disparities or unequal lives. Two methods for handling problems encountered in ranking projects with unequal lives – replacement chain and equivalent annual annuity – are illustrated with calculated examples. These two methods are adaptations of the basic NPV rule. All these discussions relate to *asset expansion* projects.

Asset replacement decisions are also important and they are illustrated using the cash flow data from the Repco Project example in Chapter 2. While management's primary focus is on investing in new opportunities to generate more cash flows and increase the value of the firm, existing projects ought also to be constantly reviewed to ensure that they are still viable. Non-viable assets should be retired. The asset retirement decision is discussed with a simple calculated example towards the end of the chapter.

The analysis in this chapter is carried out under the following assumptions:

- a single goal of wealth maximization for the firm
- all the cash inflows and outflows of the project are known with certainty
- there are no resource constraints (all the profitable projects can be accepted).

Study objectives

After studying this chapter the reader should be able to:

- use the NPV model to evaluate projects under certainty
- apply the net present value, internal rate of return, payback period and accounting rate of return criteria for investment decision-making under certainty
- understand the reasons why the NPV criterion is generally the method of choice for project evaluation
- apply the NPV criterion for ranking mutually exclusive projects and project retirement and replacement decisions
- use the NPV model to evaluate replacement chain decisions.

Certainty Assumption

In every field of human endeavour, decision-making occurs within a complex environment. In order to proceed, all decision-making relies on simplified models of the complex real world. Financial decision-making is no different. Finance theory and the financial analyst extract from the real world only those items which are immediately relevant to the decision at hand, and attempt to ignore or freeze into position those variables which may be too complex or difficult to handle. The simplest financial models operate within a very restricted world view. These models make three highly simplifying assumptions:

- financial decision-makers are rational, i.e. they are risk-averse wealth maximizers
- the financial market is perfectly competitive and efficient, i.e. there are no taxes, transaction costs or information costs
- the future is certain, i.e. future events and the outcomes of all decisions are known today with certainty.

Net present value model

The formula for the computation of net present value has been stated in Chapter 5. The NPV of a project is calculated by subtracting the present value of cash outflows from the present value of cash inflows. The difference between cash inflows and outflows is the net cash flow. Therefore, alternatively expressed, the NPV is calculated by discounting a project's net cash flows at a specified rate. This rate – often called the discount rate, opportunity cost or cost of capital – refers to the minimum return that must be earned on a project in order to leave the firm's market value unchanged.

The primary model for investment decision-making is the net present value model. Initially, the model is built and applied under the three assumptions of rationality, perfect markets and certainty. Once the structure and application of the model has been illustrated with this simplified version, the assumptions are relaxed to see how both the model and the results behave within the complex real world. One assumption – perfectly competitive efficient markets – is partially relaxed immediately by incorporating tax into the very first example. The analysis of the implications of relaxing other assumptions follows in later chapters. However, the assumption of investor rationality is not normally relaxed. Without this assumption there is no need for any decision-making. A totally irrational investor, who ignores risk completely, would be happy with any decision, or any chance outcome.

For conventional investments where there is only one capital outlay which occurs at the beginning of the first year of the project, the NPV model calculates the increase or decrease in the firm's current wealth by discounting all future net operating and terminal cash flows and netting them out against the initial capital outlay. For example: Project Alpha requires an initial outlay of $900, will have cash inflows of $300 in year 1, $400 in year 2 and $600 in year 3. The discount rate is 8% per annum. The calculation is:

$$NPV = -900 + \frac{300}{(1.08)^1} + \frac{400}{(1.08)^2} + \frac{600}{(1.08)^3}$$

$$= \$197.01$$

This positive result means that, by undertaking the project, the firm's wealth will increase by $197.01. Based on the NPV decision rule, the project should be undertaken.

We have made several assumptions in formulating and using this NPV model and decision:

- the amounts of the initial cash outflow and all future cash flows are known with certainty
- the discount rate is constant and known with certainty

- the initial capital outlay occurs at the beginning of year 1
- all operating cash flows occur at year end
- cash outflows from the firm are treated as negative; cash inflows are treated as positive
- there are no constraints on the supply of capital, or on other resources
- the firm will accept all positive NPV projects.

Certainty means that although future flows must be forecast or estimated, the estimated amounts will be received at the times they are expected to occur. Certainty makes the decision simple to model, and the outcome easy to accept.

The rate of discount is also an estimate. It will be 8% per annum, and it will remain constant, with certainty. Under the assumption of certainty, future cash flows are to be discounted at a rate which represents the time value of money. Returns on risky assets such as stock-market investments contain not only a rate for the time value of money but also a component (a risk premium) to compensate for the risk (or uncertainty) of the expected return. Rates of return on 'risk-free assets' are expected to reflect only the time value of money. Therefore, the appropriate discount rate for discounting *certain* cash flows is a suitable risk-free rate. Examples of risk-free assets in the economy are government bonds and insured banks' term deposits. Rates of returns on these assets, where their terms to maturity are commensurate with the planning horizon of the project, can be selected as discount rates.

Since capital projects extend over many years, the telescoping of within-year progressive cash flows into year-end cash flows is a reasonable assumption. It makes for less detailed computation without significant loss of information. Cash flows are timed at yearly intervals for ease of discounting, as the discount rate is expressed as a yearly rate. The name of each time point is known as 'end of year'. The time point of 'today' or 'now' is known as the end of year 0, and subsequent yearly time points count from this value. The usual cash flow table timing layout is thus:

EOY 0   EOY 1   EOY 2   EOY 3 ...

This layout may also be written as:

Y 0   Y 1   Y 2   Y 3 ...

Capital outlays which occur in any year after year 0 are subtracted from the relevant end-of-year cash flows. If a future capital outlay occurs at the immediate start of any year, it is usually included with the previous end-of-year cash flows to ensure it is correctly timed for discounting. In Project Alpha above, for example, we might have an upgrade outlay of $120 planned for the start of year 3. The $120 would be subtracted from the end-of-year flows for year 2. The cash flow table would be:

EOY 0	EOY 1	EOY 2	EOY 3
−900	300	280	600

The decision criterion in an NPV analysis is the change in a firm's current wealth. Cash flowing into the firm increases wealth; cash flowing out of the firm decreases wealth.

Table 6.1. *Delta Project: annual net cash flow*

EOY 0	EOY 1	EOY 2	EOY 3	EOY 4	EOY 5	EOY 6	EOY 7	EOY 8
−1,002,000	195,510	200,087	−295,135	379,643	384,421	608,760	618,061	638,362

This rule holds for both capital and operational flows. In defining the cash flows, then, it is important to apply the correct sign, plus or minus, and to make sure the correct sign is employed in any computerized calculation. Some computer packages have implied cash flow signs within NPV formulae, but some do not.

The amount of an NPV represents the addition to a firm's value. Rational management will accept all projects with a positive NPV and reject all those with a negative NPV. The assumption of rationality implies that projects with only $1 of positive NPV will be accepted along with projects of $1,000,000 of positive NPV. The assumption here is that capital for investment is freely available, and that projects do not have to be ranked in order of relative benefit to the firm. In conjunction with the assumption of perfect markets, this assumption will always be tenable. The 'market' will recognize the firm's beneficial project and will provide the necessary capital to the firm.

Under the assumption of certainty, a project with an NPV of $1 is perfectly acceptable. Without certainty, this small NPV may not provide an adequate buffer against errors in forecasts.

The net present value model applied

In Chapter 2, the Delta Project example was introduced to illustrate the project cash flow analysis, with Table 2.2 showing the calculation of cash flows for the project. The essential final row of data from that table, the annual net cash flow, is reproduced here as Table 6.1.

The NPV of this project can be computed by evaluating the cash flows. They begin with the initial outlay of $1,002,000 at EOY 0 and continue until EOY 8, at which time the asset salvage value is included. The NPV computation is:

$$NPV = -1,002,000 + \frac{195,510}{(1.05)^1} + \frac{200,087}{(1.05)^2} + \frac{-295,135}{(1.05)^3} + \frac{379,643}{(1.05)^4}$$

$$+ \frac{384,421}{(1.05)^5} + \frac{608,760}{(1.05)^6} + \frac{618,061}{(1.05)^7} + \frac{638,362}{(1.05)^8}$$

$$= \$1,049,852$$

With this positive NPV, the project is acceptable.

We have used the risk-free rate of 5% per annum as the required rate of return here, as the cash flows are assumed to be certain.

> Workbook
>   6.1

This calculation is also shown in the Excel workbook 6.1, where the NPV function is applied.

Other project appraisal methods

While the NPV criterion is the most appropriate method in most cases, the other discounted cash flow technique, the internal rate of return (IRR), is also frequently used, sometimes as a supplementary measure to NPV. Non-discounted cash flow methods such as payback period (PP) and accounting rate of return (ARR) have a number of serious defects but are still being used in practice in some situations. Sometimes PP is used in conjunction with NPV, particularly in making risky investment decisions. It is useful to understand these methods and their drawbacks so that the most appropriate method can be used for investment evaluation.

Internal rate of return

The IRR is the rate of discount which returns an NPV of zero. The IRR can thus be defined as the highest rate at which the future cash flows can be discounted making the project's NPV equal to zero. Since the IRR is a rate of return, the decision rule for project acceptance is: accept the project if its IRR is higher than the required rate of return.

Since the IRR cannot be expressed in terms of a solvable mathematical formula for projects, the economic life of which extends over a number of years, this rate is normally calculated by a trial-and-error process using a computer package. Using i to represent the IRR, the equation for the IRR calculation using the same cash flows as employed in the NPV calculation (Table 6.1) is:

$$\$0 \ (as \ NPV) = -1,002,000 + \frac{195,510}{(1+i)^1} + \frac{200,087}{(1+i)^2} + \frac{-295,135}{(1+i)^3}$$
$$+ \frac{370,643}{(1+i)^4} + \frac{384,421}{(1+i)^5} + \frac{608,760}{(1+i)^6} + \frac{618,061}{(1+i)^7} + \frac{638,362}{(1+i)^8}$$

> Workbook
> 6.1

The solution for i, calculated by the Excel IRR function, is 19.80%. Since this rate is above the required rate of 5%, the project is acceptable.

Accounting rate of return

The accounting rate of return uses accounting income data to calculate a ratio which is used as a decision variable. It is worth noting that, as discussed in Chapter 2, accounting income is different from cash flow. The ARR ratio is the annual average accounting income divided by an asset value. For example, an outlay of $1,000 may earn $200, $500 and $700 as accounting income over three years. The ARR is calculated as:

$$ARR = [(200 + 500 + 700)/3]/1000$$

$$= 46.66\%$$

Workbook
6.1

For the Delta Project example in Chapter 2, the accounting rate of return can be calculated by dividing the average net income by the initial outlay of $1,002,000. The average net income ($214,564) is obtained by summing the net income for the eight years (71,010 + ··· + 399,162) and dividing the sum (1,716,509) by eight. The ARR for the Delta Project is approximately 21%. If this rate is higher than a pre-determined required rate, then the project is acceptable.

There is no standard way to calculate the ARR, and this makes the definition of the ratio ambiguous. This drawback of the ARR definition is discussed later in the chapter.

Payback period

Payback period is the period of time over which the accumulated cash flows will equal the initial outlay. For example, an outlay of $1,200 may generate cash inflows of $820, $450 and $300 over three years. The total cash inflow to the end of year 2 is $1,270, so the payback period would be within two years. There is no objective time criterion associated with payback, but a period of two to three years would be generally acceptable.

Workbook
6.1

In the Delta Project example, the operating cash flows accumulate progressively to $864,526 at EOY 5 and $1,473,825 at EOY 6. As the initial outlay is $1,002,000, the payback will occur within year 6.

Suitability of different project evaluation techniques

The previous section illustrated four criteria for investment decision-making. This section briefly discusses their relative merits and demerits, and the discussion leads to the conclusion that NPV is the most suitable criterion; it can be applied in all cases and overcomes the problems of other criteria. This does not necessarily mean that the other criteria are completely irrelevant and useless. They may be used as supplementary measures to NPV to facilitate the relevant decision-making.

Net present value

The net present value model is the only decision technique which links the goal of the firm to the calculated output. The calculated NPV is the actual dollar amount by which the firm's current wealth will increase if the project is undertaken. Its calculation accounts for the time value of money at the required rate of return, and uses this as a data input, rather than as a decision output. The weaknesses and problems of the other three criteria, as discussed in the following three sections, demonstrate the superiority of the NPV criterion.

Internal rate of return

The IRR is the financial equivalent of an algebraic problem. The problem is: given a value for Y, what is the solution for x in the following equation?

$$Y = \frac{C}{(1+x)^1} + \frac{C}{(1+x)^2} + \frac{C}{(1+x)^3} + \cdots$$

This geometric progression has the same structure as a set of discounted cash flows, where the numerator of the equation is the set of cash flows, and the x value is an interest rate. In algebra this equation has meaning. Unfortunately, when it is transferred to finance it is not economically relevant. In finance, the role of x cannot be clearly defined. In the NPV model, the NPV is clearly defined. In the IRR equation, however, it is difficult to define IRR in its own terms, because it effectively means something like: 'the rate of return at which all funds, if borrowed at the IRR, could be repaid from the project, without the firm having to make any cash contribution'. The IRR criterion does not measure the project's contribution to the firm's value.

The IRR remains in use because decision-makers are used to dealing in 'rates of return' rather than the more esoteric NPV. The IRR measure is useful for easily comparing the rate of return from the project being considered with various alternative returns.

> Workbook
> 6.2

There are a number of conceptual and computational problems with using IRR. For example, the IRR calculation implicitly assumes that cash earned can be reinvested at the calculated IRR. The NPV calculation employs this assumption too, but it is probably more tenable there as it is likely that investment opportunities will be available at the general required rate of return, more so than at the unique IRR. A 'modified IRR' (MIRR) has been developed to overcome this problem. The modified IRR computational measure allows for a 'reinvestment rate' to be input to the calculation to derive the MIRR. The use of Excel's MIRR function is demonstrated in Workbook 6.2. With an assumed reinvestment rate of 8.25% per annum for the Delta Project example, the MIRR is 17.69%. This is, of course, less than the original IRR of 19.8%. The resulting MIRR figure may be defined as 'the earning rate of the project if it is assumed that funds when received are reinvested at the forecast reinvestment rate'.

> Workbook
> 6.3

There may be one or many solutions for the IRR. According to Descartes' rule of sign, there can be as many positive solutions for the IRR as there are changes of sign in the cash flows. For example, a series of flows of $-\$190$, $+\$455$, $+\$270$ can have at most one solution for the IRR, which is 189%. But, if the series is $-\$190$, $+\$455$, $-\$270$, there can be up to two positive solutions for the IRR. There are, in fact, two solutions, and these are 8.49% and 31%. Only the first solution is given by the Excel calculation. The second one is read off from the created chart, shown in Workbook 6.3. The difficulty in using the IRR as a decision-making tool in this case is that both are correct calculations, and thus both are acceptable solutions. If the required rate of return, for example, is 14% per annum, then one IRR is below and the other is above the required rate; we can come to no sensible decision as to whether the project should be accepted or rejected.

> Workbook
> 6.4

There may be *no* solution for the IRR. For example, given the set of cash flows, $-\$210$, $+\$455$, $-\$270$, there is no IRR solution, even though at an assumed required rate of 14% per annum, there is a valid NPV solution of $-\$18.63$. As shown on the graph on Workbook 6.4, there is no IRR solution, as the NPV profile line does not intersect the x-axis and the NPV is always negative.

The IRR decision can also conflict with the NPV decision for certain projects. This conflict is especially important where only one from two or more mutually competing projects can be selected. For example, let us assume Project A has cash flows of $-\$2,000$, $+\$200$, $+\$3,700$ and Project B has cash flows of $-\$2,000$, $+\$2,000$ and $+\$1,480$. The two projects differ only in the timing of the cash inflows; their initial outlays and overall lives are similar. Both have a required rate of return of 9% per annum. The outcomes from these two projects are:

	A	B
IRR	41.11%	49.50%
NPV at 9% per annum	$1,297.70	$1,080.55

A decision conflict arises here. Using the IRR, Project B should be selected; using the NPV, Project A should be selected. In such cases the NPV rule should be used, as it alone measures the absolute contribution to the firm's value made by the project. The IRR measures only the relative rates of return and not the projects' contributions to the value of the firm. Additionally, the IRR must be compared to the required rate for a decision to be made. This implies that the required rate must be known, and if it is known, then the NPV can be calculated using that rate anyway. Under certainty, as is assumed here, the required rate is known, so the NPV is easily calculated.

The ranking conflict between the NPV and the IRR for competing projects can be highlighted in an NPV profile chart (Figure 6.1). This chart shows the NPVs of both projects at various required rates of return (discount rates). The NPV schedules intersect at one point. This crossover point is known formally as the 'Fisher Intersection'. In this particular case

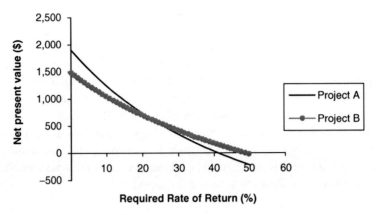

Figure 6.1.   Net present value profiles for projects A and B.

its value is given in Workbook 6.5 as approximately 23%. If the appropriate discount rate happens to be lower than this crossover rate, there is a conflict in project ranking between NPV and IRR. For example, a discount rate of 9% will produce conflicting rankings under the two criteria. The NPV criterion ranks A above B while the IRR criterion ranks B above A. If the appropriate discount rate happens to be higher than the crossover point, for example 35%, then both criteria produce the same ranking – B is preferred to A.

> Workbook
> 6.5

Payback period

Payback period (PP) is a measure of the time taken to recoup the initial outlay. Suppose for example that Project C has the following yearly cash flows: −$280, +$120, +$140, −$60, +$90. The progressive sum of the cash flows after the initial outlay is: $120, $260, $200, $290. The payback occurs in year 4. There are several problems with this measure:

- The cash flows are not discounted. As the time value of money is not taken into account, the future cash flows cannot be related to the initial outlay.
- The data outcome 'four years' is not a decision variable. It does not relate to the firm's goal of wealth maximization.
- There is no objective measure of what constitutes an acceptable payback period. Management may set an *ad hoc* target of say three years, but this value is not objectively related to the firm's goal.
- Cash flows occurring after the payback period are ignored. In the case where large outflows may occur on the termination of the project, such as the cost of rehabilitation of a mine site, a project may be erroneously accepted on the basis of a short payback term.

Payback is a very unsophisticated and misleading measure, and it is not recommended as a criterion for accepting or rejecting projects. It may be useful as a support measure to the NPV criterion, as an aid and comfort to some decision-makers when considering very risky projects. For example, suppose that a large natural resource project is to be established in a foreign country which is subject to unstable government and tribal fighting. In such a case a short payback period may be desirable to ensure that the capital expenditure is quickly recovered and repatriated so that if something goes wrong and the project has to be abandoned, at least the initial investment will have been recovered. In other words, PP may be an additional consideration for very risky foreign investments in politically and socially unstable countries. Additional risk factors in foreign investments are discussed in Chapter 16.

Accounting rate of return

The accounting rate of return (ARR) is the ratio of average accounting income to investment value. For example, suppose we have an initial outlay of $200, and subsequent annual accounting income figures of $80, $110, $70 and $120. The average annual accounting income would be $(80 + 110 + 70 + 120)/4 = \$95$, and the ARR would equal 95/200, or 47.5%.

Unfortunately, there are several variations on this simple measure. The divisor can take on several meanings and values. Examples of three of these are:

- Average of opening and closing book-values. With an opening book-value of $200, we might assume a closing written down book-value of $40. The 'average' value thus committed to the investment is $(200 + 40)/2 = \$120$. The ARR is thus 95/120, or 79.16%.
- Average of net opening and closing book-values. Given the values of $200 and $40, the 'net' average value is $(200 - 40)/2 = \$80$, and thus the ARR is $95/80$, or 118.75%.
- Average of progressive written down book-values. Written down book-values at the end of each year are: $160, $120, $80 and $40. The average is $(160 + 120 + 80 + 40)/4 = \$100$, and thus the ARR is 95/100, or 95%.

Each of the four calculated ARR values, 47.5%, 79.16%, 118.75% and 95% is 'correct'. The ARR is obviously not a reliable measure.

It also suffers other conceptual drawbacks: it does not account for the time value of money; it uses accounting data which is not directly related to the wealth of the firm; and it has no objective decision criterion. The decision criterion usually employed is a comparison of the ARR with the required rate of return. As we have seen, the ARR is only an accounting ratio; it is not a time value of money measure. It should not be compared to the time value required rate of return.

ARR is a very unsophisticated, vague and misleading measure. ARR is not recommended as a capital budgeting decision-making criterion. The ARR may play a role as an aid and comfort measure for supporting a project which is acceptable under the NPV criterion.

Summary of the suitability of the four criteria

Both the payback period and the accounting rate of return ignore the time value of money. Neither of these criteria gives an acceptable approach to the investment decision problem.

Both the NPV and the IRR acknowledge the time value of money and are worthy of consideration. Of these, the IRR technique suffers from both conceptual and computational drawbacks, and should not be the primary decision criterion. Only the NPV method relates the time value of money to the cash flows, and measures the project's direct impact on the firm's goal of wealth maximization. It is the investment model of choice. The IRR method may be used in specialized and restricted cases.

Mutual exclusivity and project ranking

The decision criterion for independent, single, stand-alone projects, such as the Delta Project, is straightforward. Projects with positive net present value or an internal rate of return greater than the required rate of return are accepted. However, this acceptance is not always possible. Firms often need to make investment decisions in the context of mutually exclusive investments where only one has to be selected from among a number of projects with positive NPVs.

As an example, consider the case of buying a machine to produce either 2,000 or 5,000 units a year. Since only one machine can be chosen, these assets are mutually exclusive. Not only does the NPV criterion have to determine whether each machine is viable in its own right, it must also provide a reliable ranking of the two assets for the investment choice.

In this case, both the size of the initial outlays and the length of the useful lives could be different, raising the question as to whether the NPV criterion will actually compare 'apples with apples'. It could be expected that the smaller machine would be cheaper and may need to be replaced every three years, whilst the larger machine would cost more, but need to be replaced only every five years. Fortunately, the NPV model can be adapted for decision support in ranking *mutually exclusive projects*.

Mutual exclusivity occurs when the acceptance of one project will exclude all competing rivals. This occurs when a number of investment proposals perform essentially the same task. For example, suppose a regional airline is considering buying a new aircraft. The choice could be between a Boeing 747 and a Boeing 737. Would these be mutually exclusive? No, the choice would depend upon the intended use. The 400-plus-seat 747 is designed for long-haul routes, whilst the 737 is designed for short-haul routes with a passenger load factor of about 100. The 747 would be uneconomical for low-load, short-haul routes. It is thus not a competing project. But an Airbus A-320, having similar range and seat characteristics to the 737, would be a competitor. In this case, these two planes would have to be directly compared and ranked.

The exclusion is based on physical factors, such as limitations of space, small market size, specialist production or integration with other parts of the production process. It is important to note that exclusion is not based on financial factors, such as having a negative rather than a positive NPV, or limitations of available capital. In the case of negative NPV, such projects exclude themselves, and in the case of resource constraints, other specialist

Table 6.2. *Cash flows, NPV and IRR for projects Big and Small*

	EOY 0 ($)	EOY 1 ($)	EOY 2 ($)	EOY 3 ($)
B	−100,000	0	0	147,000
S	−100	0	0	350

Workbook 6.6

Results	NPV ($)	IRR (%)
B	10,443	13.7
S	163	51.83

approaches, such as linear programming, are required. The point is that if competing assets all have positive NPVs, then they must be *ranked* in order of their added value to the firm, so that the firm can make a rational choice.

Mutually exclusive projects may have various differences in project size, the timing of cash flows (or cash flow patterns) and economic life. The standard NPV model can be used to rank correctly projects with size disparities or projects with cash flow timing disparities, while the use of IRR may result in incorrect ranking. Projects with unequal lives can be ranked appropriately by using extended versions of the basic NPV model. For example, replacement chain and equal annual annuity criteria used in ranking projects with unequal lives may be viewed as tailor-made extensions of the basic NPV model.

Projects with size disparities

Mutually exclusive projects with large differences in size (capital expenditures) can be ranked appropriately using the NPV criterion, while the application of the IRR method is prone to error and misinterpretation. For example, consider projects B(ig) and S(mall) with the following cash flows and a required rate of 10% per annum (Table 6.2).

On the NPV criterion, Project B is preferred, but on the IRR criterion, Project S should be chosen. The scale of the investments causes a ranking problem, depending upon the criterion used.

The asset choice should be based on the NPV rule, since the NPV gives an *absolute* amount of increase in wealth, whereas the IRR gives only a *relative* measure. When only one of these assets can be chosen, it is better for the firm to increase its wealth by $10,443, rather than to earn 51.83% on only $100.

Projects with cash flow timing pattern disparities

A second ranking problem occurs with projects which are equal in scale, but which have different cash flow timing patterns. The timing of competing cash flows is critical in project

Table 6.3. *Cash flows, NPV and IRR for projects Near and Far*

	EOY 0 ($)	EOY 1 ($)	EOY 2 ($)	EOY 3 ($)
N	−1,150	1,000	400	100
F	−1,150	100	500	1,150

Workbook 6.6			

Results		NPV ($)		IRR (%)
N		165		21.48
F		181		16.5

Table 6.4. *Cash flows, NPV and IRR for projects Short and Long*

	EOY 0 ($)	EOY 1 ($)	EOY 2 ($)	EOY 3 ($)
S	1,100	1,900	0	0
L	1,100	0	0	3,570

Results		NPV ($)		IRR (%)
S		627		73
L		1,582		48

ranking, because of the discounting process. For example, consider projects N(ear) and F(ar) with identical outlays and lives, and a required rate of 10% per annum (Table 6.3).

Again, the choice of method (NPV or IRR) leads to a difference in ranking. The NPV criterion is preferred as it shows the absolute addition to the value of the firm.

Projects with unequal lives

Assume projects S(hort) and L(ong) have the cash flow patterns shown in Table 6.4, and a required rate of 10% per annum. The results with the two criteria again conflict. This ranking inconsistency is caused by the different life-spans of the two projects. Ranking by the NPV criterion (as opposed to the IRR criterion) will not solve the problem.

A serious conceptual problem arises when mutually exclusive projects have differing life-spans. The projects are not comparable on an NPV basis because the firm will be in different financial positions according to which one is selected. If Project S has a life-span of one year, and Project L has a life-span of three years, the question arises as to what will be the firm's position at the end of Project S. Project S has the lower NPV, but it will give the firm the opportunity to reinvest the released resources for years 2 and 3, whereas the acceptance of Project L will exclude this possibility. Therefore, the comparison of the two projects by their NPVs is not a fair comparison; the ranking by NPV is not correct.

Table 6.5. *Replication chain cash flows as an annuity due ($)*

	EOY 0	EOY 1	EOY 2	EOY 3
S	627	627	627	
L	1,582			

Workbook
6.8

Two ways of handling this ranking problem have been developed by extending the basic NPV model. They are the replacement chain and equivalent annual annuity methods. The assumption underlying these methods is that the firm's reinvestment opportunities in the future will be similar to the current ones.

Replacement chains

The replacement chain method replicates each of the individual investments until the lowest common multiple life-span is reached. In our example this means that the one-year project, Project S, would be replicated three times, to equate it to one life-span of the three-year project, Project L.

The assumptions made to drive this idea are:

- the projects are repeated exactly at their replication dates
- the projects are repeated with the same physical characteristics
- the outflow and inflow streams for each project remain the same at each replication
- the discount rate is constant.

Each replication is treated as if the initial NPV is received at the repetition date of each project, and this stream of NPVs is discounted to the present day to give a 'common-life NPV'. The decision is then made on these current NPVs.

To compare projects S and L under this approach, we would replicate Project S three times, and compare it to one life-span of Project L (Table 6.5). The three NPVs of Project S form an *annuity due*, with an annual rate of 10% per annum. The present value of this annuity, which is the NPV of a three-time replication of Project S, is $1,715. As this NPV is more than the $1,582 of one replication of Project L, Project S should be chosen.

The algebraic layout of this calculation is:

$$NPV_{Short} = 627 + \frac{627}{(1.10)} + \frac{627}{(1.10)^2}$$

$$= \$1,715$$

A valid comparison of two chains of replacement can only be made when the chains are of equal length. If one project has a life of thirteen years and the other sixteen years, the lowest common denominator is 208 (i.e. 13 × 16). At this point, the first project has been undertaken sixteen times and the second project thirteen times. Thus, this approach becomes cumbersome as the number of replications increases.

This problem can be overcome by assuming that both chains continue indefinitely and then replicating the projects *in perpetuity*. The relevant calculating formula is that for a *perpetuity due*. That is, the formula for the present value of an ordinary perpetuity, with the added value of the initial NPV as at today. This formula can be expressed in two forms:

$$NPV_p = NPV_r + \frac{NPV_n}{[(1+r)^n - 1]} = NPV_r \left[\frac{(1+r)^n}{(1+r)^n - 1} \right]$$

where:

NPV_p = the NPV at the present time of all the NPVs in the replicating stream to perpetuity.

NPV_r = the NPV of the initial replication

NPV_n = the NPV of each replication at year n.

$[(1+r)^n - 1]$ = the periodic interest rate for each replication length.

For example, assume that Project E(ight) has an eight-year life, and Project T(hirteen) has a thirteen-year life with a common required rate of 10% per annum. As these projects have a lowest common multiple life-span of $8 \times 13 = 104$ years, we can emulate the present NPV calculations by assuming project replication in perpetuity. If Project E has an NPV of $432 occurring every eight years, and Project T has an NPV of $517 occurring every thirteen years, then the respective NPVs are:

E: $NPV_p = 432 + \dfrac{432}{[(1.10)^8 - 1]}$

         $= \$810$

T: $NPV_p = 517 + \dfrac{517}{[(1.10)^{13} - 1]}$

         $= \$728$

In this mutually exclusive situation, Project E ought to be chosen.

In practice, the replacement chain method could be used where firms are likely to continue to produce the same product with the same production technology. The perennial wooden mousetrap is a classic example.

Equivalent annual annuity

To allow for an easier visualization of the benefits afforded by the infinitely replicating chains, the present total NPVs can be re-expressed as streams of equivalent *annual* benefits. The dollar value of each amount in the stream is known as the equivalent annual annuity, or the equivalent annual value. The annual cash flows are simply those of a yearly ordinary perpetuity giving NPV_p at the required annual rate r. The formula is $NPV_p = \frac{EAA}{r}$.

Table 6.6. *Cash flows within timed replication chains ($)*

Year	Annual net cash flows	Salvage value
1	11,000	19,000
2	9,750	16,555
3	8,120	12,800
4	7,500	9,175
5	6,320	6,950

In our example the equivalent annual annuities will be:
Project E:

$$810 = \frac{EAA}{0.10}$$

$$EAA = \$81$$

Project T:

$$728 = \frac{EAA}{0.10}$$

$$EAA = \$72.80$$

As the equivalent annual annuity for Project E, $81, is greater than that for Project T, $72.80, E should be chosen.

The EAA method should be useful where decision-makers are able to relate more readily to a constant annual stream measure than to the total NPV value of an irregularly replicated chain.

Timing within a replacement chain

A second benefit of the EAA method is that it provides a way of determining the optimum time to replace assets, where those assets do form a natural chain. For example, a firm hiring out cars needs to know whether its fleet should be replaced every two, three or four years. It may be tenable here to assume that technological changes are irrelevant, as the firm is not producing a tangible product, but rather selling mobility. Of course, the updating cycle may be driven more by marketing requirements than by technical issues, but, even so, some analysis needs to be done to identify an optimum replacement cycle, given operational data.

Assume a new car costs the firm $25,000 and that its life can be predicted in terms of its positive cash inflows (net of increasing annual maintenance costs) and second-hand salvage values over a five-year life. The data are shown in Table 6.6.

The required rate of return is 10% per annum. The NPV for each of the separate holding periods is calculated as, for example:

One-year life cash flows:

EOY 0	EOY 1
−25,000	11,000 + 19,000

Table 6.7. *Calculated individual NPVs for various replication cycle lengths within a chain* ($)

Replication cycle length	NPV_0
One year	2,273
Two years	6,740
Three years	8,775
Four years	10,719
Five years	12,692

Workbook
6.9

$$NPV_0 = \frac{30,000}{1.10} - 25,000$$

$$= \$2,272$$

Five-year life cash flows:

EOY 0	EOY 1	EOY 2	EOY 3	EOY 4	EOY 5
−25,000	11,000	9,750	8,120	7,500	6,320 + 6,950

$$NPV_0 = \frac{11,000}{1.10} + \frac{9,570}{(1.10)^2} + \frac{8,120}{(1.10)^3} + \frac{7,500}{(1.10)^4} + \frac{13,270}{(1.10)^5}$$

$$= \$12,692$$

The NPVs for each of the singular holding periods are listed in Table 6.7.

These results are then converted to the equivalent present NPV, NPV_p, as if the assets were to be replaced at the respective intervals in perpetuity. The 'perpetuity due' formula is used for this conversion:

$$NPV_p = NPV_0 + \frac{NPV_n}{[(1+r)^n - 1]}$$

The final results are presented in Table 6.8 and indicate that the rental cars should be replaced every second year in perpetuity.

Asset replacement investment decisions

As discussed in Chapter 2, two types of investment project are *asset expansion* projects and *asset replacement* projects. The discussion so far in this chapter has related to asset expansion investment projects. Replacement chains discussed previously should not be confused with asset replacement projects. The replacement chain technique is simply used to rank mutually exclusive asset expansion projects so that the best project can be chosen.

Table 6.8. *Calculated total NPVs for perpetual replacement over various replication cycle lengths within a chain* ($)

Replication cycle length	Overall NPV (NPV_p)
One year	25,000
Two years	38,833
Three years	35,287
Four years	33,814
Five years	33,480

> Workbook
> 6.10

Table 6.9. *Repco Replacement Investment Project: incremental cash flows* ($)

	EOY 0	EOY 1	EOY 2	EOY 3
Net cash outlay	−112,400			
Operating inflows		50,800	60,550	56,800
Terminal cash flow				20,375

This section discusses the accept/reject decision for an asset replacement project. An incremental cash flow calculation for an asset replacement project was illustrated in Chapter 2 with the Repco Project example, and the relevant cash flows are reproduced in Table 6.9.

The NPV of this replacement project is:

$$NPV = -112,400 + \frac{50,800}{(1.10)} + \frac{60,550}{(1.10)^2} + \frac{77,175}{(1.10)^3} = \$41,805$$

As the NPV is positive, management should go ahead with the planned replacement investment proposal.

There is no difference in the application of the NPV or IRR techniques between asset replacement and asset expansion projects. The difference is in the calculation of the cash flows. The cash flow calculation for an asset replacement project, which involves additional steps, has been illustrated in Chapter 2 in the Repco Project example.

Project retirement

Although management's primary focus is on making new investments, existing assets also ought to be constantly reviewed to ensure that they are still viable. Non-viable assets should be retired so that their capital can be reallocated to more efficient assets.

The *retirement* decision must be differentiated from the *replacement* decision. The former means that the asset is sold and not replaced, and the capital is re-employed elsewhere; the latter means that the capital is re-employed on similar productive capacity, provided there is

Table 6.10. *Cash flow forecasts for various retirement lives ($)*

End of year	Net operating inflow	Salvage value
5	—	22,000
6	7,000	17,500
7	6,400	14,375
8	4,250	8,980

a need for such production. In reviewing an asset for retirement, management must compare its current cash *salvage* value against its current NPV as *operating in place*. Only relevant – future, changeable – flows are analysed; sunk costs must be ignored.

Assume that Torch Ltd has an asset with about three years of physical operating life remaining, today being the end of the asset's fifth year. The relevant cash flow forecasts are presented in Table 6.10.

The decision at the end of year 5 is to compare the opportunity of the available salvage value now of $22,000, with the discounted value at 10% per annum of the net operating inflow and salvage value in year 6. The computation is:

$$NPV = \frac{7,000 + 17,500}{1.10}$$
$$= \$22,272$$

As this NPV is positive, the asset should be kept at least one more year.

We can also determine whether the asset should be kept until the end of year 7 or year 8 by the same approach. The relevant NPVs are:

Hold to year 7: $$NPV = \frac{7,000}{1.10} + \frac{6,400 + 14,375}{(1.10)^2}$$
$$= \$23,533$$

Hold to year 8: $$NPV = \frac{7,000}{1.10} + \frac{6,400}{(1.10)^2} + \frac{4,250 + 8,980}{(1.10)^3}$$
$$= \$21,593$$

These calculations show that the asset should be kept until the end of year 7.

An additional case for which the retirement technique can be employed is that of determining an optimal year of harvest for a long-term growing crop. Let's assume that Woodland Inc. has a stand of timber. Woodland Inc. has no plans to grow a second crop after this crop is harvested. The projections for harvest income cash flows are as follows:

	EOY 0	EOY 1	EOY 2	EOY 3	EOY 4	EOY 5	EOY 6	EOY 7
$M	0	0	0	80	100	120	130	135

Woodland Inc. has a required rate of return of 12% per annum.

The NPV of the cash flow at each harvest date is calculated as, for example:

Harvest at EOY 3:

$$NPV_0 = \frac{80}{(1.10)^3}$$
$$= \$56.95M$$

Harvest at EOY 5:

$$NPV_0 = \frac{120}{(1.10)^5}$$
$$= \$68.09M$$

The NPVs of the various harvest flows are:

	EOY 0	EOY 1	EOY 2	EOY 3	EOY 4	EOY 5	EOY 6	EOY 7
$M	0	0	0	56.95	63.55	68.09	65.86	61.07

The optimal harvest time is at the end of year 5.

Concluding comments

This chapter has dealt with the central issue in capital budgeting: the primacy of the net present value model as the decision model in all circumstances. The NPV is preferred to its discounted cash flow counterpart, the internal rate of return, and both of these methods are far more desirable than the non-discounted cash flow methods, the accounting rate of return and the payback period. The primacy of the NPV model derives from its direct relationship to the firm's goal of wealth maximization.

This direct linkage between model output, the decision criterion and the goal of the firm, allows us to employ the NPV in unusual project evaluation tasks. These tasks include the choice among mutually exclusive projects, the setting up of asset replacement chains, the calculation of an optimum replacement cycle and the decision to retire existing assets.

In this chapter we have demonstrated the useful versatility of the NPV model, under the restrictive assumption of certainty. We relax this assumption in the following chapters to look at investment decisions under risk. The assumption of 'no resource constraints' is relaxed in Chapters 11 and 12.

Review questions

6.1 Explain and define the terms: net present value, internal rate of return, modified internal rate of return, accounting rate of return and payback period.

6.2 Explain the role of 'certainty' in project evaluation decisions.

Table 6.11. *Operational cash flows*

Year	Annual net cash flows ($M)	Salvage value ($M)
0	23.00 (Cost)	
1	4.865	21.0
2	3.956	18.7
3	2.875	16.1
4	2.115	14.3
5	1.875	12.8

6.3 Assume that Anvil Inc. has estimated the following annual data for the introduction of a new product, Ranch Hand:

	EOY 0	EOY 1	EOY 2	EOY 3	EOY 4	EOY 5
Cash flows	−14,250	3,700	2,980	6,540	7,810	6,320
Accounting income		2,870	2,540	5,890	6,720	5,780

Required rate of return: 14% per annum
Reinvestment rate of return: 12% per annum
(a) For Ranch Hand calculate NPV, IRR, MIRR, ARR and payback period.
(b) Based on the calculations in part (a), make a recommendation to Anvil's management about the introduction of Ranch Hand.

6.4 With respect to investment decisions, explain the terms: mutual exclusivity, replacement decisions, retirement decisions.

6.5 Discuss the difference in the usage of the terms 'asset replacement' and 'asset replication'.

6.6 The formula to arrive at an NPV for asset replication in perpetuity is:

$$NPV_p = NPV_r + \frac{NPV_n}{[(1+r)^n - 1]} = NPV_r \left[\frac{(1+r)^n}{(1+r)^n - 1} \right]$$

Explain how this formula works, and show how it can be set up as a generic calculation within an Excel spreadsheet.

6.7 Assume that White Knuckle Airlines Inc. operates a regional fifty-seat jet aircraft fleet. White Knuckle expects that there will be a constant demand for this type of flight service, and that the model of aircraft employed will remain in production for the foreseeable future. White Knuckle has predicted the set of operational cash flows shown in Table 6.11 for each aircraft.
If White Knuckle Inc. has a required rate of return of 12% per annum, determine the optimal aircraft replacement cycle time, in perpetuity.

6.8 Kandy Corporation is considering a replacement investment. The machine currently in use was originally purchased two years ago for $65,000. Tax-allowable depreciation is $13,000 per year for five years. The current market value of this machine is $23,000.

The new machine being considered would cost $140,000, and require $4,000 shipping costs and $2,000 installation costs. The economic life of the machine is estimated as three years. Tax-allowable depreciation is $70,000 per year for the first two years. If the new machine is acquired, the investments in accounts receivable is expected to increase by $9,000, the inventory by $13,000, and accounts payable by $15,000. The before-tax net operating cash flow is estimated as $120,000 per year for the next three years with the old machine and $143,000 per year for the next three years with the new machine. The expected resale value of the old and new machines in three years' time would be $4,000 and $6,600, respectively. The corporate tax rate is 30%.

(a) Calculate the initial investment associated with the proposed replacement decision.
(b) Calculate the incremental operating cash flows of the proposed replacement decision.
(c) Calculate the terminal cash flows associated with the proposed replacement decision.
(d) Compute the NPV of the replacement project assuming a discount rate of 6% per annum.
(e) What is the proposed investment's IRR?
(f) Use the computed IRR and NPV results and discuss the project accept/reject decision.

7 Project analysis under risk

The previous chapter discussed project analysis under certainty, i.e. in a no-risk situation. In reality, however, the future cash flows of a project are not certain. Cash flows cannot be forecast with absolute accuracy. These are estimates of what is expected in the future, not necessarily what will be realized in the future. Sometimes, even the initial capital outlay can be uncertain and subject to high estimation errors. For example, in 1987 the cost of the Channel Tunnel (between Britain and France) was estimated to be $12 billion, but later this was increased to about $22 billion. The Sydney Opera House is another famous example of a large cost increase over the initial estimate.

In the previous chapter, one single series – the best estimate of the project's future cash flows – was used to compute the net present value. This series may be viewed as the best estimate of a range of possible outcomes. For example, in Chapters 2 and 6, the Delta Project was considered and its first year's sales were *expected* to be $345,553. This was the best estimate. But this amount could eventually prove to have been under or over the actual sales that the project generated. This sales forecast was arrived at by estimating the sales units on the basis of past sales and assuming a unit selling price of $0.50. However, the actual selling price might be different to this forecast value. A change in selling price could subsequently generate a different cash flow as the project proceeds. For example, a competitor might unexpectedly open a similar business a few months later, or the economy might slow down (or go into a recession), leading to lower sales than expected. Thus, there is a risk or uncertainty associated with this cash flow. Similarly, all the forecasted cash flows have a risk or uncertainty attached to them.

Measuring the risk associated with the expected cash flows of the project and incorporating this risk into the determination of the net present value (NPV) is essential for any real-world project evaluation. There are various ways in which risk can be incorporated into the NPV computation and capital budgeting decision support. These include the risk-adjusted discount rate, the certainty equivalent, sensitivity and break-even analysis and simulation.

This chapter relaxes the certainty assumption and incorporates risk into project analysis. Risk and uncertainty are briefly discussed and two approaches to incorporating risk into project analysis – the risk-adjusted discount rate and the certainty equivalent – are discussed and applied. Another two approaches – sensitivity analysis and simulation – are discussed and applied in Chapters 8 to 10.

One way to estimate the risk-adjusted discount rate (RADR) is to use the cost of capital. This is briefly reviewed in this chapter. Another way to estimate the RADR is to use the capital asset pricing model (CAPM). Estimation of the risk premium using the CAPM, calculation of the RADR using that risk premium and application of the RADR to capital budgeting is illustrated using an extended version of the Delta Project example, which was first introduced in Chapter 2 to illustrate project cash flows and then used in Chapter 6 for capital budgeting decision support under certainty.

Study objectives

After studying this chapter the reader should be able to:

- define risk and understand the measurement of risk in finance
- evaluate capital investment proposals using the risk-adjusted discount rate (RADR) and certainty equivalent (CE) methods to incorporate risk
- define and estimate the cost of capital to be employed as the RADR in project analysis
- estimate the parameters of the capital asset pricing model (CAPM) and use the results to calculate the RADR
- understand the relationship between the CE coefficient and the RADR
- appreciate the relative merits and demerits of RADR and CE methods in the context of incorporating risk into project appraisal.

The concepts of risk and uncertainty

The term 'risk' is generally used to mean exposure to the chance of an injury or loss. In finance, the term is used in general to refer to the chance of the loss of money or of receiving less than was expected. In common-sense terms, the chance of receiving more than was expected is not considered as risk. Statistical risk measurements in finance and economics, however, do not exclude these 'better than expected outcomes' as they measure both the upside and downside variability (or fluctuations) around the expected outcome. For example, widely used risk measurements in finance and economics are based on statistical measures such as variance – or its square root, the standard deviation – covariance and correlation, all of which deal with variability around the expected outcome or 'mean'. The beta risk factor in the capital asset pricing model, estimated later in this chapter, is an example.

In the finance and economics literature dealing with risk and uncertainty, the term 'probability' is often encountered. When managers refer to the chances of something occurring, they are using probability in their decision-making process. The decision-makers are establishing in their minds the probability that some result will occur if a particular action is taken. The probability of an occurrence is the likelihood of that event expressed as a ratio or percentage. For example, an investment manager, after analysing the available information, may feel that there is a 75% chance that his proposed investment in a new car manufacturing project will earn a net cash inflow in the range of $5,000,000–$6,000,000 in its first year of operation and 25% chance that it could earn only $750,000 or less. These percentages, or probabilities, reflect the manager's expectations about the chances of the two outcomes occurring.

A distinction is sometimes drawn between the terms 'risk' and 'uncertainty'. 'Uncertainty' is used to describe situations in which the probabilities of outcomes are not known. Thus, uncertainty is defined as random variability for which it is not possible to specify the parameters of probability distributions; for example, when there is no history of observations upon which to draw. 'Risk', on the other hand, is used to describe those situations in which the probabilities of all outcomes are known. For example, these probabilities may have been estimated on the basis of past records.

In practice, the distinction between risk and uncertainty does not seem to have any realistic meaning for two reasons. First, the term 'risk' is used in ordinary conversation to refer to any situation involving the possibility of an undesired outcome (which means only downside risk), whether or not probabilities are known. Second, there is hardly ever a real-world environment, other than the gaming table, in which probabilities are known. In practice, most past events are non-repeatable and therefore accurate estimation or derivation of probability distributions of expected future outcomes of, say, project cash flows, is not possible. There is uncertainty about the accuracy of these estimates.

Nowadays, the terms risk and uncertainty are often used interchangeably. In this book, both risk and uncertainty are used in the more general sense to cover situations in which the outcomes are not known with certainty, irrespective of whether or not their probabilities are known.

Risk is a complex and multi-faceted problem. There have long been attempts to reduce risk measurements to a solid single measure. Unfortunately, however, such a single measure, which could adequately describe and assess risk in every situation, has not yet been developed and it is highly unlikely that such a measure could be developed in the years to come. Investment analysts often look at more than one risk measure in the process of incorporating risk into their project evaluation. In this book, four widely used *quantitative* methods for appraising projects under risk are discussed and applied. They are the risk-adjusted discount rate, the certainty equivalent, sensitivity and break-even analysis and simulation.

Although those *quantitative* approaches to incorporating risk into project analysis are discussed in detail, it should never be forgotten that the simplest risk analysis is *qualitative* and *subjective* and all the quantitative methods involve, at some stage or another, some element of judgement. In the simplest form of qualitative risk analysis, things that might go wrong are identified, and decision-makers are left to form their own judgement as to the importance of these things in terms of the likelihood of occurrence or the significance of the consequences. The most basic risk analysis, then, may simply involve statements such as: 'This project's estimated cash flows may not be realized if a civil war spreads'; or 'What would happen to our projected sales if a competitor suddenly enters the market?'

Main elements of the RADR and CE techniques

The main elements of the risk-adjusted discount rate (RADR) and certainty equivalent (CE) methods as well as their similarities and disparities are depicted in Figure 7.1.

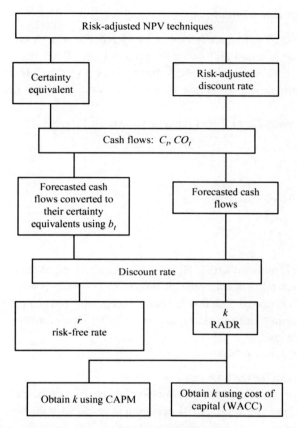

Figure 7.1. Main features of RADR and CE techniques.

The algebraic symbols in this flow chart are defined as follows:

$k = r + u + a$

$r =$ risk-free rate

$u =$ average risk premium for the firm

$a =$ an additional risk factor to account for the difference in the risk between that faced by the firm and that of the proposed project; a could be positive, negative or zero, depending upon whether the project has greater, lower or the same risk as the average risk of the firm's existing business

$b_t =$ certainty equivalent coefficient

The flow chart serves as a convenient reference point for understanding the linkages of the material presented in this chapter. The RADR method involves an adjustment for risk in the denominator of the NPV equation while the CE method makes the adjustment in the numerator of the NPV equation.

The risk-adjusted discount rate method

This seems to be the method most frequently employed by practitioners. A discount rate higher than the risk-free rate is used to allow for the project's risk. Other than that there is no conceptual difference between the basic NPV formula under certainty (presented in Chapter 6) and the NPV formula under uncertainty which uses the RADR to incorporate risk into the project analysis.

The basic NPV formula, reproduced from Chapters 5 and 6, is:

$$NPV = \sum_{t=1}^{n} \frac{C_t}{(1+r)^t} - CO$$

The NPV formula under RADR is:

$$NPV_{radr} = \sum_{t=1}^{n} \frac{C_t}{(1+k)^t} - CO$$

The only difference is that r is replaced with k. Here, k is the required rate of return (RROR) for the proposed project which takes into account the time value of money as well as the risk associated with the project's expected cash flows. Thus, conceptually and computationally, the NPV formulae under certainty and uncertainty are quite similar. However, the estimation of k is an extremely difficult task.

Conceptually, k has three components:

- a *risk-free rate* (r) to account for the time value of money
- an *average risk premium* (u) to compensate investors for the fact that the company's assets (or investments) are risky; in other words, a risk premium to account for the business risk of the firm's existing business
- an *additional risk factor* (a), which could be zero, negative or positive to account for the difference in the risk between the firm's existing business and the proposed project.

Thus, conceptually, k may be expressed in an algebraic equation form as:

$$k = r + u + a.$$

If the risk of the proposed project is the same as the average risk of the firm's existing projects, the additional risk factor a is zero. The required rate of return (or the RADR) to be employed as the discount rate for *projects of average risk*, therefore, is $(r + u)$.

Estimating the RADR

How will we arrive at an estimate for k to be employed as the discount rate in the project analysis? It has three components, although, as we will see later, the three different components may not always be estimated separately and then summed to arrive at k. For example, if the cost of capital is used to estimate the RADR, then we usually arrive at a single value for $(r + u)$, and then add to it or subtract from it a value to account for a. On the other hand, if the capital asset pricing model (CAPM) is used to estimate the RADR, then we will have separate values for r, u and a.

The risk-free discount rate, r

The risk-free rate may be arrived at by considering government bond yields or insured banks' term deposit rates. By examining data published in the financial press, a suitable figure for r can easily be chosen. Term deposits and bonds have different terms to maturity. The yield of those government bonds which have terms to maturity similar to the project life of the capital investment should be selected. For example, the yield on five-year government bonds can be used for projects with a five-year time frame.

The average risk premium for the firm, u

This may be estimated using the firm's cost of capital. The weighted average cost of capital (WACC) is usually used for calculating this. Another approach to estimating u is to use the capital asset pricing model (CAPM). Illustration and application of these involve relatively lengthy calculations. Therefore, for reasons of clarity and continuity, we will introduce the third component of the RADR before illustrating WACC and CAPM.

The additional risk factor, a

The forecast cash flows from the project may have greater or lower risk than the firm's average risk, or they may be in the same risk class as the firm. If the perceived risk of the project is greater or lower than the average risk, we need to add to or subtract from the average risk an *additional risk factor* to account for the difference between the average risk and that of the proposed project.

The additional risk factor applied to individual projects is usually established *subjectively*. For example, some firms establish a number of risk classes and then apply a different factor to each class. Projects with above-average risk, such as the expansion of existing facilities and product lines, might be assigned a value in the range 0.02 to 0.03 (i.e. 2% to 3%) for a. High-risk projects, such as investments in entirely new lines of business or the introduction of new products and services, might be assigned a value in the range 0.04 to 0.07 (i.e. 4% to 7%) for a. Below-average-risk projects, such as plant and equipment replacements, might be assigned a value in the range -0.02 to -0.03 (i.e. -2% to -3%) for a. Average-risk projects, such as plant and equipment modifications, might be assigned a value of zero for a.

Estimating the RADR using the firm's cost of capital

The cost of capital is the rate of return required by investors in the firm's debt and equity. Since investors require a higher rate of return from a risky company, risky firms will have a higher cost of capital. Similarly, less risky firms will have a lower cost of capital. Therefore, the cost of capital may be used as the RADR for projects which have the same average risk as that of the firm's existing business. In other words, the cost of capital, which is equal to $(r + u)$, is the required return for the firm's average-risk projects.

How do we estimate the cost of capital? Capital that a firm has or will use to finance new projects usually comes from more than one source. Possible sources include common stock, preferred stock, retained earnings and debt. The appropriate cost of capital figure has to be weighted by the proportions of the various capital components in the firm's target capital structure. Therefore, this figure is called the weighted average cost of capital. The basic calculation of a WACC is illustrated for a highly simplified case in the following example.

Example 7.1. Computation of the WACC for Costor Company

Costor Company has a target capital structure consisting of 50% common stock, 40% debt and 10% preferred stock. The marginal cost of common stock has been estimated to be 10%; the marginal cost of preferred stock is 8%; pre-tax marginal cost of debt is 7%. The company tax rate is 30%.

The weighted average cost of capital for Costor is:

$$WACC = 0.5 \times 0.10 + 0.10 \times 0.08 + 0.40 \times 0.07 \, (1 - 0.30)$$

$$= 0.05 + 0.008 + 0.0196$$

$$= 0.0776 = 7.76\%$$

Often the (debt and equity) proportions of the firm's long-term capital structure are not known with certainty. The best approximation in such situations may be to use the existing capital structure for allocating weights. The marginal cost of each debt and equity component is approximated by the relevant current market rates. For example, the pre-tax cost of debt may be approximated by the relevant market interest rates for similar debts.

The marginal cost of common stock, k_e is calculated from the dividend growth model of share valuation:

$$P_0 = \frac{D_0 \, (1 + g)}{(k_e - g)}$$

where:

$P_0 =$ current share price
$D_0 =$ current dividend per share
$k_e =$ investors' required rate of return on common stock
$g =$ annual expected growth rate of dividends.

Estimating the RADR using the CAPM

It was mentioned that one approach to incorporating risk into project analysis is to discount the forecasted cash flows by a risk-adjusted discount rate, k. An important component of k

is the average risk premium, u. One way to estimate u is to resort to the widely used capital asset pricing model (CAPM). This section will:

- state the basic CAPM equation
- extend the previously introduced Delta Project to demonstrate the application of the RADR to project analysis
- estimate the CAPM's beta risk coefficient using hypothetical financial market data, which are introduced to the extended Delta Project example
- estimate the CAPM and the RADR for the extended Delta Project example, and
- compute NPV for the extended Delta Project example using the RADR estimated from the CAPM.

The basic CAPM equation

The basic CAPM equation may be written as:

$$\bar{r}_i = r_f + (\bar{r}_m - r_f)\beta_i$$

where:

$\bar{r}_i =$ expected (average) return on individual firm i's shares
$r_f =$ risk-free rate (of assets from which the expected returns are certain)
$\bar{r}_m =$ expected (average) return on the market portfolio
$\beta_i =$ the beta risk factor of firm i's stock returns

In concept, the *market portfolio* represents the total value of all stocks listed on the stock exchange on which firm i is listed. In practice, this (market) portfolio is represented and measured by a representative stock market index. Beta measures the degree of systematic risk of firm i's stock returns relative to the risk of the (stock) market portfolio's returns. For example, if β is equal to 1, firm i's stock returns have the same risk as that of the market portfolio's returns; if β is less than 1, say 0.5, the risk of firm i's stock returns is about half that of the market portfolio. If β is greater than 1, say 2, firm i's stock returns are twice as risky as the market portfolio's returns. β measures the extent to which the firm i's returns are correlated with the market portfolio's returns.

The CAPM measures the expected rate of return on an asset commensurate with its risk relative to market-wide risk. An asset with returns which are expected to be more volatile than expected market returns will attract a required rate higher than that for the market in general. Conversely, an asset with returns which are expected to be less volatile than expected market returns will attract a required rate lower than that for the market.

The part $(\bar{r}_m - r_f)\beta_i$ of the basic CAPM equation above is the average risk premium for the firm's existing business, which we denoted as u. (Recall that $k = r + u + a$.) The term r_f in the basic CAPM equation is the risk-free rate, which was denoted as r earlier.

Table 7.1. *Stock-market index value and Delta Company share price*

Year	Stock-market index	Share price ($)
1990	2005	5.00
1991	2201	5.50
1992	2410	5.75
1993	2520	5.90
1994	2602	6.00
1995	2835	6.10
1996	2650	6.00
1997	2502	5.90
1998	2854	6.50
1999	3210	7.00
2000	3420	7.25

Estimation of the CAPM and its application to capital budgeting: extension of the Delta Project example

The Delta Project example was introduced in Chapter 2 for project cash flow identification, and was used subsequently for demonstrating the NPV calculations under certainty in Chapter 6. It is now extended to incorporate risk into project analysis. Two further sets of data are now added into the Delta example. They are the historical data on Delta's share price and a stock-market index. Year-end prices of the Delta Company's shares and a country's stock-market index values are presented in Table 7.1. A relevant stock-market index in Australia would be the All Ordinaries Index, whilst in the United States it would be the Dow-Jones Industrial Average, or the New York Stock Exchange Index.

The CAPM equation is expressed in terms of market and individual-company stock returns. Therefore, the first step is to calculate returns from the stock-market index values and share prices.

Calculation of returns from stock-market index values and share prices

Returns can be calculated in two ways. To allow their straightforward identification by two convenient terms, they are defined here as 'arithmetic returns' and 'logarithmic returns'.

The formula for arithmetic returns on firm i's shares is:

$$r_{it} = \frac{P_{it} - P_{it-1}}{P_{it-1}} = \frac{P_{it}}{P_{it-1}} - 1$$

where:

$r_{it} =$ return on firm i's shares over time period t

$P_{it} =$ price of firm i's shares at end of time t

$P_{it-1} =$ price of firm i's shares at end of time $t - 1$.

Table 7.2. *Stock-market index and share price returns*

Year	Stock-market Index Returns (r_{mt})	Share price returns (r_{it})
1991	0.0977	0.1000
1992	0.0949	0.0454
1993	0.0456	0.0260
1994	0.0325	0.0169
1995	0.0895	0.0166
1996	−0.0652	−0.0163
1997	−0.0558	−0.0166
1998	0.1406	0.1016
1999	0.1247	0.0769
2000	0.0654	0.0357
Average	0.0570	0.0386

> Workbook
> 7.1

Arithmetic returns on the stock-market index can be expressed in the same way, but with different symbols. As a way of demonstrating the arithmetic return calculation, the returns for the first full year in the data set, year-end 1991 to year-end 1992, will be:

Stock market

$$r_{mt} = \frac{I_{mt} - I_{mt-1}}{I_{mt-1}}$$

$$= \frac{2201 - 2005}{2005}$$

$$= 0.0977, \text{ or } 9.77\%$$

Delta Company

$$r_{it} = \frac{P_{it} - P_{it-1}}{P_{it-1}}$$

$$= \frac{5.50 - 5.00}{5.00}$$

$$= 0.10, \text{ or } 10\%$$

Returns for each of the subsequent years are calculated in the same way, and the full set of annual returns over the ten years for the stock market and the Delta Company are provided in Table 7.2. The return calculations can be viewed in Workbook 7.1.

The formula for logarithmic returns on firm i's shares is:

$$r_{it} = \ln \frac{P_{it}}{P_{it-1}} = \ln P_{it} - \ln P_{it-1}$$

where ln denotes natural logarithms.

> Workbook
> 7.1

The calculation of logarithmic returns is demonstrated in Workbook 7.1 and is reviewed in the questions at the end of the chapter. There is no significant difference between logarithmic and arithmetic returns except when the index values or share prices vary substantially between the time periods. Logarithms are often taken to convert skewed distributions to approximately normal distributions. For the purpose of illustrations in the Delta Project example, arithmetic returns are used.

Estimating β

The value of β can be estimated as the regression coefficient of a simple regression model:

$$r_{it} = a + b_i r_{mt} + u_{it}$$

where:

$r_{it} =$ rate of return on firm i's shares at time t
$r_{mt} =$ rate of return on the market portfolio at time t
$u_{it} =$ random error term (as defined in regression analysis)

The random error term may include other factors which have negative and positive influences on the individual firm's stock return; the expected value of these influences is assumed to be zero. With this standard regression assumption, the estimated regression equation can be written as:

$$r_{it} = \alpha + \beta r_{mt}$$

The value of the coefficient β can be estimated by ordinary least squares (OLS) regression of observed values for the dependent variable r_{it} on the independent variable r_{mt}. The mathematical formula for estimating β can be expressed in various forms. To relate the regression formula to the statistical measurement of risk in finance and to provide an intuitive explanation of what is involved in the CAPM β, the calculation may be expressed in terms of covariance and variance or correlation and standard deviations:

$$\beta = \frac{\text{cov}\,(r_i, r_m)}{\text{var}\,(r_m)} = \frac{\rho_{i,m}\sigma_i}{\sigma_m}$$

where:

$\text{cov}\,(r_i, r_m) =$ covariance between the rate of return on firm i's shares and the rate of return on the market portfolio
$\text{var}\,(r_m)$, or $\sigma_m^2 =$ variance of the rate of return on the market portfolio
$\rho =$ correlation between the rates of return from firm i's shares and from the market portfolio
$\sigma_i =$ standard deviation of the rate of return on firm i's shares
$\sigma_m =$ standard deviation of the rate of return on the market portfolio

The computation of the regression coefficient is based on variations about the means of the two variables. Therefore, the β risk factor is a statistical measurement dealing with variations around the means of the individual company stock returns and the market portfolio returns, and with their association (covariance or correlation) with one another.

Workbook
7.1

The regression equation is estimated using the Excel regression function and the details can be viewed in Workbook 7.1. The estimated regression equation is:

$$r_{it} = 0.0083 + 0.532\, r_{mt}$$

Excel provides various test statistics useful for assessing the reliability of the estimates. Two such measures relevant in the context of β estimation are the t value of the β coefficient and the R^2 value for the regression equation. For the current example, the t value is 5.04 and the adjusted R^2 value is 0.73. These values suggest that the β estimate is highly significant statistically and that the goodness of fit of the regression equation is quite acceptable: the explanatory variable – market returns – explains approximately 73% of the variation in the explained variable – returns on the firm's shares.

Estimating the CAPM and the RADR for the Delta Project

The parameter needed from the regression equation to establish the required rate of return in the CAPM is the value for β (i.e. 0.532). This value is substituted into the CAPM with a given risk-free rate of 5% per annum, giving the required rate of return of 5.37%. This rate is commensurate with the risk of the firm's existing business.

$$\bar{r}_i = r_f + (\bar{r}_m - r_f)\beta$$
$$\bar{r}_i = 0.05 + (0.0570 - 0.05) \times 0.532 = 0.0537$$

An additional risk factor, a, can be added to this rate to allow for the additional risk of the project, if the proposed project's risk is above the average risk of the firm's existing projects. The Delta Project is said to have the same risk as that of the firm's existing projects. Therefore the value of a is zero. Thus, the RADR to be applied to the Delta Project will be 5.37% per annum.

The next step is to use the estimated k as the discount rate and compute the NPV for the Delta Project.

NPV computation for the Delta Project using the RADR estimate from the CAPM

Discounting the Delta Project's cash flows (which were estimated in Chapter 2), by the RADR estimated from the CAPM, an estimate of the net present value under risk can be obtained.

$$NPV_{radr,\,capm} = -1,002,000 + \frac{195,510}{(1.0537)} + \frac{200,087}{(1.0537)^2} - \frac{295,135}{(1.0537)^3} + \frac{379,643}{(1.0537)^4}$$

$$+ \frac{384,421}{(1.0537)^5} + \frac{608,760}{(1.0537)^6} + \frac{618,061}{(1.0537)^7} + \frac{638,362}{(1.0537)^8}$$

$$= \$1,008,826$$

| Workbook |
| 7.2 |

The NPV in Workbook 7.2 is $1,008,457. The negligible difference (which is less than 0.04%) between the manual and Excel calculations is due to rounding errors in the manual calculation. The NPV under certainty (which was calculated using a risk-free discount rate of 5% in Chapter 6), was $1,049,852. The slightly lower NPV now is due to the marginally higher discount rate applied to allow for the risk. In this particular example, the β value was approximately 0.5 suggesting the risk of the firm's existing business is about half of that of the stock market. Thus, the average risk of the firm's business is relatively low. It was also assumed in the example that the proposed project is not expected to have any greater risk than the firm's average risk. Therefore, the RADR (of 5.37%) was only marginally higher than the risk-free rate (of 5%). Consequently, the risk-adjusted net present value is slightly lower than the risk-free level.

The certainty equivalent method

Up to this point, risk has been incorporated into project appraisal by employing the risk-adjusted discount rate. The project's expected cash flows were discounted using the RADR, where adjustments were made to the *denominators* of the NPV equation.

The *certainty equivalent* (CE) method is an alternative approach to incorporating risk into project analysis. This approach incorporates risk into the analysis by adjusting the expected *cash flows* rather than the *discount rate*. The CE approach thus involves adjustments to the *numerator* of the NPV equation.

The basic formula for the calculation of NPV using the certainty equivalent method is:

$$NPV_{ce} = \sum_{t=1}^{n} \frac{b_t C_t}{(1+r)^t} - CO$$

where:

NPV_{ce} = net present value calculated using the certainty equivalent approach
C_t = expected (risky) net cash inflow in period t
b_t = certainty equivalent coefficient which converts the expected risky cash flows (C_t) into their perceived certainty equivalent values
r = risk-free rate (assumed to remain constant over the life of the project)
n = number of years in the project's economic life
CO = capital outlay

Table 7.3. *Cecorp: CE coefficients and cash flows*

End of year	b_t	Expected cash flows ($)
0	1	−3,500 (capital outlay)
1	0.8	2,500
2	0.7	3,300
3	0.65	4,000

Compared to the basic NPV formula under certainty, the only difference in the certainty equivalent method's NPV formula is the term b_t. In the certainty equivalent method, the uncertain cash flows are first converted into their certainty equivalents using CE coefficients. These certainty equivalent cash flows are then discounted by a risk-free rate.

A certainty equivalent may be defined as the *certain* amount we would be willing to accept in exchange for an expected *uncertain* cash flow. For example, if the expected uncertain cash flow in the first year of the project is $20,000 and if, in exchange for this, we are prepared to accept $15,000 with *certainty*, then the certainty equivalent of an uncertain $20,000 is $15,000. The CE coefficient b_t in this case is 0.75 (which is equal to 15,000/20,000).

Estimation of CE coefficients

The certainty equivalent coefficient b_t ranges from 0 to 1. The greater the certainty of the expected cash flows, the higher the value of the CE coefficient. Conversely, the greater the uncertainty, the lower the value of the coefficient. For example, 0.9 for a particular year's cash flow suggests a lower risk associated with that year's cash flow than does 0.2 for another year's cash flow. A value of 1 implies that there is no risk associated with that cash flow.

CE coefficients reflect subjective management perceptions of the degree of risk of the cash flows. In more formal words, they reflect the decision-makers' perception of the degree of risk associated with the forecasted cash flow distribution and their degree of aversion to perceived risk. The product of the expected cash flow and the coefficient b_t represents the amount that management would be willing to accept for certain in each year of the project's life as opposed to accepting the cash flow distribution and its associated risk. Thus, the values for b_t are essentially subjective and the management will determine these values based on their experience and expert knowledge.

Example 7.2. Computing NPV using CE: Cecorp

The Cecorp Company is evaluating an investment proposal. CE coefficients and the expected cash flows are presented in Table 7.3. Government bond yield is a suitable proxy for the risk-free rate. Data in the financial press indicate that the government bond yield for two- to five-year maturities is around 6% per annum. In this example, the CE coefficients decline into the future. This reflects the fact that most cash flows are viewed as being more risky the further into the future they are forecasted to occur.

Expected cash flows are converted to their certainty equivalents and then discounted at the risk-free rate.

$$NPV_{ce} = \frac{2,500 \times 0.8}{(1.06)^1} + \frac{3,300 \times 0.7}{(1.06)^2} + \frac{4,000 \times 0.65}{(1.06)^3} - \frac{3,500 \times 1}{(1.06)^0}$$

$$= 1,886.79 + 2,055.89 + 2,183.01 - 3,500 = \$2,625.69$$

The certainty equivalent NPV for the project is \$2,625.69, and the project is therefore acceptable.

The relationship between CE and RADR

In discounting forecasted uncertain cash flows to their present values, two factors are taken into account: *time* and *risk*. The CE method first converts the forecasted uncertain cash flows into their certainty equivalents and then discounts them using a risk-free rate to allow for the time value of money. The RADR method, on the other hand, discounts the forecasted uncertain cash flows using a risk-adjusted discount rate, which comprises a risk-free rate for the time value of money and a risk premium to account for the uncertainty of the future cash flows.

Theoretically, if all variables are correctly specified, the present value calculated from any future cash flows must be identical in the RADR and CE methods. Therefore, the following condition must hold:

$$\frac{C_t}{(1+k)^t} = \frac{b_t C_t}{(1+r)^t}, \text{ and, therefore, } b_t = \frac{(1+r)^t}{(1+k)^t}$$

This concept is illustrated with a calculation in Example 7.3.

Example 7.3. Ceradr Company investment project

Ceradr is considering an investment project with an initial capital outlay of \$250,000 and forecast cash flows of \$150,000, \$100,000 and \$120,000 at the end of years 1, 2 and 3, respectively. The risk-free rate is 5% and the estimated risk premium $(u + a)$ for the project is 3%.

The RADR in this case is 8% (i.e. 5% + 3%).

$$NPV_{radr} = -250,000 + \frac{150,000}{(1.08)} + \frac{100,000}{(1.08)^2} + \frac{120,000}{(1.08)^3}$$

$$= -250,000 + 138,889 + 85,734 + 95,260 = \$69,883$$

Certainty equivalent coefficients, b_t, are calculated as:

$$b_1 = \frac{1.05}{1.08} = 0.972222, \quad b_2 = \frac{(1.05)^2}{(1.08)^2} = 0.945216,$$

$$b_3 = \frac{(1.05)^3}{(1.08)^3} = 0.918960$$

Using these, the certainty equivalent NPV is calculated as:

$$NPV_{ce} = -250,000 + \frac{150,000 \times 0.972222}{1.05} + \frac{100,000 \times 0.945216}{(1.05)^2}$$

$$+ \frac{120,000 \times 0.91896}{(1.05)^3}$$

$$= -250,000 + 138,889 + 85,734 + 95,260 = \$\ 69,883$$

The NPV under each method is the same. If all the relevant variables are properly specified and estimated, the two methods should yield the same NPV. Thus, on the face of it, there appears to be no reason for preferring one method to the other. However, in reality, we cannot specify all the variables properly and estimate the relevant certainty equivalent rates accurately. All those rates – whether they are risk premiums, risk factors, risk-free rates or certainty equivalent coefficients – are only best estimates.

There are also other considerations which will make the two methods different and one method can be more suitable than the other in particular circumstances. We now discuss these differences and the suitability of each method.

Comparison of RADR and CE

When discounting cash flows, it is necessary to account for the time value of money and risk. In the RADR technique, this is done by adding a risk premium to the risk-free rate. This may produce a present value factor which is not highly meaningful, because the risk premium component is also increasing exponentially. To allow for the time value of money, only the risk-free rate component needs to be increased exponentially. The exponential increase in the risk-free component, r, of the discount rate may be viewed as:

$$\frac{1}{(1+r)}, \quad \frac{1}{(1+r)^2}, \dots, \frac{1}{(1+r)^n}$$

For the RADR, however, both the risk-free rate *and* the risk premium component, which is equal to $(u + a)$, increase exponentially, as k contains both these components (r and $(u + a)$). This can be demonstrated mathematically as:

$$\frac{1}{(1+k)}, \quad \frac{1}{(1+k)^2}, \dots, \frac{1}{(1+k)^n},$$

$$\text{or} \quad \frac{1}{(1+r+u+a)}, \quad \frac{1}{(1+r+u+a)^2}, \dots, \frac{1}{(1+r+u+a)^n}$$

The use of a discount rate which is higher than the risk-free rate over the project's entire economic life implies that the project's risk is increasing over time exponentially. However, this may not be the case. The project's risk structure may be such that the uncertainty of the cash flows may remain constant over time, increase exponentially over time, gradually decrease over time, or dramatically decrease after a given critical time period has passed. Different projects can have different risk profiles over time. The RADR is suitable only when the project's risk increases over time exponentially.

In contrast to this, the CE method discounts cash flows using a risk-free rate and the adjustment for risk is made by applying appropriate certainty equivalent coefficients to forecast cash flows. Therefore, it correctly allows for the time value of money by applying an exponentially increasing risk-free rate to discount the future cash flows, after converting the uncertain cash flows into their certainty equivalents. The CE method permits the decision-maker to adjust separately each period's cash flows to account for the specific risk of those cash flows. It thus allows for different time patterns of a project's risk to be analysed according to their risk levels. Therefore, the CE method is most suitable when a project's risk varies over time. The CE method is, however, not popular in practice, although it is conceptually superior to the RADR method. The main reason for this is that a satisfactory procedure has not yet been developed to generate the necessary certainty equivalent coefficients.

Readers who wish to find more about the relationship between the certainty equivalent and risk-adjusted discount rate methods and the conceptual problems in the use of the RADR method will find a *Journal of Finance* article by Robichek and Myers (1966) interesting.

Concluding comments

This chapter has focused on two approaches to incorporating risk into project analysis. They are the risk-adjusted discount rate and certainty equivalent methods. Although the CE method is conceptually and theoretically superior to the RADR method, the CE method is not widely used in practice owing to the lack of a satisfactory objective quantitative procedure for the estimation of certainty equivalent coefficients. On the other hand, well-established quantitative approaches are available for the estimation of a risk-adjusted discount rate. The capital asset pricing model and the weighted average cost of capital are two such methods discussed in this chapter. It may be noted that even when using these quantitative methods, the estimation of the final discount rate does (and always should) involve some subjective judgements by the decision-makers about the risk of the proposed project.

Another two approaches to incorporating risk into project analysis, sensitivity and break-even analysis and simulation, will be discussed with applications in Chapters 8, 9 and 10.

Review questions

7.1 The CapmBeta Company is considering a new capital investment proposal. This project's risk structure is very similar to that of the company's existing business. Returns for this company's stock for the past ten years are given in Table 7.4, together with returns for a country's stock-market index (e.g. the All Ordinaries Index in Australia or the S&P Index in the United States). The government treasury bill rate was around 5.6% per annum. The total capital outlay of the proposed project is estimated

Table 7.4. *CapmBeta Company stock returns and stock-market index returns*

Year	Company's stock returns (r_{it})	Stock-market index returns (r_{mt})
1992	0.09	0.07
1993	0.10	0.09
1994	0.10	0.10
1995	0.11	0.12
1996	0.10	0.11
1997	0.11	0.10
1998	0.11	0.10
1999	0.10	0.09
2000	0.09	0.08
2001	0.07	0.07

Table 7.5. *CapmBeta Company: forecasted project cash flows*

Year	Net cash inflows ($ million)
1	25
2	2,000
3	4,000
4	6,000
5	6,500

as $3,000 million and it is to be incurred at the beginning of year 1. The forecasted after-tax net cash inflows of the project are provided in Table 7.5.

(a) Compute the average stock-market (index) return.
(b) Compute the average company stock return.
(c) Compute the variance and standard deviation of the stock-market return: var(r_m), or σ_m^2, and SD(r_m), or σ_m.
(d) Compute the variance and standard deviation of the company stock return: var(r_i), or σ_i^2, and SD(r_i), or σ_i.
(e) Compute the covariance between company stock return and stock-market index return.
(f) Compute the correlation between company stock return and stock-market index return.
(g) Estimate beta as $\beta_i = \frac{\text{cov}(r_i, r_m)}{\text{var}(r_m)}$
(h) Estimate beta as $\beta_i = \frac{\rho_{i,m}\sigma_i}{\sigma_m}$
(i) Calculate the average risk premium, u, for the firm.
(j) Estimate the RADR to be used as the discount rate for this project.
(k) Compute the project's NPV using this RADR.

(l)   Compute the certainty equivalent coefficients using the relevant information from the question under the condition that if risk adjustments are made correctly, the net present value calculated from any given future cash flows must be identical in the RADR and CE methods.

(m) Calculate the NPV using the RADR and CE methods to show the answer is the same under both methods.

7.2 What are the relative merits and demerits of the RADR and CE methods of incorporating risk into project analysis.

7.3 Describe the relationship between the RADR and the CE coefficient.

8 Sensitivity and break-even analysis

In Chapter 7, two methods of dealing with risk in investment analysis were covered. These focused on capturing risk by using an appropriate discount rate, or by employing a certainty equivalent coefficient. The risk-adjusted discount rate method sought to find a discount rate that reflected the comparative risk of the project. The presumption in this type of risk measurement is that the higher the risk, the higher the required rate of return. The certainty equivalent method sought to convert all uncertain future cash flows to their equivalent amounts to be received with certainty, and then to discount these flows at the risk-free rate.

This chapter introduces two mechanical methods for analysing projects under risk. The aim of these methods is to discover which variables (or parameters) have the greatest impact on the project's outcome. The first method is known as *sensitivity analysis*. In this process, individual forecasted variables are progressively stepped through their pessimistic, most likely and optimistic levels, to determine which variables cause the largest shifts in the project's net present value. For example, management may wish to know whether optimistic or pessimistic unit sales prices have greater impacts than optimistic and pessimistic values of sales growth rates.

The second method is known as *break-even analysis*. This process determines how low an income variable can fall, or how high a cost variable can rise, before the project breaks even at a net present value of zero. For example, management may wish to know how low a product's price could go in a price war before the project becomes uneconomic.

Information about the critical variables allows management to make decisions at two points in time in the investment analysis. During the planning phase, management can commit extra funds to develop more reliable forecasts for variables which will be critical to the venture's success. Decisions made at this stage are known as *ex ante* (before the event) decisions. In the operating phase, management can pay special attention to the behaviour of identified critical variables so that the project behaves as expected. Decisions made during this phase are known as *ex post* (after the event) decisions.

Study objectives

After studying this chapter, the reader should be able to:

- define 'sensitivity analysis' and 'break-even analysis'

- understand the role of these analyses in project evaluation
- understand methods by which variables within a project may be selected for sensitivity and break-even analysis
- discuss the establishment of pessimistic, most likely and optimistic forecasts for variables of interest
- calculate net present values for a project under pessimistic, most likely and optimistic values for the set of selected variables
- calculate the break-even values for the set of selected variables
- report the relevant calculations to management
- make appropriate recommendations to assist management in decision-making.

Sensitivity analysis

There are numerous ways to analyse projects for risk. One of these is to evaluate the project under various scenarios in which selected variables are stepped through their pessimistic, most likely and optimistic values. In this analysis, only one variable at a time is changed. The resulting set of net present values for the project will show management which variables have material impact on the financial outcome. Management can then decide either to invest time and effort in establishing more reliable forecasts for these variables, or to abandon the project because of excessive risk.

Terminology used within sensitivity analysis

The terminology used within sensitivity analysis is neither unique nor exclusive. This chapter uses the following definitions to avoid confusion.

- *Sensitivity analysis:* the process of analysing risky projects by estimating a net present value for each of the pessimistic, most likely and optimistic values for each variable under consideration. Only one variable at a time is analysed, and all other variables are held at their most likely value[1] whilst this one variable is analysed. The process is designed to set apart those variables which have material impacts on the project's estimated net present value. The term 'sensitivity analysis' here encompasses other common, similar terms such as 'scenario analysis' and 'what-if analysis'.
- *Sensitive variables:* variables which return wide ranges of estimated net present values, or which return negative net present values, and hence are those most likely to receive management's attention. Since all variables are forecast variables, all will have some impact on the project's estimated net present value. Those which have the largest relative impacts are known as the sensitive variables.
- *Optimistic, most likely and pessimistic values:* these are estimated values at three identified points along the range of possible forecast values for the variables under consideration. The terms, 'optimistic' and 'pessimistic' are used in the context of impact on net cash flows and the positive wealth of the firm. For example, an optimistic unit sales price will

---

[1] The term 'most likely value' is used here to refer to the best-guess level of a variable or parameter, and could correspond with either the expected value (mathematical expectation) or the modal value.

be above the most likely unit sales price, whilst an optimistic unit production cost will be below the most likely unit production cost.

- *Best case, base case and worst case results:* the name of each individual net present value estimate when the optimistic, most likely and pessimistic forecast value for an individual variable is used in calculation. The terms are sometimes used to define the three individual special cases when all the optimistic, all the most likely, or all the pessimistic values are used in calculation. That meaning is not used in this book, as the term 'sensitivity analysis' has been restricted to the analysis of individual variables one at a time. The term 'results' here encompasses other common, like terms such as 'scenario', 'outcome', 'output' and 'solution'.

Procedures in sensitivity analysis

The steps in the analysis are:

(1) Calculate the project's net present value using the most likely value estimated for each variable.
(2) Select from the set of uncertain variables those which management feels may have an important bearing on predicted project performance.
(3) Forecast pessimistic, most likely and optimistic values for each of these variables over the life of the project.
(4) Recalculate the project's net present value for each of the three levels of each variable. While each particular variable is stepped through each of its three values, all other variables are held at their most likely values.
(5) Calculate the change in net present value for the pessimistic to optimistic range of each variable.
(6) Identify the sensitive variables.

It is important to note that most textbooks treat sensitivity analysis as a mere mechanical procedure. That is, in working examples, little attention is paid to the selection of appropriate variables, and to the setting up of the relevant pessimistic and optimistic values for the selected variables. This book attempts to redress that situation by discussing ways in which management might go about identifying important variables and establishing valid upper and lower forecast values.

Sensitivity analysis example: Delta Project

In Chapter 7, the Delta Project proposal was evaluated using the most likely values for all variables. The resulting net present value was $1,008,457. This project is now subjected to sensitivity analysis.

The variables

In this project the forecast variables, expressed at their most likely values, are:

- initial outlay: $1,000,000

- upgrade cost: $500,000 at the end of year 3
- project life: eight years
- various outlays of working capital after year 0
- total asset salvage value: $16,000 at the end of year 8
- tax depreciation rate: 12.5% per annum
- time-trend forecast of sales volume: an upward trend beginning with 691,106 units in the first year of operations, plus an additional 500,000 units per year following the upgrade
- predicted selling price: $0.50 per unit, rising to $0.75 per unit after the first five years
- predicted production cost: $0.10 per unit
- predicted other costs: $50,000 per annum, rising to $55,000 per annum after five years
- company tax rate: 30% per annum
- estimated required rate of return: 5.37% per annum.

Considerations in the selection of variables for sensitivity analysis

In this simple example, it may be practicable to analyse all the variables for sensitivity of project performance. In a larger, more complex project, it may not be practicable to do so, given the time available for the analysis and the number of variables in the model. There are five characteristics which management could consider in choosing a set of variables for analysis.

Ability of management to control variables

Management may feel confident of controlling variations in some variables but not in others. For example, internal variables, such as unit production cost and the timing of the upgrade, will be subject to some control, whilst external variables, such as the unit selling price and the company tax rate, will not be controllable. Sensitivity analysis would then be undertaken only on the uncontrollable variables, because management would feel confident in being able to respond positively *ex post* to changes in levels of the controllable variables.

The project's economic setting will influence the distinction between controllable and uncontrollable variables. For example, in a monopoly supply situation, management will have control over the unit selling price or the volume made available for sale. In a perfectly competitive market, management will not be able to control these variables. In both cases, management is likely to have control over the physical production processes and the scale of production.

Conversely, in some projects management may not have control over the required rate of return. Even though management sets a required rate of return for determining the project's initial economic viability, this rate is subject to general rises and falls in interest rates in the economy as the project unfolds. Management may be restricted in its ability to react to these changes *ex post*.

In the Delta Project, the controllable variables would include: initial outlay, upgrade cost, project life, outlays of working capital and the other costs. The uncontrollable variables might include: total asset salvage value, tax depreciation rate, forecast unit sales, required rate of return and the company tax rate. Since management might feel comfortable in exercising control over the controllable variables whatever the future brings, sensitivity analysis would be conducted on the uncontrollable variables only.

Management's confidence in forecasts of variables

If management is confident that forecasts for some variables are reasonably reliable, then these variables could be left out of the analysis. All others could be included. For example, the forecasts about which management might feel confident, and the reasons for this confidence, are:

- initial outlay – probably an agreed contract price; management is also likely to have a good estimate of the figure as information is readily available and the outlay occurs in the first year
- tax depreciation rate – historically relatively stable
- company tax rate – historically usually varies within a narrow range
- unit production cost – the engineering costs and labour costs for physical production are generally well known from experience, or from engineering studies.

Historical experience held by management

Management may be aware from experience that new capital projects tend to be championed by promoters who traditionally downplay the extent of investment required and are overly optimistic about future returns. Management may also know that cash flow forecasts for elements of production such as unit costs for physical facilities and outlays of working capital are not as important as forecasts of unit sales and unit selling prices. With the benefit of such experience, management might judge that the only variables that it is necessary to test are:

- initial outlay
- forecast sales
- unit selling price

Variables which give rise to extrinsic project benefits

Income from private sector projects is taxable. Tax savings against this income are available in the form of plant and equipment depreciation, and plant and equipment salvage value tax adjustments. Whilst these are beneficial to the project, the project ought not to rely on them for viability. One way of testing this attribute is to remove or reduce these tax savings by setting their benefits at a pessimistic level.

Some projects also rely heavily on recovering a substantial portion of the capital outlays as salvage values at the end of the project. This reliance can be misplaced, as salvage value forecasts are for the very long term and assume that the assets will still have some value in a technologically advancing market. A pessimistic treatment of such benefits ensures that the project is accepted on its operating viability.

Time available for analysis and cost of analysis

In an ideal world, all forecast variables in a project would be subject to sensitivity analysis. With practical constraints on time and cost, only those variables which can be investigated quickly and cheaply will be investigated. While the actual mechanical analysis using a spreadsheet is relatively trivial, the time and effort involved in establishing pessimistic and optimistic values for some variables is not. This constraint might rule out variables such as forecast unit sales and forecast unit selling price, as these may require extensive empirical data-gathering and detailed economic analysis. Unfortunately, these may also turn out to be the critical variables.

The actual choice of variables for sensitivity analysis

The choice of variables should be based on mature and experienced judgement combined with a knowledge of the sensitivity analysis process. The choice ought to be made by management in conjunction with the project analyst.

In the Delta Project example, any suite of variables could be chosen. The following set has been chosen as a demonstration of the selection procedures just discussed, and as a demonstration of how the values for different forecasts can be established:

* initial outlay: $1,000,000
* total asset salvage value: $16,000 at the end of year 8
* time-trend forecast of sales volume: an upward trend beginning with 691,106 units in the first year of operations, plus an additional 500,000 units per annum following the upgrade
* predicted selling price: $0.50 per unit, rising to $0.75 per unit after the first five years
* Predicted production cost: $0.10 per unit
* Predicted other costs: $50,000 per annum, rising to $55,000 per annum after five years
* Estimated required rate of return: 5.37% per annum.

Developing pessimistic and optimistic forecasts

There are two general methods by which pessimistic and optimistic values for the variables of interest can be established. The first of these treats the establishment of such values as an extension of formal forecasting techniques. The method places emphasis on the actual variable-estimating process, and in that sense attempts to arrive at values which represent foreseeable events.

The second method uses a more mechanical approach, in which the upper and lower levels of variables for sensitivity analysis are chosen in an *ad hoc* manner without reference to any knowledge about their likely future values. Rather, the level of each variable of interest is allowed to vary by plus or minus a constant percentage of the most likely value, for example plus or minus 20%, or plus or minus 30%. The idea here is to highlight 'sensitivity' without reference to expectations of what levels might occur as obtained within a formal forecasting framework. In that the same percentage variation is adopted for each variable, the changes in NPV can be examined to express sensitivity in the form of 'elasticities', i.e. percentage change in NPV relative to percentage change in the level of the variable or parameter.

Developing pessimistic and optimistic values by using the forecasting approach

By definition, the static set of values adopted in the initial project analysis represents the most likely values for each variable. The discussion of forecasting in Chapters 3 and 4 demonstrates that these values will be the averages, smoothed values or extrapolated values from historical patterns, or will be the consensus of opinion from various experts. To establish pessimistic and optimistic limits around these central values, it is necessary to return to that discussion.

Pessimistic and optimistic values established from average values

If the forecast is a set of extrapolated averages, upper and lower bounds could be set around this central value by allowing for plus or minus a fixed number of standard deviations around the mean. This of course assumes that the distribution of historical observations is normal, and that the forecasts have been established on a formal statistical footing. The mean value plus or minus two standard deviations, which provides a range between optimistic and pessimistic values covering 95% of the area under the normal curve, provides a suitable forecast range. Taking one standard deviation above and below the mean would generate a more narrow range, of 68% of the area under the normal curve. As a rule of thumb, the first of these two ranges is to be recommended since it provides a high probability that the realized value will fall in the forecast range. Where the forecast mean value has been established by moving average, weighted moving average or exponential smoothing, then pessimistic and optimistic values would be set up by guided guesswork. For example, with a moving average forecast, the pessimistic and optimistic range might be the lowest and highest values within the series. A similar approach could be used for both weighted average and exponentially smoothed series.

Pessimistic and optimistic values established from extrapolated values

Some forecasts have been set up by extrapolating trend lines fitted to historical data sets. The trends have been established by simple or multiple linear regressions. The statistical output from the regression analysis will include the standard error of the estimate, and a multiple of this figure can be used to create pessimistic and optimistic limits around the forecast values. The calculated variations around the trend line are known as the prediction interval. Again, plus or minus two standard deviations could be used to give the pessimistic and optimistic forecasts at the upper and lower prediction interval values respectively.

Pessimistic and optimistic values established by using expert opinion

This approach does not necessarily employ any statistical inference techniques. In the absence of any core values with attendant boundaries, the pessimistic and optimistic values could be set up as the lower and upper values given by expert opinions.

Pessimistic and optimistic values established by using management input
Pessimistic and optimistic forecasts can be made by following the above methods. In practice, each of these will be adapted by management opinion. Where management has had experience in similar projects, or where management is experienced in risk analysis generally, pessimistic and optimistic values could be established by experience.

Pessimistic and optimistic values established by physical constraints
Where there are physical limitations to production and sales levels, these limits could become the lower and upper bounds. For example, the optimistic value for annual output could be set by the upper level of physical capacity. This could be either machine capacity (after allowing for downtime) or shipping capacity. The pessimistic value could be set as the minimum throughput required to keep the physical process operating.

Developing pessimistic and optimistic values by using the ad hoc approach

Pessimistic and optimistic values are sometimes set by selecting a standard positive and negative percentage change around the forecast value. For example, standard values of plus or minus 20%, or plus or minus 30% of the forecast values could be used. The selection of the actual percentage variation may be based on experience or in accord with management's wishes. In some cases, such as in a consulting arrangement, the client may require a standard approach to all analyses from various consultants. In such cases, the client will specify a particular variation. A figure of plus or minus 30% is often used.

As this adjustment is applicable to all variables, and is simply mechanically applied, detailed forecasts of the pessimistic and optimistic values are not required. The process does not require any justification for any particular extreme value so created. In the computational sense, these sensitivity analyses are relatively simple and straightforward.

Comparison of the forecasting approach and the ad hoc approach

A choice between these two approaches can be made by evaluating the cost and benefits of each method.

Forecasting approach
This approach has the following benefits:

• emphasizes the process of forecasting
• emulates expected real-world behaviour
• forces identification of physical sales and production limits
• forces a selection from the full range of variables which might be considered

and these costs:

• consumes time and resources in creating special forecasts
• may develop extremes that are highly unlikely

- may erroneously select variables that are not material
- may omit material variables
- may cause repeated analyses as forecasts are continually refined
- may paralyse decision-making by excessive analysis.

Ad hoc *approach*

This approach has the following benefits:

- simple to apply
- time efficient
- easily applicable to all variables
- can be used as an indirect test of the model
- may give some relative comparability across the range of variables
- may allow clients to compare consultants' reports

and these costs:

- selection of the variation percentage is not guided by what is likely to be experienced
- particular variation percentage may not discover sensitive variables
- extreme values cannot be logically justified
- some variables with fixed future values may be erroneously tested
- percentage change is relative; variables with a small base value may not capture real extremes
- extensive analysis of all variables could waste resources.

Pessimistic and optimistic forecasts of variable values for the Delta Project example

The pessimistic and optimistic forecasts for each of the variables to be analysed are set out below. The rationale for these forecasts is also given.

Initial outlay, for the fixed asset: Pessimistic $1,200,000; optimistic $800,000. With a fixed asset, the initial outlay is usually a fixed contractual amount, and there should not be much variation in its value. The value can vary when there are time delays in delivery, or in the construction of specialized equipment which has not been proven. Management experience with projects similar to the Delta Project suggests that this range should incorporate most foreseeable values.

There have been many celebrated cases of construction cost blowouts in large projects around the world. Two classic examples were the Sydney Opera House and the Montreal Olympic Stadium. In the analysis of a large, unproven project, especially where there is some public or political component, a large variation in initial cost should be included.

Total asset salvage value: Pessimistic $0; optimistic $32,000. The most likely value has been estimated at $16,000. This is a forecast for eight years forward for an asset depreciating at 12.5% per annum. It is highly unlikely that any such forecast figure could be regarded as 'reliable', particularly in a world where technology is changing so rapidly. A wide variation, of plus or minus 100%, has been chosen to demonstrate this point. Again, this adjustment is based on management experience.

In this particular project, given an initial outlay of $1,000,000, a salvage value of only $16,000 is immaterial. The salvage value has been included in the analysis to demonstrate testing of salvage values generally. A pessimistic value of $0 has been chosen to emphasize the point that any project should not rely on a salvage value for its viability.

Time-trend sales volume: Pessimistic: minus one standard error of the regression; optimistic: plus one standard error of the regression. This adjustment, of 16,701 per annum, is applied to the sales forecast given by the regression equation. The adjustment amount of plus or minus one standard deviation has been chosen because management is confident the trend will fall within this range.

The sales forecast of an extra 500,000 units for year 4 onwards should be adjusted also. This sales forecast is only a management expectation and is not supported by any formal analysis. In the absence of a formal forecast, management feels that a variation of plus or minus 20% around the most likely value should cover all foreseeable variations. This variation will be equal to plus or minus 100,000 units per year. As a comparison, the standard error of the regression for the original sales units is 16,701 units, which is only 2.4% of the forecast value of 691,106 units for the first year. This variation is relatively small as the R^2 value for the regression is relatively high at 0.92.

Unit selling price: In many capital budgeting analyses, this variable will be the one of most concern. It represents the firm's interactive face with the consumer, is not subject to management control and is at the mercy of competitors. Initial product pricing is a decision of management in consultation with the production and marketing departments, and will always be a difficult figure to determine. Additionally, it is this estimate which is most likely to vary in response to changes in the market-place. For these reasons, the figure should be carefully tested for sensitivity.

The lowest (i.e. pessimistic) price which can be set is equal to the direct costs of production. This value allows production to proceed by covering merely the direct costs of labour and materials, without contributing to fixed costs or wealth creation. Obviously, this is a figure which can be maintained only over the shortest possible term. In the example, this figure is $0.10. However, this is not a sensible value for a sensitivity test because it cannot be maintained over the full life of the project. An alternative value of $0.30 per unit is chosen as the pessimistic value for the test, because it can be assumed to represent the lowest price a competitor could set to drive the product from the market.

The highest (or optimistic) figure which can be set is the price which the market will bear. There is no direct information about this value in the example. In practice, it could be equal to the highest price being charged by a competing product. A value of $0.90 is assumed for the analysis.

In both the pessimistic and optimistic cases, the price tested is held constant over the full life of the project. That is, the price increase expected to take place in year 5 is ignored. The expected price increase could be tested for sensitivity, but that extra effort might not be worthwhile as it would probably only confirm the discovered degree of price sensitivity.

In using the pessimistic and optimistic prices in the sensitivity analysis, it is assumed that the price variation will not affect the sales forecast. Forecast sales units and forecast sales price will be inversely related variables. The only way in which these can be analysed independently is to assume that at the sales and price levels chosen the interdependencies will be small. If it is known that the relationship will be material, then an algebraic price/volume calculation will have to be set up to allow the analysis to proceed. If that is the case, then independent sensitivity tests for each variable cannot be undertaken.

Unit production cost: The figure given as the most likely value ($0.10 per unit) should be reasonably stable because it represents the consensus of production and cost accounting opinion. It should be reasonably accurate. As extremes around this value, it is assumed that the accounting and engineering staff have arrived at a pessimistic value of $0.13 and an optimistic value of $0.08 per unit. These are changes of +30% and −20% respectively.

Other costs: The values here, $50,000 per annum rising to $55,000 per annum after five years, are probably global values representing 'overhead'. The amounts should be reasonably accurate since they are engineering/production oriented. Again, it is assumed that the relevant professionals have developed a forecast pessimistic value of $70,000 per annum, and a forecast optimistic value of $35,000 per annum, over the project's life. These figures represent a rise of 40% and a fall of 30% respectively. These values are held constant over the whole life of the project, and are assumed to encompass the step increase at year 6.

Estimated required rate of return of 5.37% per annum: In addition to sales volume and sales price, this variable is subject to considerable change due to macro-economic influences. It is usually well tested in sensitivity analyses because of the traditional belief that the firm should have a reasonable buffer against unexpected upward shifts in the required yield. Management feels that current interest rates are at a historically low value, and that interest rates are likely to rise. To accommodate these changes, the interest rates chosen for the sensitivity analysis are an optimistic value of 4% per annum and a pessimistic value of 12% per annum. The pessimistic level is relatively high compared to the most likely rate. However, management feels that it is a valid expectation.

| Workbook |
| 8.1 |

Table 8.1. *Pessimistic, most likely and optimistic forecasts*

	Pessimistic	Most likely	Optimistic
Initial outlay	$1,200,000	$1,000,000	$800,000
Total asset salvage value	$0	$16,000	$32,000
Sales forecast by regression	−16,701 units	regressed value	+16,701 units
Extra sales	400,000 units	500,000 units	600,000 units
Unit selling price	$0.30	$0.50	$0.90
Unit production cost	$0.13	$0.10	$0.08
Other costs	$70,000	$50,000; 55,000	$35,000
Required rate of return	12%	5.37%	4%

The values discussed are summarized in Table 8.1. They are held, together with all their relevant calculated sensitivity tests, in Workbook 8.1.

Applying the sensitivity tests

There are important points to bear in mind when applying the sensitivity tests:

• Results of the test are measured against the objective of the project. This is the project's net present value.
• Changes in the variables are made over the whole project life. It is difficult to interpret the sensitivity results for variables changed for, say, only one or two years within an eight-year project.
• Each variable is stepped through its range individually while other variables are held at their most likely values.
• It may not be feasible to test variables which are interdependent. For example, an optimistically high selling price per unit ought to be associated with a moderate or low sales volume. If interdependent variables are tested, then some assumptions have to be made about the relationship between their values. These assumptions could be that the one variable will assume a value proportionate to the other, or that one variable will be held at its most likely level provided the other variable changes within a limited range. Interdependent variables can be fully examined within a multi-variable simulation test. This type of test is demonstrated in the following chapter.
• Optimistic and pessimistic values are not necessarily achievable targets; they are only expected extreme values on a forecast variable. In that sense, they cannot be used as goals which have to be achieved so that a project can proceed. In other words, the project should not be accepted by arguing that it would be viable 'if only sales could be made to reach that high level'.
• Sensitivity testing only provides information for guiding management decision-making about the variables identified as 'sensitive'. Management must use the outcomes to guide *ex ante* decisions about the search for better forecasts, and/or the *ex post* management of controllable variables as the project unfolds.

Table 8.2. *Results of sensitivity tests*

Variable	Sheet number	Pessimistic NPV ($)	Optimistic NPV ($)	Range ($)
Initial outlay	2(1,2)	856,208	1,160,706	304,498
Total asset salvage value	2(3,4)	1,001,089	1,015,825	14,736
Sales forecast by regression	2(5,6)	972,600	1,044,314	71,714
Extra sales	2(7,8)	869,480	1,147,434	277,954
Unit selling price	2(9,10)	−431,798	2,379,109	2,810,907
Unit production cost	2(11,12)	870,393	1,100,500	230,107
Other costs	2(13,14)	926,608	1,082,594	155,986
Required rate of return	2(15,16)	427,220	1,166,326	739,106

Sensitivity tests are performed on each variable in turn, while all other variables are held constant at their most likely values. There will be sixteen net present value outcomes since there are eight variables to be tested.

The tests could be performed using the initial spreadsheet by changing the relevant variables one at a time. These findings could then be merged into an overall tableau by using Excel's Sensitivity, Merge command. However, some of the analytical detail is lost if this method is used. It is better to run the sensitivity test over sixteen copies of the original worksheet. Each one of these sheets then becomes a record of a test. This method provides an audit trail for later follow-up of particular results. Sensitivity analysis can also be performed using Excel's Scenario function. This produces a summary table and also provides sufficient information for an audit trail. Chapter 10 uses this function for sensitivity analysis. The Table function in Excel can be set up to perform all the sensitivity tests within the same spreadsheet run.

> Workbook
> 8.1

Outcomes from each of the sixteen tests are given in Table 8.2.

Sensitivity test results

The coverage of variables here is quite extensive. Using the guidelines above, it may be possible to reduce the number of variables subject to testing. With experience in sensitivity testing, it may become apparent that only a few variables, such as forecast sales units, selling price, production cost and required rate of return, need to be routinely tested. In this example, it is useful to test most of the variables to observe their behaviour.

Individual spreadsheets have been used here for each test. Alternatively, the test could have been run on the main spreadsheet, with individual answers being recorded after each test. The use of individual spreadsheets gives a reliable audit trail, and allows for follow-up testing.

Identification of the sensitive variables

Naturally, all the variables will have some impact on the project's net present value. Management is concerned with those having the largest impacts. The sensitivity test results show that the rank ordering of these by the dollar size of the range is:

- forecast unit selling price
- required rate of return
- initial outlay.

Other variables such as the sales forecast (in units) and the unit production cost are also important.

The rank ordering is useful in that it focuses management attention on variables which have large dollar impacts on the net present value result. When the extremes of the values (i.e. pessimistic and optimistic values of each variable) have been determined using the forecasting approach (rather than the *ad hoc* approach) discussed previously, the rank ordering can indicate the 'relative importance' of the variables. This is because the extremes of the values have been based on forecasts of what the likely extremes could be. As such, the range of the NPVs that result when the pessimistic and optimistic values are used represents a reasonable estimate of the likely extremes of discounted cash flows. In contrast, the *ad hoc* approach uses arbitrary percentage variations to set the pessimistic and optimistic values. The resulting range of NPVs using arbitrarily determined pessimistic and optimistic values is not necessarily indicative of the likely range of discounted cash flows that are possible. Hence, the rank order of the dollar impacts on NPVs produced using an *ad hoc* approach to sensitivity analysis are less useful in indicating the relative importance of the variables.

The variable having the largest dollar impact on the calculated net present value is the forecast unit selling price. It has an NPV range of over $2,810,907. If the forecasts of a pessimistic price of $0.30 and an optimistic price of $0.90 are realistic, then this variable will be critical to the project's viability. Management can take three approaches to this problem of expected price variation:

(1) Be confident that the unit price in the market-place will rarely fall to $0.30 and then only for a short period. If the price remains high for the rest of the investment period, then this variable will be immaterial. Additionally, management might be confident that the price will seldom rise to $0.90 per unit, and even if it does, the project will be highly beneficial anyway. In other words, the prices of $0.30 and $0.90 are only extreme values and are unlikely to occur. Management may expect prices to vary, but only across a moderate range.

(2) Go ahead with the project as it stands, and resolve to monitor closely the selling price throughout the project's life. This would be an *ex post* solution to the problem. If the unit price falls in future, management can alter production to suit market conditions in the short term. Alternatively, if management believes it can exert some control over price in the market-place, then price can be increased to enhance the project's net present value. However, if the product's price is subject to market forces, price manipulation may not be a realistic option.

(3) Expend further resources now to develop more accurate price forecasts. This would be an *ex ante* solution to the problem. The expected price range of $0.30 to $0.90 per unit may be only a coarse approximation which could be refined by expert market knowledge. The sensitivity test could be rerun with a more 'accurate' range.

In the tests of price sensitivity, it has been assumed that price variations will not affect sales volume. If volume and price are interdependent variables, then the test may not be reliable.

Variations in the required rate of return also have material impacts on the project's net present value. Within the given range of rate of return values of 4% per annum to 12% per annum, the NPV shifts from $1,166,326 to $427,220, a range of $739,106. The good news about this is that at all rates of return, even at the extremely high rate of 12% per annum, the NPV is positive. The bad news is that management has no control over this variable, as it will be subject to macro-economic forces.

There are various ways to insulate a project from rate of return changes. These are: including the project within a broad portfolio, employing sophisticated financing techniques such as forward rate agreements and options or setting up secured financing with fixed rates of return. These are financing techniques which may or may not be applicable to this or any particular project. The problem with such techniques is that they are likely to be more short-term than long-term, and are likely to be expensive to set up and maintain.

The third variable which has a strong impact on project performance is the initial outlay. Initial outlay estimates range from $1,200,000 to $800,000. This variation gives an NPV range of $856,208 to $1,160,706. If the forecast extreme costs are valid, this variable is a problem for the project. Again, the good news is that under all variations, the project NPV remains positive. Further good news is that management will have some control over this variable. It is possible that the start-up costs could be reviewed, construction contracts relet or the production processes redesigned to reduce the initial outlay. Additionally, management should spend further time in examining the range of expected outlay levels, because this range seems quite wide for such a near term expenditure.

Further analysis of the identified sensitive variables

The above analysis shows how the singular extreme values of the sensitive variables affect the project's NPV. It is also worthwhile to analyse the behaviour of the project over the full pessimistic–optimistic range of these variables. This analysis is usually done with NPV profile charts. The variable of interest is plotted on the horizontal (x) axis and the NPV is plotted on the vertical (y) axis. This type of chart is most commonly used in plotting NPV behaviour with respect to required rate of return. It is particularly useful for analysing mutually exclusive projects, because it normally reveals a crossover in ranking between the projects at a particular rate of return.

NPV profile charts have been drawn for the three variables which have been identified as sensitive: forecast unit selling price, required rate of return and forecast production cost per unit. They have been drawn on independent worksheets within the sensitivity analysis, and are reproduced in Figures 8.1–8.3.

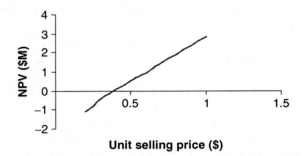

Figure 8.1. Project NPV versus unit selling price (from Worksheet 2(17)).

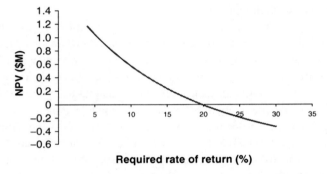

Figure 8.2. Project NPV versus required rate of return (from Worksheet 2(18)).

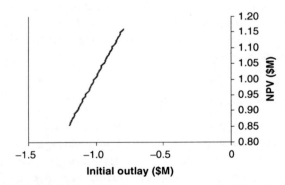

Figure 8.3. Project NPV versus initial outlay (from Worksheet 2(1)).

Other sensitive variables which may be investigated

The rank ordering of variable impacts reveals that forecast extra sales units and unit production cost are also material variables in project viability. Management may wish to expend some effort in obtaining better forecasts of these variables, or in allowing for their close monitoring during project set-up and execution. The point is that management ought to be aware that these (and other) variables will have an impact on project performance, and that they should be carefully planned and managed.

Break-even analysis

Break-even analysis is a special application of sensitivity analysis. It endeavours to find the value of individual variables at which the project's NPV is zero. For example, management may wish to know how low the unit selling price can fall before the project becomes unsuccessful. If managers know that this 'cut-off' price is likely to be reached, then they may decide not to proceed with the project. In common with sensitivity analysis, variables selected for break-even analysis can be tested only one at a time. Management can select the particular variables by following the guidelines given for sensitivity analysis.

The calculations may be carried out using one of the following methods:

(1) Creation of a data table for a range of values from which is read the appropriate value at a zero NPV;
(2) Trial-and-error substitution of variable values within a spreadsheet;
(3) Use of the Excel Tools, Goal Seek function.

Method 1: Figures 8.1 and 8.2 demonstrate this first approach. The graphs for unit selling price and required rate of return both show zero NPVs for particular values of the variable. As the graphs use large scales, the actual break-even values must be read from the relevant data table. From Worksheet 2(17) the break-even unit selling price lies between $0.35 and $0.40. Limited trial-and-error substitution within this range reveals a break-even unit selling price of $0.3830. A special worksheet, 2(20), has been created for this calculation. The analysis assumes that this price is constant through the whole life of the project. The original projection was that the price would rise in year 6.

> Workbook
> 8.1

The break-even value for the required rate of return is, by definition, the internal rate of return (IRR). The value calculated in the initial sheet, 2, is 19.8% per annum. This rate can be also interpolated from the data table on Worksheet 2(18). The original required rate of return was 5.37% per annum, so the high 'cut-off' rate of 19.8% allows for large rises in macro-economic rates of return before the project becomes untenable.

Method 2: Production cost per unit has been identified as the third critical variable. The calculated data table on Worksheet 2(19) does not extend far enough to find a zero NPV. On this sheet, various values which are greater than $0.20 for unit production cost can be substituted to find a zero NPV. The substitution process reveals the break-even unit cost to be $0.3084. When using trial-and-error substitutions within a worksheet it is important to ensure that the original values are reinstated to restore the worksheet to its original result.

Method 3: To demonstrate the Tools, Goal Seek function, a non-critical variable, forecast sales units, has been chosen. This variable is used so that the NPV does not fall below zero before the break-even sales level has been achieved. Within Excel, the Goal Seek function alters one cell to accord with the desired outcome in the target cell. In this case, the target cell will be the NPV value. The variable 'forecast sales units' runs across eight cells, with one value for each year. To make the Goal Seek function work, the cell value for each year is set equal to the initial year's cell value, and only this one initial cell is altered. The results are shown on Worksheet 2(21). The break-even sales level per year is 613,272 units. This is a constant figure for all years, and includes the notional 500,000 extra units in years 6, 7 and 8. In this analysis, the originally expected price rise from $0.50 to $0.75 per unit in years 6, 7 and 8 has been maintained.

Break-even analysis and decision-making

Management can use the break-even results in two ways. Initially, management can decide to abandon the project if forecasts show that below break-even values are likely to occur. Later, management can prepare for a worst-case scenario involving the investigated variables being realized during the project's life. This action could be to suspend production, to try to make production more efficient or to adjust the unit selling price.

In using the figures the following points must be borne in mind:

- The variables have been adjusted one at a time. It is unlikely in reality that only one variable will change during the tenor of the project. If decisions are made by observing the behaviour of only one variable, then those decisions may be invalid.
- Variables have been analysed as if they are independent. Pairs of variables such as sales volume/sales price and production volume/production cost are not independent. Break-even figures are only reliable if it is assumed that the range over which the variables change is sufficiently modest so as not to affect the related variable.
- Any project ought to be reviewed at regular points during its life. Analyses taken at particular points in time must refer only to future events, and not to past ones. Thus, break-even values calculated at the outset may not be accurate, and they should be recalculated at the chosen point in time.
- Break-even analysis is essentially pessimistic. Management should be interested in break-even figures only as a last line of defence in project analysis.

Concluding comments

Numerous analyses of the original project can be carried out using the flexibility and power of spreadsheeting. These analyses should be guided by rational predictions, and should be able to be sensibly interpreted by management. Analysts should be aware that too much analysis overwhelms management decision-making, although too little analysis may provide management too few options. Further, analysts must be careful to maintain the integrity of the original calculated spreadsheet result, and to avoid inadvertent errors. An audit trail can be maintained and computational errors minimized if multiple spreadsheets (or, alternatively, the Excel Scenario or Table functions) are used.

Sensitivity analysis is designed to identify those variables which have a material dollar impact on the project's calculated net present value. The identification of these variables should help management to refine its forecasting function, or to plan for more detailed management of those variables as the project unfolds.

In comparing the fixed percentage change (say plus or minus 20%) and pessimistic–optimistic range approaches to sensitivity analysis, the latter can be seen to provide greater information to the decision-maker. Using the fixed percentage approach, it is necessary to interpret the extent of change in the performance variable in the light of uncertainty in the parameter estimates. Using the pessimistic–optimistic approach, this uncertainty is to some extent built into the sensitivity analysis.

Both sensitivity and break-even analyses add to the strength of project investigation, and should be carried out to the satisfaction of both management and analyst. Both of these analytical methods are limited in their scope because each method alters only one variable at a time, while all other variables are held at their most likely values. In a dynamic world, many variables will be changing in different directions at the same time. This dynamic world is investigated through the methods of simulation and Monte Carlo analysis in Chapter 9.

Review questions

8.1 Define and discuss the following terms:

- sensitivity analysis
- break-even analysis
- base-case solution
- optimistic and pessimistic forecasts
- *ex ante* and *ex post* management decision-making.

8.2 Pacific Products Inc. is considering the introduction of a new product, Alpha. The firm has gathered the following information relevant to the project:

Initial fixed capital outlay: $120,000
Initial working capital outlay: $9,800
Life of the project: 5 years
Capital recovery at project end: fixed $18,000; working $7,200
Sales units forecast: 50,000 units in year 1, growing at 6% per annum thereafter
Unit selling price: $2.75
Unit production cost: $1.28
Annual fixed overhead cost: $35,000
Annual tax rate of depreciation claimable: 20% per annum

Annual income tax rate: 38%

Required rate of return: 9% per annum

For these data:

(a) Calculate an NPV for the project under the given base-case scenario.

(b) Perform sensitivity analyses on the following variables: initial fixed capital outlay, unit selling price, annual sales growth rate, unit production cost.

(c) By the use of Data Tables and appropriate graphs, calculate the break-even points for unit production cost and the required rate of return.

(d) Advise management of the analyses regarding the new product Alpha, and make appropriate investment recommendations.

8.3 Compare and contrast sensitivity and break-even analyses with other risk analysis methods such as the risk-adjusted discount rate and the certainty equivalent approach. Describe how each of these methods might influence management decision-making.

9 Simulation concepts and methods

The term 'simulation' is widely used nowadays, and most people have their own view of its meaning. In general, to 'simulate' means to mimic or capture the essence of something, without attaining reality. In management applications, simulation typically involves developing a model of a business or economic system, and then performing experiments using this model to predict how the real system would behave under a range of management policies. In that financial models have been used repeatedly in earlier chapters, the importance of modelling will come as no surprise here. But when discussing simulation, attention to aspects of modelling becomes even more important since simulation models are often highly complex representations of business systems.

While many quantitative techniques take a well-recognized form, simulation differs in its great flexibility, variety of applications and variations in form. These features, while highly valuable for modelling complex business systems, make this a difficult methodology to explain and to comprehend. In fact, simulation has been described as 'more art than science'. Proficiency with this technique cannot readily be gained in the classroom. Considerable hands-on experience from repeatedly designing, developing and performing experiments with a number of different models is also necessary. But even for readers who will not be engaged in developing complex models, an understanding of simulation concepts is indispensable because of the widespread use of this methodology.

The financial models encountered in earlier chapters, typically developed on a spreadsheet, may be regarded as a form of simulation. These simulate or mimic the financial performance of a project, including the annual cash flows, so as to predict performance measures such as net present value. However, for the purposes of this book, we will take a somewhat narrower view, and place particular emphasis on *stochastic* simulation models, i.e. that form of simulation modelling which explicitly makes allowance for financial risk by generating random observations of uncertain cash flow variables during simulation experiments.

The four methods for dealing with project risk discussed in Chapters 7 and 8 – risk-adjusted discount rate, certainty equivalent, sensitivity analysis and break-even analysis – provide additional information for the decision-maker with regard to acceptance or rejection of a single project. In this chapter, it will be seen that simulation can provide a powerful approach to measurement of project risk. This application is known as risk analysis, risk simulation or Monte Carlo simulation.

A further role of simulation is to aid in the design of projects and the choice between various resource commitments within the project alternatives. For example, it may be possible to identify a number of decision variables in the design of a project, such as the output quantity for a new product or the price to charge for a commodity or service. If the relationship between the levels of these decision variables and the project cash flows can be determined, simulation experiments may be used to assist in the design as well as the evaluation of the project.

This chapter will demonstrate the use of simulation to aid two types of decision: (1) whether to accept or reject a given project; and (2) choice of the best combination of resource commitments from among various alternatives. In this chapter, some of the basic concepts of the so-called 'systems approach' and the steps fundamental to simulation studies will be reviewed, with particular attention to model development, performing experiments and testing the reliability of the model. This is followed by a risk analysis example (of a computer project). The use of simulation as a planning technique is then demonstrated by experimenting with a deterministic and a stochastic simulation using the same data for a single project (FlyByNight).

Study objectives

After studying this chapter the reader should be able to:

• have a general appreciation of the 'systems method' and 'simulation models' in capital budgeting
• understand the application of simulation to the evaluation of project risk
• recognize the difficulties in developing and testing simulation models
• understand the basic concepts of carrying out computer-based experiments with simulation models
• recognize the range of experimental designs which may be appropriate for simulation experiments.

What is simulation?

Simulation consists of a number of disparate concepts and techniques, with different terminologies adopted by different disciplines. Hence it is useful to establish the terminology which will be adopted in this discussion of the application of simulation in capital budgeting. The essence of simulation is the development of a *model* to represent a *real system*, and then the performance of *experiments* using this model to gain an understanding of how the real system would behave under a variety of circumstances.

Various terminologies have been adopted in presentations of simulation methodology. In particular, the terms *systems analysis, systems research* and *simulation* have been used interchangeably. The term 'systems research' is typically applied to describe all the steps in the study of an organized system. 'Systems analysis' was originally used in this broad context, but is now more often applied to just one step in systems research, viz. that of identifying the boundaries, elements and interrelationships of a system prior to modelling it. The term 'simulation' is sometimes applied to the overall procedure of developing a model and generating decision support information, but sometimes to the experimentation stage only. In this chapter, the term 'simulation' will be used in the broader context, as a synonym for systems research.

The systems philosophy

Proponents of simulation usually subscribe to what is called the 'systems approach'. According to Shannon (1975), a system is 'a group of objects united by some form of interaction or interdependence to perform a specified function'. In other words, any system consists of a number of interrelated and interacting parts; further, these parts should not be studied in isolation but rather in the context of the overall system and its complex interdependencies. The whole is more than just the sum of the parts, and any change to one part of the system may cause unexpected changes elsewhere.

As the body of scientific knowledge has increased, there has been a tendency for greater specialization of research, with a loss in overall perspective and loss of communication between researchers in different disciplines. This 'spread of specialized deafness' has led to the study of more narrowly defined systems. However, from a management point of view, an holistic view of the system under study is required. The 'system' in which we are interested is usually the level of aggregation at which planning and control decisions are made, which is often that of an overall business firm. Various human, institutional, technical and financial sub-systems and interactions take place at this level of aggregation.

Practitioners of the systems approach need to have a clear understanding of the overall system, and the ability and willingness to consult with experts on various aspects of the system. In fact, systems research is often conducted by groups or teams rather than individuals, since these can take on board a broader range of expertise on various aspects of the system.

Simulation tends to be used where a solvable model is not available (i.e. would not represent the system adequately). The simulation experiments may be likened to observing how the real system would perform if particular management policies were to be adopted, except that the real system is not interfered with, real resources are not used (apart from computing resources) and time is greatly compressed. Computer simulation experiments can provide a great deal of information about how an actual system would behave, under a host of different policies or assumptions, and this may provide a greatly improved understanding of how best to manage the system.

The nature of simulation models

Opting for a systems approach begs the question of how a complex real-world system can be represented by an abstract model, and how we can define the relevant system, e.g. what are the boundaries and what are the important variables and relationships. From a capital budgeting perspective, the models we are interested in are usually *algebraic models* of business systems. The model is an abstract representation of the business system under investigation. The real system under study could be a factory, transport system, hydropower plant, recreation resort, information system, accounting process and so on.

Nowadays, people are familiar with building algebraic models, through the widespread use of spreadsheets. Any spreadsheet – including one to derive the NPV of a project – is in effect an algebraic model. Implicitly or explicitly, models have been used throughout the previous chapters. In this chapter, we will refer to *simulation models*, though it should be borne in mind that they share the features of financial models in general. What is different here is that greater emphasis is placed on the characteristics of these models, and the way in which models can be used as both *planning* and *evaluation* tools. A further distinguishing feature of simulation models is that they are often *stochastic* – i.e. have the random variability in one or more variables built into the model – and indeed this is one of the features for which simulation is particularly well suited.

Performing experiments

The model once developed is used to simulate or mimic how the real system would behave under particular circumstances, by conducting experiments on a computer using the model. In these experiments, measures of system performance are generated for various levels of the input variables. In this way, an understanding is gained of how the real system would perform under a variety of situations, which provides guidance to management about the likely outcomes of various policies. Were such experiments performed on the real system, they would be time-consuming and costly to conduct, and could have extreme adverse financial outcomes; on a computer, in contrast, they may involve just a few seconds of processor time. 'Running' a spreadsheet of a project evaluation model may be thought of as a form of experiment in which 'what if' questions can be asked by varying the input parameters and observing how this affects the performance estimates. However, the form of simulation experiments can become much more complex than the simple examples we have seen in earlier chapters.

Elements of simulation models for capital budgeting

In a simulation model for capital budgeting, the investment project becomes the 'system' under study, and we wish to mimic all those inputs and outputs and expenditures and receipts which are associated with the incremental cash flows for the project. These are represented by a set of equations or relationships between variables, in a *discrete multi-year symbolic* model. The model may be *deterministic* or *stochastic*. In a deterministic model, single-point estimates are made of the values of variables and parameters. These best-guess values are typically the expected value or most likely value.[1] In stochastic models, probability

---

[1] Technically, the expected value is the mean, while the most likely value is the mode, and these may differ for a non-symmetric distribution.

distributions are attached to one or more variables or parameters. It is generally considered that a refinement in modelling introduces a need to incorporate uncertainty. That is, as we move to model a business or economic system in more detail, one of the important aspects to consider is the introduction of stochastic variables.

The discussion of simulation models becomes easier if we introduce some terminology to describe the various elements of these models. A convenient classification (drawing on a book by Naylor, Banintfy, Burdick and Chu (1966), written when simulation first started to be used as a management tool) is given in the following subsections.

Components of the simulation model

These are the basic building blocks of the model, which may be identified in order to break the model-building task into workable sub-tasks. They may form relatively self-contained modules in a computer implementation of the model. For example:

- a construction project could include components of design, construction and utilization of the facility
- a transport project could include components of equipment acquisition, maintenance and replacement, or of transport demand and logistics management
- a retailing project could include components of staffing, premises, inventory and financial control.

Variables in the model

These may be divided into *exogenous* variables, the levels of which are determined outside the system, *endogenous* variables, the levels of which are determined within the system, and *status* variables, which describe the state of the system. Exogenous variables may be under the control of management (*decision* or *policy* variables) or not controllable (*environmental* variables). Thus, the level of capital outlays is typically a controllable decision variable, the market demand for a product when a particular price is set is an exogenous non-controllable variable and net cash flow is an endogenous variable.

In simulation experiments, exogenous variables form the inputs which drive the model. Those variables under the control of management form the decision or policy instruments, the levels of which are adjusted during simulation experiments. Non-controllable exogenous, or environmental, variables may be modelled as either fixed values (or predetermined time series) or as probability distributions from which random values are generated.

The desirability of particular management policies is assessed in terms of one or more model outputs or levels of endogenous performance variables. In capital budgeting, net present value is typically adopted as the performance variable, though other discounted cash flow performance criteria such as internal rate of return may also be considered. As well, some measure of overall investment risk may be used as a performance criterion.

Status variables record the state of the system at each period in time. Examples for an individual firm include amounts of inventory, cash and debts. The level of a status variable in any time period will depend on its level in the previous time period (a feedback loop).

Functional relationships

These indicate how variables are interrelated, e.g. by linear or non-linear equations, and with or without time lags. Included are *identities* and *operating characteristics*. Identities are true by definition, e.g.

Net cash flow = Annual cash inflow − Capital outlays − Operating costs

An operating characteristic is a hypothesized relationship between two or more variables, which may be estimated by statistical analysis or subjectively, e.g. the trend in product demand over time at a fixed price:

Demand = Current level + (Trend coefficient × Time)

Functional relationships give the system its unique behaviour, and needless to say the reliability of any systems model depends vitally on how accurately the relationships are identified and estimated.

Parameters of the model

These are the coefficients of the operating characteristics, values of which can only be estimated within given confidence levels. The constant (i.e. Current level) and trend coefficient in the above demand equation are examples of parameters.

Given this terminology, any systems model may be summarized by the following *symbolic relationship*:

$$Z = f(X, Y, S, A)$$

where:

Z is a set of performance variables
X is a set of policy variables
Y is a set of environmental variables
S is a set of initial levels or status variables (including initial resource endowments)
A is a set of parameter values
f signifies that a functional relationship exists between the variables in the various sets (i.e. f represents the model).

Steps in simulation modelling and experimentation

Having explored the nature of models in some detail, let us now look more closely at the procedures of model construction and experimentation. Carrying out a simulation study is like carrying out any other quantitative study (though sometimes slightly more complicated). The 'scientific method' is employed, which means a series of steps are performed in a logical fashion to achieve the overall task. The terminology for simulation steps varies between experts, but the following is a workable classification:

(1) identification of the problem
(2) analysis of the system
(3) system synthesis
(4) programming the model on a computer
(5) testing the model
(6) experimentation with the model
(7) interpretation of results, and reporting to the relevant authority.

These steps are performed in the sequence listed, except that there is usually some cycling between them, e.g. testing the model may reveal the need to modify the structure and then revise the computer program. Each of the individual steps will now be discussed briefly.

Identification of the problem

It is most important to identify clearly the study objectives in terms of the research or managerial problem which is being examined. The nature of the model to be developed will depend on the problem to be analysed. Is the objective to understand the system or to prescribe management policies? If the latter, who is responsible for the system, what are their goals and what is wrong with present policies?

Analysis of the system

Once the problem is identified, the systems analysis stage can be performed, in which the boundaries of the system, the relevant variables and their interrelationships are identified. This may involve drawing various charts or diagrams of the system.

System synthesis

The next step, 'system synthesis', consists of expressing the relationships between variables in symbolic form and estimating the parameters of these relationships. Because of the high degree of flexibility possible, it is difficult to lay down rules for this major step, though some guidelines can be given. Where possible, statistical (including econometric) techniques should be used to estimate relationships between variables. Distributions or random variables can be obtained by testing the goodness of fit of alternative probability models using, say, the chi-squared test. Where historical data are scarce or are not considered relevant to future behaviour of the system, subjective estimation by people regarded as experts on the system may be preferable. It is usually recommended to start with a relatively simple model, and gradually extend and refine it. To the extent that sub-systems are sufficiently independent, the model should be constructed in the form of a number of relatively self-contained modules, which can then be programmed and tested separately. Existing models of similar systems should be examined for relevance, since it may be possible to obtain ideas or even adapt modules from them.

Programming the model on a computer

Once a prototype version of the model has been constructed, computer programming can commence, using a spreadsheet package or – if the model is too complex for this – using a computer programming language such as Visual Basic, FORTRAN, C, Stellar or Simile.

Testing the model

In simulation, rather than using an off-the-shelf software package implementing a well-known solution algorithm, a model is conceived and developed by the analyst. This places greater responsibility on analysts to ensure and to demonstrate to others that their creation is structurally sound and the predictions it produces are reliable; that is, some amount of testing of the model is necessary.

There is far from general agreement on how systems models should be tested, but a workable approach is to divide testing into *verification, validation* and *sensitivity analysis*. Verification is the process of testing whether the model takes its intended structure, i.e. whether the model is free of logical errors and whether the computer program performs as intended. Validation examines the broader question of whether the intended structure truly represents the real system, and often leads to further refinement of the model.

Once a model has been validated as far as practicable, the effect of remaining errors on parameter estimates may be assessed through sensitivity analysis. If the purpose of the model is to identify optimal management policies, errors in estimates of performance due to inaccurate parameter values may not be of concern unless they lead to identification of inferior policies as optimal. That is, we are not concerned with the predictive ability of the model in absolute terms so much as the model's ability to correctly rank alternative management policies. For this reason, it is desirable to include a sensitivity analysis with respect to optimal values of decision variables.

Sensitivity analysis as a stage in model-testing involves adjusting parameter values by small amounts and calculating various sensitivity criteria. Sensitivity may be expressed quantitatively in terms of 'elasticity' of performance with respect to parameter levels, or elasticity of optimal management policies with respect to parameter values. High sensitivities (elasticities) give cause for concern about the reliability of a model.

The most difficult part of model-testing is normally validation. A variety of statistical tests have been proposed for this purpose, in which output from the model is compared with that of the real system for the same levels of decision and environmental variables. However, in practice it has been found that often the assumptions underlying these statistical tests are violated, and that confidence in a model is typically built up over time, as the model proceeds through a number of prototypes and is exposed to various users.

Performing experiments

Once sufficient confidence has been gained in a model, a variety of simulation experiments may be conducted. Typically, these experiments provide predictions of the performance variable (or variables), for various levels of one or more decision variables. Where there are two or more decision variables, care may be needed to adopt a suitable *experimental design* to provide meaningful decision support information without using excessive computer time or generating excessive computer output.

In the language of experimental design, the performance variable is known as the *response variable*, the decision variables are known as *experimental factors*, and any combination of levels of these factors (i.e. any management policy) is known as a *treatment*. A computer run in which a number of treatments are evaluated is known as a *simulation experiment*. If random variability is built into the model (i.e. if the model is stochastic), then it is necessary to evaluate each treatment or policy under a number of different environments, i.e. to include *replication* of each treatment in the simulation experiment. Experiments conducted on a computer also have important differences from real-world experiments. Three main sources of difference arise.

(1) *Compression of time.* Because of the speed of computing and the low cost of computer time, it is usually possible to include a larger number of treatments and a greater degree of replication.

(2) *Sequential processing.* Traditionally, each of the treatments in a real-system experiment is evaluated at the same time. For example, in a crop fertilizer experiment, the complete experimental design is decided, then the plots of land for each combination of fertilizer levels are all planted on (or as near as possible to) the same day, all plots are cultivated on the same day, and so on for watering, spraying and harvesting. The objective here is to minimize the effect of influences other than the experimental factors on the response variable. On the other hand, because a computer is a sequential processor, treatments are evaluated sequentially in a computer simulation experiment. This means that we know the performance level for the first treatment before the second is evaluated, and we know the performance for the first and second treatments before evaluating the third, and so on. Sequential processing opens the opportunity to use information gained from earlier treatments to adjust factor levels in later treatments within the same experiment, giving rise to what are known as 'optimum-seeking' experimental designs.

(3) *Control over experimental variability.* In a computer simulation experiment, the variability in the 'environment' is under the control of the researcher. A random number generator is used to produce numbers between 0 and 1, and these are transformed to random observations from the distributions specified for the random variables. If the random number generator is given the same seed for each treatment then the treatments are evaluated under the same sequences of random numbers, i.e. under the same environments. This reduces random variability in response levels between treatments compared to the alternative

of independent seeding (i.e. not reseeding the random number generator). The result is greater power to detect differences between treatments for a given sample size (or number of replicates).

Analysis and interpretation of computer output

Simulation experiments often generate large volumes of information, and this output must be distilled and interpreted to a form usable by managers to assist their decision-making. In the case of stochastic simulation models, which indicate a range of possible outcomes, estimated performance levels should be thought of in a probability distribution context.

Risk analysis or Monte Carlo simulation

A relatively simple application of simulation is to the evaluation of investment projects the returns from which are subject to a high level of uncertainty. Here, probability distributions are attached to a number of non-controllable exogenous variables which determine annual net cash flows, and synthetic sampling from these distributions is carried out on the computer, so as to generate the probability distribution of one or more financial *performance* criteria. This overall distribution (of, say, net present value or internal rate of return) is then presented to the decision-maker, perhaps with some summary information, to aid in making a project accept/reject decision.

This technique is known by a variety of names, including *risk analysis, venture analysis, risk simulation* and *Monte Carlo simulation*. There is lack of agreement on the name, since in a general sense any method of measuring the risk of a project could be referred to as risk analysis. The term *venture analysis* is perhaps inappropriate, since in this context 'venture' is simply a synonym for 'project', though there is an implication that the project is a risky one. *Risk simulation* is in a sense an abbreviation of the concept of 'project performance simulation taking into account risk in cash flow variables'. The term *Monte Carlo simulation* or *Monte Carlo method* arises because of the historical association of gambling and roulette wheels, to which the generation of random values of cash flow variables is likened, with the city of Monte Carlo. Two factors favouring use of the name *risk analysis* are the use of the term by David Hertz in his 1960s pioneering work on allowing for project risk, and the adoption of the term in the software add-on to the Microsoft Excel and Lotus 1-2-3 spreadsheet packages known as @RISK.

Risk analysis differs from other forms of treatment of risk in project evaluation, where sources of variability are recognized but point values are used for the variables without any attempt to attach a probability estimate to the likelihood of these values. The probability distributions fitted in risk analysis can be discrete or continuous distributions, although in practice continuous distributions are normally used. Various forms of probability distributions could be specified for these variables, e.g. normal, log normal, beta, gamma, exponential, uniform, triangular. Some of these distributions require specification of parameter values, e.g. mean and variance. Others require estimation of specific points, e.g. lower and upper extremes (uniform distribution), or pessimistic, modal and optimistic levels (beta distribution, triangular distribution). The normal distribution takes the familiar bell-shaped symmetric curve. In the log normal distribution, large values are compressed more than small values so that a positive skew is compressed, which is a better representation of the distribution for some variables. The beta distribution allows both positive and negative skew and has been found particularly useful for fitting to task durations in the project management tool, program evaluation and review technique (PERT); hence, it is sometimes referred to as the PERT beta distribution.

Risk analysis is best explained through a worked example. The following example of investment in the highly volatile computer industry, in which technology change is rapid and the failure rate of firms high, illustrates the modelling, simulation process and output of this technique.

Example 9.1. Computer project

A personal computer dealer is planning to introduce a new and more stylish model, and would like to know the likely financial performance and the extent of financial risk of this investment. Initial outlays of $50,000 are required in arranging contracts for the supply of components, tooling up and hiring computer technicians who would assemble the new PCs.

Computer components are to be imported from various sources. There is sufficient underutilized workshop space to assemble the PCs. No reduction is planned in other product lines at present. Component costs are falling over time, but this trend is expected to be offset by the need to increase the performance specifications each year. Landed costs of components will also fluctuate with the exchange rate. Because the PC market is highly competitive, the firm has limited discretion in price-setting, and has to match closely the going market price. The number of units which will be sold through the firm's three outlets is uncertain.

Management of the computer firm has identified four uncertain variables which will be important in determining the performance of this project, viz. annual sales quantity, market price, component cost and labour cost. As well as these items, it is estimated that overhead and marketing costs will amount to $500 per unit sold. Management considers that after five years the particular style of PC will have run its useful life, and hence adopts a planning horizon of five years for the project. A discount rate of 7% is judged appropriate.

Management of the computer firm has heard that the triangular distribution has proved quite useful in risk analysis and is relatively easy to specify, and has decided that this is an acceptable approximation for the cash flow variables. The financial analyst, in consultation with the head of the new project section, has specified three levels for each of the four uncertain cash flow variables, as indicated in Table 9.1. These three levels are the *pessimistic* value, the *modal* (or most likely) value and the *optimistic* value. As discussed in Chapter 8, the pessimistic value is that value which would lead to the poorest investment outcome (e.g. the lowest product price or highest input cost), while the optimistic value is the most favourable value in terms of investment outcome. These may not be absolute extremes such that it is not possible to experience values outside them, but the probability of a value more

Table 9.1. *Computer project: pessimistic, modal and optimistic values for selected cash flow variables*

	Pessimistic level	Modal value	Optimistic level
Sales quantity (no./year)	50	100	130
Market price ($/unit)	2,200	2,500	3,000
Component costs ($/unit)	1,200	1,000	900
Labour cost ($/unit)	350	300	200

extreme than either should be not more than about 0.01 or 1%. The modal value represents the highest point in the probability distribution, and for a discrete variable would be the most likely value.[2]

It should be noted that these levels of the uncertain variables, and hence the probability distributions, have been estimated *subjectively*. This has involved management using judgement and intuition, drawing on its past experience and knowledge of the PC market. Of course, it would be preferable to use *objective* probabilities. However, unfortunately, there is not likely to be a history of relevant sales records to draw upon (the new PC model may have different style and performance characteristics to previous models) and market conditions in the future will not necessarily mirror closely those of the past.

```
Workbook
  9.1
```

In specifying the probability distributions, it is not necessary that these distributions be symmetric in shape. In Example 9.1, the sales quantity distribution is skewed to the left (the modal value is towards the upper end of the distribution), while market price is skewed to the right (the longer tail of the distribution is in the higher range of values of the variable).

Since probability distributions have been specified for only four of the variables determining annual cash flows, not all of the performance variability for the project has been captured. In practice, probability distributions are usually specified for only the most important cash flow variables, but it is hoped that these capture most of the investment uncertainty. If levels of cash flow variables are expected to have clear trends over time, e.g. if there is likely to be an increasing or decreasing trend in the number of computers sold each year, then the strength of the trend can also be included as one of the uncertain cash flow variables. The choice of which variables to treat as stochastic in the risk analysis, and the estimation of their optimistic and pessimistic values, is essentially the same challenge as faced when applying sensitivity analysis to examine project risk.

---

[2] For a continuous variable, the probability that any exact value will be realized approaches zero as the width of interval under the probability distribution approaches zero, hence it is not statistically meaningful to speak of the 'most likely value'.

Derivation of annual net cash flow and NPV under modal values

The cash flow model for each year of the project life is:

$$NCF_t = REV_t - CO_t - OC_t$$

where:

$$REV_t = PRICE_t \times QTY_t$$
$$OC_t = QTY_t \times (COMP_t + LAB_t + OTHER_t)$$

and:

$$NCF_t = \text{net cash flow}$$
$$REV_t = \text{gross sales receipts from computer sales}$$
$$PRICE_t = \text{sale price per unit}$$
$$QTY_t = \text{quantity sold in the year}$$
$$CO_t = \text{capital outlay}$$
$$OC_t = \text{annual operating cost}$$
$$COMP_t = \text{component cost per unit}$$
$$LAB_t = \text{labour cost per unit}$$
$$OTHER_t = \text{overhead and marketing costs per unit.}$$

Net present value (NPV) is determined in the usual way as:

$$\sum_{t=0}^{5} NCF_t / (1 + r)^t$$

where r is the discount rate. The NPV for the project could be obtained using the modal values of each of the uncertain cash flow variables (sales of 100 units, priced at $2,500, with per unit component and labour costs of $1,000 and $300, respectively). If NPV is found to be positive, the project would be judged acceptable, assuming that the cash flow variables experienced modal values. It should be noted that the discount rate r does not include an allowance for risk aversion, since risk is measured explicitly in the analysis and quantified in the output; hence the decision-maker is able to consider risk explicitly.

Replicated sampling

Workbook
9.1

Using modal values of the uncertain variables would provide only a single NPV value, or *point estimate*, of financial performance of the project. In contrast, in the risk analysis, the cash flow variables are allowed to take random values from within their triangular probability distributions during the project evaluation. This is achieved by sampling, or *generating*, sets of values for each of the random variates for each year of the project life, and then computing the NPV for each series of cash flows obtained.

Table 9.2 presents the random numbers and generated values of the four random variables for the first five replicates of the risk analysis. In each column (i.e. for each replicate), 20 random numbers and then 20 corresponding random observations of the variables are presented. The random numbers, which range between 0 and 1, are generated using the Excel random number generator, and these numbers are applied to the triangular distributions to obtain the random observations of the cash flow variables using the method explained in the appendix to this chapter. Specifically, for a triangular distribution with three points labelled a (lowest value), b (modal value) and c (largest value), a random value y is obtained using the formulae:

For $r \leq d$: $\qquad y = a + \sqrt{r(c - a)(b - a)}$

For $r > d$: $\qquad y = c - \sqrt{(1 - r)(c - a)(c - b)}$

where $d = (b - a)/(c - a)$, and r is a random number from the uniform distribution with range 0 to 1.[3]

As an example, consider the sales quantity variable. The parameter d for this variable – which measures the proportion of the area under the probability distribution to the left of the mode – is obtained as

$$d = (100 - 50)/(130 - 50) = 50/80 = 0.625$$

In Table 9.2, the first random number for sales quantity is 0.2546. Since this is less than 0.625, the generated value for sales quantity is less than the modal quantity and is obtained as:

$$y = 50 + \sqrt{0.2546\,(130 - 50)(100 - 50)} = 81.91$$

which on rounding to the nearest integer becomes 82, as reported in the table.

The sales quantities for years 2 to 5 in the first replicate are obtained in the same way. Sales quantities in this first replicate over the five-year planning horizon range between 63 and 112 units. Similarly, observations for the other three uncertain cash flow variables have been generated in the Replicate 1 column. This procedure has been repeated 100 times, i.e. there have been 100 replicates of the DCF analysis.[4]

Applying the above annual cash flow model, the values of the cash flow variables for Replicate 1 in Table 9.2 have been used to obtain the net cash flows for this replicate in Table 9.3. The net cash outflow in year 0 is simply the project set-up cost of $50,000. For year 1, the revenue is $REV_1 = 2,636 \times 82 = \$216,152$ and the operating cost is $OC_1 = 82 \times (988 + 299 + 500) = \$146,534$, hence $NCF_1 = \$69,618$. Net cash flows for subsequent years are derived in the same manner.

Table 9.3 presents the corresponding annual net cash flows and NPV estimates for the first five replicates. The initial capital outlay is timed for year 0 and other net cash flows are

---

[3] More precisely, r is a *pseudo-random* number, and is obtained in Excel by the call to the random number generator '=rand()'.

[4] Often the term *iteration* is used to represent the process of obtaining a set of random variates from each of the probability distributions and deriving a point estimate of the performance criterion. Technically, this is not correct since an iteration is more precisely a set of steps in the solution procedure for a mathematical technique such as linear programming.

Table 9.2. *Computer project: random numbers and generated values under triangular distributions for the four stochastic variables*

Variable	Year	Replicate				
		1	2	3	4	5
Random numbers for sales	1	0.2546	0.5624	0.0138	0.4651	0.6666
	2	0.8654	0.1318	0.6674	0.2691	0.7802
	3	0.7044	0.2915	0.0166	0.2964	0.1963
	4	0.0432	0.2219	0.7905	0.0774	0.2686
	5	0.4194	0.5922	0.4623	0.7642	0.6090
Random numbers for price	1	0.6696	0.0859	0.2738	0.1789	0.8249
	2	0.7634	0.5465	0.1862	0.6624	0.8751
	3	0.8199	0.6051	0.2669	0.7659	0.8268
	4	0.4823	0.2060	0.2418	0.6317	0.3793
	5	0.5247	0.6133	0.6252	0.2579	0.1353
Random numbers for component costs	1	0.2562	0.0837	0.7600	0.0093	0.3327
	2	0.2580	0.3249	0.8085	0.9496	0.0801
	3	0.0694	0.7337	0.7810	0.8635	0.2082
	4	0.1853	0.1213	0.4338	0.8264	0.2752
	5	0.2280	0.6614	0.4277	0.1575	0.8425
Random numbers for labour cost	1	0.6508	0.3186	0.2081	0.8905	0.3415
	2	0.3937	0.7434	0.4131	0.5663	0.7577
	3	0.6355	0.4734	0.7607	0.3670	0.6478
	4	0.5525	0.2959	0.6359	0.6626	0.7794
	5	0.6215	0.6111	0.2159	0.2920	0.0073

Variable	Year	Replicate				
		1	2	3	4	5
Sales	1	82	97	57	93	102
	2	112	73	102	83	107
	3	103	84	58	84	78
	4	63	80	108	68	83
	5	91	99	93	106	99
Price	1	2,636	2,344	2,456	2,407	2,735
	2	2,692	2,574	2,411	2,633	2,776
	3	2,732	2,603	2,453	2,694	2,737
	4	2,545	2,422	2,441	2,616	2,502
	5	2,564	2,607	2,613	2,449	2,380
Component costs	1	988	950	1,080	917	1,000
	2	988	999	1,093	1,145	949
	3	946	1,074	1,085	1,109	979
	4	975	960	1,016	1,098	991
	5	983	1,057	1,015	969	1,103
Labour cost	1	299	269	256	321	272
	2	277	306	279	292	307
	3	298	284	308	274	299
	4	291	267	298	300	309
	5	297	296	257	266	210

Table 9.3. *Computer project: annual net cash flows and NPVs for first five replicates*

Year (EOY)	Net cash flow ($)				
	Replicate 1	Replicate 2	Replicate 3	Replicate 4	Replicate 5
0	−50,000	−50,000	−50,000	−50,000	−50,000
1	69,618	60,625	35,340	62,217	98,226
2	103,824	56,137	54,978	57,768	109,140
3	101,764	62,580	32,480	68,124	74,802
4	49,077	55,600	67,716	48,824	58,266
5	71,344	74,646	78,213	75,684	56,133
NPV($)	277,125	202,414	164,986	205,422	282,661

Table 9.4. *Computer project: ordered NPVs and cumulative relative frequencies*

NPV ($)	155,421	155,930	157,449	165,138	183,182	...	315,975	321,943	323,975
Cum. rel. freq.	0.01	0.02	0.03	0.04	0.05	...	0.98	0.99	1

assumed to take place at the end of the relevant years. The NPV estimates range between $165,000 and $282,000. The random numbers, generated values for uncertain variables and NPV calculations for the full 100 replicates are provided in Workbook 9.1.

The cumulative relative frequency distribution

The relative frequencies of financial performance could be summarized in the form of a histogram. However, it is more useful to express these in cumulative relative frequencies. The set of 100 NPVs has been sorted into ascending order. Table 9.4 presents some of these NPV values; to save space these are reported for the lower and upper ends of the distribution only. The lowest NPV is $155,421 and the highest is $323,975, indicating a wide range of possible payoff levels. Cumulative relative frequencies are also provided in the table, obtained simply by dividing the rank position by the total sample size (100).

The full cumulative relative frequency curve is shown in Figure 9.1. For any NPV value along the horizontal axis, the vertical axis indicates the estimated probability that the NPV will be this value or less. The graph has end points with cumulative relative frequencies of near zero (0.01 to be precise) and 1.0, and provides estimates of the likelihood, or probability, that the project if implemented would yield NPVs of less than the various levels within the range $155,421 and $323,975.

The curve of Figure 9.1 may be viewed as an estimate of the cumulative (probability) density function (CDF) of the performance variable, here NPV. The term 'estimate' is used because it is derived from sampling, not from a precise knowledge of the overall behaviour of NPV (the statistical concept of a 'population'). However, in practice we may refer to the

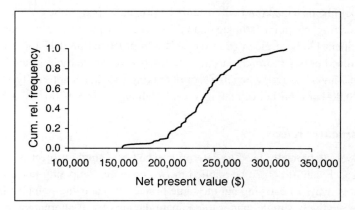

Figure 9.1.   *Cumulative relative frequency curve for NPV of computer project.*

curve, if somewhat loosely in statistical terms, as the CDF. Note that the CDF is ragged rather than smooth in shape. The degree of smoothness is a function of sample size (number of replicates). The larger this number the more smooth this curve will become. For example, a sample of size 5,000 could be taken. However, this would yield little if any additional information to that provided in Figure 9.1.

The CDF curve provides us with a good deal of information about the likely financial performance of the project. The estimated probability of various ranges of performance levels can be read from this graph. For the computer investment project, it would appear that a payoff of less than \$200,000 is highly unlikely, with an estimated probability of only about 0.1. Also, because the probability of a payoff of less than \$300,000 is about 0.95, a payoff of more than \$300,000 is extremely unlikely (estimated as $1-0.95$ or 0.05). The median payoff (middle of the distribution or probability of 0.5) appears to be about \$240,000. In fact, it can be found from the spreadsheet that the median NPV (the average of the 50th and 51st values of the ordered set) is about \$238,500. The symmetrical shape of the CDF (i.e. similar slopes at the lower and upper ends) suggests the mean payoff will be similar to the median value; the mean as computed from the spreadsheet is, in fact, \$239,141.

Determining whether a project is financially acceptable

In discounted cash flow analysis as presented in earlier chapters, the output of the analysis is a single, or point, estimate of one or more performance criteria, e.g. the NPV or IRR of the project. It is then a simple task to say, for example, the NPV is positive at the chosen discount rate or the IRR exceeds the required rate of return so the project is financially acceptable. While risk analysis provides information about the overall distribution of project payoff to the decision-maker, this makes the assessment of project acceptability somewhat more difficult, precisely because of the greater amount of information to assimilate. Risk analysis has sometimes been criticized for this reason. The decision-maker obviously cannot take in all of the, say, 100 point estimates of project performance. The expected (i.e. average) or median NPV could be provided (and will usually be printed as part of the computer output anyway), but reverting to a point estimate undermines the very purpose of risk analysis. So what is management likely to glean from the CDF? In practice, the decision-maker may have some reference points in mind, and may be interested for example in the estimated probability of making a loss (NPV negative), or of making less than a notionally acceptable payoff (say $200,000 or more) or of making a very high payoff (say $300,000 or more).

Comparing alternative projects

While risk analysis is typically used to determine whether a single project is financially viable, the approach can of course be applied to two or more competing projects or two or more alternative ways of carrying out the same project. When using point estimates of, say, NPV, it is a relatively simple matter to compare the payoffs of alternative investment options. Comparing overall CDFs can be more difficult. When the CDFs of two projects are plotted on the same graph, if the CDF of one is entirely to the right of another, then it can be said that the former project has superior financial performance over the entire probability range. But if the CDFs cross over it becomes more difficult to make a judgement between the projects. A technique known as *stochastic dominance analysis* (not discussed here) will in some cases allow one project to be judged as superior to another when the CDFs cross.

Independent versus correlated sampling of cash flow variables

In the above risk analysis, the cash flow variables have been sampled independently, i.e. no allowance has been made for correlations in their levels, in the same time period. In practice, it is likely that some cash flow variables will be positively correlated, for example price levels of inputs and outputs. Also, some may be negatively correlated, for example the price charged for the PCs and the number sold. Further, the levels of individual random variables are likely to be correlated between years within the planning horizon. For example, if the labour cost is higher than the median level of the estimated distribution in year 1, then it would tend to be higher than the median level in year 2.

Methods of generation of correlated random variates are available, so that if the analyst can estimate the degree of association between cash flow variables then this can be built into the analysis. Some software packages for risk analysis allow correlations to be specified between cash flow variables, e.g. @RISK. In general, if cash flow variables are positively correlated then overall project performance variability will be increased; if they are negatively correlated then it will be decreased. However, this pattern will be influenced by which cash flow variables are correlated with which others. For example, if cash inflow and cash outflow variables were negative correlated, this would lead to increased variability in overall financial performance.

Software packages available

Various software packages have been developed for risk analysis. For example, the packages @RISK and Insight have been designed as add-on software for spreadsheet programs including Excel. Some risk analysis packages are relatively expensive, and often it is possible to perform risk analysis simply using the facilities of the spreadsheet program (as in the example presented here).

Design and development of a more complex simulation model

A more complex example of simulation modelling is now presented to illustrate some of the more advanced features of simulation methodology. This example initially involves a multi-period deterministic financial model of an airline investment. The model is then extended to a stochastic format, and the nature of simulation experiments is illustrated.

Example 9.2. FlyByNight project

The FlyByNight airline company is planning to introduce a new country run, to provide two return services a week (104 per year) to a rural city with a population of 30,000 persons. This project is named FlyByNight. The airline will use a forty-passenger aircraft, which it can purchase for $4.5M. An airstrip owned by the local government in the rural area is available without charge, but the company will have to carry out restoration of the disused airstrip and terminal at a cost of $200,000. A financial model is to be developed to simulate the cash inflows and outflows from this venture over a ten-year period, and to provide an estimate of the net present value of the investment.

Other relevant information for model development includes:

- *Passenger demand:* This is predicted to be initially 5,000 passengers per year (in one-way flights), increasing at the rate of 300 per year.
- *Mail service revenue:* In addition to passenger services, the company has a contract to transport mail to the rural city for a fixed annual payment of $200,000.
- *Annual fixed costs:* The annual cost of the air crew is $200,000 and that of ground staff is $50,000. The annual maintenance cost for the aircraft is 7% of the initial price.
- *Fuel cost:* Aviation fuel costs $800 per flight, plus $10 per passenger.
- *Handling cost:* The cost of booking and other services is $15 per passenger flight.
- *Air fares:* A charge of $280 is made for each one-way flight ($560 return).
- Company tax is 30% of the annual operating surplus; the aircraft and ground facilities can be depreciated at a rate of 10% per annum for taxation purposes.
- After ten years, the aircraft has a salvage value of $1M.
- The appropriate discount rate is 8%.

Development of the FlyByNight basic simulation model

Given the above information, a model may be set up which predicts the cash surplus each year t:

$$NPV = \Sigma \, AS_t/(1+r)^t, t = 0 \text{ to } 10$$

$$AS_t = AR_t - CO_t - AC_t - TAX_t$$

$$AR_t = NPAS_t \times FARE_t + MAIL_t$$

$$AC_t = MAINT_t + STAFF_t + FUEL_t + HAND_t + ADV_t$$

$$NPAS_t = 5000 + 300\,t$$

$$TY_t = AR_t - AC_t - DEPN_t + SALV_t$$

$$TAX_t = ART_t \times TY_t$$

where:

AS_t = annual net cash flow

AR_t = annual revenue from passenger and mail services

CO_t = capital outlay

AC_t = annual costs

TAX_t = annual company tax payable less tax benefit arising from depreciation allowances, in relation to this investment.

$FARE_t$ = fare per passenger per flight

$MAIL_t$ = annual revenue from mail services

$NFLT_t$ = number of one-way flights per year

$NPAS_t$ = number of passengers per year

$MAINT_t$ = annual maintenance expenditure on the aircraft (purchase price × maintenance rate)

$STAFF_t$ = annual wage bill (air crew and ground staff wages)

$FUEL_t$ = annual expenditure on aircraft fuel (fixed component × no. of flights + variable component × number of passengers)

$HAND_t$ = annual passenger handling cost (number of passengers × handling cost per passenger)

ADV_t = annual advertising cost (zero in the initial model)

$DEPN_t$ = annual depreciation allowance (capital invested × depreciation rate)

$SALV_t$ = end-of-project salvage value on capital outlays (fully taxable)

TY_t = annual taxable income

ART_t = average rate of tax

r = annual real rate of interest

t = time in years.

The model has been implemented on the computer as an Excel spreadsheet.

> Workbook
> 9.2

Structure of the FlyByNight basic model

In terms of the earlier discussion of elements of a model, it may be noted:

- Aircraft costs, passenger numbers, taxation etc. could be treated as separate *components* of the model, or modules of the computer implementation. In this case, the model is relatively simple so it is not necessary to break it down into components.
- The performance or response variable is NPV.

Table 9.5. *FlyByNight: parameters of the basic model*

Cost of aircraft	$4,500,000
Restoration of airstrip and terminal	$200,000
Seating capacity	40
Number of one-way flights per year	208
Initial passenger number	5,000
Annual increase in passengers	300
Mail service revenue per year	$200,000
Annual aircraft maintenance cost (% of cost)	7%
Air crew cost per year	$200,000
Ground staff cost per year	$50,000
Fuel cost, fixed per flight	$800
Fuel cost, variable per passenger carried	$10
Handling cost per passenger	$15
Air fare (per passenger per flight)	$280
Income tax rate	30%
Aircraft salvage value at year 10	$1,000,000
Required rate of return (per annum)	8%

- Examples of *identities*, which are true by definition, include the definitions of annual surplus and annual project revenue (taxable income):

$$AS_t = AR_t - CO_t - AC_t - TAX_t$$

$$TY_t = AR_t - AC_t - DEPN_t + SALV_t$$

- An example of an *operating characteristic* is the equation for predicting passenger numbers:

$$NPAS_t = 5000 + 300\,t$$

- Various parameters are present in the model, as summarized in Table 9.5. These are listed at the top of the spreadsheet, making the assumptions clear to the viewer and making for ease of adjustment of parameters in sensitivity analysis.
- Values of various *endogenous* variables are generated in the simulation experiment.
- The fare per flight is a controllable exogenous, or *decision*, variable, but has been set at a fixed level ($280).
- The model as formulated here has no non-controllable exogenous, or *environmental*, variables.

Testing the FlyByNight basic simulation model

Before using a model such as this to derive quantitative decision support information, some testing would be highly desirable. In this context the model would first be verified by testing that it had been programmed correctly on the computer, which means checking that the logic and formulae in the spreadsheet conform with the model design. For this model, which involves only a few equations, verification is a relatively simple task.

Table 9.6. *FlyByNight: output from the basic model simulation run (all cash flows in dollars)*

Year (ending)	0	1	2	3	4	5	6	7	8	9	10
Capital outlays											
Initial outlay	4,700,000										
Salvage value											1,000,000
Project revenue											
Number of passengers		5,000	5,300	5,600	5,900	6,200	6,500	6,800	7,100	7,400	7,700
Fare revenue		1,400,000	1,484,000	1,568,000	1,652,000	1,736,000	1,820,000	1,904,000	1,988,000	2,072,000	2,156,000
+ Mail revenue		200,000	200,000	200,000	200,000	200,000	200,000	200,000	200,000	200,000	200,000
= Total revenue		1,600,000	1,684,000	1,768,000	1,852,000	1,936,000	2,020,000	2,104,000	2,188,000	2,272,000	2,356,000
Operating costs											
Aircraft maintenance		315,000	315,000	315,000	315,000	315,000	315,000	315,000	315,000	315,000	315,000
+ Air crew cost		200,000	200,000	200,000	200,000	200,000	200,000	200,000	200,000	200,000	200,000
+ Ground staff cost		50,000	50,000	50,000	50,000	50,000	50,000	50,000	50,000	50,000	50,000
+ Fuel cost		216,400	219,400	222,400	225,400	228,400	231,400	234,400	237,400	240,400	243,400
+ Handling cost		75,000	79,500	84,000	88,500	93,000	97,500	102,000	106,500	111,000	115,500
+ Advertising cost		0	0	0	0	0	0	0	0	0	0
= Total costs		856,400	863,900	871,400	878,900	886,400	893,900	901,400	908,900	916,400	923,900
Tax calculations											
Net operating revenue		743,600	820,100	896,600	973,100	1,049,600	1,126,100	1,202,600	1,279,100	1,355,600	1,432,100
− Depreciation		470,000	470,000	470,000	470,000	470,000	470,000	470,000	470,000	470,000	470,000
= Notional taxable income		273,600	350,100	426,600	503,100	579,600	656,100	732,600	809,100	885,600	962,100
+ Salvage value tax adjustment											1,000,000
= Total taxable income		273,600	350,100	426,600	503,100	579,600	656,100	732,600	809,100	885,600	1,962,100
Tax payable		82,080	105,030	127,980	150,930	173,880	196,830	219,780	242,730	265,680	588,630
Net cash flow	−4,700,000	661,520	715,070	768,620	822,170	875,720	929,270	982,820	1,036,370	1,089,920	1,843,470
NPV =	1,454,148										

Second, the model would be validated by checking whether the overall behaviour of the model corresponds with that which would take place in the real system (i.e. the airline). In other words, the validity of the structure and relationships in the model – such as the travel demand function – would be checked. This might involve examining the costs, demand and sales receipts experience of previous airline operators on this run, or those of other airlines with similar characteristics. If possible, data used for model validation should exclude that used in constructing the model. If the purpose of the model is to compare management policies, then checking of the ranking of policies is more important than checking the ability to predict NPV accurately.

Once the model had been validated as far as possible, sensitivity analysis would be used to determine what effects inaccuracies in parameter estimates would have on NPV estimates from the model, and on the ranking of management policies (experimental treatments) compared in the simulation experiments. Sensitivity analysis will indicate which parameters warrant further estimation efforts.

> Workbook
> 9.2

Since the model is implemented on a spreadsheet (Workbook 9.2) the simulation is performed automatically when the formulae in the spreadsheet are executed to generate the cell values. Running this model on the computer may be thought of as simulating passenger numbers and hence financial performance over the ten-year planning horizon. Output from this model is presented as Table 9.6. The lower part of the table presents the annual cash flow estimates. The NPV function of the spreadsheet is used to derive net present value for the investment in the final line of output.

Deterministic simulation of financial performance

Simulation has been defined as modelling and performing experiments with the model (on a computer). In this example, it may seem odd to describe estimation of project performance by simply evaluating each of the spreadsheet formulae as an 'experiment'. Only one set of values is used for the variables, and this is in fact a standard NPV calculation. However, with minor modification, the financial model may be used to carry out more complex experiments so as to improve the understanding by management about the behaviour of the system which is being modelled.

Example 9.3. FlyByNight deterministic model

Suppose that the airline wishes to increase seat sales, and has identified two methods by which this can be achieved, viz. advertising or price discounting. Research indicates that:

(1) the number of passengers in any year, $NPAS_t$, is related to the advertising expenditure in that year (x_1, in thousands of dollars) by the quadratic function with linear coefficient 50 and quadratic coefficient -1.4;

Table 9.7. *FlyByNight: NPV levels from the deterministic simulation ($M)*

			Annual expenditure on advertising ($)		
		0	8,000	16,000	24,000
Price discount ($/flight)	0	1.45	1.79	1.91	1.81
	20	1.94	2.19	2.27	2.19
	40	2.02	2.15	2.17	2.11
	60	1.65	1.66	1.62	1.58

(2) the number of passengers in any year increases linearly by 500 for each $10 decrease in fare ($x_2$).

This information has been built into the operating characteristics for passenger numbers:

$$NPAS_t = (5000 + 300\,t) + 50\,x_1 - 1.4\,x_1^2 + 500\,x_2$$

where x_1 is expenditure on advertising in thousands of dollars and x_2 is the price discount in $10 steps. In addition, there is a capacity constraint that $NPAS_t \leq 8,320$ (208 flights of 40 passengers). For simplicity, it has been assumed that any advertising or discounting policy will be employed throughout the whole ten-year period. (Allowing these to vary each year would lead to a very large number of decision variables.) Flight operations over ten years have been simulated for the following promotion policies: advertising expenditures of 0, $8,000, $16,000 and $24,000; price discounting of 0, $20, $40 and $60.

> Workbook
> 9.3

Note that each advertising level is to be combined with each price discount level. Any combination of *levels* of each variable may be thought of as a treatment in the simulation experiment; the simulation experiment therefore involves 4 × 4, or 16, treatments. In Excel, the Data Table function is used to evaluate these combinations of factor levels, producing the NPV levels shown in Table 9.7. The spreadsheet employed to produce this table, indicating all of the calculations involved, is provided as Workbook 9.3. Details of how to use the Data Table function are provided in the Excel Help files. (Advertising is treated as the row variable and price discount as the column variable, and a table frame with selected treatments or combinations of levels of these is set up before the Data Table function is used.)

The figures in the body of Table 9.7 may be thought of as points on an NPV *response surface* in two dimensions. It is apparent that NPV – which was $1.45M in Table 9.6 – can be increased considerably by the promotion activities. The optimal levels of the decision variables can be read off as approximately $x_1 = \$16,000$ and $x_2 = \$20$, i.e. spend $16,000 annually on advertising the airline and discount fares by $20 per flight. This information would be conveyed to management.

Stochastic simulation of financial performance

The above examples relied on a *deterministic* simulation model. In practice, simulation models are often *stochastic* in nature, i.e. they include random variates, the values of which are obtained through some random variate generator; this is sometimes referred to as *Monte Carlo sampling*. The use of such models is referred to as *stochastic simulation* or *Monte Carlo simulation*.

Example 9.4. FlyByNight stochastic simulation

Suppose that the number of passengers – the main source of uncertainty for the airline – can be represented by the demand function of Example 9.3, but with the addition of a random component, y:

$$NPAS_t = (5000 + 300\,t) + 50\,x_1 - 1.4\,x_1^{\,2} + 500\,x_2 + y$$

where this random component has a normal distribution with a mean of 0 and standard deviation of 500 passengers. The financial model may now be used to conduct a simulation experiment in which the demand function includes this non-controllable environmental variable. Every time the program is run on the computer (each *encounter with the model*) a different set of demand levels is generated, and hence a different NPV obtained. For this reason, it is necessary to include in the simulation experiment a number of replicates and to average NPV performance over these replicates, if we are to gain a sound comparison of treatments or sales promotion policies.

A method of generating normal random variables is explained in the appendix to this chapter. Random variates from the $N(0,500)$ distribution of this example are obtained as

$$y = \left(\Sigma^{12} r_i - 6\right) \times 500$$

where the twelve r_i values are observations from a uniform distribution with range 0 to 1 (i.e. the spreadsheet random number generator).

```
Workbook
   9.4
```

A simulation experiment is performed with the same sixteen treatments as above, and with four replicates, and NPV estimates are reported in Table 9.8. The spreadsheet used to produce Table 9.8 is provided as Workbook 9.4. For this experiment, the levels of the random demand variable have been obtained using the above procedure for generating normal variates and the random number generator of the spreadsheet package. The set of random numbers to generate annual demand for air flights for one of the encounters with the model is indicated in this workbook. An alternative approach to generating random variates is to use purpose-built risk analysis software, such as the @RISK add-on package for Excel.

Table 9.8. *FlyByNight: NPV estimates for individual replicates and mean of replicates ($M)*

		Annual expenditure on advertising ($)			
Rep. 1		0	8,000	16,000	24,000
	0	1.55	1.50	1.79	1.90
Price discount ($/flight)	20	1.61	2.29	1.93	2.24
	40	1.86	2.15	2.24	2.20
	60	1.59	1.64	1.61	1.52
Rep. 2		0	8,000	16,000	24,000
	0	1.08	1.54	1.63	1.93
	20	1.85	2.08	2.23	2.22
	40	1.97	1.90	2.19	1.98
	60	1.51	1.62	1.60	1.58
Rep. 3		0	8,000	16,000	24,000
	0	1.81	1.64	1.90	2.09
	20	2.05	1.97	2.34	2.16
	40	2.18	2.16	2.25	2.00
	60	1.63	1.62	1.58	1.49
Rep. 4		0	8,000	16,000	24,000
	0	1.27	1.54	1.97	1.82
	20	2.09	2.00	1.87	1.94
	40	1.86	2.06	1.98	2.02
	60	1.61	1.66	1.59	1.48
Means		0	8,000	16,000	24,000
	0	1.43	1.55	1.82	1.93
	20	1.90	2.08	2.09	2.14
	40	1.97	2.07	2.16	2.05
	60	1.58	1.63	1.59	1.52

It is notable that there is considerable variation in performance among replicates. For example, NPV is highest for advertising expenditure of $16,000 a year in replicates 2 and 3 but for expenditure of only $8,000 in replicates 1 and 4. Averaging the NPV values over the four replicates removes some of the variation between treatments found when individual replicates are compared. The NPV values for the highest fare discount rate exhibit little variation, because the capacity constraint is reached early in the project life. The fact that the optimal policy is to spend $8,000 to $16,000 a year on advertising and to discount prices by $20 to $40 would be conveyed to management. But as well, some information could be conveyed on the extent to which the NPV for a particular policy varies among replicates, and the extent to which the optimal policy varies among replicates.

Choice of experimental design

In the simulation experiment producing the response data of Table 9.8, each level of each experimental factor (decision variable) was combined with each level of the other experimental factor, giving rise to what is known as a *full factorial* design. There are four replicates in this experiment, hence $4 \times 4 \times 4$, or 64, encounters with the model are required. If there is a greater number of decision variables, the number of treatments can become unmanageable. For example, if there are six factors, each at four levels, and four replicates, then the number of encounters with the model is 4^7, or over 16,000. In such cases, it may be necessary to resort to alternative experimental designs to reduce the overall number of treatments and associated computer time and amount of computer output. Alternative types of design include:

- *Incomplete factorial designs*: here some of the combinations of factor levels are omitted so as to reduce computing time.
- *Optimum-seeking designs*: in these designs, the factor levels are decided within the computer run (simulation experiment) rather than prior to it. As each treatment is evaluated, the response level is compared with that of previous treatments, and the next treatment is strategically placed so as to seek a higher NPV performance level. In this way, it is often possible to identify near optimal management policies with a relatively small number of treatments.

Advantages and disadvantages of simulation compared with other techniques in capital budgeting

In the sense that simulation is both a project evaluation and project planning tool, it may be compared with other approaches in both these areas. Various methods of incorporating risk in project evaluation models were discussed in earlier chapters, including the risk-adjusted discount rate, the certainty equivalent, and sensitivity and break-even analysis. Risk analysis, or risk simulation, is an alternative to these approaches which provides more information to the decision-maker. For example, compared to sensitivity analysis not only is the range of possible outcomes indicated, but also probabilities are attached to these ranges. Further, the variables are allowed to vary simultaneously, to yield a probability distribution of overall project performance. In this sense, a more comprehensive measure of risk is obtained. From the CDF, the decision-maker can gain an idea of the overall range over which project financial performance is likely to vary, and can read off probability estimates for various sub-ranges of project performance.

On the other hand, more information is required to carry out risk analysis, and the computer modelling can be more demanding (though availability of spreadsheet add-on software for risk analysis tends to overcome this problem). As mentioned above, interpretation of the computer output becomes more complex, and this may be a drawback for managers who are not familiar with this form of information. Perhaps a more serious concern is that of the additional effort estimating correlations between cash flow variables over time. In cases when these are high, this additional effort may be worthwhile to provide an improved picture of project risk.

As a project planning tool, simulation may be compared with other planning and resource allocation techniques, for example linear programming. Since this technique is not discussed until Chapters 11 and 12, little can be said about the comparison at this stage. Experience indicates that simulation has the advantage of providing much greater flexibility in modelling, in terms of being able to represent complex systems in a realistic way. The disadvantage is that often much greater model development and testing effort is required.

Concluding comments

This chapter has introduced some of the concepts and methods of the technique of computer simulation, as it is applied to capital budgeting decisions. Computer simulation relies on a total systems philosophy, which asserts that components of a system should not be viewed in isolation but rather in terms of the complex interrelationships and interactions among variables. An attempt is made to analyse carefully all the components of the system and their interrelationships, and to represent these in a simplified and abstract model. This model is used to conduct experiments in which the behaviour of the system is simulated under various assumptions or management policies.

This is a highly flexible technique, where the analyst has the ability to develop a complex model, using a spreadsheet package or computer programming language, and to use this model to mimic the behaviour of a real system over time. With the flexibility comes the requirement for testing of the model to ensure it is a realistic representation of the real system. In general, adopting the 'systems philosophy' tends to impose greater discipline on model development and testing.

While many simulation models are deterministic in nature, including random variates to represent the major sources of uncertainty in project performance generates additional information for the decision-maker concerning the level of uncertainty of project performance. Risk or venture analysis is sometimes used when probability distributions can be attached to the variables governing cash flows for a prospective investment. Simulation experiments with a stochastic model superimpose decision variables on this risk analysis, so that project planning as well as evaluation becomes possible.

Review questions

9.1 Explain the basic steps in risk analysis or Monte Carlo simulation.

9.2 Suppose the number of customers at a proposed restaurant is expected to follow a triangular distribution with pessimistic, modal and optimistic levels of 40, 60 and 100, respectively, on weeknights and 60, 90 and 140, respectively, on weekends. Using the random number generator on your computer spreadsheet, generate a sample of customer numbers for a two-week period.

9.3 Is risk analysis a complement or an alternative to sensitivity analysis? Discuss.

9.4 Consider the Delta Project example of Chapter 2. Suppose probability distributions have been estimated in terms of pessimistic, modal and optimistic values as in Table 8.2 of

Chapter 8. Develop a simulation model to derive a cumulative relative frequency curve for this project.

9.5 Develop a simulation model in an area in which you are familiar, along similar lines to that of Example 9.2. Incorporate two or more decision variables in this model, and conduct a deterministic experiment to identify the optimal management policy. Explain how this model could be made into a stochastic simulation model.

Appendix: Generation of random variates

A critical step in any stochastic simulation model is to generate values of random (stochastic) variables or 'variates'. In Example 9.1, annual demand was recognized as a random variable, and values were obtained by sampling from the demand distribution using random numbers. In simulation practice, variables are frequently recognized as stochastic. It has been said that a refinement in modelling introduces a need for stochasticity. A wide variety of forms of probability distributions have been recognized as reflecting the behaviour of particular random variables. Three examples will be presented here.

The starting point for producing (or 'generating' or 'sampling') values from any form of probability distribution is to use a random number from a known distribution. In practice, this is usually a number from a uniform distribution over the range 0 to 1, as illustrated below. 'Uniform' implies that the probabilities over the range are equal. Since the area under a probability function must be unity, the height of this curve is also 1. When a random number generator is called in a computer spreadsheet or programming language (e.g. using the statement '= rand()' in Excel) a number from this distribution is obtained. The procedure used on the computer is typically to divide a very large number by another large number, and to take the remainder as a fraction of the divisor (hence yielding a number between 0 and 1). As well, the remainder is multiplied by a third large number, and the product divided by the original divisor. By repeating this process, a series of random numbers can be generated. The numbers are sometimes called 'pseudo-random' because given the same three large numbers (and the same computer accuracy), the same series will always be produced.

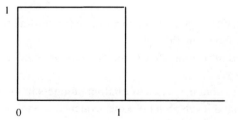

Generating uniform variates over a specified range

Perhaps the simplest form of *continuous* probability distribution used in simulation models is the uniform distribution, as illustrated in the following diagram. Here a is the smallest value and b the largest value that the variable is expected to take. Since the area under a

Table 9A.1. *Probability distribution of number of tickets sold*

Number of tickets sold	3,000	4,000	5,000	6,000
Probability	0.2	0.3	0.3	0.2

probability function must be unity, and the range of values of the variable is $b - a$, the height of the curve must be $1/(b - a)$.

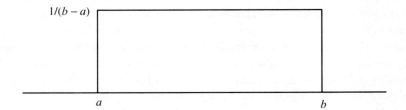

A value y from a uniform distribution can be generated by taking a random number r and applying the expression:

$$y = a + r(b - a)$$

i.e. the lower limit plus the random number times the distance between the upper and lower numbers. To obtain a series of values on the random variable, simply repeat this process a number of times (on your computer).

Generating values from an empirical probability distribution (discrete probability table)

Suppose it has been found from experience that a random variable (say airline ticket sales) can be described by the distribution shown in Table 9A.1.

This distribution may be converted into cumulative form, and random numbers attached to demand levels, as shown in Table 9A.2.

It is now a relatively simple task to obtain a series of random numbers in the range 0 to 1, and to use these to 'look up' demand levels. Suppose the sequence of random numbers 0.2765, 0.8346, 0.1207, 0.4533 and so on has been obtained. The first of these numbers falls in the range 0.2 to 0.4999, hence demand of 4,000 seats is generated. The second random number falls in the range 0.8 to 0.9999, corresponding to a demand of 6,000 seats. Proceeding in this way, a random series of demand levels is generated, in which the relative frequency in each demand class will approximate the estimated probability.

Table 9A.2. *Cumulative probability distribution of number of tickets sold, and ranges of random numbers*

Demand level (tickets sold)	Probability of this demand level or greater	Range of random number
3,000	0.2	0.0–0.1999
4,000	$0.2 + 0.3 = 0.5$	0.2–0.4999
5,000	$0.2 + 0.3 + 0.3 = 0.8$	0.5–0.7999
6,000	$0.2 + 0.3 + 0.3 + 0.2 = 1.0$	0.8–0.9999

Generating normal variates

The normal distribution is widely recognized in statistical methods as a commonly occurring or approximated distribution. Further, many distributions can be converted to approximately normal distributions by applying a suitable transformation, e.g. by taking of logarithms or square roots.

There are several methods for generating normal random variates (values from a normal distribution). The simplest is to take the sum of 12 random values from a uniform 0–1 distribution (e.g. a computer random number generator), subtract six, then multiply by the target standard deviation (500) and add the target mean (0), i.e. to derive:

$$y = \left(\Sigma^{12} r_i - 6 \right) 500,$$

where the twelve r_i values are observations from a uniform distribution with range 0 to 1 (e.g. from a spreadsheet random number generator). Since the expected value of a single uniform 0–1 random number is 0.5, the expected sum is 6, hence $(\Sigma^{12} r_i - 6)$ has an expected value of 0. Further, it can be shown that the variance of a single uniform 0–1 number is $1/12$, hence the sum of twelve *independent* numbers from this distribution has a variance of 1.0 (and this is unaffected by subtracting 6). The sum of twelve numbers from the same distribution will approach a normal distribution, especially if the distribution is not heavily skewed – this follows from the Central Limit Theorem. It follows that $(\Sigma^{12} r_i - 6)$ is approximately a standard normal or $N(0, 1)$ variable.

Any normal variable can be converted to a standard normal variable by subtracting the mean and dividing by the standard deviation. Conversely, a standard normal variate z can be converted to a value from a target normal distribution by multiplying by the standard deviation and adding the mean. That is, if y is a normal variable, and $z = (y - \mu)/\sigma$, then $y = z\sigma + \mu$ must be a normal variate from the target distribution.

Generating values from a triangular distribution

The triangular distribution is popular since it is often easy for people to make estimates of the most pessimistic, most likely (modal) and most optimistic values of a random variable.

For any variable, these values (denoted a, b and c, respectively) can be used to define a triangular distribution as in the following diagram.

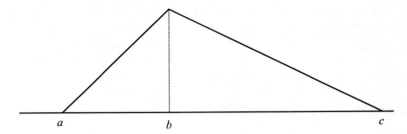

If a distance parameter d is defined as $d = (b - a)/(c - a)$, then, using a random number r, a value from this distribution y can be generated by applying the formulae:

For $r \leq d$ $y = a + \sqrt{r(c - a)(b - a)}$

For $r > d$ $y = c - \sqrt{(1 - r)(c - a)(c - b)}$

10 Case study in financial modelling and simulation of a forestry investment

Forestry projects are a form of capital investment with a particularly long time horizon, and as such present an interesting case of capital budgeting. In many countries, plantation forestry has traditionally been the domain of government agencies, e.g. the national Forestry Commission in the UK and the various state forestry services in Australia. Timber was considered to be a critical economic resource but the long production period meant that only governments had the long-term perspective and capacity to enter into forestry investments. This situation has changed markedly in the past fifty years, with probably the bulk of forestry investment in most countries being undertaken by private companies and individuals. The need for the establishment of plantations has been stimulated by decreasing supplies of timber from native forests through unsustainable logging practices, and the withdrawal of large areas from logging because of their being set aside as protected areas, particularly in tropical counties.

An integral component of investment in forestry is the need for financial information about the likely cash flows associated with the establishment, management and final harvest of a plantation. This chapter uses the development of a financial model for forestry investment as a case study of financial modelling. The financial evaluation of forestry projects poses many challenges and this chapter examines the key parameters for forestry appraisal and some of the problems faced by developers of financial models. The development of a model for the evaluation of forestry projects is outlined, following the step-by-step approach which was actually used by the model developers. This basic model framework is then used to illustrate how to undertake a sensitivity analysis and risk simulation.

Study objectives

After studying this chapter the reader should be able to:

- appreciate the need for estimates of forestry returns
- identify the problems encountered in developing a forestry financial model
- appreciate the difficulty in establishing cash flow estimates for long-lived forestry projects
- discuss the methods of allowing for risk in the evaluation of forestry projects

- develop a simple forestry model
- apply sensitivity and risk simulation to forestry projects.

Key parameters for forestry models

The most common cash outflows associated with forestry operations include establishment costs (e.g. land and site preparation such as clearing, fencing and preparing the soil; purchase of planting stock; planting, mulching and watering), weed control, fertilization, pruning and thinning to waste, and commercial harvesting. The major cash inflows come from the sale of commercial thinnings and the final harvest, and perhaps tree residues such as firewood. In some situations, revenues are also derived from non-wood forest products such as wild berries, mushrooms, honey and hunted game, all of which are made possible by the environment created by the forest.

Cash flow estimates of growing native timbers as a business enterprise will vary depending on a variety of factors, some of the more important of which are:

- Site characteristics (e.g. climate, soil, aspect)
- Species mixture
- Silvicultural system (e.g. planting density, weed control and pruning)
- Harvest age and harvest scheduling
- Final yield or mean annual increment of individual species
- Interactions between species in mixed-species plantations
- Stumpage price (affected by a number of supply and demand factors)
- Costs (land preparation, planting and establishment, maintenance, harvesting)
- Amount of government assistance
- Harvest rights (buffer zones, harvest on steep land, roading permission)
- Taxation regime (deductions allowable, treatment of harvest revenue)
- Allowance for non-wood benefits
- Discount rate

In principle, a spreadsheet could be devised which incorporates each of these factors. One factor that can have a major impact on eventual cash flows is timber yield from plantations. Yield is commonly expressed as 'mean annual increment' (MAI) which is the aggregate volume of harvestable timber produced in a year from the growth of trees in a plantation. It is usually expressed as cubic metres of timber produced per hectare per year. Other factors, such as site productivity, species mixture, harvest ages and timber prices (usually expressed as $ per cubic metre) may also strongly affect eventual cash flows.

As well as direct and measurable financial benefits, forests provide a variety of non-market services that are more difficult to quantify in terms of cash flows. These include: crop benefits (e.g. windbreaks, insect control); visual amenity, including wildlife viewing; environmental products and services (e.g. carbon sequestration, erosion control, wildlife habitats, biodiversity); soil protection and stream bank stability; improvements in water quality; and acting as a store of wealth for the owner. In some cases, forestry activities may impose non-wood costs such as the opportunity cost associated with conversion of cropland to forest, increased fire risk for adjacent properties, and crop damage from feral or native animals using the forest as a habitat. Non-wood benefits and costs may be private (i.e. borne by the company or individual) or social (public). Private non-wood benefits and costs are relevant to the private capital budgeting process and investment decision and hence should be included in a financial model for a forest company, though their estimation often presents considerable difficulty.

In general, social (or public) non-wood benefits and costs are not included in forestry financial analysis. However, they are sometimes included in more extended economic analysis, such as a governmental economic cost/benefit analysis. The importance of these non-market benefits is apparent when it is realized that trees are often grown to obtain these benefits with no intention of logging. Furthermore, in some cases the multiple uses of forests have a direct impact on management or harvesting practices and need to be incorporated in the financial analysis.

The choice of an appropriate discount rate is a contentious issue. For example, in Australia, the Queensland state forest agency (Department of Primary Industries), which is required to make a commercial return on plantations under its control, currently uses a rate of 7% when assessing their industrial softwood plantations. It is sometimes argued that a lower rate (such as 3% or 4%) is more appropriate for assessing forestry activities, to allow for the important non-wood benefits produced by growing trees. Whilst some government initiatives can be investigated by adjusting the discount rate in this manner, discount rate adjustment as a method of benefit incorporation is not usual in commercial projects generally. Forestry investments judged not viable at the commercial rate may become acceptable using a lower rate. This is particularly important for forestry investments under consideration by government, which must satisfy multiple objectives when establishing and managing forests.

Sources of variability in forestry investment performance

Plantation forestry is not a risk-free investment. A variety of factors contributes to the uncertainty in revenue generated. Most cash inflows from plantations occur with the final harvest of trees when they reach maturity, although some additional cash inflows may be generated from the sale of trees that are thinned as part of the normal management practices. Typically it is thirty or more years until plantations are ready for final harvest, hence long-term predictions of physical and financial performance have to be made. The main sources of variability in the financial performance of forestry are summarized in Table 10.1.

Most of the costs of establishing forestry are incurred in the first few years of plantation life and are reasonably predictable. Contract rates for the various plantation operations are generally well known. The cost of land preparation can vary to some extent, depending on site characteristics. Seedling costs should be known in advance, as well as initial fertilizer costs. Weed control practices and labour requirements can be predicted within a narrow range. Should unusually dry weather be experienced after planting, there may be additional costs in watering and replanting lost trees.

Table 10.1. *Sources of risk in farm forestry*

Risk category	Major sources
Risk of poor establishment	Dry weather, poor weed control
Production (timber yield) risk	Storm or cyclone Fire Pest (insect, disease) Unsuitable species or mixture for the site Collateral damage at harvest
Timber quality and product type risk	Inappropriate pruning and thinning regime Insect damage Product type and fashion changes in demand
Sovereign risk	Regulatory changes concerning machinery use and roading Changes in taxation arrangements Uncertain harvest rights and compensation
Market risk	Uncertain future timber prices

Plantation establishment success and growth rates are less predictable, particularly when species are used for which only limited experience has been gained. Even with the best of intentions, there is no guarantee that thinning and pruning will be carried out at optimal times. The type of product which will be produced is also uncertain: high-quality poles are likely to be more profitable than sawlogs due to earlier harvest and favourable prices.

With mixed-species plantings and differing harvest ages for different species, there is a risk of damaging retained trees at the various harvest stages. This is overcome to some extent by planting whole rows of individual species, but even then it presents problems in that growth within rows will not be uniform and it may be desired to retain some individual trees. Helicopter or balloon lifting at harvest is highly expensive, but financially viable for high-value trees.

Sovereign risk relates to changes by government in the rules relating to farm forestry. Over the life of a plantation, it is probable that there will be numerous changes in taxation arrangements. Also, environmental regulations have a tendency to become more stringent over time, and these could increase management and harvesting costs or even lead to the outlawing of harvest. The extent to which compensation will be provided for such limitations on property rights is quite unpredictable.

In general, these sources of risk do not pose a threat of total crop loss. Even with severe storm damage or fires, it is usually possible to salvage a considerable proportion of the timber.

In summary, a variety of sources of risk arise with respect to timber quantity, quality and price. Superimposed upon the various risk components, landholders often have little information about likely plantation performance and payoff. This is particularly the case for species which have not been widely used in industrial forestry, and for which little 'growth curve' data are available. In Australia, most industrial forestry relies on exotic conifers, and there is little information available about growth rates of native tree species, even though these species are increasingly being favoured by growers and markets. One native conifer species which is widely grown in plantations is hoop pine (*Araucaria cunninghamii*), but this is limited to favourable sites in terms of soil fertility and climate.

Some opportunity exists to minimize these risks. While plantation insurance is not normally taken out, the relatively non-perishable nature of the product allows harvesting to be timed for when timber prices are relatively high. Also, forestry may be conducted as a risk-reducing business diversification, with harvesting when other income is low. In fact, forestry is sometimes viewed as a form of superannuation or savings, with harvest when there is a particular need for cash, say to assist in intergenerational property transfer or to buy out the equity shares of siblings.

Methods of allowing for risk in the evaluation of forestry investments

It is typical of projects spanning a number of years into the future that costs and benefits (especially the latter) are estimated subject to a high degree of uncertainty. That is, the cash flow estimates are simply best-guess point values arising from (unknown) probability distributions of random cost and benefit variables. This is certainly the case with forestry investments. Some of the methods used to deal with investment risk in forestry are now outlined.

Taking conservative benefit estimates. This is probably the simplest and most widely adopted method of allowing for risk in forestry projects. However, benefits tend to be adjusted in a rather arbitrary manner, and the approach provides little information to the decision-maker about the extent of risk faced. The emphasis is on protection against 'downside risk', and no recognition is given to the possibility of payoffs above the single-point estimates. As a result, projects which are financially sound could easily be rejected.

Requiring a short payback period. Sometimes projects are favoured because they lead to recovery of expenditure in a relatively short period. The payback period in forestry is usually the number of years from plantation development to clearfell (i.e. when all remaining mature trees are harvested at the same time), since thinnings (even the later commercial thinnings) cannot be expected to recover plantation establishment costs. Favouring a short payback period usually means adopting a short rotation system such as production of pulpwood from eucalypts with harvest after about seven to ten years. A shortened payback period means that there is less uncertainty about whether a market will exist for the timber harvested and, associated with this, the stumpage price which will be achieved.

Including a risk margin in the discount rate. In Chapter 7 we discussed how the discount rate (k) has three components, i.e.:

$$k = r + u + a$$

where r is the risk free rate, u is the average risk premium for the firm and a is an additional risk factor to account for the difference between the average risk faced by the firm and the risk of the proposed project.

Adjusting a to reflect the additional riskiness of forestry would result in an appropriate discount rate commensurate with the risk of the investment project being considered.

Sensitivity analysis can be employed to measure the investment risk for forestry projects. Timber yield (progressively calculated through mean annual increment in total cubic metres) at a nominated harvest age and timber price are frequently subjected to sensitivity analysis. These parameters may be defined for a number of product lines from the same plantation, e.g. thinnings and final harvest, or poles, peelers (high-quality logs used to produce veneer) and sawlogs. It is also usual to test sensitivity with respect to the discount rate, or alternatively to plot the NPV profile with respect to discount rate.

Risk or venture analysis. This is sometimes carried out (e.g. Harrison, Herbohn and Emtage, 2001) to provide an overall estimate of project risk (this compares with sensitivity analysis which is usually designed to estimate risk with respect to one variable at a time). Risk analysis provides an estimate of the probability that a plantation will be profitable (positive NPV or required rate of return achieved), which can be particularly useful information for decision-makers. Commonly, Monte Carlo simulations are used here.

Problems faced in developing forestry financial models

There are numerous problems that may be encountered in developing financial models for assessing forestry investments. These problems usually arise from the particular nature of forestry – a long investment period over which world timber prices are likely to fluctuate, combined with the multiple-use nature of forests and the interaction of forestry with other ventures in a diversified firm.

Forestry is a long-term activity. Typically it takes twenty to thirty years for pine plantations to mature in temperate countries such as Australia and New Zealand. In Europe, rotations (the time taken from planting to final harvest of plantations) are typically fifty to eighty years for pines and up to two hundred years for broad-leaf species such as English oak. At the opposite end of the scale are some fast-growing hardwoods that can be harvested after only eight to ten years in some tropical countries. The long investment period typical of forestry projects provides a number of challenges when developing financial models. In particular, timber prices are likely to fluctuate over this period and it is difficult to predict the price that will be obtained for timber when it is harvested. The problems with forecasting timber prices thus pose a challenge in estimating cash inflows as part of the financial modelling process. Timber prices may increase over time in real terms, i.e. the price increase may be greater than the rate of inflation. For example, an annual increase in the real price of timber of 1.3% has been suggested (Russell *et al.*, 1993). Furthermore, there is a risk that technological change or fashion change could result in weak demand for some timber types (e.g. satellite communications reducing demand for poles for phonelines, consumer preferences for wood colour changing over time). Regulatory change in response to changing community attitudes could increase costs and restrict areas which can be harvested.

The long time required for trees to grow also means that there is sometimes a lack of biological growth data that can be used to predict growth rates (and hence timber yield). Timber yield and harvest timing are critical variables in forestry financial models. The lack of such data is most critical when new (non-traditional) species for which there is no past history of cultivation are being used in plantations. As seen in Chapter 4, the Delphi and other group forecasting methods can be used to develop estimates of growth and harvest ages which can be used in financial models.

The multiple-use nature of forests has also been recognized in the management of large industrial and government plantation estates. These management practices can have direct impact on the financial performance of the investment and thus should be considered in the appraisal process. For example in Finland, when a plantation estate is harvested, a number of habitat trees must be retained. The failure to harvest these trees directly reduces cash inflows to the investor. Similarly in the United Kingdom, there is recognition that native Scots pine and native broad-leaf species provide greater non-timber benefits than the exotic Sitka spruce. The result has been the harvesting of Sitka spruce plantations earlier than their optimal rotation age and their subsequent replacement with plantations of Scots pine and broad-leaf species. In many countries there are also large incentives provided to establish plantations, ranging from tax benefits to direct cash payments. Where they exist, these also need to be incorporated in the appraisal.

As with any appraisal of a capital project, it is necessary to gain an understanding of the social environment in which the project is being undertaken. In the case of a forestry investment, the way in which a forest is managed, and the ultimate quantity of timber which can be harvested, can be greatly affected by the increasing need for forests to be managed for multiple uses.

Developing a financial model: a step-by-step approach

As with any project appraisal, undertaking a financial analysis of a forestry project can be broken down into a number of individual and relatively simple steps:

(1) Identify the forestry system to be adopted – for example, the type of trees to be planted and at what density, when they will be pruned, the types of product intended (e.g. sawlogs, veneer logs, pulpwood, poles, or some combination of these) and when harvesting is likely to occur.
(2) Estimate the likely cash outflows.
(3) Estimate the cash inflows from harvest.
(4) Develop the financial model and estimate financial performance measures.
(5) Evaluate investment risk.

These steps will now be illustrated with respect to a case study.

Example 10.1. Flores Venture Capital Ltd forestry project

Example 10.1 (see Box 1 for the relevant background) will be used as a case study to illustrate the development of a financial model to assess investment in establishment of a large plantation estate.

Box 1.   Background to the case study forestry project

Flores Venture Capital Ltd (FVC Ltd) is considering diversifying its operations into forestry. It has been presented with a proposal involving the establishment of a plantation estate of 1,000 ha in an area with suitably high rainfall and soil quality. To encourage investment in the region, a local government has offered the required land rent-free for the period of the project on the condition that native species are used rather than an exotic pine. The company has decided to establish a mixed species (eucalypt and rainforest species) plantation. The finance department of FVC Ltd has indicated that a rate of return of 7% is required for the project.

Step 1: Identifying the forestry system

In Chapter 4 it was demonstrated how the Delphi method could be used to develop estimates of key parameters. The example used was of a forestry project involving the use of two species for which little quantitative growth and harvest age data existed. In this section we demonstrate how a forestry financial evaluation can be undertaken using similar data. The example in Chapter 4 was based on a real-life Delphi survey and the associated financial analysis was quite complicated; the basic information from that example will be used here, but will be simplified in a number of ways. The forestry system to be adopted is outlined in Box 2.

Box 2.   Identification of the FVC Ltd forestry system

FVC Ltd has engaged a forestry consulting company to provide technical advice on the project. Because there was no past experience in growing native species in the region, the consulting company has used the Delphi method to develop an appropriate silviculture (tree-growing) system. Based on the results of their investigation, it is recommended that trees be planted at a density of 660 stems per hectare. It is expected that extensive weed control will need to be undertaken in the first year, with further weed control required in the second and third years. Pruning of the trees to ensure good form will be required in years 2, 4 and 6. A number of experts involved in the Delphi survey indicated that the amount of pruning required is difficult to estimate because no one knows how much branching will occur on the sites and it could range from minimal to requiring high labour inputs. The consultants explain that pruning is crucial because it ensures that the trees produce a straight, knot-free log for which high prices can be obtained. It was also recommended that each pruning event should be certificated by an external party because this will increase the likelihood of being able to obtain a premium price for knot-free wood. A non-commercial thin is required at year 8, at which time 320 trees per hectare will be removed.

The first revenue from the plantation will come when a commercial thinning occurs at the end of year 17, at which time about eighty-five trees will be harvested. At year 26, eighty-five further trees will be cut and sold for telephone and electricity poles. The best eighty-five trees will be left to grow until year 34, when about half (forty-two) will be cut for sawlogs. The remaining trees will be allowed to grow to year 60, when they will be harvested and sold as high-quality veneer logs.

From the information about the plantation system contained in Box 2, the major cash outflow and inflow categories have been identified, and these are listed in Table 10.2.

Table 10.2. *FVC Ltd. forestry project: main cash categories and predicted timing*

Cash flow category	Nature of cash flow	Timing (year)
1. Establishment (capital) costs	Planning and design	0
	Incidental clearing	0
	Site preparation and cultivation	0
	Cover crop establishment	0
	Pre-plant weed control	0
	Cost of plants	0
	Planting and refilling	0
	Fertilizer	0
	Fencing	0
2. Maintenance costs	Post-plant weed control (1)	1
	Post-plant weed control (2)	2
	Post-plant weed control (3)	3
	First prune (plus certification)	2
	Second prune (plus certification)	4
	Third prune (plus certification)	6
	Thinning – non-commercial	8
3. Annual costs	Protection and management	
	Land rental (if applicable)	
4. Cash Inflows	Thinning revenue	18
	Revenue from poles	26
	Revenue from first harvest	34
	Revenue from second harvest	60

Table 10.3. *FVC Ltd. forestry project: cash outflows and timing associated with a two-species plantation*

Cash outflow category	Nature of cash outflow	Timing (year)	Cost ($/ha)
1. Establishment costs	Planning and design	0	74
	Incidental clearing	0	158
	Site preparation and cultivation	0	265
	Cover crop establishment	0	88
	Pre-plant weed control	0	92
	Cost of plants	0	450
	Planting and refilling	0	645
	Post-plant weed control	0	540
	Fertilizer	0	83
	Fencing	0	560
	Sub-total		2,955
2. Maintenance costs	Post-plant weed control (1)	1	1,300
	Post-plant weed control (2)	2	800
	Post-plant weed control (3)	3	200
	First prune (plus certification)	2	600
	Second prune (plus certification)	4	600
	Third prune (plus certification)	6	600
	Thinning – non-commercial	8	500
3. Annual costs	Protection and management		40
	Land rental		0

Step 2: Estimating cash outflows

Estimates are now made of the likely amount of the cash outflows associated with the categories of Table 10.2. This has drawn on information from a number of sources, e.g. quotes sought for the cost of establishing the plantation; pruning costs based on past experience. Table 10.3 provides the financial estimates of each of these activities provided by the consultant. For convenience, all estimates are expressed on a per hectare basis.

Step 3: Estimating cash inflows

Table 10.4 presents the estimated cash inflows. Cash inflows arise from the harvest of the trees. Harvest revenue is determined by the volume of timber produced (typically measured in cubic metres) multiplied by the stumpage price paid per cubic metre. For example, if a commercial thinning occurs at year 17 (as in the current example) and yields 170 m^3 of timber with an estimated sale (stumpage) price of $30/m^3, this will result in estimated cash inflows of $5,100 per hectare.

Estimates of cash inflows are particularly difficult to make for forestry investments. The long production cycle means that it is difficult to estimate what stumpage prices will be many years in the future. In rare cases, long-term supply contracts may be signed with a

Table 10.4. *Estimated cash inflows for 1,000 ha plantation*

Activity resulting in cash inflow	Year of harvest	No. stems/ha	Yield (m³/ha)	Stumpage ($/m³)	Revenue ($'000)
First thinning	17	170	170	30	5,100
Second thinning (poles)	26	85	—	148 per pole	12,580
First harvest (sawlogs)	34	42	100	200	20,000
Second harvest (sawlogs/veneer logs)	60	43	270	300	81,000

guaranteed sale price. Even in these circumstances the uncertainty associated with harvest volumes means there is still considerable uncertainty when estimating cash inflows from harvests. Some revenues may be obtained from commercial thinnings part way through the production cycle, though stumpage price is usually low because of the small diameter of these trees and the low quality of the timber. Typically there is no market for thinnings of a very young age, in which case the thinning process results in a net cash outflow. This is the case in year 8 of the current example where a non-commercial thin was required costing an estimated $500.

The largest cash inflows from plantations will come at the end of the production cycle. In the current example, final harvest revenue is obtained after sixty years, although another significant harvest occurs at thirty-four years. For this case study, estimates of harvest volumes and timing were collected as part of the Delphi survey undertaken by the consultants. These estimates, combined with estimates of future timber prices (in nominal dollars and also collected as part of the survey) can be used to estimate cash inflows (Table 10.4). The expert panel used in the Delphi survey thought high-quality sawlogs of a native hardwood produced at year 34 would achieve a price of $200/m³. Furthermore, it was thought that it was likely that logs harvested at year 60 would be suitable for the production of veneer, and attract a premium of 50% above the price of high-quality sawlogs.

Step 4: Developing the financial model

Workbook 10.1

The Excel spreadsheet program provides a convenient platform for financial analysis with the object of calculating key financial parameters such as NPV and IRR. Such a spreadsheet is provided in Workbook 10.1.

The tax component of the analysis has been simplified. It is assumed that all cash outflows are fully allowable as deductions in the year that they are paid. In most years there is no revenue from the plantation against which to offset these tax losses. It is, however, assumed that FVC Ltd will be able to claim these losses against income generated from other operations. As such, these losses produce a tax benefit equivalent to the amount of the net cash outflows multiplied by the prevailing tax rate (30%). The results of this analysis from Workbook 10.1 are provided in Table 10.5.

Table 10.5. *NPV calculations for FVC Ltd forestry project ($'000)*

Cash flow item	Timing of cash flow (end of year)																
	0	1	2	3	4	5	6	7	8	9–16	17	18–25	26	27–33	34	35–59	60
1. Establishment costs (capital costs)	−2955																
2. Operating costs																	
Post-plant weed control		−1300	−800	−200													
First prune (plus certification)			−600														
Second prune (plus certification)					−600												
Third prune (plus certification)							−600										
Thinning (non-commercial)									−500								
Annual protection and management		−40	−40	−40	−40	−40	−40	−40	−40	−40	−40	−40	−40	−40	−40	−40	−40
Total operating expenses		−1340	−1440	−240	−640	−40	−640	−40	−540	−40	−40	−40	−40	−40	−40	−40	−40
3. Operating revenue																	
Thinning revenue 1 (year 17)											5,100						
Thinning revenue 2 (year 26)													12,580				
Harvest revenue 1 (year 34)															20,000		
Harvest revenue 2 (year 60)																	81,000
Total operating revenue	0	0	0	0	0	0	0	0	0	0	5,100	0	12,580	0	20,000	0	81,000
Tax paid or tax benefit (30%)	886.5	402	432	72	192	12	192	12	162	12	−1,518	12	−3,762	12	−5,988	12	−24,288
Net cash flows (Operating revenue − Capital outlays − Operating costs)	−2,068.5	−938	−1,008	−168	−448	−28	−448	−28	−378	−28	3452	−28	8,778	−28	13,972	−28	56,672
Net present value of cash flows at discount rate specified	−58.214																
Internal rate of return	6.96%																

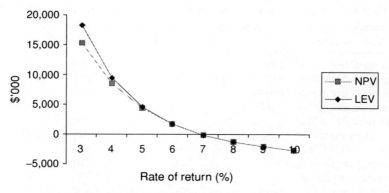

Figure 10.1. NPV and LEV profiles of FVC Ltd forestry investment.

Step 5: Undertake a sensitivity analysis

Once the financial model has been set up, it is a simple task to examine the effect of changes in parameter levels on the project performance criteria. This includes analysis with respect to the required rate of return and with respect to parameters which are not under the control of FVC Ltd.

The Excel Table function has been used to derive NPV values for a range of discount rates, and these have been plotted in Figure 10.1. Note that the IRR is the discount rate for which the net present value is zero, i.e. the point where the curve crosses the *x*-axis.

This analysis suggests that the project is marginal in terms of financial acceptability. At the rate of return of 7% required by management, the NPV for the project is −$58,214, and the IRR is just below 7% (6.96%). Figure 10.1 also presents the *land expectation value* (LEV) or *site value* for the project, which was defined in Chapter 5. This is the NPV for an infinite sequence of identical rotations, and is useful for comparing projects of unequal duration. The LEV will be considerably higher than the NPV for short rotations, but for long rotations (such as is the case with the investment under consideration by FVC Ltd) LEV will differ little from the NPV.

Parameters outside the control of FVC Ltd. which are likely to have most effect on NPV have been identified, and pessimistic, most likely and optimistic levels identified for each, as in Table 10.6.

The spreadsheet used in the calculation of NPV and IRR for the most likely values in Step 4 has been used to recalculate these values for the optimistic and pessimistic values for each of the parameters of Table 10.6.

Only one variable is changed at a time, while the other variables are held at their most likely values. The Scenario function within Excel allows multiple scenarios to be developed and the results reported in a table in a separate spreadsheet. This function has been used in Workbook 10.1 to undertake the sensitivity analysis, results of which are reported in Table 10.7.

The results of the sensitivity analysis could now be used by FVC Ltd to guide it in which variables it may need to investigate further. From the sensitivity analysis it is clear that the

Table 10.6. *FVC Ltd forestry project: parameters selected for sensitivity analysis*

Uncontrollable variable	Pessimistic	Most likely	Optimistic
Stumpage price, first thinning ($/m³)	25	30	35
Stumpage price, poles ($/pole)	110	148	200
Stumpage price, first harvest ($/m³)	100	200	300
Stumpage price, second harvest ($/m³)	150	300	450
Yield, first thinning (m³/ha)	120	170	190
Yield, poles (number/ha)	70	85	85
Yield, first harvest (m³/ha)	80	100	150
Yield, second harvest (m³/ha)	220	270	350
Establishment costs ($/ha)	3,455	2,955	2,655
Post-plant weed control, year 1 ($/ha)	1,800	1,300	1,000
Post-plant weed control, year 2 ($/ha)	1,100	800	600
Post-plant weed control, year 3 ($/ha)	400	200	0
Pruning, years 2, 4, 6 ($/ha)	1,000	600	500
Thinning costs, year 8 ($/ha)	800	500	400

> Workbook
> 10.1

Table 10.7. *NPVs for FVC Ltd forestry investment ($'000)*

Parameter	Pessimistic estimate	Optimistic estimate	Range	Rank
Stumpage price, first thinning ($/m³)	−247	130	377	10
Stumpage price, poles ($/pole)	−448	475	922	4
Stumpage price, first harvest ($/m³)	−760	643	1,403	1
Stumpage price, second harvest ($/m³)	−547	431	978	3
Yield, first thinning (m³)	−391	75	465	9
Yield, poles (number)	−326	−58	268	12
Yield, first harvest (m³)	−339	643	982	2
Yield, second harvest (m³)	−239	232	471	8
Establishment costs ($)	−408	152	560	6
Post-plant weed control, year 1 ($)	−385	138	523	7
Post-plant weed control, year 2 ($)	−242	64	306	11
Post-plant weed control, year 3 ($)	−172	56	229	13
Pruning, years 2, 4, 6 ($)	−703	103	806	5
Thinning costs, year 8 ($)	−180	−17	163	14

stumpage prices for the first and second harvests and for the poles, along with the yield for the first harvest are the variables that have the greatest effect on the net present value of the project. After identifying the variables causing most impact on NPV, FVC Ltd may investigate ways to reduce their impact, such as through investing further resources into developing more accurate yield predictions or investigating further projections of future timber prices. It may also use the existing data to undertake an investigation of the three variables for a greater number of values within the range from pessimistic to optimistic.

Comparing forestry projects of different harvest rotations

In Example 10.1, NPV was the appropriate criterion for FVC Ltd to judge whether it should invest in establishing 1,000 ha of trees. The project involved a decision either to plant the trees on a sixty-year rotation or not to proceed. This analysis indicated that the project was marginal, with the NPV being negative but with an IRR almost equal to the required rate of return. NPV does, however, have its limitations when comparing alternative forestry investments or comparing forestry with other uses of the land that have different project lives. In such cases, LEV is the appropriate means by which to compare projects.

Example 10.2. FVC Ltd: comparison of one-stage and two-stage harvest options

Consider an extension of the scenario introduced in the previous example. The council offering FVC Ltd free use of the 1000 ha for the plantation project considers that there is great potential for forest-based recreation activities in the plantations after about thirty years. By this stage the remaining trees will be quite large and be somewhat irregularly spaced because of past thinning and harvesting patterns. It is also likely that a diverse understorey of native plants and shrubs will have grown under the remaining trees, which will attract many birds and other native wildlife. For this reason, a two-stage harvest at years 34 and 60 is the preferred harvesting option of the council, although under the terms of the agreement this cannot be enforced. What are the alternative NPVs for FVC Ltd for a preliminary harvest at year 34 and final harvest at year 60; or for all the trees to be harvested at year 34.

> Workbook
> 10.2

The material in Example 10.2 describes two mutually exclusive projects, one involving a two-stage harvest (at years 34 and 60) and the other a one-stage harvest with all the trees being harvested at year 34. The first scenario has already been analysed in Example 10.1. The NPV coming from that analysis is −$58,214. The spreadsheet used in Example 10.1 can be easily modified to analyse Example 10.2 by simply adjusting the amount of timber to be harvested at year 34 (i.e. a doubling) and deleting the income stream from the subsequent harvest at year 60 (see Workbook 10.2). The most likely values used in Example 10.1 were also used in this second analysis. The results of this new cash flow structure are summarized in Table 10.8. The results clearly indicate that it is better for FVC Ltd to harvest completely at year 34 as the LEV is positive at $481,000, or in other words, there is a financial cost in delaying harvest, the LEV of the project decreasing by some $540,000 (i.e. −$59,000 −$481,000). Thus FVC Ltd would choose to harvest the plantations at year 34 as this would result in the higher LEV. Another option would be if the council decided that the recreation and wildlife benefits provided by delaying the harvest were so great that they were willing

Table 10.8. *Impact of harvesting all trees at year 34 compared with the two-stage harvest in Example 10.1*

Scenario	NPV ($'000)	LEV ($'000)	IRR (%)
Two-stage harvest, with half the trees harvested at year 34 and remaining trees at year 60	−58	−59	7.0
One-stage harvest with all trees harvested at year 34	433	481	7.3

to compensate FVC Ltd. for delaying the harvest and granting access to the sites. In this case, FVC Ltd would be indifferent from a financial perspective if it received $540,000 as an upfront cash payment from the council to alter the harvest strategy to include a two-stage harvest.

Note also that the difference between NPV and LEV is more marked in the shorter rotation option of thirty-four years. This illustrates the previous observation that LEV will be considerably higher than NPV for short rotations, but will differ little from NPV for long rotations.

Risk analysis or Monte Carlo analysis

As discussed in Chapter 9, *risk analysis* is an extension of DCF analysis in which the variability of performance of a project is estimated by fitting probability distributions to risky cash flow parameters, and subsequently estimating the probability distributions of performance criteria. Random observations may be drawn from a variety of probability distributions, e.g. the normal, triangular, beta, exponential and Poisson distributions. In the following example, the triangular distribution is used.

Example 10.3. Simulation analysis of FVC Ltd forestry project

The estimates of pessimistic, most likely and optimistic values of the sensitive variables given in Table 10.6 are used to define a triangular distribution for a simulation analysis.

> Workbook
> 10.3

Workbook 10.3 has been set up to undertake the simulation analysis. This spreadsheet is a modified version of the spreadsheet used for Example 10.1, in which the 'most likely' values for the uncontrollable variables have been replaced by values for these variables drawn randomly from a triangular distribution defined at the lower and upper limits by the pessimistic and optimistic values in Table 10.6. The following steps are used to undertake a simulation analysis involving 500 replicates.

For each of the 500 replicates, parameter values are generated for the relevant years of the project life. Each replicate sets up one static picture of the project over its whole

Table 10.9. *Calculation of random values used in NPV calculations*

Variable	Pessimistic (a)	Modal (b)	Optimistic (c)	Random number	Value of random variate
Stumpage price, first thinning ($/m^3)	25	30	35	0.35161	29
Stumpage price, poles ($/pole)	110	148	200	0.050347	123
Stumpage price, first harvest ($/m^3)	100	200	300	0.66567	218
Stumpage price, second harvest ($/m^3)	150	300	450	0.649968	324
Yield, first thinning (m^3)	120	170	190	0.3696	156
Yield, poles (number)	70	85	85	0.052963	73
Yield, first harvest (m^3)	80	100	150	0.752005	121
Yield, second harvest (m^3)	220	270	350	0.546859	281
Establishment costs ($)	3,455	2,955	2,655	0.911398	3,309
Post-plant weed control, year 1 ($)	1,800	1,300	1,000	0.632912	1,503
Post-plant weed control, year 2 ($)	1,100	800	600	0.036198	674
Post-plant weed control, year 3 ($)	400	200	0	0.345005	166
Pruning, years 2, 4, 6 ($)	1,000	600	500	0.712976	878
Thinning costs, year 8 ($)	800	500	400	0.505055	646
Net present value					8,796

life-span; each year of the life-span is not separately replicated. The random values used in the simulation are derived in exactly the same way as in the example in Chapter 9. An example of the results of the calculation of one set of random values is presented in Table 10.9. The figures seen in Workbook 10.3 are not the same as the results shown in Table 10.9, because every time a simulation is run, different random numbers are generated. Even when someone uses the same Workbook 10.3 on one of their computers (which is different to what we used) the resulting output may not be the same because of the different random numbers used in the analysis. This process is repeated 500 times with a new random number being generated for each replicate, which in turn produces a new random value for each of the variables.

A macro has been written and used in Workbook 10.3 to automate this process. This macro generates a series of random numbers, which are then used to calculate the values of each of the variables (highlighted in blue in the spreadsheet). The NPV returned for the set of values of the variables listed in Table 10.8 is $8,796,000. The cells containing these variables are referenced in the calculation of NPV. In the spreadsheet, the cells referenced back to the table of variables are highlighted in yellow. Thus each set of values of the variables is used to calculate a unique NPV. This NPV is then copied and pasted in an output row as a value. Another set of random numbers is then generated and the process

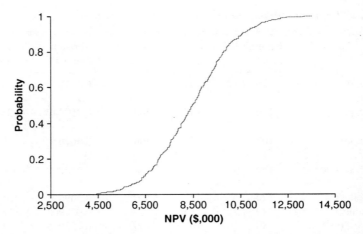

Figure 10.2. Cumulative relative frequency distribution for forestry investment for FVC Ltd.

is repeated, these steps being carried out 500 times. The macro then sorts the values in ascending order and plots them as a cumulative distribution function, which is shown in Figure 10.2.

The CDF curve in Figure 10.2 provides a good deal of information about the likely financial performance of the project. The estimated probability of various ranges of performance levels can be read from this graph. For example the downside risk of the project can be expressed as the likelihood of achieving an NPV of less than a specified amount. For the forestry investment project, it would appear that there is a probability of less than 5% that the project will return a payoff of $5.9 million or less. The upside risk of the project can be expressed as a likelihood of achieving a result greater than a specified amount. For example, there is a likelihood of less than 5% (i.e. those amounts falling in the area of the curve beyond 0.95 on the x-axis) that the project will achieve an NPV of more than $11.3 million. The median payoff (middle of the distribution, or probability of 0.5) appears to be about $8.48 million. The symmetrical shape of the CDF (similar slopes at lower and upper ends) suggests the mean payoff will be similar to the median value; the mean as computed in Workbook 10.3 is, in fact, $8.50 million. It should be noted that this mean NPV is significantly larger than the NPV for the project calculated in Workbook 10.1. This is because a risk-free discount rate of 4% has been used in Workbook 10.3 while a risk-adjusted discount rate of 7% was used in Workbook 10.1. The long time-span over which cash flows occur means that a lower (higher) discount rate will result in a significant increase (decrease) in NPV. This is illustrated in Figure 10.1.

Concluding comments

This chapter has presented a case study of the financial evaluation of a forestry project, in which a long list of sources of uncertainty in cash flows can be identified. Investment risk has been assessed using both sensitivity analysis and risk analysis.

Risk analysis has been demonstrated to provide greater information about investment risk for the decision-maker, integrating the measures of risk from various sources in the estimation of the probability distribution of net present value. The triangular distribution has been used as a relatively simple form of probability distribution for cash flow variables.

The choice of discount rate can present problems in the evaluation of forestry investments. A particular feature of forestry, particularly government-owned and small-scale plantations, is management for a variety of objectives, including non-wood benefits. It is sometimes argued that indirect allowance can be made for multiple use of forestry by downward adjustment of the discount rate. However, this is a rather arbitrary and unsystematic method, and inferior to estimation of the private non-wood benefits to the forest-owner or social non-wood benefits in the case of government-owned plantations.

While the analysis has been couched in terms of a forestry investment, the approach is relevant to other forms of long-term investment. Notably, the risk analysis has been performed using the capabilities of the Excel spreadsheet program, with macros for generation of random variates, rather than requiring special-purpose risk analysis software such as @RISK or Insight.

Review questions

10.1 What are some of the difficulties in establishing cash flow estimates for long-lived forestry projects?

10.2 What methods are available to allow for risk in the evaluation of forestry projects? Which of these methods are preferred?

10.3 In Example 10.1, the land used for the plantations was made available by a local council for FVC Ltd to use at no cost (see Box 1). Assume now that FVC Ltd had to pay rental on the land from the council at the rate of 4% of the land value per annum.

(a) Using Workbook 10.1, recompute the NPV assuming that FVC Ltd had to pay an annual land rental and that the land value on average was $2,000 per ha.

(b) What effect has payment had on IRR?

(c) Using the Goal Seek function of Excel, calculate the final stumpage price that FVC Ltd must receive in order to achieve an NPV of 0.

11 Resource constraints and linear programming

So far we have assumed that the firm's market value or the shareholders' wealth is maximized by accepting *every* investment project that has a positive NPV. In the real world, however, there are limitations on the investment programme that prevent the firm from undertaking all such projects. There may, for example, be a limit on the amount of funds available for financing investment projects. This is often called *capital rationing*.

Clearly, capital rationing does exist in the real world. If projects have positive NPVs and both management and financiers are happy with the NPV estimates, then, in an efficient capital market, one would expect funds to be available for *all* positive NPV projects. Under these circumstances, capital rationing is irrational. Nevertheless, two types of capital rationing are often encountered. Sometimes, management imposes capital expenditure limits; this is called *soft capital rationing*. Sometimes, a firm is unable to raise funds to undertake all positive NPV projects, and this is referred to as *hard capital rationing*. Various reasons have been advanced as to why hard or soft capital rationing might exist (Weingartner, 1977).

Apparently viable projects can also be rejected because firms face various other resource constraints, such as the availability of particular types of labour and raw material. Government regulations or marketing strategies may also impose restrictions.

Specific methods such as the profitability index, which involve 'juggling' positive NPV project expenditures to ensure that total combined NPV is maximized from the investment decision, can handle decisions associated with a single constraint. However, when two or more constraints are present, mathematical programming techniques such as linear programming become very handy.

Linear programming (LP) is a mathematical technique for choosing the *optimal combination* from a set of alternatives when the decision-maker has to operate within certain limitations or *constraints*. For example, a firm considering output levels for two products may wish to find out the product mix which maximizes the total dollar contribution to the firm's cash flow subject to particular constraints. These constraints may be imposed by limited supplies of capital and raw materials. There may be other requirements which necessitate the firm producing a minimum number of units of a given product, e.g. to satisfy the demand from certain customer groups or to satisfy the firm's minimum production agreements with, say, the government.

The optimal combination depends on the *objective* and the *constraints*. An objective is something management wishes to achieve, for example to maximize the total cash flow or NPV, or to minimize the total cost. The variables in the objective function are referred to as *decision variables*. Their values will be determined by the model as the *optimal solution*. The optimal solution will be obtained from maximizing (or minimizing) the objective given the limitations set by the constraints.

The objective function and constraints are stated in terms of a set of linear equations, defined in terms of decision variables and input parameters. The input parameters are values specified by the decision-maker to describe the characteristics of the system. For example, the dollar contributions per unit of each product to total cash flow can be the input parameters of the objective function. Technical (or input-output) coefficients(e.g. the amount of labour hours or the amount of each raw material required to produce one unit of each product) and the resource supply levels (sometimes called right-hand sides) can be the input parameters of the constraints.

In developing and applying an LP model for problem-solving or decision support, a number of steps are involved. They are:

(1) *Formulation of the problem.* This involves the translation of relevant information into the LP framework. We need to specify input parameters and decision variables, the objective function, and all relevant constraints.

(2) *Solving the problem.* Simple two-variable problems can be solved graphically. The graphical method is very good for understanding the LP concept and gaining an insight into what is involved in the solution procedure. Whenever there are more than two decision variables, or if there are numerous constraint equations, the graphical method is of limited value. These problems can be solved using suitable LP software packages. We use Excel Solver.

(3) *Interpretation of the optimal solution.* It is necessary to understand what the optimal solution values mean for decision-making. The optimal solution also provides *shadow prices*. They show the maximum amount that the decision-maker should be willing to pay to acquire one additional unit of each resource or to have a minimum requirement relaxed by one unit that is constrained in the problem. These are important for decision-making.

(4) *Performing sensitivity analysis.* A sensitivity analysis on the optimal solution can be performed to determine ranges for each of the input parameters wherein the optimal solution remains valid. Shadow prices remain valid only within the specific range of input parameters. Sensitivity analysis can suggest these ranges.

This chapter will illustrate and discuss LP concepts, problem formulation, graphical and computer solution approaches, and interpretation of the optimal solution, with worked examples. Since the shadow prices provided in the optimal solution are important for decision support, they are discussed in the decision support context. The sensitivity analysis provides additional information for decision-makers.

We begin with a simple LP resource allocation problem, where the decision is to choose the product mix which will maximize the total cash flow subject to two resource constraints and one minimum production requirement constraint. Next, a decision problem is discussed where the decision is to allocate capital between two investment divisions of a firm to maximize the total NPV subject to the limited investment opportunities and a by-product requirement. Application of LP to project choice (or project portfolio selection) is then discussed using a two-period capital rationing model. These examples will familiarize the reader with the concept and application of the LP technique. With that familiarity, the assumptions underlying the LP technique and its limitations will be reviewed and more advanced LP concepts and methods discussed in Chapter 12.

Study objectives

After studying this chapter the reader should be able to:

- understand the general purpose and structure of linear programming models
- formulate an LP problem from relevant information
- solve an LP problem on a computer, i.e. obtain the optimal solution
- interpret the optimal solution and associated shadow prices
- determine the combination of projects which maximizes the total NPV for the firm in relatively simple portfolio selection situations.

LP with two decision variables and three constraints

Let us begin with a simple problem in which a firm must deal with two resource constraints and a minimum contractual requirement, while seeking to maximize total dollar contribution.

Example 11.1. Roclap: product mix problem

Roclap Inc. manufactures two products, the production levels of which will be referred to as x_1 and x_2. It has been estimated that contribution margins per unit of product 1 and product 2 (to the firm's cash flow) are \$3.00 and \$4.50, respectively. Roclap wants to maximize the total dollar contribution, but the production is limited by certain constraints. The availability of raw material, used for the production of the two output lines, is limited to 80 tonnes. The firm uses 0.05 tonnes of raw material to produce one unit of product 1 and 0.1 tonnes for one unit of product 2. Products 1 and 2 require one kilogram of a particular ingredient for each single unit of output. The maximum amount of this ingredient available is 1,000 kilograms. Roclap is bound by a legal contract with the government to produce a minimum of 300 units of product 2. The firm wishes to find out the product mix which maximizes the total dollar contribution subject to these constraints.

This problem can easily be solved using LP. The LP formulation is as follows:

maximize total dollar contribution $\qquad Z = 3.00x_1 + 4.50x_2$

subject to:

availability of raw material $0.05x_1 + 0.1x_2 \leq 80$

availability of ingredient $1x_1 + 1x_2 \leq 1{,}000$

minimum contractual requirement $x_2 \geq 300$

non-negativity condition $x_1, x_2 \geq 0$

The optimal solution to this simple two-variable problem can be arrived at graphically or using an LP software package such as Excel Solver. The graphical solution will be explained first.

Graphical solution to the product mix problem

Figure 11.1 presents Roclap's decision problem in graphical form. The vertical axis represents the number of units of product 1 (i.e. x_1) and the horizontal axis represents the number of units of product 2 (i.e. x_2). Each of the three constraints and the non-negativity conditions can be entered as straight lines. For example, sufficient raw material is available to produce 1,600 units of product 1 or 800 units of product 2. The non-negativity conditions simply represent the vertical and horizontal axes. The area in Figure 11.1 labelled 'feasible region'

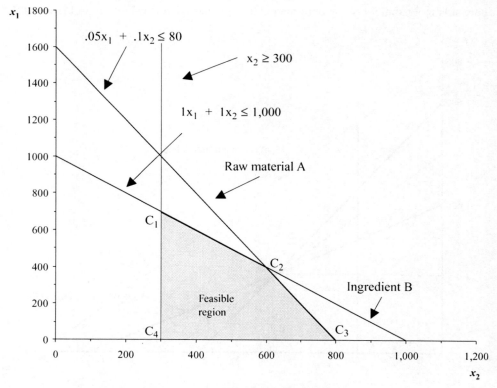

Figure 11.1.   Graphical solution to the product mix problem.

consists of all possible x_1 and x_2 values that simultaneously satisfy all the four constraints. This consists of points below or to the left of '≤' and above or to the right of '≥' constraints. We do not need to evaluate all of these possible combinations to determine the optimal solution because the optimal solution can only occur at an extreme or boundary point of the feasible region – here C_1, C_2, C_3 or C_4 – or occasionally along a straight line joining two boundary points.

Figure 11.1 reveals the physical production possibilities. To determine the optimal production levels, it is necessary to consider also the per unit contributions of the two products ($3 for product 1 and $4.50 for product 2). A diagram can be drawn, as in Figure 11.2, displaying levels of each product which will result in equal total contributions. Suppose 1,800 units of product 1 but none of product 2 were to be produced (this is an arbitrary and, in fact, infeasible level). The total contribution would then be $3 multiplied by 1,800 or $5,400. The same contribution could be achieved by producing $5400/$4.50 or 1,200 units of product 2. Also, any combination on the straight line joining these two output mixes would generate a total contribution of $5,400; thus the line can be referred as the $5,400 *iso-contribution line* (where 'iso' simply means equal). Any other iso-contribution line will have exactly the same slope as the $5,400 iso-contribution line. The further the line from the graph origin, the higher the total contribution. Hence the optimal product mix can be determined by moving the arbitrarily chosen iso-contribution line inwards or outwards in a parallel fashion until the point of greatest payoff is located. In Figure 11.2,

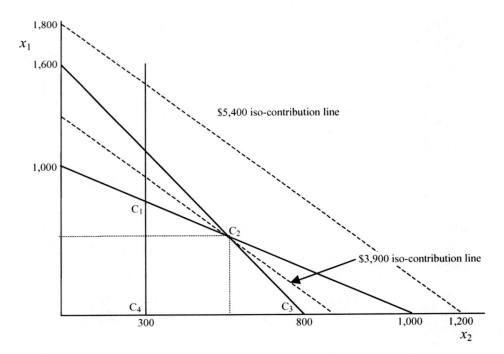

Figure 11.2.   Product mix problem: iso-contribution lines and optimal product mix.

Table 11.1. *Initial tableau for the product mix problem*

	A	B	C	D	E	F
1	Roclap decision problem					
2						
3	Constraint or objective	Product 1	Product 2	Resource use	Sign	Resource supply
4	Activity level	0	0			
5	Raw material	0.05	0.1	0	≤	80
6	Ingredient	1	1	0	≤	1,000
7	Contract		1	0	≥	300
8	Total dollar contribution	3	4.5	0		

this turns out to be at point C_2. The optimal product mix can thus be read off the graph as approximately $x_1 = 400$, $x_2 = 600$, with a corresponding objective function value of $Z = 3x_1 + 4.5x_2 = \$3{,}900$.

Whenever there are more than two decision variables (almost always in practice), it is not possible to obtain the optimal solution by graphical means. These cases can be solved by using a suitable LP software package.

Finding optimal activity levels for the product mix problem with Excel Solver

The LP problem may be entered onto an Excel spreadsheet and the optimal solution obtained using Solver, a mathematical programming solution *algorithm* provided in Excel. Some special features are required in the way the *initial tableau* for the decision problem is arranged, so that it will be amenable to solving. The solution is provided in a revised tableau, as well as in some associated reports.

The initial tableau for the product mix problem is presented as Table 11.1. This and other tableaux are included on the website as workbooks, with numbers indicated above the tableaux (in this case, Workbook 11.1). The activities are represented across the columns of the tableau (columns B and C), and the resources down the rows (rows 5 to 7), with the objective function as row 8. The *technical coefficients* form the body of the tableau (cells B5 to C7). Column F lists the initial resource supplies and other constraint right-hand sides.

```
Workbook
  11.1
```

Prior to using Excel Solver, it is necessary to introduce a row for activity levels (row 4); these activity levels are initially set at zero. It is also necessary to introduce a column for resource use (column D). As well, a column for signs of the constraints is introduced (column E), in this case containing both ≤ and ≥ signs. (If not available in the Excel version, these symbols may be copied and pasted from a word processor file.)

The most complex step in setting up the initial tableau is to enter formulae in the 'Resource use' column, i.e. column D.

(1) The resource use for the raw material constraint (cell D5) is entered as the formula '=SUMPRODUCT(B$4:C$4,B5:C5)'. This initially takes a level of zero, because the activity levels in row 4 are zero. Note that absolute cell references are required for row 4.

(2) The contents of cell D5 are then copied to cells D6 to D8. The coefficients in cells D5 to D7 represent 'resource use' with respect to the other constraints, while the value in cell D8 is the level of the objective function. Initial values in these cells are again zero.

Note that, ignoring row 4 and column D, this tableau formulation is exactly equivalent to the algebraic formulation of the decision problem. Here row 4 represents the level of each activity, rows 5 to 7 represent the constraints, and row 8 represents the objective function.

Once these data have been entered onto the spreadsheet, Solver can be used to further set up the problem for solution. Solver is to be found under the Tools menu of Excel. (If it is not currently available, seek assistance on how to access it.)

Note that the general form of the Solver window is:

> Set Target Cell:
> Equal to:
> By Changing Cells:
> Subject to the Constraints:

The target cell is the total net revenue cell, here D8. Under the 'Equal to:' option, the maximization is chosen. Cells B4 to C4 are selected as the changing cells. When adding constraints, select corresponding cells in columns D and F. It is also necessary to add non-negativity constraints. Each of these selections has been added in Workbook 11.1.

The Solve option within Solver may now be used to obtain the optimal product mix. The figures in row 4 and column D will now change to those of Table 11.2, and these provide solution information. According to row 4, the solution is to produce 400 units of product 1 and 600 units of product 2, generating a total contribution of $3,900, which agrees with the graphical solution. Comparing columns D and F, all of the raw material and ingredient are used up, and the contract is more than met.

Sensitivity or post-optimality analysis

On solving the problem, some further report information is generated if required. Three types of reports which may be selected are Answer, Sensitivity and Limits. The Answer report

Table 11.2. *Revised LP tableau after solution for the product mix problem*

	A	B	C	D	E	F
1	Roclap decision problem					
2						
3	Constraint or objective	Product 1	Product 2	Resource use	Sign	Resource supply
4	Activity level	400	600			
5	Raw material	0.05	0.1	80	≤	80
6	Ingredient	1	1	1,000	≤	1,000
7	Contract		1	600	≥	300
8	Total dollar contribution	3	4.5	3,900		

Table 11.3. *Sensitivity report for the product mix problem*

Adjustable cells

Cell	Name	Final value	Reduced gradient
B4	Activity level, Product 1	400	0
C4	Activity level, Product 2	600	0

Constraints

Cell	Name	Final value	Lagrange multiplier
D5	Raw material, Resource use	80	30
D6	Ingredient, Resource use	1000	1.5
D7	Resource use	600	0

provides little information beyond that in Table 11.2. The Sensitivity report is illustrated in Table 11.3. This repeats the optimal solution, in the Adjustable Cells section, of $x_1 = 400$ and $x_2 = 600$. The 'reduced gradient' for these activities is zero. For an activity not in the optimal solution, the 'reduced gradient' would indicate the increase in contribution required for the activity to enter the optimal solution.

Under the Constraints section, Table 11.3 reports *shadow prices* (under the heading 'Lagrange multiplier') associated with the three constraints. For constraints on resource supplies of the 'less than or equal to' type, the shadow price indicates the amount by which the value of the objective function would increase (in a maximization problem) if the original right-hand side (RHS) value associated with the slack-variable constraint were increased by one unit. In other words, the shadow price is the maximum additional amount the firm should be willing to pay to acquire one additional unit of a resource so as to expand output. The two resources of raw material and ingredient are fully used up in the optimal solution. Raw material has a shadow price of $30 per unit, and the ingredient has a shadow price of $1.50 per unit. Hence the firm should be willing to pay up to a maximum of $30 (in addition to the current price it pays) to acquire one tonne of additional raw material. If the firm currently pays, say, $60 per tonne, it is worthwhile to pay a maximum of $90 (= 60 + 30) per tonne to acquire additional amounts of raw material. For acquiring additional amounts of ingredient, it is worthwhile to pay up to a maximum of $1.50 per kg (in addition to the current price it pays).

For 'greater than or equal to' constraints (in this case the contract constraint), the shadow price indicates the amount by which the objective function would increase if the original RHS value associated with the constraint were decreased by one unit. Since this constraint is not binding in the optimal solution (a minimum level of only 300 was required, compared with the optimal level of 600), it would not make sense to pay money to relax the minimum requirement, so the shadow price is zero.

A further form of sensitivity analysis, not available in the Solver reports, is *contribution ranges* for solution stability. LP packages often provide this information. For example, solving this decision problem with another package revealed that the contribution for product 1 can range between $2.25 and $4.50 without the optimal solution changing, if all other input parameters remain fixed. Similarly, the contribution for product 2 can range between $3 and $6, *ceteris paribus*, without the optimal solutions changing. If contributions fall below their lower limits, then the level of that activity in the solution will fall; if contributions increase to above the upper limit then the level will increase. Some packages also report the new solution level for the activity.

There is in effect no limit on the number of activities and constraints which may be included in a linear programming model. For example, a model may be set up in which there are several thousand activities and several thousand constraints. This, of course, requires a considerable time input in setting up and checking the initial tableau.

Investment opportunities and by-product constraints

By going through a simple resource allocation problem, the previous section has provided familiarization with the concepts of linear programming, and illustrated how to formulate an LP problem, obtain the solution and interpret it. This section will discuss a simple capital budgeting decision problem involving capital rationing and proportionality requirement for two investments.

Example 11.2. Capital rationing problem

Capitol Inc. faces one-period capital rationing. The firm is subject to capital rationing now, but this is not anticipated in future years. Capitol has two divisions, between which it must allocate capital. For every dollar invested in Division 1, $0.25 of NPV is created, and for every dollar invested in Division 2, $0.35 of NPV is created. Total investment opportunities in Divisions 1 and 2 are limited to \$3,000 and \$1,900, respectively. A by-product from Division 1 is used in Division 2, so the amount of investment in Division 1 must be at least twice that in Division 2. The firm wishes to decide how much to invest in each division.

Let us translate this information into an LP problem. How will we translate the by-product condition into a linear constraint? Denoting the amount of investment in Divisions 1 and 2 (the decision variables) as x_1 and x_2, the condition may be stated in mathematical terms as:

$$x_1 \geq 2x_2$$

To fit into the standard LP formulation, this can be rewritten as

$$-x_1 + 2x_2 \leq 0$$

The LP problem can now be expressed as:

maximize NPV $\qquad Z = 0.25x_1 + 0.35x_2$

subject to:

investment in division 1	$x_1 \leq 3{,}000$
investment in division 2	$x_2 \leq 1{,}900$
by-product constraint	$-x_1 + 2x_2 \leq 0$
non-negativity condition	$x_1, x_2 \geq 0$

The input parameters for this LP problem are as follows:

objective function coefficients: 0.25 and 0.35
right-hand sides: 3,000 and 1,900 (capital supplies) and 0 (by-product constraint)
technical coefficients: 1 (investment in each division), -1 and 2 (by-product constraint)

The Excel Solver solution to this problem is held in Workbook 11.2. Selected extracts from the solution are presented in Tables 11.4 and 11.5.

> **Workbook 11.2**

The optimal solution is to invest \$3,000 in Division 1 and \$1,500 in Division 2. This allocation of capital will yield a total NPV of \$1,275. This is the maximum NPV that Capitol can obtain while operating within the limited investment opportunities in the two divisions and, at the same time, satisfy the by-product requirement of the two divisions.

The shadow price for the Year 1 Capital constraint is \$0.425, indicating that each extra dollar in capital available for investment in Division 1 would raise the overall contribution by 42.5 cents.

Table 11.4. *LP tableau after solution for the capital rationing problem*

	A	B	C	D	E	F
1	Capitol's decision problem					
2						
3	Constraint or objective	Division 1	Division 2	Resource use	Sign	Supply
4	Activity level	3,000	1,500			
5	Div. 1 investment	1		3,000	≤	3,000
6	Div. 2 investment		1	1,500	≤	1,900
7	By-product requirement	−1	2	0	≤	0
8	Total dollar contribution	0.25	0.35	1,275		

Table 11.5. *Sensitivity report for the capital rationing problem*

Adjustable cells

Cell	Name	Final value	Reduced gradient
B4	Activity level, Division 1	3,000	0
C4	Activity level, Division 2	1,500	0

Constraints

Cell	Name	Final value	Lagrange multiplier
D5	Div. 1, Resource use	3,000	0.425
D6	Div. 2, Resource use	1,500	0
D7	By-product requirement, Resource use	0	0.175

How should the shadow price associated with the by-product constraint be interpreted? Its value (from Table 11.5) is 0.175. This suggests that if the requirement can be slightly relaxed such that the investment in Division 1 must be at least 'twice the investment in Division 2 less one dollar', the total NPV can be increased by $0.175. In other words, if the investment in Division 2 is increased from $1,500 to $1,501, all other parameters being unchanged, the total NPV will be $1,275.175.

LP and project choice

To illustrate the application of the LP technique to project portfolio selection, the Lorie and Savage (1955) nine-project, two-period capital rationing problem will be considered. This problem is now regarded as a classic LP example in capital budgeting.

Table 11.6. *NPVs, cash outflows and available capital in the project portfolio selection problem* ($)

		Cash outflow	
Project	NPV	Period 1	Period 2
1	14	12	3
2	17	54	7
3	17	6	6
4	15	6	2
5	40	30	35
6	12	6	6
7	14	48	4
8	10	36	3
9	12	18	3
Capital available		50	20

Example 11.3. Project portfolio selection problem

NPVs for the nine projects, their cash outflows for periods 1 and 2 and the capital available in periods 1 and 2 (in current dollars) are presented in Table 11.6.

In this model, the values in the capital constraints have not been discounted back to year 0 (or the beginning of year 1) since the funds available are expressed in current dollars. Note that additional constraints have been imposed on each project j such that:

$$0 \le x_j \le 1$$

The constraint '≤ 1' is used to place upper limits. Each project can have a maximum value of 1, i.e. can be fully accepted. The condition in the above equation allows the fractional acceptance of projects. A value of zero indicates non-acceptance of the project, and a value between 0 and 1 represents the acceptance of a fraction of the project.

The Excel worksheet to solve this problem can be viewed in Workbook 11.3. The LP tableau after solution is presented in Table 11.7 and the corresponding Sensitivity report in Workbook 11.3.

Projects 1, 3, 4 and 9 have levels of one unit in the optimal solution, i.e. they are accepted in full. Only partial acceptance, of approximately 97% and 4.5%, is suggested for Projects 6 and 7. The optimal level for Projects 2, 5, and 8 is zero, indicating the complete rejection of these three projects. Fully and partially accepted projects generate a total combined NPV of $70 ($70.2727 in Table 11.7).

Final values of $50 and $20 for the two capital constraints (in Table 11.7) suggest that the entire budget allotment of $50 in year 1 and $20 in year 2 has been fully exhausted by the optimal solution. Therefore, both these constraints have become binding at the optimal solution. Their shadow prices reproduced from Workbook 11.3 sensitivity report are about $0.14 and $1.86. If the capital available in year 1 is increased by $1, the value of the objective

Table 11.7. *LP model for the project portfolio selection problem*

Project portfolio selection problem												
Constraint or objective	Proj. 1	Proj. 2	Proj. 3	Proj. 4	Proj. 5	Proj. 6	Proj. 7	Proj. 8	Proj. 9	Resource use	Sign	Supply
Activity level	1	0	1	1	0	0.9697	0.04545	0	1			
Capital, year 1	12	54	6	6	30	6	48	36	18	50	$\leq$	50
Capital, year 2	3	7	6	2	35	6	4	3	3	20	$\leq$	20
Max. project 1	1									1	$\leq$	1
Max. project 2		1								0	$\leq$	1
Max. project 3			1							1	$\leq$	1
Max. project 4				1						1	$\leq$	1
Max. project 5					1					0	$\leq$	1
Max. project 6						1				0.9697	$\leq$	1
Max. project 7							1			0.04545	$\leq$	1
Max. project 8								1		0	$\leq$	1
Max. project 9									1	1	$\leq$	1
Net present value	14	17	17	15	40	12	14	10	12	70.2727		

Workbook
11.3

function will increase by \$0.14. Therefore, the firm may consider paying an interest rate of up to 14% to increase year 1 capital. Following the same logic, it may be worthwhile for the firm to pay an interest rate of 186% to raise new capital in year 2. This, of course, is an unusually high cost of capital. This interest rate applies only within certain limits.

It is notable that this solution involves the acceptance of fractional projects. While this may be appropriate in specific situations, it would not generally be the case. For example, if a project represents an investment in 2,500 m^2 of warehouse space or 2,500 tonnes of steel plate, it may be quite possible to accept 2,000 m^2 or 2,000 tonnes and reasonably assume that cash flow will be reduced proportionately. For investment projects such as a huge shopping complex, a jumbo jet, a copper mine or an oil well, such fractional investments make little sense. If the decision-maker is compelled to consider accepting only full projects, the integer programming technique, which will be discussed in the next chapter, can be used.

Concluding comments

This chapter has demonstrated that linear programming is a powerful and versatile technique for providing decision support information in resource allocation problems, including capital budgeting decisions. Problem formulation, graphical and computerized solution approaches, interpretation of the optimal solution and associated shadow prices have all been discussed and illustrated with examples.

When it is realized that LP models may have several thousand activities and constraints, the potential uses of this technique become more apparent. The technique is, of course, subject to some limitations, for example with respect to the linear nature of the objective function and constraints, the fact that activities (including project levels) are allowed to take fractional levels, difficulties in including multiple time periods and capital accumulation over time, and failure to allow for project risk. Even these kinds of limitations can be overcome with sufficient ingenuity, as will be discussed in Chapter 12.

Review questions

11.1 Refer to Example 11.1 (product mix problem).
  (a) Demonstrate that the optimal values for x_1 and x_2 in the solution satisfy the original constraints by substituting the values into the three constraints.
  (b) Write the raw material A constraint by increasing its RHS value by 1 from 80 to 81, while keeping the other values in the problem unchanged. Solve the resulting new LP problem and demonstrate that the value of the objective function increases by the amount of the relevant shadow price, which is 30, from 3,900 to 3,930.

11.2 Refer to Example 11.2 (capital rationing problem).
  (a) Represent the problem in graphical form and find the optimal solution using the graphical method.
  (b) Solve the capital rationing problem using Excel Solver and compare your results with the solution details provided in Workbook 11.2.

(c) Confirm that the objective function increases by the value of the shadow price of the by-product requirement constraint (0.175) by appropriately reformulating the capital rationing problem and solving it.

11.3 Refer to Example 11.3 (project portfolio selection problem).

(a) Formulate the problem as an LP problem by specifying the information in terms of a set of linear equations.

(b) Solve the problem and compare your results with those provided in Workbook 11.3.

12 More advanced linear programming concepts and methods

Selecting a portfolio of investment projects from a larger group of potential projects is a common decision problem in capital budgeting. The basic concepts and applications of linear programming were introduced with reference to simple resource allocation and capital budgeting problems in Chapter 11. This chapter explores further the application of linear programming (LP) to capital budgeting, and demonstrates the power and versatility of the technique.

Recall from Chapter 11 that linear programming requires that the decision problem be represented within a mathematical framework of optimizing a linear objective function of activity levels subject to a set of linear constraints. In this context, the investment projects become *activities*, the levels of which are restricted by limited capital and other resource *constraints*. The *objective function* represents the total payoff from the investment portfolio, typically in terms of net present value. LP problems are invariably solved using a computer package.

A number of restrictive assumptions were made in the examples in Chapter 11 so that they would conform to the LP framework. The current chapter first reviews the nature of these assumptions, and the limitations they impose on the formulation of capital budgeting problems. Various model formulation approaches to overcome these limitations are then explained, and examples presented in the form of LP tableaux. The specific extensions presented include: expanding the model for greater numbers of activities and constraints; modelling indivisible investments; allowing for borrowing and transferring resources between years; representing interdependent projects; specifying investments as mutually exclusive; and dealing with threshold investment levels, economies of scale, multiple goals and investment risk. General concepts are presented for each type of extension, with simple examples and interpretive comments provided in most cases. Tableau constructions for the examples are presented as images of Excel Solver spreadsheets, for which files are provided on the website.

Study objectives

After studying this chapter the reader should be able to:

- recognize some of the main limitations of the standard LP formulation in the context of capital budgeting

- create mixed integer linear programming tableaux to accommodate investments involving indivisible assets
- incorporate borrowing and capital transfers in linear programming models
- incorporate interactions between projects, including contingent projects and mutual exclusion between projects, in a linear programming model
- understand in general terms how to deal with threshold investment levels, economies and diseconomies of size, multiple goals and risk in a mathematical programming framework.

Basic LP assumptions and their implications for capital budgeting

The limitations of the basic linear programming model as developed in Chapter 11 derive from the assumptions of additivity and divisibility within activities, independence of activities, single-valued expectations and a linear one-dimensional objective function.

Additivity within activities

The amount of each resource used per unit of each activity is assumed to be constant regardless of the level at which the activity is conducted. In practice, an investment project can typically be designed with a number of alternative sizes and configurations, and the proportionate use of land, capital and other resources is likely to vary between these alternatives. Large plants tend to benefit from economies of scale or size, that is, a large plant may generate more revenue or a greater NPV per dollar invested.

Divisibility within activities

This implies that we can implement a fraction of a project, e.g. 70% or 25% of a new hotel, power station or manufacturing plant could be constructed. While variation in the size of investment is sometimes possible, most frequently the task is to choose between discrete alternatives. Thus a number of facility sizes may be nominated, on the basis of engineering, economic and planning factors, and capital budgeting applied to each of these nominated alternatives. Management is not likely to be impressed if the capital budgeting analyst comes back with the recommendation that none of these designs exactly fits the optimal investment mix as identified by the computer and a different set of project sizes should therefore be investigated. Admittedly, LP can sometimes be used within limits to investigate the optimal sizes of investment projects under resource and other constraints.

Independence of activities

A standard assumption in LP is that whether one activity enters the optimal plan does not depend on what other activities enter the plan; there is no interaction between projects. In practice, some investment projects provide infrastructure or intermediate products to support others. Also, projects are sometimes incompatible or mutually exclusive. For example, a developer may have a building site, and has to choose among construction of a five-star hotel, casino, home-unit complex or sporting facility. Since these alternative projects compete for the same site, only one can be chosen. More complex situations arise where groups of activities are complementary or incompatible, e.g. firms will want to invest in particular project areas because it is easier to build up expertise and business alliances in more specialized areas.

Modelling of multi-period decision problems

The simplest type of LP model is one which applies to a single time period, e.g. choice of enterprises for a firm to maximize aggregate annual net revenue subject to a number of resource constraints. Example 11.3 illustrated how capital constraints for two separate years could be included in an LP model. For more serious multi-period modelling, a means for transferring supplies of unused capital and other resources between years is required. Also, if a project has positive net cash flows, it is desirable to be able to make these funds available for use in later years. This introduces another aspect of interdependence of activities, since, over time, one project can generate resources to support another activity.

Single-valued expectations

Typically, in LP applications, point estimates are made of capital outlays and operating costs and of product or service prices, though partial recognition of cost and price uncertainty may be made through sensitivity analysis. In the case of long-term investments, cost and price uncertainty are often high, as are technical, legal and institutional uncertainty. Taking account of uncertainty raises an additional challenge for mathematical programming methods.

Linear one-dimensional objective function

In the examples presented here, the objective will generally be to maximize the *total NPV*, i.e. the aggregate NPV over the set of projects selected. Variations of this objective are sometimes warranted. For example, a measure of investment risk may be included in the objective function to allow for a risk-averse decision-maker. Also, additional goals are sometimes apparent, such as paying high dividends, achieving recognition as being environmentally responsible, or being recognized as a significant source of employment.

In summary, the assumptions of the basic LP model as developed in Chapter 11 do not, in general, match well with all the realities, complexities and requirements of capital budgeting. Hence there is a need to explore ways in which the limitations imposed by these assumptions may be overcome.

Expanding the number of projects and constraints

Linear programming provides a general approach to solving project selection problems, which is applicable regardless of the number of projects from which to choose and the number of limited resources or inputs which constrain the choice. Larger choice sets and

Table 12.1. *Power generator's decision problem: alternative technologies*

Constraint or objective	Hydropower	Natural gas, site A	Natural gas, site B	Windfarm	Biofuel	Solar panels
Capital outlay ($M)	400	170	150	100	50	120
Power output (MW)	420	250	200	70	50	90
NPV ($M)	180	100	80	50	7	20

more constraints may be incorporated in the analysis simply by adding more activity columns and constraint rows, respectively, in the initial tableau. The following decision problem for an electricity generation company illustrates how a number of investments may be represented in LP format, and optimal solutions derived on the computer.

Example 12.1. Power generator's decision problem

A company in a privatized electricity supply industry is planning the construction of new generation plant. The company has identified alternative generation technologies and NPV payoffs, for which suitable sites are available. The relevant data are presented in Table 12.1.

The industry regulator has directed that at least 100 MW have to be produced from renewables and at least 200 MW from natural gas. The company is constrained by cash and credit access of $700M. Determine the construction portfolio which maximizes total NPV under the capital and output constraints.

In setting up this decision problem as an LP model, a series of constraints have been added to ensure that the maximum level of each project is one unit. (Without these constraints, the hydropower and natural gas A projects would form the solution, each at greater than one unit.) This model has been entered onto an Excel spreadsheet, and the optimal activity mix obtained using Solver. The method of setting up the Excel spreadsheet was outlined in Chapter 11. Table 12.2 presents the spreadsheet after the problem has been solved, optimal activity levels being indicated in row 4. This LP tableau is included on the website as Workbook 12.1.

> Workbook
> 12.1

According to Table 12.2, the solution is to develop the two natural gas projects and the windfarm, and to develop a 70% scale hydropower station, with a total NPV of $356M. The scaling down of the hydro plant may or may not be acceptable to the power company. Column H indicates that all capital is used, and the renewable and natural gas targets are more than met.

There is in effect no limit on the number of activities and constraints which may be included in a linear programming model. For example, a model may be set up in which there are several thousand activities and several thousand constraints. This, of course, leads

Table 12.2. *LP tableau for power generator problem after solution*

	A	B	C	D	E	F	G	H	I	J
1	Power generator's decision problem									
2										
3	Constraint or objective	Hydropower	Natural gas, site A	Natural gas, site B	Windfarm	Biofuel	Solar panels	Resource use	Sign	Resource supply
4		0.7	1	1	1	0	0			
5	Capital outlay ($M)	400	170	150	100	50	120	700	≤	700
6	Renewables output (MW)	420			70	50	90	364	≥	100
7	Nat. gas output (MW)		250	200				450	≥	200
8	Max. hydropower	1						0.7	≤	1
9	Max. nat. gas A		1					1	≤	1
10	Max. nat. gas B			1				1	≤	1
11	Max. windfarm				1			1	≤	1
12	Max. biofuel					1		0	≤	1
13	Max. solar						1	0	≤	1
14	NPV ($M)	180	100	80	50	7	20	356		

Workbook
12.1

to a considerable time input in setting up and checking the initial tableau. In practice, the number of alternative investment activities in which management is interested is usually relatively small. On the other hand, it can be useful to include other types of information which substantially increase tableau size. For example, resource constraints may be included for each of a number of years, and various activities other than those representing investment projects may be added, as discussed below.

Indivisible investments and integer activity levels

As noted in the above example, a solution to an LP problem is often generated which contains activity levels in fractional values.

Where the activities are discrete investment projects, this is often unsatisfactory, since there are sound technical reasons why a particular scale of investment is chosen. Also, once all the planning has been carried out for a particular-sized project, management would not be impressed by investment department advice that a 70% project should be implemented! Obviously, some mechanism is needed to ensure that projects can only enter the optimal mix at exactly one unit, or a 100% level, of the design size. The maximum-level constraints in Example 12.1 ensured that a one-unit level for each activity could not be exceeded, but did not prevent undersized projects from entering the solution.

Fortunately, a method has been developed, known as *mixed integer linear programming* (MILP), for overcoming this problem. This allows specific activities in the tableau to be flagged as *integer* (taking levels of 0, 1, 2, 3, etc.) or as *binary* (a special type of integer which can take levels of 0 or 1 only). The former would be appropriate when multiple units could be developed; the latter implies the project is a 'take it or leave it' investment, which is probably most often the case. The approach is called *mixed* integer programming because it is possible to force some activities to take integer levels while allowing others to have continuous levels.

Various computer solution *algorithms* have been developed for solving MILP problems, the most popular of which is the *branch-and-bound method*. MILP is automatically available in Excel Solver; when setting up a problem it is simply necessary to add 'bin' or 'int' constraints. (These choices appear in the sign box of the constraints window of Solver.) The mechanics of MILP need not concern us here, but a few implications of using this solution procedure need to be noted:

(1) MILP is much more computer-intensive than normal LP. Rather than solve one LP problem, the algorithm requires that a large number of LP problems be set up, with different combinations of integer constraints added, and that each (or at least many) of these individual LP problems be solved. In effect, a partial evaluation of all the contender integer combinations of activity levels is evaluated. For large tableaux, this can increase computing time substantially.

(2) For very large tableaux, the solution method is not always totally reliable, in terms of identifying the exact optimal solution, although at least a near-optimal solution can be expected.

(3) The sensitivity or post-optimality analysis (contribution ranges, shadow prices) provided in the Report sheets accompanying the Answer sheet generated by Excel Solver ceases to have any economic or business logic, because of the artificial nature of the constraints which are added to force activities to take integer levels.

Because binary and integer activity levels are particularly relevant in the application of linear programming to project selection, it is appropriate to examine this solution approach before proceeding to more advanced problem formulations. Also, as will soon be seen, the ability to confine activities to binary levels is a critical ingredient in other extensions to the linear programming approach to capital budgeting.

Example 12.2. Resort development problem

A Majorca-based property developer plans to construct luxury hotels at beach resorts in north-east Australia. He has identified sites where well-located land is available and the local government is extending a welcoming hand, on the Gold, Sunshine, Capricornia and Cassowary Coasts. The predicted capital investments for the four locations are $20M, $18M, $19M and $24M respectively, and the estimated NPV payoffs are $12M, $10M, $9M and $14M respectively. A total investment budget of $50M is available. Another constraint concerns the time required by the specialist resort architect to design the hotels. He can spend up to 1,000 hours on designs and modifications for the approval process. Each hotel will be unique in design, and respective time requirements are 250 hours, 180 hours, 320 hours and 400 hours. Obviously there will be various other constraints, but these will not be considered here.

This decision problem can be set up with a tableau containing four activities for the four hotel sites, and two resource constraints (capital and architect's time). Each of the activities is *flagged* to take binary (0–1) levels only. This is achieved by adding further constraints with respect to the changing cells. Specifically, in the spreadsheet (Table 12.3), the constraints are added that 'B4 = bin', 'C4 = bin', 'D4 = bin' and 'E4 = bin'. The optimal solution, indicated in row 4 of Table 12.3, is: $x_1 = 1$, $x_2 = 0$, $x_3 = 0$, $x_4 = 1$, total NPV = $26M. That is, the developer would be advised to proceed with the Gold Coast and Cassowary Coast resorts.

> Workbook
> 12.2

It is informative to compare the optimal solutions obtained in Table 12.3, with the solution which would have been obtained from continuous LP, both without and with upper bounds on activity levels (Table 12.4). Where no upper limits are imposed on activity levels, multiple units of the Gold Coast development are selected. Placing an upper bound of one unit on each activity leads to selection of the Gold Coast and Cassowary Coast sites, but also to a fraction of the Sunshine Coast site. Under MILP, the latter site is eliminated, and some resources ($44M in capital and 350 hrs in design development) are left idle. Notably, when using MILP, not only is a more precise solution obtained, but tableau formulation is simpler since it is not necessary to add the upper activity level constraints.

Table 12.3. *LP tableau and optimal plan for property developer decision problem*

A	B	C	D	E	F	G	H
1 Property developer decision problem							
2							
3 Constraint or objective	Gold Coast site (bin)	Sunshine Coast site (bin)	Capricornia Coast site (bin)	Cassowary Coast site (bin)	Resource use		Resource supply
4 Activity level	1	0	0	1			
5 Capital ($M)	20	18	19	24	44	≤	50
6 Design devpt (hrs)	250	180	320	400	650	≤	1,000
7 NPV ($M)	12	10	9	14	26		

Table 12.4. *Property developer decision problem: alternative solution methods*

Solution method	Gold Coast (x_1)	Sunshine Coast (x_2)	Capricornia Coast (x_3)	Cassowary Coast (x_4)
Continuous	2.5	0	0	0
Upper bounds	1	0.3333	0	1
MILP	1	0	0	1

Borrowing and capital transfers

Capital budgeting involves investments which generate cash flows over time. The LP models discussed above are not well suited to handling this time dimension. It would be more realistic to take account of the amount of financial capital required by a project in each year for which the net cash flow is negative. Further, it would be useful to allow for borrowing funds, and for carrying forward cash reserves to meet negative cash flows after the first year. This becomes possible when two further types of activities are introduced into the LP toolkit, namely activities for borrowing financial capital and activities for transferring unused funds from one time period to the next. These are illustrated in Example 12.3.

Example 12.3. Borrowing and capital transfer problem

An entrepreneur is considering two projects, namely purchase of an airport and construction of a light rail line to provide a transport service to the airport. The airport purchase project requires capital of $120M in the first year and $25M in the second year. Construction of the light rail facility requires $20M in the first year and $10M in the second year. After the second year, both projects will yield a positive net cash flow and no further borrowing will be required. The entrepreneur has $130M available to invest, and can borrow up to $10M

Table 12.5. *Tableau after solution for borrowing and capital transfer problem*

	A	B	C	D	E	F	G	H	I
1	Borrowing and capital transfers								
2									
3		Airport (bin)	Light rail (bin)	Borrow, year 1	Borrow, year 2	Transfer cash, yr 1 to yr 2			
4		1	0	4.2857	10	14.2857			
5	Capital, yr 1	120	20	−1		1	130	≤	130
6	Max. loan, yr 1			1			4.2857	≤	10
7	Capital, yr 2	25	10		−1	−1.05	0	≤	0
8	Max. loan, yr 2				1		10	≤	10
9	NPV	80	4	−1	−0.8696	0	67.02		

a year, at an interest rate of 15% per annum. Funds carried forward will earn 5% per year net of tax. Determine whether the entrepreneur should proceed with either or both projects.

To set up this problem in tableau form (Table 12.5), two columns are used for the two projects, which are flagged to take binary values, and two rows are used to specify the year 1 and year 2 capital constraints. An activity is then set up for borrowing in year 1. This activity supplies funds at the beginning of year 1. Note that a *supply activity* has a negative coefficient for the resource it supplies, hence the −1 in cell D5. This activity can take continuous values, defined in units of $1M. A maximum loan constraint is added, with a unit entry in the borrow funds column, to limit the amount borrowed in year 1 to not more than $10M. Similarly, an activity is added for borrowing funds at the beginning of year 2, and a constraint is placed to limit the amount borrowed in year 2 to not more than $10M.

Finally, a *transfer activity* is set up to carry unused funds in year 1 through to year 2, also defined in units of $1M. This demands unused funds in year 1 and supplies funds in year 2. The amount demanded in year 1 is represented by +1 in units of $M transferred. These funds are released in year 2, with the addition of interest earned net of tax, assumed here to be 5%, hence the coefficient of −1.05.

With regard to the objective function, borrowing funds at the beginning of year 1 generates a debt in terms of NPV. If the discount rate is taken as the borrowing rate, the present value of the debt is equal to the amount borrowed at the beginning of year 1 (assuming no capital redemption). On the other hand, each $1M of debt incurred at the beginning of year 2 has a present value of minus $0.8696M; this is based on an interest rate of 15%, i.e. 1/1.15. The present value of interest due at the end of year 2 ($-0.15/1.15^2$) could also be included in the NPV row for the two borrowing activities.

The solution to this problem is to purchase the airport only, and use both borrowing and transfer of funds to year 2 to meet the second-year capital outflow. $4.29M is borrowed in year 1, and this and the unused $10M of the firm's own capital are transferred forward, to supply $15M in year 2, which is supplemented by a further $10M in year 2 borrowings. Additional loan funds would need to be available to proceed with the light rail project. It would be possible to introduce further borrowing and capital transfer activities, perhaps with different interest rates, if additional sources of external finance were required to support this investment.

```
Workbook
  12.3
```

Contingent or dependent projects

Sometimes it is not possible to proceed with one project unless another project on which it depends, but which is defined as a separate investment, is also implemented. For example, one project may provide the infrastructure needed for another project. In this case, the two projects – infrastructure construction and infrastructure use – could be treated as a single combined activity. But what if there were several projects which could all make gainful use of the infrastructure, but not all of which need to be implemented? In this case, it is best to treat the infrastructure development as a discrete project, and to treat all the potential projects which depend on this infrastructure as distinct activities.

The LP model for this type of problem again requires binary, or 0–1 activity levels. As well, *permission constraints* must be used, such that only if the investment is made in the infrastructure can the profitable dependent investments be undertaken. Infrastructure investments *supply* units of a *permission resource* for dependent investments.

Example 12.4. Infrastructure problem

A coal-mining company wishes to open up new mines in an area where large coal deposits have been proven by geological survey. Mines at three sites – labelled Mine A, Mine B and Mine C – are being considered. Respective predicted capital outlays are $20M, $18M and $12M, and the company has $70M available for investment. To allow rail transport of coal to an export port on the coast, a railway line extension to the area at an outlay of $25M in present value terms is required. While accommodation already exists at mine sites A and B, Mine C would require a town development project costing $15M in present dollars. Predicted NPV payoffs from the three sites are $19M for Mine A, $17M for Mine B and $28M for Mine C. Markets exist for up to 45,000 tonnes (45 kt) of coal per year, and predicted mine outputs are 18, 16 and 24 kt/year respectively.

The LP tableau including solution is presented as Table 12.6. Railway construction, development of the town, and the three mine site options are each set up as activities that can take only binary levels. Capital and market constraint rows are included.

Two *permission constraints* have been added. The first is the rail–mine tie. Here the railway construction activity supplies three units of permission for mine site development. A unit of this permission is an essential resource for any mine site to proceed. The second permission constraint is the town–mine tie, whereby development of the town supplies an

Table 12.6. *Tableau with solution for coal-miner's example*

	A	B	C	D	E	F	G	H	I
1	Coalminer's decision problem								
2									
3	Constraint or objective	Construct railway (bin)	Develop town (bin)	Mine A (bin)	Mine B (bin)	Mine C (bin)	Resource use	Sign	Resource supply
4		1	0	1	1	0			
5	Capital ($M)	25	15	20	18	12	63	≤	70
6	Market (kt/yr)			18	16	24	34	≤	45
7	Rail–mine tie	−3		1	1	1	−1	≤	0
8	Town–mine tie		−1			1	0	≤	0
9	NPV ($M)	−25	−15	19	17	28	11		

essential resource for Mine C. Note that the initial supplies of these permission resources are zero, so it is only by development of the rail line and town that all three mine development projects become feasible.

> Workbook
> 12.4

For simplicity, the capital costs of the two infrastructure development projects are taken as present values. In the objective function, these become negative NPVs such that the optimal solution takes into account the impact on total NPV of the infrastructure development.

The solution to this problem (row 4) is that the railway but not the town be constructed ($x_1 = 1$, $x_2 = 0$), and Mines A and B but not C be constructed ($x_3 = 1$, $x_4 = 1$, $x_5 = 0$). Some capital is unused and some market opportunity is sacrificed; total NPV is $11M.

Mutually exclusive projects

Sometimes there are various ways in which a project can be undertaken, and a choice must be made between these. For example, a processing plant, office block or recreation resort of various discrete sizes could be constructed on a given site. Here, only one of the projects could be implemented. In more complex situations, a firm may have a number of competing project proposals, but wishes to limit the choice to a sub-set of these for reasons which cannot be specified conveniently as resource constraints. An example could be where a firm considers it should choose projects of a similar nature, because this will allow specialization of its managerial staff.

Table 12.7. *Tableau and solution for sports gear problem*

	A	B	C	D	E	F	G	H
1	Sports gear							
2								
3	Constraint or objective	Cricket (bin)	Golf (bin)	Hockey (bin)	Baseball (bin)	Resource use	Sign	Resource supply
4		1	1	0	1			
5	Capital ($M)	4	8	3	3.5	15.5	≤	16
6	Mut. excl. overall	1	1	1	1	3	≤	3
7	Hockey–baseball mut. excl.			1	1	1	≤	1
8	NPV ($M)	3	5	2	2.2	10.2		

Example 12.5. Sports gear problem

A sporting goods manufacturer is considering introducing a number of new product lines, namely cricket, golf, hockey and baseball equipment. Respective capital requirements for establishment of these product lines in $M are 4, 8, 3 and 3.5, and capital of up to $16M is available. NPV payoffs in $M are predicted to be 3, 5, 2 and 2.2. Because of the need for specialization to become technically efficient, the manufacturer decides to limit production to at most three product lines. Also, he does not wish to produce both hockey and baseball equipment, owing to lack of expertise in these product lines.

The LP tableau after solution to this decision problem is presented in Table 12.7. Production of each of the four types of sporting goods is represented as an activity, the level of which is confined to a binary value. The capital constraint is added. Two mutual exclusion rows are then included. The first has a coefficient of +1 for each activity, and a right-hand side of +3. Since the activities can only take values of 0 or 1, at most three activities at the level of one unit can enter the solution. The second mutual exclusion row has unit coefficients in the hockey and baseball columns and a right-hand side value of +1, ensuring that only one of these activities can enter the solution.

The solution to this decision problem is to produce cricket, golf and baseball equipment (row 4, read $x_1 = 1$, $x_2 = 1$, $x_3 = 0$, $x_4 = 1$). A small amount of capital is unused; the mutual exclusion 'resources' are fully used. Note that it would also be possible to have a solution in which less than three activities are present, including the case where neither hockey nor baseball equipment is selected.

```
Workbook
   12.5
```

Closer inspection of this example reveals that the first mutual exclusion constraint is not needed. If hockey and baseball equipment cannot both be included, then not more than three product lines can be selected. This is an example of a *redundant constraint*, which can be deleted from the formulation.

Some other LP extensions for capital budgeting

The range of tableau construction devices to make mathematical programming more flexible is indeed great, the above examples illustrating but a few of the possibilities. In this section, some further modelling constructs will be introduced briefly, without presenting example tableaux.

Threshold investment levels

Sometimes it is an acceptable approximation to allow an investment project to be treated as a continuous activity, i.e. to let the optimal size of investment be determined in the LP solution. However, technical issues frequently dictate that the investment is not worthwhile unless it is undertaken at a sufficiently large scale to warrant particular types of equipment and tooling-up steps. In such case, a minimum *threshold level* for the investment may be formulated as an activity which can only take a binary level, with this activity, if selected, providing permission for further units (i.e. a larger size) of the investment. The modelling approach here is similar to that in Example 12.4 for infrastructure projects.

Plant size and economies of scale

Different project sizes can lead to differences in efficiency of resource use, i.e. projects may not be additive within activities. The term *economies of scale* is widely used in reference to the relationship between long-run output quantity (related to plant size) and long-run average cost of production. Strictly speaking, scale relationships refer to the case where all inputs – not just plant but also labour and other inputs – are adjusted in fixed proportions; if quantities of some inputs are increased by relatively greater amounts than others then a *size* rather than *scale* relationship is observed. Economic theory suggests that the long-run average cost curve, or *planning curve*, is downward-sloping with respect to plant size, at least up to some large size where management control becomes difficult.

Size economies are an important reason why it is inappropriate to allow activities to enter the solution at continuous levels, i.e. to assume additivity within activities. Rather, in a capital budgeting context it is preferable to define a number of discrete investment sizes and associated resource demands.

As an example of economies of size, suppose a resort developer plans to construct a new hotel. Three size options are being examined for the site, viz. small (200 rooms), moderate (400 rooms) and mega-sized (1,000 rooms). The larger the hotel, the greater the resource demand in terms of capital, architectural design, staff required and so on. On the other hand, the mega-sized hotel may be able to form business links with airlines to attract extra patrons, support auditoria which can attract international conferences, and have its own travel, legal, laundry and other services rather than contracting out. In this way, the mega-hotel may generate a greater NPV payoff per $1,000 invested than a small one. To determine the size choice with linear programming, it is necessary to specify each of the hotel sizes as separate activities, and flag these as taking binary levels.

Dealing with multiple goals

Often, management of the firm will have multiple goals. The simplest approach for dealing with these is to use *constraint goals*. For example, if it is a goal of management that the projects selected must have a total NPV of at least $20M, create 200 jobs, ensure that a 6% dividend can be paid, or restrict the area of native vegetation which must be disturbed to 20 ha, these requirements can be included as constraints in the same way as resource supply or market size constraints. If it turns out that these constraints cannot be met in a profitable investment mix, then the constraint levels will have to be reviewed.

A more systematic way of dealing with multiple goals is through *goal programming* (GP). Here, a number of goals are identified, and a target or *aspiration level* is specified for each. For example, the firm may aspire to generate a total NPV of $20M, a dividend rate of 6%, and so on, as in the above constraint levels. *Deviational activities* are then introduced in the tableau to allow for underachievement or overachievement of goals relative to the aspiration levels. In particular, an *underachievement activity* is introduced for each aspiration floor, such as total NPV. On the other hand, an *overachievement activity* is introduced for each aspiration ceiling, e.g. area of native vegetation cleared. A series of constraints are again set up for the goals, but with equality rather than inequality signs. For example, the constraint for total NPV states that the NPVs of the investments plus NPV underachievement must equal the aspiration level of NPV.

In the objective function for goal programming, the coefficients are not the project NPV payoffs. Rather, they are the costs of underachievement and overachievement of goals relative to the aspiration levels. The objective function now states that the sum of shortfalls and over-runs, with appropriate coefficients for each, be minimized.

Because of the presence of deviational variables in goal programming, the constraints are referred to as *soft constraints*, cf. the *hard constraints* for resource limits. Even if some or all the aspiration levels cannot be met, the problem will not be found to be infeasible (with an error message when an attempt is made to find the optimal solution). Rather, levels of the deviational variables in the solution will indicate the extent to which it is not possible to meet the goal targets.

The question arises as to what coefficients or weights to place on the deviational activities. Shortfalls can be expressed in a variety of different units, such as dollars, rate of return as a percentage, jobs and hectares. One approach would be to place a weight on each deviational variable to represent the cost of goal underachievement or overachievement. Applying a system of weights to these is known as *weighted goal programming*. In practice, expressing the deviations in a common unit – say dollars – may be difficult and unnecessary.

Often a priority ordering can be established between goal dimensions, referred to as *lexicographic* or *pre-emptive* goal programming. For example, the requirement may be to achieve the target dividend rate first, then NPV payoff, then the job creation goal, and finally the environmental requirement. This could be achieved by placing weights of different orders of magnitude on the shortfall activities. However, software has been developed in which the priority ordering is stated as input data and the solution algorithm ensures this priority ordering of goals. Often, it is possible to solve lexicographic goal programming problems by using an appropriate system of weighting on deviational variables (e.g. $1M per unit shortfall for top priority goals, $0.1M for second priority goals and so on).

Incorporating risk in mathematical programming models

Keeping financial risk to an acceptable level is often considered an explicit goal of management, along with NPV maximization. The simplest way to limit exposure to risk is to avoid projects with highly uncertain payoffs. For example, if particular types of projects are known to be speculative but could create financial embarrassment for the firm, then the number of projects of this type could be limited in the project mix, through use of a mutual exclusion constraint.

A more effective but more data-demanding approach to limiting the selection of risky projects is to use *quadratic programming* (QP). Here, typically the expected payoff (NPV) and the variance of payoff for each project, and the covariance between payoffs for all pairs of projects, is estimated, often by subjective means. The model is then formulated with the objective function being the minimization of project risk, where risk is defined in terms of the variance of the total NPV, which is a quadratic function of activity (project) levels. A target level of NPV is specified as a constraint.

The quadratic programming model can be solved for various target levels of total NPV, and from the results a graph can be drawn relating level of payoff (total NPV) to level of risk (variance of NPV), enabling the decision-maker to choose their preferred trade-off point. Excel Solver can deal with quadratic programming problems. The major difficulty is, of course, to estimate the variance-covariance matrix for the payoff criterion.

Concluding comments

The various forms of mathematical programming provide a powerful means of selecting an optimal combination of investment projects subject to capital and other constraints. While the linear programming formulation appears to impose a number of limitations on the flexibility with which a model of the decision problem can be specified, in practice it is a relatively simple matter to develop a formulation which overcomes these restrictions. For example, indivisible investments can be modelled as binary variables using a mixed integer solution facility. Binary activity levels in turn can be used to model investment in infrastructure to support revenue-generating activities, threshold activity levels and mutual exclusion between activities. Inclusion of supply activities (particularly borrowing activities) and transfer activities allows more realistic multi-period models to be developed. Goal and quadratic programming allow multiple goals of management including risk aversion to be taken into consideration. In most cases, the decision models formulated for capital budgeting can be solved using widely available computer software, such as Excel Solver.

Review questions

12.1 With regard to Example 12.1:
- (a) solve this problem using MILP, with each generation project specified as a binary activity;
- (b) solve the problem using MILP, with the requirement that only one natural gas project can be selected, and at least two of the windfarm, biofuel and solar panel projects should be included. (*Hint*: Mutual inclusion requires similar formulation to mutual exclusion, except for the direction of the inequality sign.)

12.2 Suppose in Example 12.5 that the manufacturer wishes to restrict the selection to only two product lines, and that either hockey or baseball equipment is to be included in the optimal plan. Modify the model and determine which product lines constitute the optimal mix.

12.3 A gas company is planning a natural gas export project. This involves three component projects, namely to develop the gas field, construct a pipeline to a large coastal city, and develop a gas liquidification and export facility at the end of the pipeline. In the first case, gas would be sold on-site to another company. If the pipeline is constructed, the company could find domestic markets for all its production. A gas liquidification and export facility would allow substantially higher gas prices to be obtained through exporting. $160M is available for investment. Gas-field development would cost $50M, pipeline construction $60M, and development of a liquidification plant and an export facility $45M. Respective NPV payoffs are $20M if gas is sold on-site, $10M for sales domestically and $30M if gas is exported. Set up a MILP model and solve this problem, taking account of the contingency relationship between the three component projects.

12.4 A fisherman is considering expansion of his operations. He has the opportunity to purchase a new fishing boat and net licence, to set up an on-shore fish processing depot and to build a fish canning operation. His current scale of operation does not warrant setting up the processing plant. The canning operation cannot proceed unless on-shore processing is carried out. The net present values for the three projects are $2M, $1M and $1.5M. Year 1 and year 2 capital outlays for the new boat and licence are $400,000 and $200,000, for the processing plant $300,000 and $300,000, and for the canning plant $200,000 and $300,000. The fisherman has $800,000 in cash reserves, and can borrow money in years 1 and 2, of up to $1M in total, at a 12% interest rate. Set up these investment opportunities as a linear programming model, and determine the optimal investment portfolio.

12.5 A developer is planning to construct a new five-star hotel on a prime inner city site. Three alternative design and size options are under consideration, with net capital

Table 12.8. *Capital expenditure for alternative hotel designs*

	Design 1	Design 2	Design 3
Capital expenditure, EOY 0 ($M)	2	5	3
Capital expenditure, EOY 1 ($M)	12	15	11
Capital expenditure, EOY 2 ($M)	4	6	8

outlays in the first three years as shown in Table 12.8, after which the hotel should be self-funding.

The developer has $20M in readily available funds, and can borrow further finance of up to $5M at an interest rate of 14%. The three designs have estimated net present values over twenty years of $10M, $17M and $9M. Set up a linear programming model which can be used to assist in project choice.

13 Financial modelling case study in forestry project evaluation

This chapter presents a case study of the structure and application of financial models for the evaluation of investment projects in forestry. Forestry projects provide a good example of capital budgeting in that forestry is a very long-term investment, i.e. one with substantial initial outlays but with main cash inflows typically more than thirty years later. The case study illustrates principles which would apply equally well to other forms of long-term investment, e.g. in mining, energy, tourism or manufacturing.

While one-off models can be developed to evaluate individual forestry projects, the cash outflows and inflows of all forestry projects have much in common, giving rise to the opportunity to develop a *generic model* which can be used to evaluate a variety of separate investment projects by a variety of users. Generic models are often large and complex, and involve considerable development effort. A generic model has important advantages over a one-off model for investment areas where projects with similar features repeatedly arise. Development costs can be spread over a number of applications or users. Greater expertise can be brought to bear in the design, development and testing of the model, and it is often possible to include a greater range of features or capabilities in the model.

When designing and developing a generic model, a number of important questions need to be addressed: What is the model to be used for? Who is going to use the model? How is it to be used? What are the most appropriate design features? How will the model be tested for validity and user friendliness? Who will be responsible in the future for making changes to the model to accommodate unanticipated or novel applications? Who will be responsible for handling user queries and training?

This chapter examines the various questions and issues in the development and application of generic models for project evaluation. As a way of illustrating some of these issues, a financial model which has been developed to evaluate forestry investments using native tree species in eastern Australia is reviewed. Attention is paid to user groups, choice of model type, computing platform, model design options, and model testing and maintenance.

Study objectives

After studying this chapter the reader should be able to:

- appreciate the benefits which can arise from the availability of a generic model for financial evaluation of investments in a particular field
- understand the various design objectives which may be involved in developing a generic financial model to evaluate investment projects in a particular area
- identify a number of financial models available to evaluate forestry investments
- recognize the uses and user groups of forestry evaluation models
- understand how models evolve through a number of versions over time and are progressively refined, generalized and made easier to use
- appreciate the high resource requirements involved in the design, development, testing and maintenance of generic project evaluation models.

Forestry evaluation models: uses and user groups

The traditional use of financial models is to assess simply the financial viability of a proposed investment. As well as deriving single-point estimates of financial performance criteria, sensitivity analysis and risk simulation may be performed to explore the impact of variations from the core assumptions. Models can also be used to explore investment alternatives. For instance, forestry models applied to joint ventures can be used to explore the impact on cash flows of different equity participation arrangements. Large pastoral companies can also use financial models to explore the impact that forestry may have on their overall business risk. The way in which a model is to be used is a crucial consideration in design of the model.

Commonly, financial models are constructed to investigate a specific capital budgeting project, which may be independent of other projects under consideration or one of a number of mutually exclusive projects. Previous chapters have demonstrated that spreadsheets are convenient and powerful tools that can be used in the analysis of capital projects. Often the nature of the analysis means that novel spreadsheets are developed each time a new project is assessed. Because of the structured nature of project evaluation, these spreadsheets are often quite similar in nature. This is certainly true for forestry investments, where particular categories of costs and revenue are recognizable for any investment.

Recall the example in Chapter 10, where a spreadsheet was used to evaluate the 1,000 ha forestry proposal of FVC Ltd. For the company, this would have been a one-off appraisal of a forestry investment, or at most one of a limited number of forestry projects. Developing a spreadsheet model that only applied to the particular investment under consideration was thus an appropriate and cost-effective option. If, however, FVC Ltd were a promoter of forestry schemes, it would likely be undertaking such analyses on a regular basis. In such cases, it would be appropriate to develop a more generic model which could be used to assess a range of forestry investments.

Forestry financial models can potentially be used by a number of different groups and for a number of different purposes. For instance, a company which frequently promotes forestry schemes to investors would require a model that could be easily adapted to new areas and different tree species. Alternatively, a government department promoting joint venture arrangements involving only one or two species but which involve different equity-sharing arrangements with private landholders would need a model that was flexible in a different way. In both cases, it would be inefficient to develop a new spreadsheet-based model for each new situation.

Globally, forestry is a major economic activity at the farm level and can be a significant contributor to gross domestic product (GDP), particularly in many European countries. Farm operations, however, are highly diverse in terms of area planted (thousands of hectares down to very small plots), species chosen, management regime, harvest age and other variables. Forestry is also only part of the overall business undertaking of the landowner, and must be considered in this context.

Farmers also often lack the skills to develop financial models capable of modelling their activities. The provision of models to be used as a tool to undertake this type of analysis is often done as a form of assistance or extension service by governments. In such cases, models need to be highly flexible and often also take into account the impact that forestry has on the overall operations of the farm, particularly cash flows. The impact that forestry has on the farm financial structure and cash flows can be critical. In such cases, a project with a positive NPV may be rejected because it cannot be accommodated within the financial structure of the business (i.e. the question of how, if at all, the project can be financed becomes critical).

Forestry financial models are also useful for land valuers, real estate agents and lending agencies, who often have a need to place a value on immature forests when estimating market values or evaluating loan proposals for rural properties. They also have a role in training foresters and as a teaching device.

Financial models available to evaluate forestry investments

A number of publicly available models have been developed for evaluation of forestry investments. Of particular interest here are several large generic models developed recently in Australia and New Zealand.

The FARMTREE model (Loane, 1994) contains considerable detail on tree growth rates, product recoveries and stock shelter effects for *Pinus radiata* grown in parts of southern Australia. The Agroforestry Estate Model (Middlemiss and Knowles, 1996) is a whole-farm model in which estimates of timber yields are provided by the user. This is a commercial software package, used under licence, which is regularly maintained and has user support mechanisms in place, hence the adoption rate has been high. It is also actively marketed by the developers, so it has a higher adoption rate than the other models mentioned here.

The AGROFARM spreadsheet models have been developed for research and extension purposes by the Centre for Agricultural and Regional Economics (CARE) Pty Ltd and have a focus on northern New South Wales. These whole-of-business models include taxation and allow for joint-venture arrangements. Risk can be added to the model structure using the @RISK or Insight add-in for Excel.

The Australian Cabinet Timbers Financial Model, or ACTFM (Herbohn, Harrison and Emtage, 1999), estimates NPV and LEV for forestry investments in northern Australia involving non-traditional eucalypt and rainforest timber species. The Australian Farm Forestry Financial Model, or AFFFM (Emtage *et al.*, 2001) involves a combination of the features of the CARE AGROFARM models and the ACTFM model. The objective with AFFFM was to develop a stand-alone whole-farm model for use by researchers and forestry advisers, with a geographic focus on northern New South Wales and south-eastern Queensland.

While these models have much in common, each has been developed to meet a particular need. The Australian Cabinet Timbers Financial Model is now examined in greater detail, as a case study in the development of a generic forestry evaluation model.

The Australian Cabinet Timbers Financial Model (ACTFM)

The Australian Cabinet Timbers Financial Model has been developed as a flexible and user-friendly computer-based model suitable for assessing the financial viability of timber plantations using Australian native eucalypt and cabinet species in North Queensland. Little published information exists on growth rates of many of these native tree species. To provide information for the model about the growth rates and optimal harvest ages for the thirty-one species included in the model, it was necessary to undertake a Delphi survey of experts on North Queensland forestry. Details of this study are provided in later subsections.

The model contains a number of linked sheets in an Excel workbook format. Sheets are used to store or display data or information about the program, and to perform calculations of the value of the plantation scenario established by the user. The model was developed on Excel (version 7.0) software and contains a collection of Visual Basic macros. It requires the Excel program to operate. To navigate between various data input and model output screens, a system of 'button bars' is provided. Notably, the model was developed by researchers and not professional computer programmers. A schematic representation of the structure of the model is provided in Figure 13.1.

The model has been set up with an attractive opening sheet, which indicates the model name, the names of the developers and the version of the model, and acknowledges the agencies providing financial support for model development. From the title page access is gained to the Plantation Output summary sheet (Figure 13.2) by clicking on a Start button. This in turn is linked to the various other sheets in the workbook, which provide default data and instructions and other information to the user, to allow calculation of net present value and the internal rate of return. The menu system to allow the user to move freely between sheets in the ACTFM workbooks consists of a series of buttons, on which the user simply clicks the computer mouse. The various sheets provide:

- information about the program
- data relating to mean annual increments (MAI), stumpage prices, and harvest ages of thirty-one different cabinet timber species

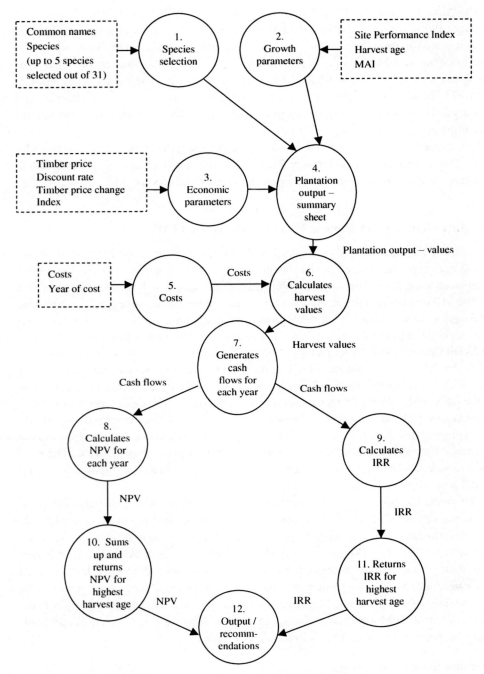

Figure 13.1.   Schematic representation of the structure of the ACTFM.

• data relating to establishment and maintenance costs
• tables for the entry of alternative MAI, price, costs and harvest age data, and
• pages containing Visual Basic code.

Users can see and access all the information about a plantation scenario with up to five species on one sheet (Figure 13.2). Users can also choose to select default data to run the model, or may enter their own growth, cost and price data.

The main outputs of the model are summarized in the Plantation Output sheet in order to make it easy to see what is happening in terms of the volumes of timber produced, the value of the harvest and the timing of returns. This sheet also assists in understanding the effects of changing each variable on the overall financial performance of the plantation. More detailed output from the financial analysis is displayed in the Economic Summary sheet which can be accessed from the Plantation Output sheet by a button bar.

Default values of the model

The model contains embedded estimates for a number of parameters used in the calculation of NPV and IRR, some of which are presented in Table 13.1. Default values for MAI and harvest ages were derived from a Delphi survey of experts on North Queensland forestry undertaken for thirty-one cabinet timber species in 1996–7, and are probably the best projections currently available of future growth of many of the species. They are, however, for restricted growth conditions (relatively fertile basalt derived soils in areas of 1,600–2,000 mm rainfall) and so users may wish to enter site-specific values. This need is to some extent overcome by the inclusion of a site index variable, which allows the user to vary the MAI (growth) data for all species in a scenario according to the conditions for which the model is being used relative to those specified for the estimates. If, for example, the soils are less fertile than basalt-derived soils or the site under consideration receives less rainfall, then the site productivity index can be set at less than 100%, reducing the estimated volume of timber produced in the scenario. However, if the rainfall regime in the area for which the plantation scenario is established is greater than 2,000 mm per year and on fertile soil, or irrigation of the plantation is planned, then the site productivity index may be set at greater than 100%. The maximum allowable value for the index is 150%, and the minimum 50%. The default value for the index is 100%.

The default values for the costs of establishing and maintaining a plantation that are supplied with the model are those for Community Rainforest Reafforestation Program (CRRP) plantings in the Atherton Tablelands region. Cost items include land preparation and planting, pruning and certification of pruning, weeding, fertilizers and fencing. Also, allowance is made for the opportunity cost of financial returns to the land foregone with plantation establishment, and for insurance and road maintenance. It is arguable whether a land rental amount should be included as part of the cost of the plantation, particularly in the case of degraded or otherwise unproductive land.

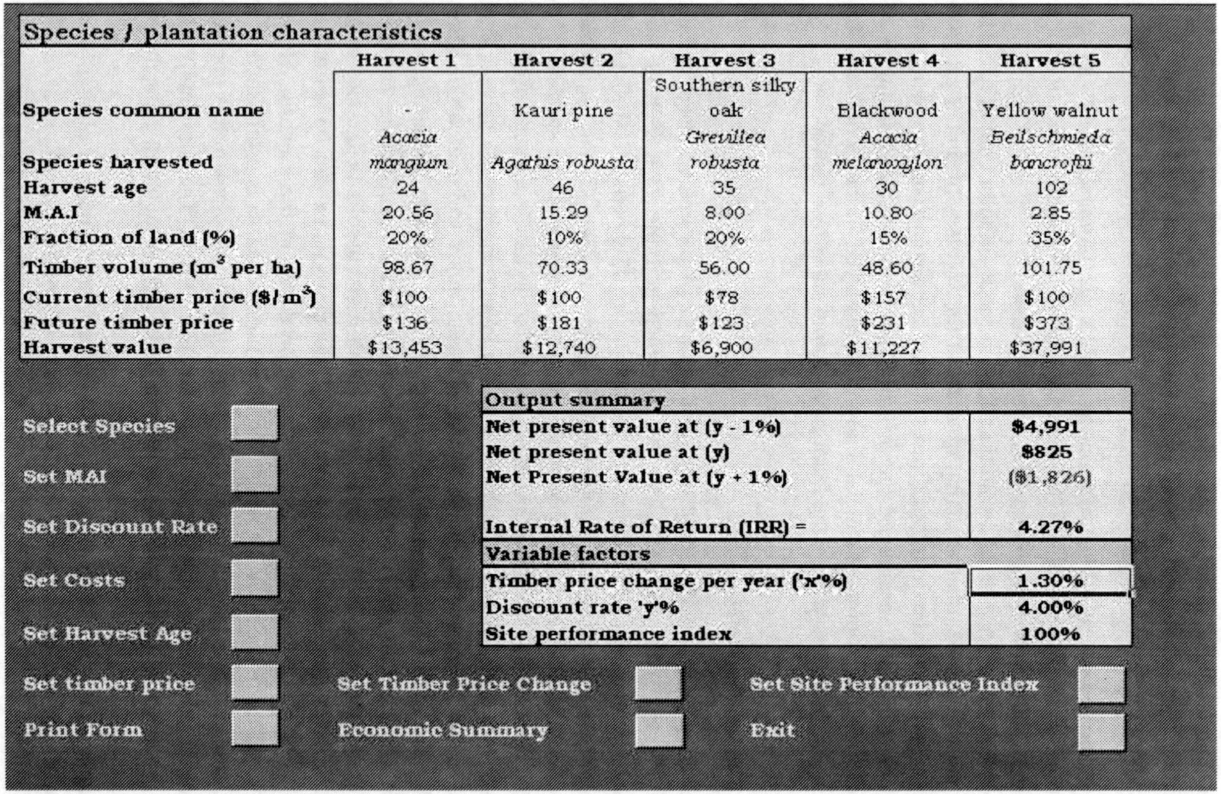

Species *j* plantation characteristics

	Harvest 1	Harvest 2	Harvest 3	Harvest 4	Harvest 5
Species common name		Kauri pine	Southern silky oak	Blackwood	Yellow walnut
	Acacia mangium	*Agathis robusta*	*Grevillea robusta*	*Acacia melanoxylon*	*Beilschmieda bancroftii*
Species harvested					
Harvest age	24	46	35	30	102
M.A.I	20.56	15.29	8.00	10.80	2.85
Fraction of land (%)	20%	10%	20%	15%	35%
Timber volume (m^3 per ha)	98.67	70.33	56.00	48.60	101.75
Current timber price ($/m^3)	$100	$100	$78	$157	$100
Future timber price	$136	$181	$123	$231	$373
Harvest value	$13,453	$12,740	$6,900	$11,227	$37,991

Output summary

Net present value at (y − 1%)	$4,991
Net present value at (y)	$825
Net Present Value at (y + 1%)	($1,826)
Internal Rate of Return (IRR) =	4.27%

Variable factors

Timber price change per year ('x'%)	1.30%
Discount rate 'y'%	4.00%
Site performance index	100%

Select Species Set MAI Set Discount Rate Set Costs Set Harvest Age Set timber price Print Form

Set Timber Price Change Economic Summary Set Site Performance Index Exit

Figure 13.2. ACTFM: example of plantation output sheet.

Table 13.1. *Estimated harvest ages, timber yields and timber prices for eucalypt and cabinet timber species in North Queensland*

Species	Harvest age (yrs)	Yield (MAI in m³/ha)	Timber price ($/m³)
Acacia mangium	23.9	20.6	
Acacia melanoxylon	29.5	10.8	299
Agathis robusta	46.2	15.3	
Araucaria cunninghamii	43.8	19.4	
Beilschmieda bancroftii	102.0	2.9	
Blepharocarya involucrigera	47.9	8.7	
Cardwellia sublimis	58.1	7.5	317
Castanospermum australe	66.7	5.9	280
Cedrela odorata	37.5	10.3	242
Ceratopetalum apetalum	113.3	5.0	355
Elaeocarpus angustifolius	33.8	16.9	317
Endiandra palmerstonii	156.0	4.5	653
Eucalyptus camalduensis	28.1	17.0	
Eucalyptus citriodora	32.0	16.1	
Eucalyptus cloeziana	35.5	17.2	47
Eucalyptus cloeziana (poles)	25.5	15.8	
Eucalyptus drepanophylla	44.4	10.8	
Eucalyptus grandis	31.4	20.6	
Eucalyptus microcorys	30.6	15.8	
Eucalyptus pellita (resinifera)	30.6	16.3	75
Eucalyptus tetreticornis	31.7	16.0	
Flindersia australis	57.5		355
Flindersia bourjotiana	52.5	10.3	373
Flindersia brayleana	43.0	13.5	205
Flindersia iffliana	56.7	8.0	243
Flindersia pimenteliana	55.0	9.0	317
Flindersia schotiana	48.3	8.5	467
Gmelina fasciculiflora	54.2	8.6	280
Grevillia robusta	35.0	8.0	149
Melia azedarach	31.1	13.7	243
Paraserianthes toona	55.0	7.1	
Toona cilata (australis)	48.8	8.9	336

Notes: Assumed biophysical conditions: basalt-derived soils, annual rainfall 1,600–2,000 mm per year. Price estimates were not available for some uncommon species.

Timber prices and price changes over time

The generic stumpage price of $100/m³ has been used as a default value, being the approximate royalty received by the state forest service for plantation hoop pine at the time of model development. The model allows users the option of selecting their own generic stumpage price. Stumpage prices have a major influence on estimates of NPV and IRR, hence sensitivity analysis is reported in the Economic Summary sheet.

1. Prescriptive costs	Cost/ha
Planning and design	74
Incidental clearing	158
Site preperation and cultivation	265
Cover crop establishment	88
Pre-plant weed control	92
Cost of plants	450
Planting and refilling	645
Post plant weed control	540
Fertilizer	83
Fencing	560
2. Additional Prescriptive Costs	
Sub-total	2955.00

Figure 13.3. Prescriptive costs sheet. Additional prescriptive costs can be added by entering the cost type and amount under section 2. They will be added to the sub-total.

Costs During Plantation	Year of Cost	Cost/ha
Post plant weed control	1	1310
Post plant weed control	2	812
Post plant weed control	3	213
First prune (plus certification)	4	880
Second prune (plus certification)	8	648.6
Third prune (plus certification)	12	864.4
Thinning	8	501
First harvest marking and inventory	49	57
Second harvest marking and inventory	58	57
Third harvest marking and inventory	55	57
Fourth harvest marking and inventory	48	57
Fifth harvest marking and inventory	102	80
Additional costs during plantation		

Figure 13.4. Costs during plantation sheet. Additional plantation costs can be added by entering cost type, year of cost and the amount under 'Additional costs during plantation'. They will be included in the calculations in the spreadsheet.

Annual costs	
Land value (per ha)	$2,000
Land rental (capitalised @ 4% of land value)	80
Protection and management	40
Insurence	
Additional Annual costs	
Total annual costs	120

Figure 13.5. Annual costs sheet. Additional annual costs can be added by entering the cost type and amount. They will then be included in 'Total annual costs'.

Figures 13.3–13.5. Default costs (CRRP costs) from the Australian Cabinet Timbers Financial Model.

Given that most of the species being planted are premium cabinet timbers it is likely that the average stumpage received for these will be considerably higher than that for hoop pine. The only available estimates of future stumpage price for many of the species in the model have been derived by a commercial consultant and are reported in Russell *et al.* (1993). No default price is supplied for species not examined by these authors. Users can set their own timber prices by selecting the Set Timber Prices button on the front sheet, and selecting the Set Own Timber Prices checkbox in the dialogue box that is subsequently displayed. This will result in a new table being displayed, showing the species and their prices, that can be altered individually by users.

A number of studies on the future of the timber trade in Australia and overseas have suggested that it is likely that cabinet timber prices will increase in real terms in the foreseeable future as world supplies from native forests diminish and the demand for such timbers increases.

The rate at which timber prices change per year can be set in the ACTFM by selecting the button Set Timber Price Change Rate. Russell *et al.* (1993) suggested a possible increase of up to 1.3% per annum in timber prices, which is considered conservative by the authors when it is compared to a number of long-term forecasts. The default value for the model is 0% although the option is available to set a real price change between +5% and −5%.

Output values generated by the ACTFM

The ACTFM calculates the financial returns that may be expected from a hypothetical eucalypt or cabinet timber plantation, expressed in the form of net present value (NPV) and internal rate of return (IRR) per hectare of the plantation. The NPV of a plantation in the model is the financial return that can be expected from harvesting the trees for timber in today's values. The model adopts a 7% discount rate, but also provides NPV estimates with the discount rate varied by +1% and −1%. Outputs from the model are displayed on screen, but a Print button is available to generate a hard-copy version.

Further comments about the model

ACTFM takes into account only financial benefits, and does not include non-wood benefits to the firm or agency establishing the plantations. If, for example, carbon credits were available from growing the trees, then this additional income could be included in the model.

The model assumes fixed harvest ages (default values or entered by the user) and does not directly allow for a trade-off between harvest age and timber revenue. However, the user could enter their own estimates of harvest age and timber price, and could rerun the model with different combinations. The model does not allow directly for any interaction between species in mixed species plantings, although again the user could adjust timber yields if they were confident about estimates of interactions.

A stochastic version of this model has also been developed (Harrison, Herbohn and Emtage, 2001), while other versions have had other features added such as the calculation of LEV and the ability to add new species for use in specific financial analyses. It has been used by a variety of forestry stakeholders, including forestry investors, consultants, farm forestry advisers, by researchers and students, by corporate users, and by valuers and real estate agents.

Evolutionary development of the ACTFM

Development of the ACTFM commenced with a very simple financial model which had been produced in a national forestry inquiry. Even though the ACTFM represents the culmination of several years of model development, it is still recognized to have limitations in terms of its suitability for evaluating a wide range of forestry investment projects. Experience in developing and trialling the ACTFM led to recognition of a need for some users to model the impact of forestry on the wider business activities, along with a more robust modelling framework not dependent on Excel. In response to this, the whole-farm planning components of the CARE Pty Ltd financial model and the ACTFM financial model have been integrated in a user-friendly stand-alone Visual Basic programmed package, known as the Australian Farm Forestry Financial Model (AFFFM). This model is designed to evaluate forestry investment proposals on mixed farming properties in eastern Australia.

Review of model development and design options

The above case study has provided insights into a number of decisions which have to be made in relation to the nature of the financial model to be used for the evaluation of forestry investment proposals in a practical setting. Similar decisions would arise in project evaluation in other investment areas, such as mining or tourism. Some of the options are indicated in Table 13.2.

The issue of one-off versus generic models was discussed above. This is basically a question of cost-effectiveness. If a model is to be used repeatedly, then greater effort in model development is warranted. It may be that a generic model is already available, which has been developed elsewhere. Regardless of whether this is 'freeware' or moderately expensive to acquire, it may be in the best interests of the firm to gain access to such a package rather than commit staff time to developing its own model.

No matter whether the model framework is acquired from external sources or developed in-house, an important consideration when planning the evaluation of a forestry project is whether the assessment is to be undertaken for the individual investment in isolation or in the context of the overall business operations and cash flows. Small-scale forestry is often an incremental investment with relatively small impact on the firm's cash flow pattern. Large forestry investments may have a severe adverse impact on the time pattern of cash flows, warranting consideration in a whole-of-business context.

Well-designed generic models can cope with a wide range of investment circumstances. However, it is not possible to predict all of the situations in which people may wish to use a model. In the design of a generic model, it is critical to give consideration to the degree of flexibility that is required for changes to be made, the availability of skilled modellers to make changes in the model to accommodate novel or unforeseen applications, and the

Table 13.2. *Modelling options for forestry investments*

Characteristic of model	Options
Model complexity and resource demands	One-off or generic
Model property rights	Developed by investor or off-the-shelf
Level of business activity	Forestry enterprise or whole-of-business
Level of flexibility	Narrow to wide range of applications
Modelling platform	Spreadsheet programs (e.g. Excel), programming languages (e.g. C^{++}, Visual Basic) or simulation languages (e.g. Stella, Simile)
Type of yield modelling	Growth curves, growth simulations using packages such as Plantgro, discrete harvest age and MAI
Source of input data	Default (trial-based, subjectively estimated, simulated) vs user-provided
User interface	Menu system, button bars
Choice of project benefit categories	Wood only vs wider benefits (financial vs economic)
Representation of investment risk	RADR, sensitivity analysis, risk analysis
Choice of project performance variables	NPV vs LEV, IRR, not payback period
User support	None, access to technical assistance, package maintenance

choice of computing platform to suit user needs. This can also be a major influence on the software used to develop the model.

For a large and complex generic model, a spreadsheet platform may not be suitable. In such cases, it may become necessary to resort to programming languages such as Visual Basic or C^{++}. In other cases, modelling environments such as Simile, which have been specifically developed for use in developing models for complex resource management decisions (as are often required in forestry projects) may be appropriate.

When traditional timber species are grown, the growth curve (yield vs age) is generally available, but this is not the case for non-traditional species such as Australian eucalypts and cabinet timbers. In this case, it may be necessary to settle for point estimates of plantation harvest age and yield (MAI) based on expert opinion. Alternatively, models such as Plantgro and other physiological models may be used to estimate the yield based on key determinants of growth such as soil type, rainfall and temperature.

In general, the user has to enter a variety of input data into the model relating to their particular investment situation. However, to the extent that forestry parameters are relatively constant between sites, a model may be made much easier to use if a variety of *default data* are embedded in it. Such data could include, for example, cost estimates for operations such as site development and planting, fertilizer, weed control and thinning, and estimates of growth rates and timber prices for a variety of tree species. If these default data can readily be viewed by the user, then the user can decide whether to accept them or enter more precise case-specific values.

For these generic models to be used by a variety of stakeholders, most of whom have little understanding of the mechanics of the model, the user interface, or series of screens for data input and output, has proved to be a critical design factor. Also, ease of navigation around the model is critical, and a convenient way to provide this is through button bars which are clickable with the mouse.

While plantations are often established primarily for timber production, the owners may have an interest in *multiple-use forestry*, and in fact government-owned plantations are usually managed from this perspective in almost all countries. As well as returns from timber sales, a forest owner may gain income, status or pleasure out of having a standing forest. Income opportunities could arise from allowing the forest to be used for recreation purposes such as hunting, berry and mushroom collecting or tramping (bushwalking). There is also a developing market for the sale of carbon fixed by trees (commonly known as 'carbon credits'), with at least one futures market already operating through the Sydney Futures Exchange. Company or personal status benefits could arise from being regarded as undertaking environmentally responsible activities (contributing to carbon sequestration, watershed protection, flood mitigation or the provision of wildlife habitats). Personal pleasure may arise from improved landscape appearance or the increased presence of native birds and animals. In the last two decades, much research has been carried out on the inclusion of these non-wood forest benefits (NWFBs) in the evaluation of forestry investments. The continued access to land on which to grow trees and the ability to harvest trees when mature are also often dependent on plantations being managed for multiple uses.

Forestry investments by their long-term nature and various sources of uncertainty (as discussed in Chapter 10) are relatively high-risk investments. In practice, sensitivity analysis and sometimes risk analysis are used to examine project risk. Inclusion of NWFBs in the evaluation may reduce the estimated investment risk.

The investment performance criterion advocated in earlier chapters has generally been the net present value. While NPV is often the appropriate criterion for judging forestry investments, it has limitations when comparing alternative forestry investments or comparing forestry with other land uses. For example, suppose we wish to compare an eight-year woodchip project and a thirty-year lumber project. It could be that the lumber project has a higher NPV per hectare of plantation. However, once the woodchip stand is harvested, a new tree crop may be planted or the land may be used for pasture or other profitable purposes. This alternative earning opportunity is not possible for many years with the longer-rotation lumber project. Use of the NPV criterion fails to take account of the future land use under different project lives. The calculation of the NPV of an infinite series of identical rotations is one way to overcome this problem of comparing plantations with different rotation lengths. The resulting value is often referred to as the *land expectation value* (LEV) or *site value*. LEV is simply a specialist case of NPV, which is used when comparing projects of unequal duration. Adopting the LEV criterion assumes the land will be used permanently for forestry, and removes any need to consider future alternative land uses. The LEV will be considerably higher than the NPV for short rotations, but for long rotations will differ little from the NPV. The IRR is again appropriate for forestry investments. There is normally little purpose in calculating the payback period for forestry projects, because this is typically the age of final harvest.

Where the model developer and user are different people within an organization, or are in different organizations, then the availability of technical support for users and further development of the model becomes important. Some problems invariably arise when a person is using a model they did not develop, and users will quickly lose confidence and abandon a computer package for which technical support is inadequate. If an existing model is used which has been developed external to the investor, then access to help in using the model (documentation within the package, user manual, help line) and the maintenance of the model become important factors.

Concluding comments

The development of a forestry financial model (the ACTFM) illustrates some of the issues which arise when developing a generic model for evaluation of proposed investments in a particular sector. It was soon found that a spreadsheet-based model was not adequate for dealing with a complex biological and financial analysis, because of capacity constraints and slow runtime. Development or purchase of generic models becomes cost-effective when one is faced with repeated decisions about investments of a similar nature. In any particular application area (such as forestry investment), there tends to be a variety of generic models available, and spending a little time investigating the accessibility and features of existing models can save a lot of time in 'reinventing the wheel'.

Both activity-specific and whole-of-business models appear to fill a need for forestry investors, the relative suitability depending on the magnitude of the forestry investment relative to other activities of the firm. The business has to be able to support the cash flow pattern and long payback period of forestry. In this context, it may be critical to know the impact of a forestry project on annual cash flows of the business.

The experience of developing these models has highlighted the fact that large multi-user financial models are not constructed in a single stage. There are always features which one would like to add to a financial model. If the model is proving useful, and there is continued enthusiasm by the developers, and someone is prepared to provide funding, then the model may keep evolving and improving. This has been the case with financial models for the evaluation of plantations of Australian native tree species. Hence, generic models typically evolve through a number of versions over time, as continued design work, modelling and testing take place and the variety of potential uses becomes clearer. In general, large models make use of components or modules developed in previous modelling efforts.

A critical stage in the development of large financial models is 'field testing' where representatives of the various potential user groups make trial runs and provide feedback on the usefulness, the user interfaces, the apparent validity of estimates and any computing problems experienced.

In terms of testing, rather than having a set of validity tests, confidence is built up in a model over time as it is used by a variety of people in a variety of applications and proceeds through a number of versions. The ACTFM has undergone this progressive development and testing.

It has also been evident that a commitment to the construction of a large and generic model has substantial resource implications. The ACTFM required about two full-time person-years in programming and evaluation of prototypes by various users. Similar inputs were required for the AFFFM model, in addition to which a professional programmer was hired to make final revisions for programming efficiency and ease of use. The cost of developing a generic model to a standard where it may be used as a commercial product will typically be over $100,000, and further maintenance costs will arise.

With a generic model, it is important to clarify the legal responsibility of the model developer in relation to commercial decisions taken using information generated by the model. Normally, the developer cannot reasonably be held responsible for commercial decisions which turn out to be less successful than anticipated, and in this context it is important to issue a clear disclaimer of this responsibility.

Review questions

13.1 Consider an investment area with which you are familiar. What (if any) software packages are available designed specifically for financial analysis in this area? What features do these packages possess which you consider useful for project evaluation?

13.2 Consider an investment area with which you are familiar. Suppose that development of a financial model which can be used to evaluate a range of investment proposals is being contemplated.

(a) Identify some of the uses to which such a model could be put.

(b) Which financial performance criteria would you consider to be most appropriate for these types of applications? Explain your logic.

(c) How would you suggest the generic model should be designed? Suggest a model structure and set of features, and illustrate with diagrams.

(d) What default data do you think would be useful to include in this model?

(e) Develop designs for:
    (i)   the opening computer screen for the model
    (ii) data input screens
    (iii) data output screens.

(f) Explain how such a model could be tested and how it might be maintained.

14 Property investment analysis

Property (or real estate) is any interest in land and its buildings. Purchasing or leasing a property is a capital budgeting decision that can be evaluated in the ways described in the preceding chapters. In many ways, the decision is no different to acquiring any asset that is expected to provide returns in the future. We apply all the usual principles of capital budgeting but there are some features of property investments and developments that require special care.

There are four main features of properties that distinguish them from most other assets. First, buying a property is an *'all-or-nothing' decision* with limited choice at any time. Investors must often compromise in their search for the right property and yet the outlay is often the largest made by both private investors and businesses. Properties are not uniform, partial acquisitions are generally impractical and there are sizable transaction costs. Except for property developments, the only way to alter the scale of the investment is to change the financing arrangements.

A second distinction of properties is that *each is financed separately*, rather than drawing on a pool of company funds. Typically, the financing may be with a mortgage secured over the legal interest of the investor or company. This is one reason why the property and its financing are commonly evaluated together. This is a significant departure from the corporate approach explained in Chapter 2, in which it was pointed out that properties are commonly evaluated by working out their 'equity' cash flows. The details and rationale for this are explained later in this chapter.

Thirdly, there are *distinct patterns in the cash flows* from properties that influence the way in which rents, expenses and values are forecast. Rents fixed for several years are common for non-residential properties, which makes the leases important in forecasting rents. The resale value or terminal value is often the most important element of the projected cash flows and hence needs special consideration. Rather than being a residual, the resale value may be the rationale for the acquisition. Severe cycles in property markets are seemingly unavoidable and must be incorporated into forecasts of rents and values. These issues and the importance of local knowledge in property forecasts are explored more fully in Chapter 15, together with the related analysis of the uncertainty of the cash flows.

Fourthly, *most tax systems have special rules for real estate*. Depreciation for tax purposes separates land, buildings, plant within buildings and acquisition costs although they are one asset. There are often special rules for calculating taxable capital gains from the sale of properties. Passive investors (those who acquire properties to receive rent) may be treated differently to businesses occupying properties. All these complications emphasize the importance of analysing cash flows after tax.

This chapter illustrates capital budgeting for three types of property decision. The first is the *acquisition of an income-producing property* by an investor. The objective of buying the property is to earn investment returns in the form of rent and/or capital gain. The investor may be a private entity, a public company or an institutional fund. The property is evaluated as an addition to the investor's portfolio, rather like a company acquiring an asset for its incremental effects on cash flows. As we saw in Chapters 2 and 6, an acceptable project has cash flows with a present value greater than the initial outlay.

The second illustration is the evaluation of premises to be used by a business. Many of these capital budgeting decisions are the same as the examples in previous chapters. They can be settled by estimating the incremental effects of acquiring the property. As well as simple decisions on whether to expand into new premises or not, businesses are confronted with choices of properties and timing choices. Sometimes, the critical choice is in the nature of a financial issue: should the business lease or buy the property? All of these are termed *corporate real estate decisions*.

The third and final illustration in this chapter is the *development of a site* for a new use. Typically, this involves the creation of an asset over many periods. The project is generally based on the acquisition of a vacant (or redevelopment) site and then a series of cash outflows whilst a building is constructed or infrastructure is provided. Upon the completion of the development, the property may be sold or retained for its use or income-producing potential.

An industrial property, which could be in virtually any metropolitan area, is used to explain these three common decisions about properties. Although the type of property is largely irrelevant to the analysis, it is helpful to have a tangible property in mind when grappling with the dollars it generates. All the examples in this chapter are based upon a modern industrial property. As with most industrial properties, it is little more than an enclosed tall space with an ancillary office or showroom at the front of the building. There is sufficient land on the site for car parking and truck deliveries. The property is located amongst similar buildings, close to major roads and a rail terminal.

Study objectives

After studying this chapter the reader should be able to:

• apply the usual methods of capital budgeting to property decisions
• work out both property cash flows and equity cash flows and know when to use each
• evaluate properties on behalf of investors, corporations and developers.

Income-producing properties

Income-producing properties are acquired by investors for their rents and growth in value. In essence, the present value of these two elements, discounted at a rate that reflects the risk of

Table 14.1. *Operating cash flows before tax*

Gross rent as if fully let
less
vacancy allowance
operating expenses
Operating cash flows before tax

not receiving them, is compared with the initial outlay on the property, based upon the asking price (as in Chapter 6). The steps in building a cash flow model to evaluate income-producing properties in this way are described here and illustrated using the industrial property.

The period of analysis

Property investments are almost always evaluated over a period that is less than the life of the asset. Their lives are much longer than our ability to forecast returns from the properties. As a general rule, property investments should be evaluated over a five-year period, or less if the investor plans to sell sooner. Some investors may have no clear idea of how long they plan to retain a property. Some may express intentions of holding onto properties for ten years or more. However, given the volatility of property markets and their links to the regional and national economy, there is little point in projecting cash flows beyond a five-year horizon (although some analysts do attempt ten- or fifteen-year projections).

For a five-year analysis, annual intervals are normally sufficient, although quarterly or even monthly analysis is relatively easy using a computer spreadsheet. If the intervals are less than annual, yearly summaries are essential to be able to review the expected performance of the investment.

Establishing the operating cash flows before tax

The owner of an income-producing property receives rent and any other charges paid by the occupants, less any loss to vacancies and less the recurrent operating expenses. The calculation of the operating cash flows for each year (or shorter interval) is shown in Table 14.1 (the terminology may vary in other markets). Operating cash flows from properties are termed 'net income' (in the UK and Australia) or 'net operating income' (in the USA). As explained in Chapter 2, income is an accounting or accrual concept that may reflect non-cash items such as depreciation.

The operating cash flows before tax during the first period can be assessed by checking the following three sources of information:

- the lease, which establishes the terms of occupation and responsibilities of the landlord;
- the current state of the rental market for the type of the property, which indicates potential rents and losses to vacancies; and

• the building management records, which confirm the recent operating expenses of the property.

The lease(s)

If the property is currently occupied, a copy of the lease(s) should be available to potential purchasers. The critical details from the lease are the current rent, when it was set, when it will be adjusted and whether there are other payments by, or responsibilities of, the tenant(s). Leases of non-residential premises often include provision for the rent to be adjusted during the lease by one or more means. The adjustment is often by a fixed percentage, by the rate of consumer price inflation, by a portion of turnover in shops or by adopting the market rent at that time. For a property with several tenants, a tenancy schedule summarizing this information should be available from the owner, selling agent or property manager.

A lease may be on a gross basis, under which the tenant pays rent and the landlord is responsible for all the operating expenses. Alternatively, the tenant may be responsible for running the property or reimbursing some or all of the landlord's operating expenses by way of what is commonly called a service charge or recovery of outgoings. The provisions of a lease on a net or partially net basis must be checked carefully to work out the operating cash flows before tax.

The current market

Investigations into current conditions in the specific market for the property are important to several elements of the analysis. The terms and volume of recent leases in the same or similar buildings must be ascertained. If leases have been granted for several years, the rents being paid when the property is evaluated may be well above or below the rent that a new tenant would agree to pay. If parts of the building are empty or if leases are due to expire shortly or have imminent rent reviews to market levels, current market rents are a better guide to net income for the first year than the lease rent.

The amount of competing vacant space will determine how quickly vacant portions of the property are leased as well as the likely ongoing loss to vacancies and bad debts. Loss to vacancy is usually expressed as a percentage of the potential gross income if the property were fully occupied. The usual practice is therefore to show the gross income as if the property were fully let and deduct the expected loss to vacancy during the year. The vacancy allowance should reflect the history of the building and the current balance between supply and demand in the locality.

The building management records

To ascertain the net income from a property, the operating expenses for which the landlord is responsible are deducted from the rent paid by the tenant(s). The categories of operating expenses vary slightly depending on the type of property and the country in which it is located. The operating expenses can be grouped as property taxes (taxes on ownership as distinct from taxes on income and capital gains received by the owner), insurances, maintenance and management. Typical categories of expenses are:

- goods and services tax (GST), value-added tax (VAT) or similar taxes on rents collected (less any input tax credits on qualifying expenses)
- local council, water authority or other government rates and charges for services or consumption
- land tax, property tax or other taxes on ownership
- insurances against damage to the building and public liability claims
- repair and maintenance of the building and upkeep of other improvements and landscaping
- contracts for servicing and maintenance of plant, such as air-conditioning and lifts, cleaning common areas of the building and security services
- provision of power and fuel for shared services such as heating, cooling and ventilation systems
- wages and salaries of caretakers, security and other staff
- wages or fees paid to property managers and leasing fees paid to find new tenants and negotiate new leases.

It is important for the potential purchaser or analyst to make sure that no items have been omitted and that the recurrent amounts are realistic. In some countries, standard charts of property accounts are used by property managers and these can be used as a checklist. Comparisons with the costs of running similar properties and, if possible, the operating expenses in previous years help to confirm whether the reported amounts are realistic. Many property investments have not lived up to expectations because the past or quoted operating expenses did not allow for the full costs of running the property, thereby overstating the operating cash flows. On the positive side, good management may achieve efficiencies that lower costs without lowering rents or future capital value.

The gross income, vacancy rates and operating expenses must be forecast for each year of the period of analysis. These projections are the most difficult part of the evaluation of property (and most other) investments and are always critical to the ultimate success of the investment. They are described further in Chapter 15. At this point, it should simply be noted that the operating cash flows before tax for all the periods of analysis must be estimated by projecting changes in the rent that tenants are willing to pay, the related changes in vacancy and the changes in operating expenses.

Estimating the resale proceeds before tax

The proceeds from the sale of the property before tax form part of the property flows at the end of the final year of the analysis. The resale proceeds are the estimated resale value less the selling costs. The resale value can be only roughly estimated because of the uncertainties in forecasting a market value many years in the future. Sometimes, the resale value is computed by applying a compound growth rate to the purchase price or current value of the property. In those markets where investors dominate, the resale value is generally estimated as the present value of the stabilized expected net income in the year after the period of analysis. This will be explained further in Chapter 15. The selling costs usually comprise the fees of a real estate agent and a legal representative to arrange for the conveyance of the property.

Setting out the property cash flows before tax

The typical property cash flows before tax comprise a large initial outlay, a series of smaller inflows and a large terminal inflow. The property cash flows are the equivalent of the project cash flows before tax, as described in earlier chapters, and are not adjusted for loan payments.

The initial outlay on the property at the start of the analysis is made up of the purchase price of the property and the acquisition costs. In most instances, real estate prices are negotiable and the cash flows will reflect either the asking price or a realistic bid for the property. The acquisition or buying costs are made up of any government transfer duty (often called stamp duty) and legal and other professional fees incurred by the buyer to confirm that the building is in reasonable condition.

The subsequent flows from an income-producing property are the operating cash flows during each year of the analysis, with the resale proceeds added in the final year. Following the usual capital budgeting rules, operating cash flows during each year are treated as though they are received at the end of the year.

Example 14.1. Property cash flows from the industrial property

The derivation of the property flows before tax for an industrial property is shown in Table 14.2 (and more fully in the accompanying Workbook 14.1). An investor is considering the acquisition of a modern property that is available at a price of $2,150,000. Buying costs of 4% of the price would also be incurred, making a total outlay on the property of $2,236,000. This outlay is the property outflow at the end of year 0 (EOY 0), which is the beginning of year 1.

During the first year after the purchase, the tenant will pay a gross rent of $302,500. As a precaution, some allowance for possible losses to vacancy during the period of analysis will be made. Although this is unlikely to be the same in each year, 5% per annum of gross rent will be allowed in this and subsequent years. Careful investigations suggest that operating expenses will total $95,000 in the first year of ownership. The operating cash flow to the end of year 1 (EOY 1) is therefore $192,375.

Initial market research suggests that the gross rent is likely to increase at 5% per annum (to $317,625 for EOY 2, $333,506 for EOY 3 etc.) and that operating expenses are likely to increase at 2% per annum during the period of analysis (to $96,900 for EOY 2, $98,838 for EOY 3 etc.). Table 14.2 shows the operating cash flows in each year to be the gross rent less vacancy and operating expenses ($204,844 for EOY 2, $217,993 for EOY 3, etc.). Whilst the period of analysis is only five years, the resale proceeds have been calculated, in this instance, by projecting the operating cash flows to a sixth year ($261,884) and dividing this amount by the expected market yield of 9.5%, giving a resale value of $2,756,673, and then deducting selling costs of 3% of the value, leaving $2,673,971. The rationale for this calculation is explained in Chapter 15.

The property cash flows before tax are made up of the initial outlay and the operating cash flows for each year, with the resale proceeds added in the fifth year.

Table 14.2. *Property cash flows before tax* ($)

	EOY 0	EOY 1	EOY 2	EOY 3	EOY 4	EOY 5
Outlay	−2,236,000					
Gross rent		302,500	317,625	333,506	350,182	367,691
Vacancy (5%)		−15,125	−15,881	−16,675	−17,509	−18,385
Operating expenses		−95,000	−96,900	−98,838	−100,815	−102,831
Operating cash flows		192,375	204,844	217,993	231,858	246,475
Resale proceeds						2,673,971
Property cash flows	−2,236,000	192,375	204,844	217,993	231,858	2,920,446

Workbook
14.1

Measuring the return on the property flows before tax

Much analysis of property investments is carried out using the property cash flows before tax. The property is acceptable provided that its net present value is positive at the required discount rate (implying that its internal rate of return will be greater than this required rate). The discount rate would be derived from comparisons with similar investments, perhaps adjusted for different risks. For public funds, the discount rate would also reflect the weighted average cost of capital before tax.

The property flows in Table 14.2 show a net present value at a discount rate of 11% per annum of $148,835 and an internal rate of return of 12.68% per annum. This confirms that the property is acceptable at the price of $2,150,000. If the net present value had been negative, a lower offer could have been made for the property. Even if the vendor had not reduced the price sufficiently, favourable terms, such as delayed payments or rental guarantees by the vendor, might have been conceded and the return recalculated.

At this level of analysis, the property can be evaluated knowing little about the potential buyer apart from a required discount rate. The cash flow projections are drawn from the property and are independent of the circumstances of the investor. The sources of finance and the tax status of the buyer are not explicit. This is the level of analysis favoured by those assessing market values of property investments for which a variety of buyers may be competing and for which the discount rate can be drawn from an analysis of recent sales of similar properties.

Adjusting the property flows before tax for loans

Most property investors use loans to meet part of the purchase price. For private investors who secure debt such as mortgages against the property, the flows are adjusted to reflect the impact of such loans. These adjusted flows are shown in Table 14.3. After describing these adjustments, the reasons for deviating from the usual practice of separating the project and financing decisions are explained.

The initial capital outlay is reduced by the loan amount, net of any fees required to establish the loan. The loan is a positive flow to the investor, making the outlay smaller. The net income is reduced by the loan payments (and possibly service or 'line' fees). The resale proceeds are reduced by any outstanding loan balance, together with any prepayment penalties charged by the lender for redeeming a loan before its full term. These penalties are prescribed in the loan contract and may be a specified number of months of payments, months of interest, a percentage of the outstanding balance or other compensation for the lender's losses.

Example 14.2. Equity cash flows before tax from the industrial property

The calculations in Table 14.3 are based upon a loan of $1,505,000, being 70% of the price. There will be loan establishment fees of $6,000, meaning that the initial outlay is reduced from $2,236,000 to $737,000 (i.e. $2,236,000 − ($1,505,000 − $6,000)). The investor can borrow on a monthly amortizing loan over fifteen years at an interest rate of 7.25% per annum, fixed for the first five years of the loan. This would require total annual payments of $164,863. This and the other calculations for amortizing loans are explained in Chapter 5. In the final period, the outstanding balance of $1,170,227 is repaid, together with a prepayment fee of $27,477 (being two monthly payments).

With a required return on equity of 16% per annum, the net present value of the equity cash flows before tax is $129,194 and the internal rate of return is 20.10% per annum. These are positive signals for the acquisition of this property *at this level of borrowing*. The higher discount rate for the equity flows compared to that for the property reflects the risks of using debt.

Reasons for analysing project and financing flows together

The use of equity cash flows to analyse property investments enables us to evaluate the property and its sources of finance together. Private property investors are generally well served by a model that explicitly shows cash flows as the return on their equity. They can see clearly their yearly cash receipts and any shortfall between rent and loan payments. Generally, private investors do not use many sources of funds; they use only a mortgage and their own savings as equity. It is unnecessary to amalgamate the sources and terms of finance into a weighted average cost of capital to discount the property cash flows (see Chapter 7). Further, if each property is held in isolation, with debt secured against it, any growth in value or loan amortization will change the debt-to-value percentage, making it impractical to use a weighted average cost of capital.

On the other hand, public corporations and funds are more likely to evaluate property cash flows. Public funds can estimate the return required by their investors and subscribers. This required return can be based on recent capital issues or can be imputed from the current prices of shares or units in the companies or funds or in their competitors. Public companies

Table 14.3. *Equity cash flows before tax ($)*

	EOY 0	EOY 1	EOY 2	EOY 3	EOY 4	EOY 5
Property cash flows	−2,236,000	192,375	204,844	217,993	231,858	2,920,446
Payment		−164,863	−164,863	−164,863	−164,863	−164,863
Loan	1,505,000		Outstanding balance			−1,170,227
Loan initial fee	−6,000		Prepayment penalty			−27,477
Equity cash flows	−737,000	27,512	39,981	53,130	66,995	1,557,879

Workbook
14.1

and funds typically have a target debt percentage without necessarily allocating debt to particular assets. They can combine the required returns of investors and the current costs of borrowing to determine their weighted average cost of capital, which can be used to discount the property flows. This approach is illustrated later in this chapter in the context of corporate real estate decisions.

It is important to understand that these two approaches (discounting the equity cash flows at a required return on equity and discounting the property cash flows at a weighted average cost of capital) are not inconsistent. However, whenever the debt-to-value percentage changes during the investment, the two approaches may support slightly different prices. As a general rule, equity cash flows are more meaningful for private investors and property cash flows are more appropriate for property decisions by public corporations and investment funds.

Adjusting the cash flows for income and capital gains tax

Both property and equity cash flows should be adjusted for the effects of income and capital gains tax, unless the investor's tax status is not known or the investor does not pay tax. Listed property trusts and pension funds are major property investors that do not pay tax in some countries.

Whether evaluating property flows or equity cash flows, the expected liability for tax can influence the outcome from property investments. Although savings in tax rarely justify buying properties, tax liability may influence the choice and pricing of properties. Because the same portion of tax is not deducted from all properties, it is important to incorporate the tax liability when evaluating investments.

This chapter does not attempt to explain the details of any tax system. The tax rules vary around the world and change over time within countries. The following brief description of the typical features of tax laws that influence returns from income-producing properties is provided in order to demonstrate how after-tax cash flows are established and evaluated.

Rents and operating expenses

Rents and almost all other recurrent receipts from property investments are assessable income for taxpayers. As operating expenses are tax-deductible, it is usual to begin the calculation of tax liability with the operating cash flows or 'net income'. On rare occasions, some expenses are not tax-deductible (for example, property taxes in a few countries and money paid into sinking funds for future expenses).

Depreciation allowances

The two principal differences between cash flows and taxable income from property investments are depreciation allowances and deductions for loan interest. Depreciation and investment allowances on some elements of the purchase of a property may be permitted for tax purposes. This will often require an apportionment of the purchase price between land, buildings, plant within the buildings and acquisition costs. Some tax systems permit the apportionment of the acquisition costs between the other three elements. The land cannot be depreciated for tax purposes although, in a few countries, investment allowances are given to those who purchase industrial land.

In some countries, buildings can be depreciated for tax purposes if the owner is using them to earn taxable income. This would normally be at a prescribed rate per annum, which may be faster than the actual rate of depreciation. Accelerated depreciation rates for tax are used by governments to encourage the purchase or construction of particular types of property. The plant within buildings may be depreciable in the same way as other plant used to make profits. Items of plant within buildings can include the heating and cooling equipment, lifts, carpets and other fittings. Plant depreciation can be claimed under most tax regimes and is usually allowable at considerably higher rates than depreciation for buildings.

Tax deductions for depreciation are attractive to tax-paying investors when the rates of depreciation are faster than the decline in value of the asset. It is often difficult to tell how the land and buildings are separately changing in value over time but certainly a property may be increasing in value whilst the owner is claiming substantial depreciation allowances. However, many tax systems have devised ways in which excess depreciation deductions are reclaimed when the property is sold. The recapture of excess depreciation may be either by an adjustment to taxable income in the year that the property is sold or by increasing the taxable capital gain on resale.

Loan interest

If we are carrying out an equity cash flow analysis, the effects of the sources of finance upon the tax liability should be incorporated. This is not the case if we are analysing the property or project cash flows.

Interest paid on loans taken out to purchase property investments is generally tax-deductible. In some countries, the interest deduction cannot exceed the net rental income from the property (additional interest payments are carried forward as losses until the investment or pool of investments earns taxable income). Elsewhere, investors are able to offset tax payable on salaries and other sources against tax losses generated by property investments. Generally, the loan must have been taken out to earn investment income to give rise to a tax deduction, although in some countries the tax deduction may be regardless of the purpose of the loan. The loan principal within each payment of an amortizing loan does not give rise to a tax deduction. Loan establishment fees are either deductible immediately or apportioned over several years.

Capital gain

Capital gains on the resale of a property investment are generally taxed differently to recurrent income, unless the investor is deemed to be running a business buying and selling properties for profit. In most countries, capital gains are taxed leniently. Under some tax systems, capital gains are taxed at a lower rate than income; other systems tax only a portion of the capital gain; sometimes the portion taxed declines if the property is held for longer; some systems only tax the gain if the property is held by a business. The capital gain is calculated after allowing for acquisition and selling costs. It is calculated on the gain in value of the asset, irrespective of the equity.

After-tax equity cash flow analysis

These features of the tax system are used to calculate the taxable income and gain as if the property is added to the investor's other income. Usually a marginal tax rate is used to determine the expected tax liability although it is possible to use a progressive tax scale to calculate the liability more accurately. The marginal tax rate is the rate that would be applied to additional income (or would have applied to taxable income that is sheltered by losses generated by the property). The tax liability is deducted from the cash flows before tax to arrive at the cash flows after tax (or tax savings generated by the property are added back to the cash flow before tax).

Example 14.3. Equity cash flows after tax from the industrial property

Table 14.4 illustrates how the tax liability, including the tax deduction for loan interest, is deducted from the equity cash flow before tax to arrive at the equity cash flow after tax. The example is based upon the tax regime in Australia at the time of writing. The net income in working out the tax liability from the property is the same as the operating cash flows before tax. Tax deductions for elements of the loan and for depreciation are used to compute the taxable income. In this example, the investor's tax rate is 40% on taxable income and taxable capital gain.

The interest portion of the annual loan payments is tax-deductible (Chapter 5 explains how this is calculated). Initial fees to establish loans are deductible over the first five years of the loan. The building attracts a 'capital allowance' of 2.5% per annum of its construction cost of $1,500,000. Items of plant within the building, with a value of $400,000, are depreciable over an average effective life of nine years. Depreciation for these items is calculated on a straight-line basis. During the first year, the taxable income is $2,008, of which 40% is paid in tax. This tax liability of $803 is subtracted from the equity cash flow before tax of $27,512 to arrive at the equity cash flow after tax in the first year of $26,709.

In the final year, the tax consequence of selling the property must be incorporated in the analysis. The balancing adjustment (an amount added to the taxable income based on

Table 14.4. *Equity cash flows after tax (an Australian example)* ($)

	EOY 0	EOY 1	EOY 2	EOY 3	EOY 4	EOY 5
Equity cash flows	−737,000	27,512	39,981	53,130	66,995	1,557,879
Tax liability						
Net income		192,375	204,844	217,993	231,858	246,475
Loan interest		−107,222	−102,901	−98,257	−93,264	−87,897
Loan initial fee		−1,200	−1,200	−1,200	−1,200	−1,200
Building allowance		−37,500	−37,500	−37,500	−37,500	−37,500
Plant depreciation		−44,444	−44,444	−44,444	−44,444	−44,444
Balancing adjustment						22,222
Taxable income		2,008	18,798	36,592	55,449	97,655
Income tax payable (40%)		−803	−7,519	−14,637	−22,180	−39,062
Capital gains tax						−125,094
Equity cash flows after tax	−737,000	26,709	32,462	38,493	44,815	1,393,722

Workbook
14.1

the resale value of the plant) and the capital gains tax payable under current Australian rules are rather complex and are calculated in the accompanying Workbook 14.1. These rules ensure that if the building and the plant have been written down for tax purposes to less than their resale values, the excess depreciation is recaptured when the property is sold. Their effects on the equity cash flow after tax in the final year are shown in Table 14.4.

The after-tax cash flows have an internal rate of return of 16.77% per annum and a net present value of $159,440 at a discount rate of 12% per annum − positive signals for the acquisition at this level of borrowing after adjusting for expected tax liability. This method of evaluating property investments shows the effects of growth in rents and value, the effects of borrowing and the effects of tax. It requires careful consideration of the investor's circumstances and likely cash flows generated by the property. Although it is never easy to make the necessary forecasts, the calculations can be set up as a proforma for use with any property, as in the accompanying workbook.

Because some elements of the after-tax cash flows are derived from the purchase price, it would be incorrect to conclude in this example that the investor could pay $159,440 more than the existing price to earn exactly 12% per annum. Increasing the price will alter the transfer costs, the capital gains tax and possibly the loan amount if this is a percentage of the price. The exact price that will earn this discount rate can be determined using the Goal Seek command provided in Excel (by setting the NPV to zero and varying the purchase price). In this example, a purchase price of $2,363,127 would earn a 12% per annum after-tax return on equity. Using the workbook will confirm that with a loan of $1,654,189, being 70% of this purchase price, the initial equity is $809,463 including $6,000 initial loan fees and buying costs of $94,525.

Corporate real estate

Decisions by businesses to occupy additional properties or move to a new location are critical to their operations and profitability. A wide range of decisions can be evaluated within the capital budgeting framework expounded in this book. In essence, the premises are an expense of operating the business and contribute to the value of the firm. Corporate property decisions are made as part of the overall strategy by which the business maximizes its value. The details of such analysis can vary with the circumstances and scale of the property investment. Two typical decisions are illustrated – the choice to move premises and the choice between leasing and buying a property – and other corporate property decisions that can be evaluated similarly are mentioned.

Moving to new premises

Small firms and sole traders considering new premises might evaluate their whole business in a potential new location: would the business be more profitable in the new property? For larger firms, it is generally possible to identify the specific effects of operating from different facilities or location. The effect on profitability is weighed against the initial outlay and running costs of the property. Occasionally, new premises are required solely for one project, in which case the costs of the property can be evaluated as outflows within that project. However, new premises are usually required for general expansion or change of direction for the firm and obtaining a new property is itself a project.

This is best evaluated by measuring the differences in the inflows and outflows resulting from the move to the new property. These are known as *incremental*, or *differential*, cash flows. The principles are the same as those illustrated in replacing a machine in Table 2.4 in Chapter 2. The initial outlay is the difference between the costs of purchasing the new property and the amount that can be realized from a sale of the existing property. During the interim periods of the analysis, there may be higher profits and different costs in operating from the new property than from the existing one. The period of analysis cannot extend beyond realistic projections for the business. In the final year of analysis, the difference between the likely resale proceeds from the new and existing properties should be added to the other flows.

Example 14.4. Acquiring the industrial property for operations

The following example shows how a firm might evaluate the decision to sell an existing property in order to purchase a larger property. The period of analysis is four years. The larger property is the same industrial building used in the previous examples but now assumed to be vacant and available for occupation. The move would enable the firm to make savings in its transport costs and expand its business to meet unsatisfied demand. The savings in transport costs have been identified to be about $15,000 during the first year, growing at 4% per annum in later years. The expansion of the business is estimated to increase net cash flows (excluding the property expenses and transport savings) by $20,000 in the first year and

$65,000 in the second year, while the new operations are being established, and $105,000 and $110,000 in the third and fourth years. These items would be estimated in consultation with the works and transport managers for the company. In practice, this analysis should also show the differences in the tax shelter from the new and existing properties but, to illustrate the principles, the cash flows before tax suffice.

The purchase of the new property for $2,150,000 requires an outlay, including buying costs, of $2,236,000. From market enquiries, it is believed that the existing property could realize $1,410,000, net of selling costs, if sold today. The operating expenses of the new property are estimated to be $95,000 in the first year, growing at 2% per annum. The operating expenses of the existing property are estimated to be $64,000 in the first year, growing at 2.5% per annum (a slightly higher percentage increase as costs are likely to increase faster for older buildings).

If it is assumed that the new property will increase in value at 5% per annum, it will have a value of $2,613,338 at the end of the fourth year. From this, selling costs of 3%, being $78,400, are deducted, giving resale proceeds of $2,534,938. The existing property is older and assumed to be growing in value at a slower rate than the new one, suggesting resale proceeds, less selling costs, of $1,600,000.

Table 14.5 calculates the differential flows created by acquiring and moving to the new property and selling the existing one. The differential cash flow today (EOY 0) is an outflow of $826,000, being the difference between the costs of acquiring the new and the proceeds of selling the existing property. The differential cash flow in subsequent years is the sum of any financial benefits from the new property and savings resulting from the sale of the existing property (positive amounts at EOY 1 and subsequently), less any costs of the new property and benefits given up by selling the existing property (negative amounts at EOY 1 and subsequently). In the final year (EOY 4), the differential cash flow includes the potential resale proceeds of the new property, $2,534,938, and an opportunity cost of $1,600,000 because the existing property would not be available for sale.

For corporations, the effects of loans would not normally be shown. However, the discount rate is based upon the firm's weighted average cost of capital before tax (see Chapter 7). In this example, the firm aims to retain about 40% debt and can borrow at 7% per annum. Shareholders require about a 15% per annum return. This suggests a discount rate of 11.8% per annum, being 40% of the 7% per annum cost of debt and 60% of the 15% per annum cost of equity. In this example, the net present value of the differential flows is negative, suggesting that the purchase of these new premises is *not* justified.

Differential cash flow analysis such as this can be used in several ways. If the business is renting premises, the analysis would show the rent and operating expenses of the new property compared to those of the old one, rather than the acquisition and resale values. If a mortgage were secured on the new property, it would be legitimate to reflect the new and existing loans and loan payments in the differential flows (as in Table 14.3 above). If equity cash flows are used, the discount rate should be the required return on equity (as the cost of debt is explicit in the loan payments).

Sometimes, a business is committed or obliged to move and wishes to choose between alternative premises. Occasionally, the alternative premises do not have major effects on the

Table 14.5. *Evaluating moving to new premises* ($)

	EOY 0	EOY 1	EOY 2	EOY 3	EOY 4
Purchase price, plus costs	−2,236,000				
Sale of existing property	*1,410,000*				
Operating expenses (of new property)		−95,000	−96,900	−98,838	−100,815
Operating expenses (of existing property)		*64,000*	*65,600*	*67,240*	*68,921*
Savings in transport costs		15,000	15,600	16,224	16,873
Net increments from expanded business		20,000	65,000	105,000	110,000
Resale proceeds from new property					2,534,938
Resale proceeds from existing property					*−1,600,000*
Differential cash flows	−826,000	4,000	49,300	89,626	1,029,917
Net present value at a weighted average cost of capital of 11.8%					−59,616

```
Workbook
  14.2
```

operations of the business and the analysis is simplified to the selection of the premises with the lowest net present value of the costs of occupation. More often, however, the choice of premises will lead to differences in transport costs, labour costs and property operating expenses; larger premises might also enable a larger scale of operations or accommodate future expansion. Each alternative can be evaluated separately, seeking the one with the highest net present value. Or, one of the possible new properties can be used as a benchmark against which to evaluate the alternatives, as in Table 14.5.

Lease or buy

Businesses can often choose between buying and leasing their premises. In recent years, many companies have sold their properties and leased them back, freeing capital for their operations. Leasing gives the company more flexibility but less control over their premises. Although, in theory, leasing and buying should be financially equivalent (Miller and Upton, 1976), firms often maintain that they can take advantage of market conditions to enhance the value of their business by the appropriate choice of tenure.

The choice is best evaluated by comparing the net present value of the costs of buying with the net present value of the costs of leasing. The costs of buying are the initial outlay and the subsequent expenses of operating the property (less tax deductions for those operating expenses). The resale value of the property is added to the final year's property flows. The costs of leasing are the rent payable in each year (less tax deductions for the rent). The cheaper option is the one with the smaller (negative) net present value.

It is generally important to incorporate the tax implications of buying, which may provide depreciation allowances, and leasing, which gives tax deductions for the rent. The financing can either be reflected in the after-tax cost of debt within the discount rate or by adjusting the property flows for the loan, its repayments and the tax deduction for interest.

Example 14.5. Leasing or buying the industrial property for operations

Using the same industrial property as in the previous examples, the costs of buying or leasing can be compared. This example is calculated after tax, using a company tax rate of 30%, and is based upon the property cash flows (in other words, before financing). We first consider the costs of buying, as set out in the top part of Table 14.6. The initial outlay is the price of $2,150,000 plus the acquisition costs, totalling $2,236,000. The operating expenses in the first year of $95,000 are reduced to their after-tax cost of $66,500 because they will give rise to tax deductions of $28,500 (being 30% of the expenses). These expenses have been increased at 2% per annum as in the earlier example.

As a tax-paying owner, the company would be able to claim $37,500 per annum as a building allowance and $44,444 per annum as plant depreciation (explained in Example 14.3). This provides a tax deduction or tax shield of 30% of the claims, being $24,583. If it is assumed that the property will increase in value at 5% per annum, it will have a value of $2,613,338 at the end of the fourth year. From this, selling costs of 3%, being $78,400, are deducted and capital gains tax of $134,681. The resale proceeds of $2,400,257 are added to the final year's property cash flow after tax.

We then consider the costs of leasing, as set out in the bottom part of Table 14.6. The gross rent in the first year of $302,500 would be based upon the asking rent and rents recently agreed for similar premises nearby. The rent will be deductible for tax purposes and hence is reduced by 30% to its after-tax cost of $211,750 in the first year. Growth in rents has been projected at 5% per annum, which is consistent with the growth applied to the value of the property.

These alternative property cash flows after tax are discounted to their net present values using the weighted average cost of capital, adjusted from the previous example to an after-tax cost (see Chapter 7). The cost of debt has been reduced to an after-tax rate of 4.9%, being an interest rate of 7% per annum, less 30% tax deduction. This suggests a discount rate of 10.96% per annum, being 40% of the 4.9% per annum cost of debt and 60% of the 15% per annum cost of equity. Table 14.6 shows that the net present value of leasing is less than the net present value of buying, and leasing would therefore be preferred.

A similar conclusion would be derived from evaluating the purchase as an investment outlay that leads to *savings in rent* and an asset with a residual value. These flows would be rather like those of purchasing an income-producing property (see Table 14.3 above) and could be adjusted similarly for the tax deductions created by depreciation allowances and the tax deductions forgone on the rent. However, the comparison between leasing and buying is less clear if set out in this manner.

Table 14.6. *The costs of leasing or buying* ($)

	EOY 0	EOY 1	EOY 2	EOY 3	EOY 4
Costs of buying					
Purchase price plus costs	−2,236,000				
Operating expenses after tax deduction		−66,500	−67,830	−69,187	−70,570
Resale proceeds, net of costs and gains tax					2,400,257
Tax shield of depreciation allowances		24,583	24,583	24,583	24,583
Property cash flows after tax	−2,236,000	−41,917	−43,247	−44,604	2,354,270
Net present value at 10.96%					−788,453
Costs of leasing					
Rent after tax deduction		−211,750	−222,338	−233,454	−245,127
Net present value at 10.96%				−704,009	

> Workbook
> 14.2

Sale and leaseback of a property

A property strategy that has been followed by many companies in recent years is to sell their real estate. This is generally done to free up capital for other investments. As such, it is a financial decision similar to the choice between leasing and buying. A sale and leaseback of a property results in inflows and outflows that are the inverse of the purchase of a property. The sale is an initial inflow and the rent a subsequent outflow. Depreciation allowances are given up but the rent will provide tax deductions. In evaluating the consequences of selling the property now, it must not be forgotten that the company gives up an asset. The analysis must show a further outflow in the final year that is the estimated resale proceeds *had* the property been retained. If this incremental cash flow is discounted at a rate reflecting the costs of alternative sources of capital, a positive net present value suggests that the property should be sold (because selling the property is a cheaper source of capital than the alternatives).

> Workbook
> 14.2

A wide variety of corporate real estate decisions can be analysed by estimating either the incremental or differential effects of acquiring, selling or leasing suitable premises. Some of these decisions may appear complex but, provided the analysis of alternatives is consistent in its treatment of inflows and outflows, financing, tax and discount rates, the usual capital budgeting rules can be adopted.

Development feasibility

The purchase and development of sites is an entrepreneurial activity like any other business. The business produces completed buildings or subdivided parcels of land for sale. Property development may be undertaken by trading companies or investors intending to retain the completed building but the development phase is generally evaluated separately. The cash flows and the risks during this phase are quite distinct from those when operating the property.

Any property development has four principal elements. These are the site and its ancillary purchase and holding costs, the construction costs and related professional fees, the return for the risks taken, and the value of the completed property. In simple terms, the development is viable if the completed value is greater than the sum of the other three elements. Typically, a developer evaluates a project to determine either how much can be paid for the site or, if the price is not negotiable, whether the estimated return is sufficient. Many different versions of the project may be considered, such as buildings of different size and quality, or perhaps various sites might be considered for the same project. Many development projects are speculative (that is, they are built on the expectation that occupants will be found) and the eventual selling price of the completed development is the key to the success of the project. Some projects are only undertaken if the completed buildings have been 'pre-let' or 'pre-sold'. Some projects are completed by corporations for their own occupation.

In this section, a preliminary method to screen development projects is contrasted with an evaluation of the project cash flows. The preliminary method, or some variation of it, is so widely used that it needs to be demonstrated. However, it is not consistent with the rules of capital budgeting, as will be evident when the same project is shaped into a cash flow model. The preliminary evaluation ignores the time value of money but gives a rough indication of whether the project is worthy of detailed investigation. This preliminary or 'static' analysis calculates a notional 'profit' as a percentage of the total expenditure. It approximates holding or opportunity costs whilst the site is not producing income by a simple interest calculation. Provided that this form of analysis is done using current costs and values, its assumptions will tend to be more conservative than a cash flow model. However, the way that it allows for 'profit' and interest means that the results cannot be directly compared with a cash flow analysis of the project.

Example 14.6. Initial screening of an industrial building project

Let us imagine that a developer is considering putting up an industrial building on a vacant site adjoining the property illustrating earlier examples in this chapter. On completion of a new but otherwise similar building to the adjoining one, the developer might anticipate selling the property for $2,400,000, less selling costs of about 5% of the price. Planning approvals for the building would take two months and construction a further seven months. Design and engineering fees of $130,000 would be payable in the second month and construction costs of $1,100,000 spread evenly over the remaining seven months. The site can be acquired for $550,000, plus 4% buying costs. The developer can utilize funds that cost 11% per annum for both the acquisition and the development.

Table 14.7. *Preliminary analysis of a property development* ($)

Sale of the completed property		2,400,000
less Costs of sale		−120,000
Net proceeds of sale		2,280,000
Purchase price of land, plus buying costs	−572,000	
Holding costs of land	−47,190	
Construction costs and design fees	−1,230,000	
Opportunity or financing costs on construction	−39,463	
Total outlays on development	−1,888,653	
'Profit' on total outlays		391,347
'Profit' as a percentage of total outlays		21%

> Workbook
> 14.3

Table 14.7 shows these items in the typical preliminary format. The net proceeds of sale are expected to be $2,280,000. Holding costs on the site cost of $572,000 at 11% per annum for nine months are shown as $47,190. Opportunity cost for *half* of the construction costs and design fees of $1,230,000 at 11% per annum for seven months are shown as $39,463 (the halving approximates the gradual use of these funds during the construction period). The preliminary analysis shows a 'profit' of $391,347, or 21% of the total outlay of $1,888,653. The development would be further investigated if this 'profit' is considered to be a sufficient percentage to justify the risks. Bearing in mind that speculative property development is highly risky, a required percentage 'profit' on outlay of 20–30% is typical.

More thorough evaluation of development projects uses cash flow models. In fact, it is difficult in many countries to obtain funds for development without detailed cash flow analysis of the project. Property developments that can be completed in about one year are usually evaluated on a monthly basis. Longer projects may be evaluated quarterly and extended, staged projects over five or more years may be evaluated annually. All the revenue and expenses are allocated to their expected time during the project. This is one of the main benefits of projecting cash flows rather than relying on the preliminary screening in Table 14.7. The discount rate would reflect both the opportunity cost of money involved in the project and a return for the risks taken.

There is likely to be a series of outflows during most of the project, starting with the purchase of the site, followed by design fees, construction costs and concluding with marketing costs (if the project is a speculative one). The components of the construction costs are often shown in great detail to ensure that no items are overlooked in assessing the feasibility of the development. Later, there will be one or possibly more inflows, which estimate the consequences of the sale of the completed property or properties. If the property is to be retained by a long-term investor or for occupation by a company, it can be shown in the project cash flows as a notional transfer on completion.

Table 14.8. *Project cash flows from a property development* ($)

	EOQ 0	EOQ 1	EOQ 2	EOQ 3	EOQ 4
Sale of completed property					2,400,000
Costs of sale					−120,000
Land plus buying costs	−572,000				
Design fees		−130,000			
Construction costs		−157,143	−471,429	−471,429	
Project cash flows before tax	−572,000	−287,143	−471,429	−471,429	2,280,000

Workbook
14.3

Example 14.7. Project cash flows from a property development

Using the same project as in the previous example, Table 14.8 shows the quarterly development flows for the industrial property. These would generally be calculated monthly but the principles are clearer if the cash flows are displayed quarterly. The flows have been calculated by allocating the expected revenue and costs to the quarter when they are likely to be received or paid. The initial outlay is the purchase of the site at the start of the first quarter (EOQ 0). This is followed by payments for design and then construction payments over seven months in the first to third quarters. It is assumed that the property will be sold in the quarter following its completion (EOQ 4).

A net present value has been computed based on the quarterly project flows before tax at a discount rate of 9% per quarter. The positive net present value of $18,954 indicates that the development shows sufficient return. The high discount rate is indicative of the degree of risk that developers take. The risks of property development without a commitment of a purchaser upon completion (without what is referred to as a 'take-out') can be seen as similar to venture capital or trading in futures contracts.

Basic NPV sensitivity analysis for a property development

Alternative schemes can be tested to see if variations in the value on completion, the construction costs or the price offered for the land might result in a higher net present value. On the accompanying spreadsheet (Workbook 14.3), the Goal Seek command can be used to set the NPV to zero by changing one of these three elements. The land value is often treated as a residual and the cash flow model can be used to work out the most that the developer can bid for the site whilst earning the required rate of return.

The ability to adjust the components of the project flows to show the effects of different timing during the development makes this form of analysis much more realistic and more flexible than the preliminary screening in Table 14.7. The tax consequences of the development project can also be incorporated, although development for sale does not usually attract depreciation allowances. Project cash flow analysis can be extended to show the

Table 14.9. *Equity cash flows from a property development* ($)

	EOQ 0	EOQ 1	EOQ 2	EOQ 3	EOQ 4
Project cash flows before tax	−572,000	−287,143	−471,429	−471,429	2,280,000
Loan drawdowns	211,600	287,143	471,429	471,429	
Cumulative loan	211,600	504,562	989,866	1,488,516	0
Loan repayments					−1,529,450
Equity cash flows before tax	−360,400	0	0	0	750,550

> Workbook
> 14.3

effects of borrowing upon the developer's return and liquidity. Much property development is carried out by small businesses and individuals who learn more from a 'bottom line' that shows their equity than from the project flows.

Funding for development is offered by financial institutions on different terms than mortgages for long-term property acquisitions. It is often available on terms that enable the developer to draw down portions of a loan when they are required to pay for stages of the construction. Typically, the developer is expected to contribute all the equity before any portion of the loan is taken and to repay all the loan before receiving any of the sales revenue. Some lenders will lower their interest rate if they are given an equity stake in the project. The equity cash flows from these and other joint ventures can be made explicit, showing the returns to each party.

Example 14.8. Equity cash flows from the development project

Assuming that the developer has arranged a loan facility for 80% of the estimated project costs (excluding the costs of sale), Table 14.9 extends the project cash flows from Table 14.8 to calculate the equity cash flows before tax. The developer will be required to contribute the first 20% (the equity cash outflow of $360,400 at EOQ 0) of the estimated total project costs of $1,802,000. The balance of the project costs will be covered by drawing down the loan in stages. Interest on the cumulative amounts borrowed will be charged at a rate of 2.75% per quarter (one quarter of 11% per annum) and added to the cumulative loan. For example, the cumulative loan at the end of the first quarter is $504,562, being the total loan from the previous quarter ($211,600) plus interest at 2.75% ($5,819), plus the amount drawn down ($287,143).

The loan has the first claim over the proceeds of selling the completed industrial building. In this case, the net proceeds of sale of $2,280,000 at the end of the fourth quarter are used to pay off the accumulated debt of $1,529,450 (being the debt of $1,488,516 plus interest of 2.75%, $40,934). This shows an equity cash flow at EOQ 4 of $750,550.

A net present value has been computed based on the quarterly project flows before tax at a discount rate of 20% per quarter. The positive net present value of $1,555 indicates that the equity contributed to the development shows sufficient return. The discount rate has been increased considerably to reflect the volatility of the equity cash flows when large loans have prior claims on the project. The degree of risk is evident if you consider a decline in the industrial property market. If property prices should fall 15% (which is quite possible), the developer will get the initial equity back and nothing more. Further risks of property development are described in Chapter 15.

One of the benefits of working out the equity cash flows is to be able to see the timing and magnitude of the developer's contribution. The equity cash flows in Table 14.9 show quite a different pattern to the project cash flows.

Concluding comments

This chapter has applied capital budgeting techniques to three types of property decision. It has been shown that the evaluation of properties requires particular attention to some elements of the cash flows that might be unnecessary for many other capital outlays. The allowance for financing should be given careful attention as, in many instances, the practice varies from other uses of capital budgeting techniques. There are four ways of constructing cash flows from properties – before and after financing and before and after tax. The chapter has shown that each may be suitable under different circumstances and each will require a different discount rate.

It should be evident that the evaluation always depends upon forecasting flows from the property in the foreseeable future. The techniques are only as reliable as the forecasts. The following chapter considers how to make these forecasts and how to measure the risks that arise because the forecasts are inherently uncertain.

Review questions

14.1 Consider an office building which is available for sale at $3,200,000, plus $150,000 of acquisition costs. The property is leased to a variety of tenants under short leases which permit regular reviews of rent to the current market level. Fully leased, the building would earn rents of $287,000 in the first year but the current vacancy level of 4% is likely to be typical over the holding period. Operating expenses, including property taxes and management fees, are estimated to be $76,000. Market rents are expected to increase at 6% per annum for the next four years. Operating expenses are expected to increase at 3% per annum during the period of analysis.

The property is entitled to depreciation allowances for tax purposes of $94,000 per annum which will not be reclaimed upon resale of the property. It is believed that the property will be saleable after three years for $3,750,000, less selling costs of 1.5% of the resale price.

(a) Use the equity cash flows *after* tax to evaluate the returns over the next three years, assuming that $1,340,000 is borrowed on a monthly amortizing loan over fifteen years at an interest rate of 8% per annum with no loan fees. The investor pays tax at a rate of 30% and has a required return on the equity after tax of 9%. Should the investor proceed with the acquisition at this price?

(b) Now, assume that the building can be acquired vacant and is suitable for the occupation of a company in need of this additional accommodation. The prices, rental value and resale value are as above.

Apply the company's weighted average cost of capital after tax to the property cash flows after tax over the next three years to evaluate the purchase of the property over a three-year period of analysis. The company plans to retain its current 40% debt-to-asset values. It can borrow at an effective fixed interest rate of 8% per annum. It can issue shares provided that investors believe they will earn 11% per annum. The company pays tax at a rate of 30%.

Given these assumptions, would it be better to lease the property rather than buy it?

15 Forecasting and analysing risks in property investments

Property investments put capital at risk. The outcomes almost always vary from the best estimates that we make when evaluating the property. Forecasting outcomes and gauging the risks of not achieving those outcomes are critical in applying capital budgeting techniques to property decisions. This chapter can therefore be seen as a supplement to Chapter 14 which illustrated the methods of property investment analysis.

The early part of Chapter 15 provides guidelines for forecasting cash flows arising from property investments. There will always be doubts about the reliability of forecasts of property rents, operating expenses and capital values, but what is the alternative to forecasting? Purchasing (or leasing) real estate without forecasting cash flows would require that the company or other investor accept the asking or market price (or rent). The 'going price' is derived from other people's opinions of the prospects and worth of the property to them. Thus, however difficult forecasting may be, it is surely better than investing blind. The solution lies in selecting the information and methods of forecasting that are most likely to help in estimating cash flows. The most reliable forecasts for real estate often combine the use of quantitative techniques (Chapter 3) and judgemental techniques (Chapter 4).

The later part of this chapter describes ways in which we can assess the risks of not achieving the investment objectives. Risk analysis is needed because of the uncertainty of the cash flows that we forecast. The risks can be revealed by testing the sensitivity of the investment to variations in the cash flows (as in Chapter 8) and simulating the alternative outcomes (as in Chapter 9). Having assessed the risks of a property investment, we can determine whether the investment shows sufficient return. This might lead us to reject the investment or adjust the discount rate, changing the present value.

The examples used in this chapter illustrate forecasting and risk analysis for the three types of property decision described in Chapter 14. Most of this chapter is devoted to forecasting for, and the risks of purchasing, *income-producing properties*. Similar cash flow forecasts are required for *corporate real estate* decisions, but *development feasibility* requires a slightly different approach to forecasting. The risks of each type of property decision are somewhat different although the methods of analysing them are the same. The examples in the text are available in the accompanying Excel workbooks.

Study objectives

After studying this chapter the reader should be able to:

- identify the typical factors that determine cash flows from property investments
- make forecasts combining past data with judgement about the future direction of the specific property market
- identify the main risks that property investors face and incorporate them in the analysis of properties.

Forecasting

There are no sure ways to forecast cash flows from properties with complete accuracy if they are leased or traded in open markets. The problems of any economic forecast are compounded by the lack of reliable data and the local variations. Information about past changes in rents and values may only be available as broad averages across the region and this is sometimes of limited relevance to the property in question. Therefore, forecasting tends to be largely judgemental, supported by aggregate data, trends and local market knowledge. The difficulties of forecasting are the main reason why Chapter 14 recommends that we restrict cash flow models for property analysis to five years.

Judgemental forecasts are based upon a sound understanding of the factors that cause changes in rents and values. These are often referred to as *market drivers*. This section suggests an approach to forecasting property cash flows that makes use of available information about these market drivers, whilst leaving room for qualitative adjustments to suit current local conditions. The stages in forecasting operating cash flows before tax, generally termed 'net income' in property circles, are described in this chapter. Each stage is then demonstrated by refining the projected cash flows for the property used as an example in Chapter 14.

Rent under the lease

For properties acquired with existing tenants, there is reasonable certainty about the rent under the terms of the lease. Therefore, the starting point in forecasting the rents from leased properties is a study of the covenants in the lease. Most leases of commercial and industrial properties are granted for several years. The leases fix the rent but often contain mechanisms for the rent to be adjusted occasionally. The typical provisions for changing rent during the lease are:

- fixed percentage changes or dollar adjustments on the anniversary of the start of the lease
- adjustments each year in line with the rate of increase in an index of consumer prices or construction costs (as published by government statisticians)
- less frequent reviews to the then current market rent, as agreed by the parties or independently assessed
- additional rent as a percentage of the turnover of shops.

For an income-producing property, the rent is projected in accordance with the lease terms. If the rent is adjusted during the year, the lease rent may comprise some months at one level and the remainder of the year at a different level. It is relatively easy to model cash flows to this degree of accuracy when using computerized spreadsheets.

Forecasting the operating expenses

The lease also dictates which party is responsible for the various expenses of running the property. Each of the expenses (itemized in Chapter 14) can be projected separately if there are foreseeable changes or if major outlays are required to keep the property in good condition. Sometimes, changes to property taxes, insurance premiums or servicing contracts are announced and can therefore be built into the projections. Sometimes, it may be necessary to upgrade a property to retain tenants or to renew plant at the end of its economic life. If there are no obvious irregular or unusual outlays, it may be adequate to assume that operating expenses will change at the rate of increase of an index of consumer prices (obtained from government sources or economic forecasting groups).

Estimating market rents

For a leased property, the rent collected will be adjusted to the prevailing market level for each tenancy either at a 'market rent review' during the lease or at the expiry of the lease. Estimating rent at these times is a two-stage process. The first stage is to establish the market rent today and the second stage (described later) is to forecast what the market rent will be at the time of the market rent review. To establish the market rent today, we must compare the property with other similar ones that have been leased recently. The objective is to estimate what a likely tenant would pay if the property were offered for lease today. Because of the distinct characteristics of each property, this may require a careful investigation of recent rents paid for similar premises. Rents are not generally public information and rents for comparable properties can only be gathered by personal enquiries of those involved in the deals. Commercial and industrial properties are not uniform, nor are their leases, making comparisons awkward.

The common practice of granting new tenants hidden incentives to sign leases (such as granting periods free of rent or paying to fit out the premises to the tenant's specification) can make it more difficult to estimate market rents. The practice of granting leasing incentives is common in many markets for commercial and industrial properties. It adds to the dangers of buying income-producing properties by assessing only the initial rent being paid by the tenant(s) – this rent should always be checked against current market rents. Because of leasing incentives and changes in the market since the premises were leased, there are often substantial differences between the rent fixed under the lease and the rent that would be agreed if the premises were available to lease.

Allowing for vacancy

Both the loss of rent arising from vacancy at the end of the lease and any monetary incentives to attract new tenants should be built into the forecast of operating cash flows. The loss will be determined by the suitability of the property for occupants and by market conditions when the lease expires. Typically, this will be expressed as months without rent and costs of attracting new tenants. The alternative (which is commonly used when there are many tenants) is to subtract an annual average loss to vacancy as a percentage of the lease rent.

Determinants of market changes

To estimate market rent when the review will occur and loss to vacancy when the lease expires, we must forecast changes in the state of the market for the type of property. Although long-term trends in past average rents can be measured as compound growth rates or by using statistical methods such as regression analysis, these are of limited help in monitoring rental changes. There are two reasons for this. Long-term trends in rents and property values are heavily influenced by consumer price inflation. Therefore, past growth rates can only be used to forecast future trends if the rate is adjusted to reflect likely inflation rates in the future. The second (and more important reason) is that property markets are strongly cyclical, often displaying startling booms followed by equally startling but more sobering contractions. Forecasts over a five-year period of analysis cannot afford to ignore the likely movement through a cycle that will occur.

Much has been written about the persistence of property cycles. They are tied to cycles in the national and regional economy and to the long lead-time between decisions to build more space and its availability for occupation. Smoothing techniques can help to reveal the cycles more clearly than a time series of rents. For the analyst forecasting changes in market rents (and property values), there are some signs to observe. The vacancy rate is the unoccupied percentage of the stock of a certain type of property within a defined geographic area. Some vacancy is necessary to enable occupants to move. When vacancy rates decline below this 'equilibrium' or 'natural' vacancy level, rents are likely to rise as occupants compete for limited supply. When vacancy rates are above this level, rents are likely to be stable or declining. In many markets, there is published data indicating vacancy rates in recent years for particular types of property and the trends can be monitored.

Changes in vacancy rates are brought about by changes in supply and/or demand. It is possible to anticipate most changes in supply because of the length of time to develop new buildings. Buildings under construction are evident and market enquiries will reveal how much of this new space is already committed to occupants. Local government authorities maintain records of building approvals (which in some countries are collated and published by government statistics offices) and generally monitor how much land is suitable but not yet approved for development.

It is more difficult to anticipate changes in demand. Past absorption rates (being the amount of additional property occupied per period) are indicative of average expansion in demand. However, the demand for properties is derived from various economic and social factors that are themselves difficult to predict. For example, the demand for further dwellings in a city is determined by household formation, job security, interest rates and many other factors. The demand for offices is determined by growth in employment in professions and services, business confidence and gradual shifts in the required floor area per person.

Table 15.1. *Forecasting rent from leased properties*

	EOY 1	EOY 2, EOY 3 etc.	
Market rent	From comparisons with recent lettings	Forecasts based on market dynamics	
Lease rent	From lease(s)	Changes based on lease provisions	Market rent when lease permits
Vacancy	Loss to vacancy and reletting costs at lease expiry		
Operating expenses	Allowance for operating expenses for which the landlord is responsible		
Operating cash flows	Lease rent, less vacancy and operating expenses		

It is helpful to have available both the aggregate regional data for any of these factors and local data. Property markets operate locally and we often observe slightly different patterns in rents and values in different suburbs for commercial and residential properties. However, because occupants and suppliers can switch localities, regional trends cannot be ignored in projecting market rents in one locality.

The sources of the forecasts of rent to derive the operating cash flows (before tax) and the relationship between changing market rents and lease rents are summarized in Table 15.1.

Combining judgement and statistics in forecasts

Despite much research, property analysts have been unable to establish any consistently reliable quantitative relationships between rents (and prices) and vacancy rates, supply and demand. Therefore, most forecasts of rents are made by assembling data that show how the market has changed in recent years and using this data informally to develop judgemental forecasts. The judgement of someone with wide experience may recognize turning points and idiosyncrasies in markets that most statistical techniques do not detect. Experience also makes it easier to detect differences between average rents and the likely changes in the particular property under scrutiny. However, forecasts based on judgement would undoubtedly benefit from formalizing the process (as described in Chapter 4), as casual approaches to qualitative forecasting are open to bias and may simply reinforce passing market sentiment.

Example 15.1. Forecasting operating cash flows for the industrial property

This example illustrates one method of forecasting the rent from the industrial property described in Chapter 14. The approach uses averages and trends to support judgement about the direction of the market and the particular characteristics of the property being evaluated.

The lease rent
To show the relationship between the lease rent and the market rent, it is assumed in this chapter that the property was leased *one year ago* for five years at a gross rent of

Table 15.2. *Lease rent for the industrial property*

	EOY 1	EOY 2	EOY 3	EOY 4	EOY 5
Lease rent	$283,250	$291,748	Market rent	3% increase	Market rent

$275,000 per annum in the first year. The lease specifies that the rent will increase by 3% per annum at the end of the first and second years (hence the rent during the first year of our evaluation (EOY 1) is $283,250 per annum and will increase to $291,748 per annum for the third year of the lease, being EOY 2).

The lease states that at the end of the third year the rent is to be renegotiated to the then market rent (with provision for independent opinion to settle any dispute). Therefore, the rent during year 3 will be the market rent at that time. The lease specifies a further 3% increase at the end of the fourth year of the lease (which will apply during year 4). At the end of the lease, the parties are free to terminate their agreement or to negotiate a new lease. Therefore, the rent during year 5 will be the market rent as agreed for a new lease with either the existing tenant or someone else. Table 15.2 shows the rent that can be expected under the lease and after it expires.

The market rent

To forecast the future market rent first requires an estimate of the market rent today, which can be ascertained by research into recent lettings of similar properties and under similar terms. In this case, rents in the range $50–$60/m² per annum are currently being agreed for similar premises nearby. Although this property is on a main road (an advantage for industrial properties), it has a low roof height, a small portion laid out as offices and a short road frontage (all disadvantages). On balance, its current market rent is estimated to be $55/m² per annum, equating to $302,500 per annum. This is 10% higher than the rent agreed when this property was leased last year, which is consistent with the average change in industrial rents since last year in this neighbourhood.

We must now consider how market rents are likely to change between now and when the market rent can be collected from the tenant. This property is similar to others in the area (average rents in the current year are $58/m² per annum). From statistics, such as those shown in Table 15.3, we can form a picture of the direction of the market, supported by commentary from real estate managers and agents who are active in the area.

In the last two years, rents for industrial premises in this neighbourhood have increased substantially, after many years of largely stable rents. A boom in the need for industrial premises can be attributed to the expansion of the minerals sector of the regional economy with the discovery of valuable deposits in the hinterland where mining has begun. As a response to increased demand and higher rents, there has been a substantial increase in the construction of industrial buildings in the last two years with projected completions of new buildings next year well above the annual average. The result is that the percentage of vacant space is currently edging upwards, perhaps indicating that increased demand has largely been satisfied. Although the regional economy is still

Table 15.3. *Industrial property market statistics*

Year	Gross rents ($/m^2 p.a.)	Time trend in rents ($/m^2 p.a.)	Difference from time trend ($/m^2 p.a.)	Estimated vacant (%)	New building (m^2)
−10	37.00	37.14	−0.14	4	27,000
−9	41.00	38.67	2.33	6	13,000
−8	44.00	40.21	3.79	9	47,000
−7	42.00	41.75	0.25	14	58,000
−6	41.00	43.28	−2.28	18	21,000
−5	42.00	44.82	−2.82	15	8,000
−4	44.00	46.35	−2.35	14	15,000
−3	44.00	47.89	−3.89	6	6,000
−2	47.00	49.43	−2.43	3	18,000
−1	53.00	50.96	2.04	4	24,000
0	58.00	52.50	5.50	9	29,000
1		**54.04**			37,000
2		**55.57**			12,000
3		**57.11**			
4		**58.65**			
5		**60.18**			

> Workbook
> 15.1

buoyant and benefiting from the mining expansion, it seems likely that only moderate, if any, growth in rents can be expected whilst the new buildings are absorbed into the market.

These directions are confirmed by simple quantitative analysis. A time trend regression (as explained in Chapter 3) shows that 73% of the change in rents can be explained by straight-line growth of $1.54/m^2 per annum. A continuation of this linear growth for the next five years would show the levels of rent in bold type in Table 15.3 and represented by the straight line in Figure 15.1.

It is probable that adjustments to this linear projection will improve the accuracy of a forecast of rents. First, we should check prevailing levels of inflation during the last ten years. The gross rents in the second column of Table 15.3 have grown at an average annual compound rate of 4.6% per annum during a period when the rate of inflation averaged around 4% per annum. As economists are predicting lower rates of inflation in the next few years (the consensus is about 2% per annum), our trend line should be tempered to reflect lower expected inflation during the next five years.

Second, it is evident that rents increased rapidly in some years but were stable or declined slightly in other years. The ten-year pattern of rents looks to be a little more than one cycle in this market, as is evident in Figure 15.1 and in the differences between the actual rents and the time trend in Table 15.3. With data that spreads over several cycles, we might be

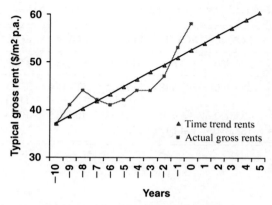

Figure 15.1. Trend in industrial rents per square metre.

able to build a cyclical index (as described in most business statistics primers as an element in time series decomposition). With one cycle only, a less formal adjustment to the time trend is all that is practicable. This can be based on three series in Table 15.3: the difference from the time trend (the regression residuals); the estimated vacancy percentage; and the new building completions.

Such adjustments to the trend are partly subjective. They are incorporated in this example informally prior to considering whether this approach to forecasting could be enhanced by the recognized techniques described in Chapters 3 and 4. Current rents are $5.50/m^2$ per annum above their long-term trend. This is the furthest above the trend that they have been during the last ten years. The vacancy rates in Table 15.3 have an average of 9.1%. In the previous cycle, when vacancy reached this percentage, rents in the following year actually declined. Average new building over the last eleven years has provided a further $24,182/m^2$ per annum. In the previous cycle, construction reached more than twice this average. The forecast construction for the next two years does not show anywhere near this amount of new space in the pipeline.

Distilling this information and discussing the implications with local professionals, typical rents are forecast to rise by 3% next year in this neighbourhood. For the following two years, market rents are expected to be stable (as the market absorbs substantial new construction) and thereafter 4% per annum growth is projected in a gradually recovering market (2% per annum above expected inflation).

In applying these forecasts to the property in question, some comments from real estate agents concerning its favourable position lead to a final adjustment. Work has started on a new road link that is due for completion in two years and this will provide substantially quicker access from the property to the city and the freight terminals. Real estate agents believe that this will create a preference for those industrial buildings that will benefit from this road link over other buildings in the neighbourhood. For this reason, the forecast for the rent that might be achieved for this property is adjusted upwards by 2% to 5% next year (to $317,625 during year 2 to year 4).

Table 15.4. *Operating cash flows for the industrial property* ($)

	EOY 1	EOY 2	EOY 3	EOY 4	EOY 5
Market rent	302,500	317,625	317,625	317,625	330,330
Lease rent	283,250	291,748	317,625	327,154	330,330
Vacancy					−110,110
Operating expenses	−95,000	−96,900	−98,838	−100,815	−102,831
Operating cash flows	188,250	194,848	218,787	226,339	117,389

> Workbook
> 15.1

Operating expenses

In this case, operating expenses are forecast to grow at the same rate as consumer price inflation (estimates of 2% per annum over the next three years were obtained from government sources and economic forecasting groups). As this property is leased to a single tenant, vacancy is allowed by way of a period of four months without rent at the end of the lease (an amount of $110,110 deducted from the lease rent during year 5). The length of this potential vacancy at the end of the lease is one of the risks considered later in the chapter. Vacancy and operating expenses are deducted from the lease rent to calculate the operating cash flows in Table 15.4.

More formal methods of incorporating these effects on forecast rents

There are many ways in which forecasts of rents can be made more sophisticated than in the above example. However, none is suitable for all occasions. A few alternative approaches are outlined but a business statistics primer should be consulted for details.

There are inconsistencies between linear growth (as predicted by regression) and compound growth. Because rental growth is more likely to compound year by year, it may be appropriate to use the natural logarithms of the rents in a simple regression with time as the independent variable.

The strength of the negative relationship between rental growth and the vacancy rate in previous years can be tested in a simple regression with vacancy as the independent variable. For the data in Table 15.3, the vacancy rate in one year explains 47.5% of the rate of rental growth in the following year. Lagged dependent variables such as this can help in making short-term projections but the strength of the relationships is rarely sufficient to forecast rents accurately.

In gathering the opinions of those active in the market, property analysts rarely follow the guidelines suggested for the qualitative forecasting methods described in Chapter 4. When collecting information for the analysis of a single property, opinions are virtually never sought by formal surveys (although these are occasionally used to uncover general market perceptions). Few analysts would rely on the opinions of one market expert but would consider both published commentary and discussions with several experts. Many of the experts in each local property market are involved in the sales, leasing or management of those properties. The analyst must guard against their bias (typically to 'talk up the market'). Analysts must avoid being overly influenced by passing waves of market sentiment that tend to assume that the current direction of the market will continue indefinitely. If there is a team of experts employed by the property investor, more structured group approaches to qualitative forecasts might be utilized (such as the Delphi technique explained in Chapter 4) but these are often impracticable if the analyst seeks the advice of outsiders for their local market knowledge. Nevertheless, some elements of structured group forecasting may lessen bias and careless aggregation of inconsistent opinions. For example, using a proforma with a set of questions when discussing market influences and trends will make the opinions easier to synthesize. Discussing the local market with four or five experts will avoid giving too much weight to one opinion. Probing to establish the reasons for stated opinions can help to reconcile their differences.

The choice of forecasting technique is a trade-off between reliability and convenience. Property markets differ in the availability of data for statistical analysis and the reliability of independent local experts. To some extent, the factors that determine changes in rents also vary with the type and locality of the property. Forecasting techniques must therefore be varied to suit the circumstances, aiming to utilize accessible, relevant data that can improve projections.

Forecasting the resale proceeds

The final year of the analysis of an income-producing property requires an estimate of its resale value, which is then reduced by the costs of sale. The value of the property at the end of the final year is added to the operating cash flow in the final year. The value must be drawn from an assessment of the likely strength of the market at that time.

In many markets for property investments, the capitalization rate is the prevailing unit of comparison. The capitalization rate is a simple measure of the initial return on a property investment, being the initial operating cash flow divided by the purchase price. In similar fashion, the resale value can be estimated by dividing the operating cash flow in the month *after* sale by a *resale capitalization rate*. We use the operating cash flows after the period of analysis as they will be the first available to a purchaser. Capitalization rates have been relatively stable over time in most markets, increasing up to 2% in times when investors are pessimistic and increasing gradually as a property ages. The stability of capitalization rates over time explains the preference for forecasts of values that are linked to changes in rents.

Example 15.2. Forecasting resale proceeds for the industrial property

As we can only guess at the terms under which this property might be leased for the fifth year of the period of analysis, it will be assumed that the market rent can be obtained in the month after resale. Using 4% growth in the market rent in year 5 in Table 15.4 gives a

Table 15.5. *Property cash flows before tax for the industrial property* ($)

	EOY 1	EOY 2	EOY 3	EOY 4	EOY 5
Operating cash flows	188,250	194,848	218,787	226,339	117,389
Resale proceeds					2,261,411
Property cash flows	188,250	194,848	218,787	226,339	2,378,800

> Workbook
> 15.1

sixth year's rent of $343,543, less an average vacancy allowance of 5% and operating expenses of 2% more than in year 5 (being $104,888 in the sixth year). This leaves an initial annual operating cash flow or 'net income' available to a buyer of $221,478. This is capitalized to indicate a resale value.

The capitalization rate if this property is purchased now for $2,150,000 is 8.8%, being $188,250 divided by $2,150,000. As the market for these types of property is currently buoyant, capitalization rates are towards the low end of their range. In calculating resale value, a capitalization rate of 9.5% is used. This suggests a resale value at the end of the fifth year of $2,331,351, being the operating cash flow of $221,478 divided by 9.5%. Selling costs of 3% are deducted to give resale proceeds of $2,261,411, as shown in Table 15.5.

Table 15.5 can be compared with the assumed constant rental growth used to demonstrate the principles of cash flow analysis in Table 14.2 in Chapter 14.

Forecasting for corporate real estate decisions

Although corporate real estate is not acquired for the same reasons as income-producing properties, it requires forecasts of similar elements of the property market. Evaluating corporate real estate requires projections of either the likely rent under the typical leasing arrangements that the company could negotiate or the likely resale or residual value of a property that is acquired. This would follow the market-based methods described above.

If the company is evaluating the advantages of moving premises, it may be necessary to estimate increased revenue or cost savings in the new premises. Many of these changes can be estimated by those who manage the existing operations, using the techniques described in Chapters 3 and 4.

Forecasting development cash flows

Cash flows from development projects are quite different to those from other properties. As pointed out in Chapter 14, the cash flows are generally assigned to months or quarters and the development phase evaluated separately from the subsequent use of the completed building(s). The critical but most difficult element is the assessment of the sales price(s) or value(s) of a completed development. Much property development is speculative, which means that it is commenced without a commitment from users or buyers. If a speculative development cannot be sold (or at least rented) reasonably quickly for roughly the amount estimated, it is unlikely to show an acceptable return.

The first skill lies in imagining the amount for which buildings on a currently vacant site would sell or rent if they were completed today. This is done by researching current prices for similar properties and adjusting them to reflect the superior and inferior features and location of the proposed development. In many markets dominated by investors (rather than owner-occupiers) prices are set by capitalizing the initial operating cash flow (as explained in the subsection 'Forecasting the resale proceeds' earlier in this chapter). In these markets, the value on completion is found by estimating the likely rent and dividing this by the going capitalization rate that investors are paying for similar income-producing properties.

The second skill lies in adjusting these prices or rents for changes between today and when the buildings will be sold either to owner-occupiers or to investors (after finding tenants). Because property development is carried out in dynamic and highly competitive markets, it is common for opportunities to be recognized by several developers simultaneously. As a consequence, today's shortage can lead to a glut of new buildings offered at about the same time. The importance of monitoring other development activity is obvious. This is usually done from records of development approvals, visits to competing development sites and enquiries into sales activity and vacancy levels.

A speculative development often creates several properties for sale, such as a group of dwellings or commercial or industrial buildings which are sub-divided for sale as individually titled units. Forecasts of the rate of sale are made, based on past 'take-up rates' for similar projects and the likely state of the market when the development nears completion. The speed at which the completed properties are sold can make a considerable difference to the viability of the development. Simplistic forecasts of constant growth in prices in the future can mask this, because the delay will appear to be offset by higher expected prices. In reality, sluggish sales may force the developer to reduce asking prices, may incur more loan interest and consequently lower the present value of the cash flows.

The outflows in a development project are the construction costs and the purchase of a site. Construction costs are generally estimated by specialists, except in preliminary evaluations, which may utilize published costs per square metre or other unit rates. Most building contracts involve payments by the developer at the completion of each stage. For cash flow analysis, each stage payment is allocated to its likely month or quarter. Some building contracts have fixed prices for each stage and penalties for delays beyond given dates. Others are adjusted at each stage for interim changes in the prices of materials and labour and are less stringent in the imposition of penalties for time and cost over-runs. Because the decision whether to develop will generally precede the signing of a building contract, some assumptions must be made about likely or typical building contracts that the developer will be able to negotiate and the probable construction time.

Example 15.3. Forecasting development cash flows for a residential project

To illustrate project cash flows when a series of sales occurs in more than one period, a project to develop and sell a group of five townhouses is introduced. The developer is

Table 15.6. Development project cash flows before tax ($)

End of month	0	1	2	3	4	5	6	7	8	9	10	11	12	13	14
Sales of townhouses											283,500	284,850	286,200	287,550	288,900
Costs of sale											−25,000	−10,000	−10,000	−10,000	−10,000
Land plus buying cost	−234,000														
Design fees			−60,000												
Site works				−45,338											
Building costs					−157,813		−158,594		−159,375		−160,156				
Landscaping											−32,800				
Project cash flows	−234,000	0	−60,000	−45,338	−157,813	0	−158,594	0	−159,375	0	65,544	274,850	276,200	277,550	278,900

Workbook
15.2

considering buying a site for $225,000, plus 4% acquisition costs. Zoning would permit the construction of five townhouses. From comparisons with similar townhouses currently selling nearby, it is estimated that these could be sold for $270,000 each if available today. Prices in this market are rising at 6% per annum and it is likely that one townhouse could be sold per month upon completion. The developer anticipates paying initial marketing fees of $15,000 and then $10,000 in brokerage and legal fees on the sale of each townhouse.

Current building costs for the townhouses would be $625,000, paid in quarterly stages over an eight-month building period starting after two months. This excludes design and planning fees of $60,000, preliminary site works of $45,000 and landscaping of $32,000. These expenses are currently increasing at about 3% per annum. The construction contract would be let on a basis which adjusts each of the stage payments for any changes in the costs of building materials or wage rates since the signing of the contract.

Table 15.6 shows how these inflows and outflows would be allocated to months and the (net) project cash flows before tax is calculated. Land and buying costs are an outlay today (end of month 0). Design fees are an outlay in the second month. All construction costs are inflated by one-twelfth of 3% per annum to the month when they will be incurred. For example, the site works, which would cost $45,000 today, will be carried out in three months; the cost is increased by 0.75% to $45,338. Similarly, the first payment of one quarter of the building contract is increased from $156,250 by 1% (because of the contractual adjustment) to $157,813 in the fourth month.

The sales of the townhouses have been allocated to the months in which they are expected to be settled. Their prices are inflated by one-twelfth of 6% per annum to their month of sale. For example, the first sale is expected in the month that construction is completed; the current price of $270,000 is increased by 5% to $283,500 in the tenth month. The initial marketing fees of $15,000 would be payable at about the time the townhouses are ready for sale. The brokerage and legal fees, totalling $10,000, are allocated to each of the months of sale.

These projects are very risky, compared with other small business activities, and a required rate of return might be 4% per month. The net present value of these project cash flows at 4% per month is $16,607 (and the internal rate of return is 4.27% per month). The net present value indicates that the scheme is viable and that the developer could even increase the initial outlay on land and buying costs by $16,607 to $250,607.

Adjusting for tax and financing

The effects of taxation on a property investment, corporate real estate or a development are forecast using the current tax laws and therefore follow directly from the forecasts of income, expenses and sales. Most changes to tax systems are prospective, meaning that the relevant rules for tax assessment are those prevailing when the property is acquired. Every tax system has its tax shields and anomalies that should be incorporated in the after-tax cash flows. Depreciation and investment allowances, being major items that distinguish cash flows from taxable income, are built into the analysis. Announced changes to tax rules and rates can be accommodated if they will apply to properties that are already held by investors and companies.

Whenever the equity cash flows are used to evaluate investments, the potential changes in loan interest rates should be considered. For loans at variable interest rates, the expected changes can be projected and the sensitivity of the investment to different interest rates can be tested. For investors and developers using high levels of debt, the projected equity cash flows provide a clear indication of any shortfalls in rent and sales revenue in the early periods of the investment.

Risk analysis

Because forecasts of cash flows from real estate are largely determined by our interpretation of the direction of the specific, local market, there is inevitably scope for inaccuracy in our projections. We should not despair of the forecasts but rather gauge the scale of the potential variations in the investment outcomes. Measuring the range of foreseeable outcomes indicates the extent of risks to the investor or company. This section describes the typical risks that may affect the returns from income-producing properties, corporate real estate and development projects. They are accompanied by one example of each of four forms of risk analysis: sensitivity analysis, scenario analysis, break-even analysis and simulation, as explained in Chapters 8 and 9.

Risks of income-producing properties

Most of the risks in purchasing an income-producing property are based on four related concerns:

- default by the tenant
- the uncertainty of changing market rents
- losses caused by vacancy
- the uncertainty of the resale value.

After it has been shown how these risks are linked, the industrial property from earlier in this chapter and Chapter 14 will be used to illustrate the sensitivity of the property to changes in the forecast cash flows. Further risks arise from such factors as unexpected expenses in running the property, increasing interest rates, regulations limiting the use of the premises and retrospective tax changes.

Default by the tenant

There is a risk that the tenant may default on lease payments. The lease is rather like a bond issued by the tenant agreeing to pay rent until the lease expires. The default risk is partly gauged by credit checks on the tenant before acquisition. However, the difference between the market rent and the lease rent influences the likelihood of default by the tenant. Whenever the lease rent is greater than the market rent, there is an incentive for the tenant to avoid the commitment. Whenever the lease rent is below the market rent, there is a reduction in the risk of default.

The uncertainty of changing market rents

In most cases, the market rent today can be assessed with reasonable accuracy. It is much harder to forecast changes in the market rent. If the growth potential of a property is a significant reason for its acquisition, the uncertainty of future market rents is the biggest risk for property investors.

If the market rent is below the lease rent when the lease expires, the tenant will argue for a rent reduction on renewal of the lease. Given the cyclical nature of property markets, this may occur if the lease expires during a trough in the market. If the market rent is above the lease rent at the end of the lease, the risk lies in any doubts over the ability of the current tenant to afford a higher rent.

Losses caused by vacancy

When the lease expires, there is the risk that the tenant may not renew the lease and the premises may sit empty, not producing rent. This is most likely to occur during a trough in the market. At such times, vacancy rates may already be high if firms have been giving up surplus space, households avoiding new commitments or if new construction from a previous boom has not been fully absorbed. It is therefore likely that decisions not to renew leases will coincide with periods when it is difficult to attract new tenants. The owner is then confronted with the choice of prolonged vacancy or locking into an unattractive rent (in order to receive sufficient income to meet commitments such as loan payments).

The uncertainty of the resale value

Because the resale value of the property generally accounts for more than half of the present value of the cash flows, it is critical to the performance of the investment. The amount and timing of the resale are dependent upon the state of the market several years away, posing a considerable risk to the owner.

The resale value of a property investment is usually tied to its potential rental income. If the market for the property has contracted, rental growth will be lower than expected, depressing the resale value. This in turn may adversely affect investors' beliefs about future growth potential and capitalization rates may increase, further lowering resale values. Similarly, if interest rates rise, not only will equity cash flows decline but capitalization rates may increase, again lowering resale values.

Example 15.4. Net present value of the industrial property – sensitivity analysis

Using the industrial property that was described in Chapter 14 as available for sale as an income-producing property, we can test the sensitivity of the net present value of the property cash flows before tax using the Excel Data, Table command. Table 15.7 shows output on the changes to the net present value that would occur if:

(1) the rental growth rate per annum varies from the original forecast of 5% per annum
(2) annual loss to vacancy varies from the original forecast of 5% of the gross rent.

The variations across the columns are greater than the variations down the rows. Therefore, the table suggests that the uncertainty of rental growth is of more concern than

Table 15.7. *Sensitivity table for net present value ($)*

Vacancy loss (%)	Rental growth rate (%)				
	0	3	5	7	10
2	−343,525	3,190	255,709	526,464	969,015
4	−402,545	−62,906	184,460	449,689	883,209
5	−432,055	−95,954	148,835	411,302	840,306
6	−461,565	−129,001	113,211	372,914	797,403
8	−520,585	−195,097	41,962	296,140	711,596

> Workbook
> 15.3

the portion of rent lost to vacancy, provided that the ranges for the inputs are realistic. The production of these tables in a computer spreadsheet (such as in Workbook 15.3) permits one to vary the inputs and observe the effect on the outcome from the investment instantly.

It is evident that the above four risks are related and it may be misleading to measure the effects on the investment of one or two variables at a time. A change in one is likely to lead to a change in some or all the others (as described in relation to the uncertainty of resale values). It may be more realistic to carry out a simulation of an alternative scenario and its simultaneous effects on all of these concerns.

Example 15.5. Overbuilding for the industrial property – scenario analysis

A downturn in the market brought about by overbuilding of competing industrial properties in the region and the locality is often a scenario which causes concern. The example in Table 15.8 is based upon a scenario for the industrial property which recognizes its vulnerability in the event of an increase in the level of construction. The outcomes from the scenario were calculated using the Excel Scenario Manager (found under the Tools command).

The three variables that would be affected by overbuilding were re-estimated, showing lower rental growth of 2% per annum over the period of analysis, increased vacancy of 10% of rent and a higher resale capitalization rate of 10.5%. The combined effect of these changes upon the property cash flows before tax, the internal rate of return and the net present value are shown in Table 15.8.

It is evident from Table 15.8 that the effects of overbuilding would be to make the investment a poor one. The net present value at the discount rate of 11% per annum would become negative (−$484,083) and the internal rate of return would drop to 4.75% per annum. The likelihood of such a scenario occurring must be assessed to determine whether it is an unacceptable risk.

Buying versus leasing – break-even analysis

Businesses acquiring or renting properties for their use are exposed to the uncertainty of changes in market rents and capital values but not the risks of tenant default and vacancy.

Table 15.8. *Cash flows and returns from contrasting scenarios*

	Scenarios	
Uncertain variables	Market overbuilding	Expected outcome
Rental growth (%)	2.0	5.0
Vacancy loss (%)	10.0	5.0
Resale capitalization rate (%)	10.5	9.5
	Varying outcomes	
Cash flows		
EOY 1	$177,250	$192,375
EOY 2	$180,795	$204,844
EOY 3	$184,411	$217,993
EOY 4	$188,099	$231,858
EOY 5	$1,999,741	$2,920,446
IRR	4.75% per annum	12.68% per annum
NPV	−$484,083	$148,835

Workbook
15.3

To illustrate the use of break-even analysis for corporate real estate managers, the choice between buying and leasing is used. One of the critical unknown factors that influences this choice is the consequence of changing levels of rental growth. In the example in Table 14.6 in Chapter 14, leasing showed a lower cost over the four-year analysis than buying. This was based upon an assumption that rents would grow at 5% per annum if the property was leased, as would the resale value if the property was acquired. If both grow at a higher (but the same) rate per annum, leasing will become less attractive. We can answer the question, at what rate of rental (and capital) value growth will leasing no longer be cheaper? The full calculations are shown in Workbook 15.4, which uses the Excel Goal Seek command to confirm that, if the rental growth rate is 6.53% per annum, leasing and buying cost the same. At this growth rate, the net present values of leasing and buying are the same and, if the rent grows faster than this rate, buying would be cheaper. This indicates how much margin for error there is in our forecast before the decision to lease becomes the more costly alternative.

Workbook
15.4

Risks in property development

The typical risks of property development fall into three categories. First, the completed development may prove harder to sell than expected. This may result in lower prices and a protracted selling period. This may be caused by more severe competition from new buildings than was anticipated; or, it may follow a decline in demand for the completed

Table 15.9. *Monte Carlo simulation of office development*

	Stochastic variables		Deterministic variables	
Net rent	Triangular distribution	Minimum $110,000, most likely $130,000 and maximum $140,000	Marketing costs	8% of rent
Letting period	Uniform distribution	Minimum of 1 month and maximum of 6 months		
Capitalization rate	Triangular distribution	Minimum of 9%, most likely 9.5% and maximum 10.5%	Costs of sale	3% of the price
Building costs	Normal distribution	Mean of $600,000 and standard deviation of $50,000	Design fees	10% of building cost
Building period	Discrete distribution	5% chance of finishing in 7 months, 5% in 8 months, 40% in 9 months, 30% in 10 months and 20% in 11 months	Site purchase	$250,000 plus 4% buying costs

Summary of results of simulation (with 500 replications (iterations))

Expected net present value	$120,690
Standard deviation of net present value	$83,934
Minimum net present value	−$140,331
Maximum net present value	$332,104
Percentage of negative net present values	8%

Workbook
15.5

Forecasting and analysing risks in property investments 293

properties that is attributed to changes in economic conditions or tastes. Second, the development may become more expensive than the budgeted cost or the building period may overrun. Third, the development may suffer because its costs of finance have increased. Because developers typically use a high proportion of debt finance, their projects are particularly susceptible to increases in interest rates.

A combination of these three adverse outcomes can be enough to halt work on half-completed buildings and to bankrupt developers. Because property development is such an uncertain enterprise, it is suitable for demonstrating a form of computer-based risk analysis known as Monte Carlo simulation (which was explained in Chapter 9).

Example 15.6. Development risks – Monte Carlo (risk) simulation

This example evaluates the risks of developing an office building for lease and sale. Details are in Workbook 15.5. Possible distributions are defined for five critical random variables. These are the net rent, the number of months to find a tenant, the capitalization rate to be applied to the net rent on sale of the development, the building costs and the number of months taken to build the offices. The type of distribution applied to each of these stochastic variables is shown in Table 15.9, together with the deterministic variables. A computer worksheet has been used to calculate the project flows for 500 replications, selecting at random from the distributions of the stochastic variables. The lower part of Table 15.9 shows a summary of the output from the Monte Carlo simulation.

The Monte Carlo simulation can be viewed and rerun in Workbook 15.5. The use of Excel to achieve the random generation of values and the calculation of the distribution of net present values and some further statistics is explained in the workbook.

The combination of random values led to an average (or expected) net present value of $120,690 and only 8% of the runs through the project resulted in negative net present values. The potential variations in the outcome from the development are displayed in the probability distribution of net present values in Figure 15.2.

Despite the ease with which computers can generate these variations in possible outcomes from a development, Monte Carlo simulation is rarely used in development feasibility. This may be because of the difficulties of specifying the distributions for the critical inputs. However, random simulations such as this are one way of gauging the effects of uncertainty in property developments.

Concluding comments

This chapter illustrates the forecasting of cash flows from properties and the measurement of the risks to those cash flows. It suggests that the best methods of forecasting property cash flows are a mixture of quantitative analysis and judgement. It demonstrates that we can assess the main risks by testing how much they affect the forecast outcomes.

However, the evaluation of a property should not stop when it is acquired or leased. Opportunities for enhanced returns emerge and unforeseen problems must be tackled.

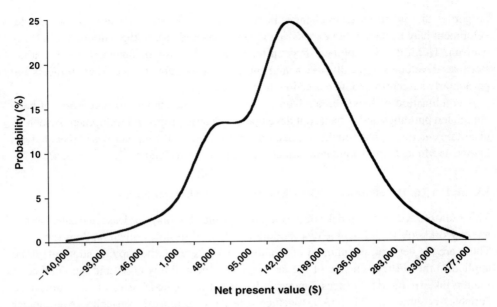

Figure 15.2.   Distribution of possible net present values.

Consequently, the initial capital budgeting decision should be reviewed regularly as the circumstances of the investor and the market change, using revised forecasts and perhaps revised discount rates. This is part of the function of good property management.

As well as measuring risks that arise in property decisions, it should not be forgotten that properties are *active investments*, for which the risks can be anticipated and controlled to some extent. Properties only perform well if they are managed well. A few examples will suffice to illustrate this point. For owners of income-producing properties, the risks of vacancy are limited by renegotiating leases well before expiry; the risks of rapid obsolescence can be anticipated by timely renovations; the risks of rising interest rates can be removed by choosing fixed rates or hedging against rising rates. For both investors and corporate real estate owners, good management will minimize operating expenses by avoiding waste, negotiating favourable service contracts and reviewing other charges carefully.

For corporate real estate owners, the risks of acquiring properties include the possibilities that they will be unsuitable for the operations of the company, unduly expensive to operate or difficult to resell. Good management will ensure that the premises are fully utilized and maintained in good order to minimize these risks.

Properties acquired for development are inherently risky propositions. However, developers can lower some of the risks by arranging buyers or tenants prior to commencing construction, by using fixed-price building contracts with penalties for delayed completion and by reacting to competing developments quickly through changes to marketing strategies.

Table 15.10. *Lease terms for suburban office building*

Tenants	Floor area (m²)	Current gross rent ($)	Lease terms
First floor	321.7	67,500	Leased three years ago for a fixed rent; lease expires at the end of next year.
Second floor	460.4	87,500	Leased last year for five years; with a fixed 10% increase at the end of this year and a market rent review at the end of next year.

Table 15.11. *Market data for suburban offices*

Year	Gross rents ($/m² p.a.)	Time trend in rents ($/m² p.a.)	Difference from time trend ($/m² p.a.)	Estimated vacant %	New building (m²)
−10	165.00	173.41	−8.41	12	7,000
−9	165.00	176.73	−11.73	11	11,000
−8	170.00	180.05	−10.05	8	8,000
−7	180.00	183.36	−3.36	3	9,000
−6	200.00	186.68	13.32	4	21,000
−5	215.00	190.00	25.00	7	29,000
−4	215.00	193.32	21.68	9	36,000
−3	205.00	196.64	8.36	12	19,000
−2	195.00	199.95	−4.95	17	17,000
−1	190.00	203.27	−13.27	11	6,000
0	190.00	206.59	−16.59	8	7,000
1					12,000
2					9,000

> Workbook
> 15.6

Review questions

15.1 Assess the property cash flows before tax of a leased suburban office building that an investor is considering buying with a view to holding for five years. The property is leased to two tenants on the terms shown in Table 15.10.

Study the data for the suburban office market in Table 15.11. It can be used to help in forecasting market rents for the office building. Assume that this building is typical of those in the suburb and has a current gross market rent of about $190/m² per annum.

(a) What has been the compound growth rate in office rents in the last ten years? During this period, the rate of increase in the index of consumer price inflation has averaged 2% per annum. Economic forecasters are predicting an average rate of inflation of about 4% per annum for the coming years. How might this impact your forecast for the next five year's rental growth?

(b) Work out the linear trend in rents over the next five years using simple regression to extend the time trend of the past ten years. How much of the past variation in rent is explained by the trend line?

(c) Study the table above to estimate how market cycles might influence the rent over the next five years. Consider the relationship between construction, vacancy and rental changes. Suggest a pattern for market rents over the next five years. Use this pattern and the details about the existing leases to project lease rents for a five-year analysis.

(d) The landlord is currently paying $68/m^2 per annum in operating expenses for the property. These can be assumed to increase at the projected rate of inflation. Allow for six months' loss of rent (or an equivalent leasing incentive of six months' rent-free at the start of each new lease). Using this information, work out the operating cash flows before tax.

(e) The property can be acquired for $1,200,000, plus 4% buying costs. It is believed that the property should be saleable at the end of the fifth year at a capitalization rate of 8.5% applied to the sixth year's forecast operating cash flows before tax (less 3% costs of sale). Using this information, work out the property cash flows before tax. At a discount rate of 12% per annum on the property cash flows before tax, would you recommend the purchase?

16 Multinational corporations and international project appraisal

So far in this book, investment projects have been analysed on the understanding that they were domiciled completely within a single country. This approach has allowed the discussion to proceed in the absence of the extra layer of analysis that is required when investments are located outside a firm's home country. In this chapter, we will relax this assumption and investigate the situation where a firm is considering investing in a project in another country.

Multinational corporations (MNC) frequently invest in foreign countries through their subsidiaries established in those foreign countries (also called 'host countries'). These subsidiaries may be viewed as the MNCs' 'investment arms', or 'business arms', in host countries.

Multinational corporations' foreign investment analysis is complicated by a variety of factors and risks that are not encountered by purely domestic firms or purely national investments. These complicating factors and risks stem from:

- involvement of more than one company – the existence of parent and subsidiary
- involvement of more than one country – home (or parent's) country and host (or foreign or subsidiary's) country
- tax differentials between home and host countries
- requirement to convert funds from one currency to another currency and the associated risks due to unpredictable exchange rate movements
- country risk: the host country's political, social, economic and financial risk factors.

The basic concepts, principles and techniques of project analysis still apply to multinational corporations' foreign investments. The net present value concept and criterion are still valid, but the analysis required for the application of the NPV criterion to foreign investments is usually more complicated.

This chapter defines and clarifies the terms often used in multinational foreign investment analysis. A distinction is made between cash flows to the subsidiary and to the parent company, and an analysis of a foreign investment is illustrated from the view points of both the parent and the subsidiary. Two risks in foreign investments are 'exchange rate risk' and 'country risk'. These are briefly discussed and strategies to reduce them are reviewed. These strategies can reduce the exchange rate and country risks but cannot eliminate them.

Therefore, foreign investments, unlike other risky investments, need to be evaluated taking account of exchange rate and country risks. Techniques for incorporating these risks into the foreign investment analysis are reviewed towards the end of the chapter. Throughout this chapter, for clarity and ease of comprehension, a number of selected countries, currencies and financial institutions are sometimes used.

Study objectives

After studying this chapter the reader should be able to:

- define an international investment project from the perspectives of both an MNC (parent company) and its local subsidiary
- analyse the investment project from these parent company and subsidiary perspectives
- identify and incorporate into the analysis the additional computational steps associated with foreign investments
- comprehend the additional risk factors involved in international investments
- identify and define exchange rate risk
- identify the more common forms of country risk for MNCs' foreign investments
- review strategies to reduce the impact of these additional risks.

Definition of selected terms used in the chapter

Terms often used in this chapter are now defined.

Host country and home country

The host country is the country in which a subsidiary of an MNC carries out its local investment projects. For the discussion in this chapter, Asia-Pacific nations are selected as host countries (e.g. Sri Lanka, Singapore, Malaysia and Thailand). The home country is the home of the MNC (or the parent company) where the MNC's headquarters are located. The one specific home country used as an example is the United States.

Parent and subsidiary

'Parent' refers to the parent company, which is the MNC with its headquarters in the home country (here, the United States). The subsidiary firms are domiciled in the named host countries such as Sri Lanka and Singapore. Subsidiaries are the host country investment arms of the MNC. Local investment projects are carried out through the MNC's subsidiaries established in the host countries.

Local currency

In this chapter, local currency specifically refers to the currency of the host country concerned – for example, the Sri Lankan rupee (SLRs.) or Singapore dollar (SIN$). This is to distinguish host country currencies from MNCs' home country currencies (e.g. the US dollar).

The parent's perspective versus the subsidiary's perspective

The issue of whether a foreign investment project should be evaluated from the subsidiary's or the parent's viewpoint arises because the project's net after-tax cash flows to the subsidiary are different from those to the parent. The parent does not receive (or have access to) all of the project cash flows which are received by the subsidiary. As a result, a project which produces a positive NPV for the subsidiary may have a negative NPV for the parent; a project acceptable from the subsidiary's point of view may not be acceptable from the parent's point of view.

Given the differences between project and parent cash flows, the question arises as to what is the relevant perspective from which a multinational corporation's international investment in a subsidiary's project should be evaluated. If the subsidiary is wholly owned by the parent company and the project is wholly financed by the parent, the owners of the project are the parent company's shareholders. Therefore, each project, whether foreign or domestic, should ultimately generate sufficient NPV to the parent in order to increase its shareholder wealth.

If the foreign subsidiary is not wholly owned by the parent and the foreign project is partially financed with retained earnings of the parent and of the subsidiary then both the parent and subsidiary perspectives need to be considered. The project must increase the wealth of both shareholder groups. In such situations, the NPVs from the perspectives of both the subsidiary and the parent need to be positive for the project to be acceptable.

Differences in cash flows to the subsidiary and the parent are caused by tax differentials, exchange controls, exchange rate movements, management fees and royalties.

Host and parent country tax differentials

Various taxes result in a difference between the cash flows received by the subsidiary and those received by the parent. The subsidiary's after-tax cash flows are those cash flows which remain following the payment of host country corporate tax. If these cash flows are remitted to the parent, a host country withholding tax might also apply. This tax, to be paid to the host country taxing authority, will reduce the cash flow to the parent. The cash flows received by the parent after these two taxes may be subjected to a third tax in the home country. Despite double-taxation agreements, income received by the parent may be subjected to another tax in the home country in the form of some corporate tax. Thus, the after-tax cash flow to the parent can be substantially lower than that to the subsidiary.

Management fees and royalties charged by the parent company

Administration of the foreign project is generally carried out by the subsidiary. Sometimes, the parent company may facilitate the project with the provision of advice, guidance and supervision. For these services the parent company may charge a service fee. At times, management may be highly centralized at the parent's headquarters and the subsidiary may be charged excessively high administration fees. These fees are classed as expenditures (cash outflows) by the subsidiary, and as revenues (operating cash inflows) by the parent. The fee revenue received by the parent may well exceed the actual cost of managing the subsidiary, the result being higher net cash flows for the parent and lower net cash flows for the subsidiary.

Remittance restrictions in the host country

As part of the permission to operate, a host country government may limit the outward flow of a subsidiary's earnings to the parent. This restriction may be employed to encourage the MNC to lengthen the time period of the project's operation within the host country. If only a fraction of a subsidiary's cash flows can be remitted to the parent, it will take a longer period to generate a positive NPV for the parent. Accordingly, the local project has to be continued for a longer period of time.

The parent will have no access to these restricted funds, which could have been used for distribution as dividends to the home country shareholders, repayment of debts sourced from the home country, reinvestment in the home country, or reinvestment in another subsidiary located in a different country. When there are remittance restrictions, a project viable from the subsidiary's perspective may become non-viable from the parent's perspective, because the cash flows to the parent can be considerably less than those to the subsidiary.

A possible strategy to overcome this problem is for the subsidiary to obtain a considerable proportion of funds for the project from within the host country, for example in the form of local currency debt. Cash flows from the project that cannot be remitted to the parent (and retained in the subsidiary within the host country) can be used to repay the local currency debt and its interest. As discussed later in this chapter, it is quite possible for subsidiaries in some countries, such as Singapore, to raise considerable funds within the host country at competitive rates. This strategy of local-currency borrowing also helps to reduce foreign exchange risk (which is discussed later in this chapter).

Exchange rate movements

When funds are remitted to the parent, they are converted from the host country currency to the parent country currency. The amount received by the parent is therefore affected by the exchange rate at the time of transfer. If the host country currency depreciates over the life of the project, the amount received by the parent will decrease.

For example, assume that the parent country is the United States and the local project is in the host country of Sri Lanka. At the time of project evaluation, the exchange rate is US$1 = Rs.100. The Sri Lankan rupee now depreciates over time and when the funds are to be remitted – say at the end of the project's third year – the actual exchange rate is US$1 = Rs.120. If the amount of funds being transferred is Rs.120 million, the parent will receive US$1 million (Rs.120 million/exchange rate 120). If the Sri Lankan rupee has not depreciated, the parent would receive US$1.2 million (Rs.120 million/exchange rate 100).

If a host country currency is expected to depreciate considerably over time, a project which is viable from the subsidiary perspective can become non-viable from the parent perspective.

Parent perspective versus subsidiary perspective: an example

To illustrate how a project analysis may vary depending upon whether the project is evaluated from the perspective of the subsidiary or the parent, consider the following example.

Example 16.1. Garment project

Durango Corporation, a US-based MNC, has a subsidiary in Sri Lanka called Lekano. A new line of business, a garment manufacturing project, is being considered for Lekano. The following data have been compiled for the analysis.

- The initial capital outlay is estimated as SLRs.800 million. At the existing exchange rate of 80 rupees per US dollar, this converts to US$10 million.
- The projected net operating cash flow of the proposed garment project is SLRs.500 million per year for three years.
- According to contractual agreements with the Sri Lankan government, the garment project will have to be handed over to the Sri Lankan government in three years' time; no compensation will be paid. In return for this concession, the Sri Lankan government will tax only the funds remitted to the US parent at a rate of 20%. This can be called a 'withholding tax' in the sense that this tax encourages the funds to be withheld in the host country.
- The exchange rate forecasts are SLRs.85, 95 and 102 per US dollar at the end of the first, second and third years, respectively, of the project.
- The US government will tax any dollar earnings received by the parent company at a 15% rate.
- The required rate of return for the project is 22% per annum.
- The subsidiary is wholly owned by the parent company and the project is wholly financed by the parent.

The project analysis, conducted in terms of NPV, from the perspective of the subsidiary and the parent company is presented in Table 16.1.

The NPV of the project, from the subsidiary's perspective, is a positive SLRs.220 million whilst it is a negative US$2.48 million from the parent's perspective.

There are three main causes for this discrepancy. They are withholding tax, depreciation of the host country local currency (rupee) and US government taxes. This example shows that while a project may be acceptable when analysed from a subsidiary's perspective, it may not be acceptable from the parent's perspective. In this example, the subsidiary is wholly owned by the parent and the project is wholly financed by the parent. Therefore, the relevant perspective is the parent's. Since the NPV from the parent perspective is a negative US$2.48 million, the project is not acceptable.

Table 16.1. *Analysis of the proposed garment project (SLRs. millions or US$ millions)*

Cash flow item	EOY 0	EOY 1	EOY 2	EOY 3
From subsidiary's perspective				
Capital outlay	Rs.800			
Operating cash flows		Rs.500	Rs.500	Rs.500
Present values (at 22%)	Rs.800	Rs.409	Rs.336	Rs.275
Net present value	Rs.220			
From parent's perspective				
Capital outlay	$10			
Total operating cash flows from project		Rs.500	Rs.500	Rs.500
Withholding tax if cash flows were remitted to parent (at 20%)		Rs.100	Rs.100	Rs.100
Remitted funds after withholding tax		Rs.400	Rs.400	Rs.400
Exchange rate (Rs. per $)		85	95	102
Funds to parent company		$4.71	$4.21	$3.92
US government taxes (at 15%)		$0.71	$0.63	$0.59
After-tax funds to parent company		$4.00	$3.58	$3.33
Present values (at 22%)	$10	$3.28	$2.41	$1.83
Net present value	−$2.48			

> Workbook
> 16.1

Possible alternative arrangements to make the project viable to both parent and subsidiary

> Workbooks
> 16.2 and 16.3

The project may become viable for both parties if some expenses such as management and administrative fees are paid by Lekano to Durango and are treated as non-taxable income in the United States. Alternatively, or additionally, Durango could negotiate with the Sri Lankan government to provide compensation to Durango when the project is handed over to the Sri Lankan government in year 3. Some examples of such calculations are presented in Workbooks 16.2 and 16.3. These computations may be viewed as an application of the simulation of alternative combinations (as in the airline example illustrated in Chapter 9), but here the process is designed to provide to the MNC's management some points of negotiation on the project, rather than as an assessment of risk.

Workbook 16.2 demonstrates an alternative analysis, with a single change to Example 16.1. The change is that the Lekano subsidiary pays a management fee of SLRs.200 million a year for three years to Durango. These fees are remitted to Durango and they are not subject to any tax. In this situation, the NPV from the subsidiary's point of view becomes negative (SLRs.187.33 million) and from the parent's point of view also it is negative (US$1.07 million).

Workbook 16.3 provides calculations with the following changes to Example 16.1.

- The Sri Lankan government pays SLRs.200 million compensation at the end of year 3 to Lekano. This is repatriated to Durango without any tax from the Sri Lankan and US governments.
- Lekano pays a management fee of SLRs.200 million a year for three years to Durango. These fees are remitted to Durango and they are not subject to any tax by the Sri Lankan and US governments.

In this situation, the NPV from Lekano's point of view is negative (SLRs.77.19 million) and from Durango's perspective it is positive (US$0.01 million). The purpose of these calculations is to demonstrate that simulation experiments can be performed under various alternative scenarios to assess the conditions under which Durango can implement the project in Sri Lanka, the information from which can be used as a basis for negotiating the terms and conditions for the project with the Sri Lankan government. If the project creates great employment opportunities for Sri Lankans and helps maintain the political, social, financial and economic stability of the country, then the Sri Lankan government may consider providing various incentives for the project.

Exchange rate risk

Exchange rate risk is usually a major concern in foreign investments. Exchange rate risk in capital budgeting can be broadly defined as the risk that a project's performance or NPV will be affected by unexpected movements in exchange rates. Exchange rates cannot be forecast with a high degree of reliability. Generally, the longer the forecasting period the higher the forecasting errors. Hedging methods to reduce exchange rate risk, such as forward exchange contracts, futures and options, are generally not available for long time horizons. The larger the amount of foreign exchange and the longer the period of time involved, the greater the risk. MNCs' international investments involve not only the conversions of *large amounts* of foreign currencies but also very *long-term* debt financing. For example, in 1993, the large Dutch consumer electronics company, Philips Electronics NV, borrowed US$500 million by selling US$250 million in ten-year notes and US$250 million in twenty-year bonds in US capital markets. In such situations, the exchange rate risk is further compounded by the MNCs' *long-term* borrowings of *large* sums for foreign investment projects.

This exchange rate risk (associated with foreign debt) stems from the 'transaction exposure'. This is defined as future exchange gains or losses on foreign currency denominated transactions or financial obligations already committed. Suppose a US-based MNC finances its Sri Lankan subsidiary project with a US$100 million borrowing converted to rupees at the exchange rate of US$1=SLRs.95. The US dollar debt is equivalent to Rs.9,500 million. If the rupee depreciates over time and the exchange rate at the time of debt repayment is US$1=SLRs.150, the subsidiary needs Rs.15,000 million. This is Rs.5,500 million more than the rupee equivalent of the borrowing. The currencies of many developing countries, where multinationals operate their subsidiaries, often depreciate dramatically and unexpectedly. This subjects the debt repayments to considerable transaction exposure and the associated exchange rate risk.

Country risk

One of the country risks faced by an MNC is the *political risk*. An extreme form of political risk is *expropriation*. Expropriation is the seizure of the subsidiary's assets by the host country's governments (or an illegal regime), with or without compensation. In a situation of expropriation, the cash flows to the subsidiary and parent diverge. With expropriation, a project which was viable from the perspectives of both the subsidiary and the parent can easily become non-viable from the parent's perspective. For example, suppose a project's cumulative net present value will not turn positive until well after its fourth year of operation. Should expropriation occur at some point during the first four years, it is unlikely that the project will ever be viable from the parent's perspective unless the compensation is sufficiently great.

At times, some host countries become hostile to the presence of multinationals and suddenly block the repatriation of funds. Fund transfers from the subsidiaries to the parent are often required for dividend repatriation, loan repayments, purchases of supplies, management fees and other purposes. If the fund transfers are unexpectedly restricted or completely blocked, a project which was initially viable may become non-viable for the parent. In the event of these *blocked funds*, the project would be viable (in the face of this risk) only if the blocked funds could earn an adequate return (in the host country) to compensate the opportunity cost of these funds.

Wars, tribal clashes and civil armed conflicts can cause both the project and parent cash flows to decrease or even disappear. Such circumstances may even require the sudden abandonment of the project. In the 1990s, some tribes in Papua New Guinea armed themselves and rebelled against the operation of the Bougainville mine, one of the largest gold and copper mines in the world. This rebellion caused a dramatic loss of cash flows to the parent companies' consortium, and to the national government of Papua New Guinea. The terrorist attack on 11 September 2001 on New York's World Trade Center and the following Afghanistan war (or the war against terrorism), caused disruptions not only in New York and Afghanistan, but all around the world. Thus, in assessing country risks, both the particular host country's current and future state of affairs and the global economic, political and financial conditions have to be taken into consideration.

Bureaucratic 'red tape' and corrupt practices in some countries can cause considerable delay and interruption to normal cash flows. For example, necessary approvals may be deliberately delayed by bureaucrats seeking unethical inducements (i.e. bribes) and this may hinder the efficient and smooth implementation of projects. All these country risks can be reduced if the project has considerable participation from within the host country and will contribute to the host country's development. Examples of measures which can have a favourable influence in securing support for the project include: host country government involvement in terms of partial equity injections and the appointment of directors to the subsidiary's board; debt financing for the project from influential host country financial institutions; considerable employment of skilled and unskilled host country labour; and large use of host country raw materials as inputs for the final product of the project.

Many host country governments are sceptical about MNCs' contribution to the host country's socio-economic development. Host countries would like to see that the MNCs' investment projects contribute to employment creation, financial stability, foreign exchange and balance-of-payments enhancement, worker-skill development and infrastructure development. Host countries would like to see these MNCs as friendly, contributory and helpful organizations, well assimilated and integrated into the host country's socio-economy (as opposed to being alien and exploitative). Therefore, a strategy which includes these elements would contribute to reducing country risk.

A strategy to reduce a project's exchange rate and country risks

MNCs' foreign exchange risk management has been discussed in the international financial management literature, e.g. Madura (1995) and Shapiro (1996). The elements of some of these risk management techniques include local-currency borrowing and reinvestment. A strategy which can reduce foreign exchange risk and financing cost has been presented in the form of a 'model for thought' in Dayananda (1999). This strategy can also help to reduce the country risk, because operation of the strategy involves local-currency borrowing from the host country's most respected and influential financial institutions, and an increased 'presence' of the MNC in the host country as a friendly, contributory and helpful organization, well assimilated and integrated into the host country's socio-economy.

A strategy (to reduce exchange and country risks) is outlined using a model which has three basic participants: (1) MNCs (2) host country national provident funds (NPF), and (3) host countries. These three participants, along with their preferences or characteristics pertaining to the model operation, are placed in the three boxes in Figure 16.1. The main flows between the MNC subsidiary and the other two participants in the model are depicted by arrows linking to and from the MNC.

NPFs in Asia-Pacific host countries may be viewed as equivalent to superannuation or mutual funds in the Western countries (such as the USA, Australia and the UK). The NPFs are government-sponsored institutions which operate the compulsory national superannuation schemes. In the model, the host country's NPF acts as a *lender* to the MNC's subsidiary in the host country. This financial flow is shown in the figure by the arrow labelled 'borrow'. The Central Provident Fund (CPF) of Singapore and the Employee Provident Fund (EPF) of Malaysia are two examples of Asia-Pacific host country NPFs. Reference is primarily made to the CPF in the illustrations. These NPFs are located in the middle box in Figure 16.1.

Asia-Pacific countries are identified in this model as host countries, and from this group of countries, Singapore, Malaysia and Thailand are selected for illustrative purposes, with the primary focus being on Singapore. These host countries are placed in the upper box of the figure.

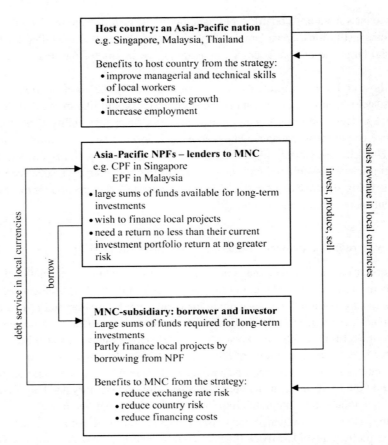

Figure 16.1. A strategy for an MNC to reduce a host country project's exchange rate and country risks.

The chosen MNC in the model has subsidiaries in Asia-Pacific countries, particularly in Singapore, Malaysia and Thailand. The MNC is a US-based company and therefore the parent's home country is the USA. The MNC and its subsidiary in the host country are represented in the lower box of Figure 16.1.

Basic elements and operational features of the strategy

The basic activities and operational flows of the strategy (to reduce country and exchange rate risks) are outlined below using the MNC as the main actor in the model. The main features of this strategy are depicted in Figure 16.1. For clarity and to allow a quick grasp of the overall strategy, in points 6–9 below, references are made only to particular host countries – Singapore being the focus host country, and Malaysia and Thailand being mentioned where it is necessary to refer to another host country. Also a specific national provident fund, the

CPF, and a specific home country, the USA, are used in points 6–9. These points can be generalized without loss of validity.

(1) Carefully select the projects such that they will greatly contribute to the host country's economic growth, employment creation and social development. These investments in the host country are shown by the arrow going from the MNC-subsidiary box to the host country box labelled 'invest, produce, sell', meaning the MNC will invest in projects which will benefit the host country and produce and sell in the host countries. Product may also be sold in other countries, such as that exported to the home country (e.g. the United States).

(2) Hire local labour to the maximum extent possible and contribute to the development of the skills of the local labour force. This action of the MNC will benefit the host country and therefore it is listed as a benefit in the host country box.

(3) Use raw materials from within the host country or other countries in the region which maintain close commercial and social ties with the host country.

(4) Finance a considerable proportion of the project funding by *direct* local-currency borrowing from the host country NPF, for example from the CPF in Singapore dollars. These borrowings can include *large* amounts of *long-term* debt. This project financing flow is depicted by the arrow labelled 'borrow' in Figure 16.1. The arrow runs from the NPF box to the MNC-subsidiary box.

(5) Invest these borrowings (along with other capital from the MNC) in projects in the host country from which the local currency is borrowed (i.e. in Singapore if Singapore dollars are borrowed from the CPF), and also, if desirable, in another host country in the region (e.g. Malaysia). This is shown by the arrow titled 'invest, produce, sell' going from the MNC-subsidiary box to the host country box.

(6) Export, at least partly, the final product from the MNC's Malaysian subsidiary's project to Singapore. Sell the final product from the Singaporean project in Singapore, Malaysia or other Asia-Pacific countries and in the USA.

(7) Price the product sold in different countries in the local currency of the country of sale. For example, exports from Malaysia to Singapore are priced in Singapore dollars, as is product made and sold in Singapore.

(8) Receive Singapore dollars from the portion of product made and sold in Singapore and the portion of product made in Malaysia and exported to Singapore. This flow is shown in Figure 16.1 by the arrow running from the host country box to the MNC-subsidiary box labelled 'sales revenue in local currencies'.

(9) Use these Singapore dollars to service the debt to the CPF. This flow is shown in Figure 16.1 by the arrow running from the MNC-subsidiary to the NPF box labelled 'debt service in local currencies'.

(10) Maintain close business and social ties with the host country NPF, e.g. borrowing considerable sums on a long-term basis from the NPF, consulting the NPF in relation to the

MNC's investment decisions in the host country, allowing NPF representation (as a director or simply as an observer) in the MNC's subsidiary in the host country.

How the strategy reduces host country risk

National provident funds are highly regarded in the host countries and therefore their involvement in financing the MNC's projects in the host country (point 4 above) and the MNC's close business and social ties (through the subsidiary) with the NPF (point 10 above) can reduce country risk. For example, a host country government would be reluctant to take any actions such as expropriation or blocking the repatriation of funds if the NPF had provided considerable finance to the MNC's projects in the host country or if the NPF had close and friendly business and social ties with the MNC subsidiary in the host country. Under these situations, the NPF may pressure the host government to avoid possible 'takeover' or 'block fund' actions.

Country risk is reduced because both the NPF and the host country will have a positive social attitude to the MNC's project. This positive attitude stems from the fact that the MNC borrows from the NPF and invests in projects which benefit the host country (point 1 above). For example, the CPF in Singapore is highly valued by the nation and its government and most, if not all, workers in the country contribute to the CPF. If the Singapore subsidiary borrows from the CPF, the country risk of potential government takeover will be reduced to a minimum because of the considerable influence the CPF has on the nation and its government. Generally, all the features in the strategy (points 1–10) help to reduce the project's country risk, because they all contribute to the host country's socio-economic development and skill development.

How the strategy reduces a project's exchange rate risk

The proposed strategy will reduce transaction exposure and the associated exchange rate risk, because the NPF loans are denominated in local currencies and debt is serviced using local currency earned from sales in the host countries. For example, a CPF loan to the MNC is denominated in Singapore dollars and the debt is serviced from Singapore dollars earned by sales in Singapore. If the MNC had borrowed in US dollars (or UK pounds) and converted them into local currency (e.g. Singapore dollars) for investing in the host country (e.g. Singapore), then the subsidiary would face the foreign exchange risk of the value of local currency depreciating over time. This is because the amount of local currency required for the repayment of a given amount of US dollar-denominated debt would increase. This is particularly so for long-term (say, twenty-year) loans, because the value of many Asia-Pacific currencies has depreciated in the past and is expected to depreciate in the future.

Is it feasible to obtain a considerable amount of finance for a host country project from an NPF?
It is quite possible because the NPFs (e.g. CPF or EPF) have *large sums* of accumulated funds which can be lent for *long terms* as long as they can earn risk-adjusted returns similar to those from their current investment.

Can the NPFs earn risk-adjusted returns similar to their current investments? Current NPF investments are mostly in government securities and bank term deposits. Considering the rates of return on government securities and term deposits, the MNCs should be able to pay comparable (if not higher) rates to NPF monies used for a host country project. The MNCs largely borrow through financial intermediaries. Therefore, by *direct* lending/borrowing between the NPF and an MNC, it is possible for the NPF to earn a return at least equal to what it earns from its current investment portfolio and at the same time for the MNC to pay an interest not greater than what it otherwise pays. Financial intermediaries always retain a margin when lending their depositors' money to borrowers. This difference between the financial intermediary's 'average lending rate' and its 'average borrowing rate' is called the financial intermediary's 'spread'. The direct lending/borrowing between an NPF and an MNC avoids the intermediary, and therefore the 'spread' of the financial intermediary can be shared between the NPF and the MNC. The transaction cost of NPF–MNC direct lending/borrowing is minimal, because the amount involved in a single debt transaction is *large* and it is arranged for a considerably *long* period of time (e.g. fifteen to twenty years). Therefore, direct lending/borrowing can be beneficial to both the NPF and the MNC.

It may also be argued that the risk associated with these loans is not greater than that of the NPFs' current investment portfolios, because the project will mimic current investments, and the MNC's investments will be larger, and thus more internationally diversified, than the host country's traditional investments. One may also argue that an NPF's investments with an MNC (in terms of loans to the MNC) are safer than the term deposit investments with host country banks, because many MNCs are large and have a diversified portfolio of investments spread over different industries and countries. Many MNCs may be prudentially more sound than many host country banks.

Other country risk reduction measures

The most serious country risk is that of a host government takeover of the subsidiary (which means the takeover of an MNC's projects in the host country run through the subsidiary). Blockage of fund transfers (by imposing 'exchange controls' or through direct and specific government orders), civil or international wars, terrorism and host country government bureaucracy can also cause unexpected adverse outcomes for the project's NPV. In some situations, projects will have to be abandoned, causing major losses.

Insurance against country risks

Purchasing insurance against selected country risks may also be considered as part of a comprehensive risk reduction strategy. Some home countries have insurance schemes which provide cover for several country risks. For example, the US government has been providing insurance through the Overseas Private Investment Corporation (OPIC) to cover the risk of expropriation. Many home countries of MNCs have investment guarantee programmes that partly insure the risks of host country government takeovers, wars or blockage of fund transfers. An important point to remember is that even if a subsidiary qualifies for insurance, the insurance policies usually cover only a portion of the country risk and there is a cost to the MNC in terms of an insurance premium. A subsidiary must weigh the benefits of the insurance against the cost of the policy's premiums and potential losses in excess of the coverage. While the insurance may reduce the risk at a cost, it does not by itself prevent losses arising from host country risk factors (Madura, 1995, pp. 593–4).

Using a short-term planning horizon for the project

The payback period for project evaluation was discussed in Chapter 6. Payback period may provide supplementary decision support (in addition to NPV) in selecting projects in host countries. A shorter payback period is helpful for recovering cash flows quickly, so that in the event of expropriation or war, losses are minimized.

Incorporating exchange rate and country risk in project analysis

Standard NPV risk adjustment methods, such as the risk-adjusted discount rate (RADR) and the certainty equivalent (CE) approaches, can be applied to international projects. However, the estimation of RADR and CE coefficients becomes more difficult.

There is no precise formula for adjusting the discount rate to incorporate country risk and exchange rate risk. One way to arrive at a suitable discount rate is to first estimate a discount rate for a similar domestic project and then to add a risk premium to represent added exchange rate and country risks. This basically involves the inclusion of a high 'additional risk premium' in the discount rate. In Chapter 7, we discussed how the RADR has three components, i.e.

$$k = r + u + a$$

where r is the risk-free rate, u is the average risk premium for the firm and a is an additional risk factor to account for the difference between the average risk faced by the firm and that of the proposed project.

Adjusting a to reflect the additional risk of foreign investments stemming from exchange rate and country risks would result in an appropriate discount rate for use in foreign investment analysis. In arriving at a suitable estimate for a, at least some of the information can be collected using the Delphi method discussed in Chapter 4. For example, independent opinions on country risk can be collected without group discussion by expert assessors. The assessors may be the corporation's employees or outside consulting firms which have established networks for collecting the relevant country risk information. The MNC can average the country risk scores provided by several independent assessors and, if necessary, establish the degree of disagreement by measuring the dispersion of opinions.

The certainty equivalent approach allows the analyst to adjust each annual cash flow by taking into account the potential impact on the cash flow of each different risk factor. For example, if there is a high degree of risk that the cash flows will be adversely affected in the second year of the project because of the eruption of a civil war or a tribal fight, that year's estimated cash flows can be multiplied by a relevant certainty equivalent factor, say 0.5. This will halve the value of that year's estimated cash flow.

Sensitivity analysis and the simulation methods discussed in Chapters 8 and 9 can be used to obtain more information to aid the decision-maker, and to highlight variables which should be monitored during a project's operation with the aim of early intervention. For example (using sensitivity analysis as discussed in Chapter 8), alternative NPV estimates can be prepared on the basis of various scenarios for volatile variables such as the exchange rate and political risk. Scenario projection, discussed in Chapter 4, is also useful for preparing alternative estimates under selected possible circumstances and for preparing contingency plans.

In the face of potential risks of takeovers, wars and blocked funds, the NPV analysis may be used in conjunction with a payback period to determine a suitable approach for an international investment project. When faced with these additional risks, shorter payback periods become an important consideration.

Concluding comments

The basic concepts, principles, techniques and methods of project evaluation do not differ between domestic and international investment projects. The application of these concepts, principles, techniques and methods becomes more complex, detailed, lengthy and cumbersome in the case of international projects. The additional complications and risks emanate from the involvement of more than one country and more than one currency.

Given the additional risk factors and the greater uncertainty associated with the expected cash flows, the challenge in multinational capital budgeting revolves around making reliable forecasts of the parameter values relevant to the project evaluation. If poor data (inaccurate forecasts) are input into the analysis, then the output generated will also be poor; the financial performance estimates will be unreliable. Consequently, an MNC might wrongly go ahead with a project. Most international investment projects are irreversible and decisions which seem right at the time they are made, turn out to be unfavourable. Therefore, MNCs' foreign investment projects need thorough evaluation and considered judgement by experienced project analysts well conversant with exchange rate and country risk analysis.

Review questions

16.1 Define the following terms:
- international investment
- multinational corporation
- home country
- host country
- exchange rate risk
- political risk
- expropriation
- transaction exposure

16.2 What are the benefits of international investment for the two main parties involved, the MNC and the host country.

16.3 Explain why the host country as an entity is recognized as a party to international investment, whilst the home country is not.

16.4 By performing simulation experiments with alternative combinations of parameter values and introducing new variables (or conditions) to Example 16.1, establish a mix of cash flows to Lekano and Durango which would result in a positive NPV for both parties. In your experiments, possible compensation payments to Lekano by the Sri Lankan government and US government tax exemption for Durango may be considered.

16.5 Assume that Lekano in Example 16.1 can raise SLRs.600 million of the required initial SLRs.800 million from the country's national provident fund as a loan at 11% per annum. Explain how this new financing arrangement would affect the calculated NPV results, and discuss how Lekano's transaction exposure to possible Sri Lankan rupee depreciation would be reduced.

16.6 Explain how both the RADR and the CE approaches might be employed to assess a project under an international risk scenario.

References

Alreck, P.L. and Settle, R.B. (1995), *The Survey Research Handbook: Guidelines and Strategies for Conducting a Survey*, Chicago: Irwin Professional Publishing.

Brealey, R., Myers, S., Partington, G. and Robinson, D. (2000), *Principles of Corporate Finance*, Sydney: Irwin McGraw-Hill.

Byrne, P. (1996), *Risk, Uncertainty and Decision-Making in Property Development*, 2nd edn, London: Spon.

Carn, N., Rabianski, J., Racster, R. and Seldin, M. (1988), *Real Estate Market Analysis – Techniques and Applications*, Englewood Cliffs: Prentice-Hall.

Dayananda, D. (1999), 'Reducing multinational corporations' foreign exchange risk and financing cost by sourcing debt from Asia Pacific national provident funds: a model for thought', in T. Fetherston and T. Bos (eds.), *Advances in Pacific Basin Financial Markets*, vol. V, Greenwich, Conn.: JAI Press, pp. 135–43.

DiPasquale, D. and Wheaton, W.C. (1996), *Urban Economics and Real Estate Markets*, Englewood Cliffs: Prentice-Hall.

Ducot, C. and Lubben, G.J. (1980), 'A typology of scenarios', *Futures* 12: 51–7.

Emtage, N., Harrison, S., Herbohn, J., Davidson, J. and Thompson, D. (2001), 'The Australian Farm Forestry Financial Model: a software package developed for the Rural Industries Research and Development Corporation', draft report, Brisbane.

Gujarati, D.N. (1995), *Basic Econometrics*, 3rd edn, New York: McGraw-Hill.

Hamilton, J.D. (1994), *Time Series Analysis*, Princeton: Princeton University Press.

Harrison, S.R., Herbohn, J.L. and Emtage, N.F. (2001), 'Estimating investment risk in small-scale plantations of rainforest cabinet timbers and eucalypts', in S.R. Harrison and J.L. Herbohn (eds.), *Sustainable Farm Forestry in the Tropics: Social and Economic Analysis and Policy*, Cheltenham: Edward Elgar, pp. 47–60.

Herbohn, J.L. and Harrison, S.R. (2000), 'Assessing financial performance of small-scale forestry', in S.R. Harrison, J.L. Herbohn and K.F. Herbohn (eds.), *Sustainable Small-Scale Forestry: Socio-Economic Analysis and Policy*, Cheltenham: Edward Elgar, pp. 39–49.

(2001), 'Financial analysis of a two-species farm forestry mixed stand', in S.R. Harrison and J.L. Herbohn (eds.), *Sustainable Farm Forestry in the Tropics: Social and Economic Analysis and Policy*, Cheltenham: Edward Elgar, pp. 39–46.

Herbohn, J.L., Harrison, S.R. and Emtage, N. (1999), 'Potential performance of rainforest and eucalypt cabinet timber species in plantations in North Queensland', *Australian Forestry* 62: 79–87.

Hertz, D.B. (1964), 'Risk analysis in capital investment', *Harvard Business Review* 42: 95–106.

Jaffe, A.J. and Sirmans, C.F. (1995), *Fundamentals of Real Estate Investment*, 3rd edn, Englewood Cliffs: Prentice-Hall.

Janis, I.L. and Mann, L. (1977), *Decision Making*, New York: Free Press.

Janssen, H. (1978), 'Application of the Delphi method to short-range price predictions on the fruit market', *Acta Horticulturae* 77: 223–30.

Jungermann, H. and Thüring. M. (1987), 'The use of mental models for generating scenarios,' in G. Wright and P. Ayton (eds.), *Judgmental Forecasting*. Chichester: Wiley, pp. 245–66.

Kmenta, J. (1990), *Elements of Econometrics*, 2nd edn, New York: Macmillan.

Loane, B. (1994), 'The FARMTREE model: computing financial returns from agroforestry', paper to conference *Faces of Farm Forestry*, Australian Forest Growers, Launceston, Tasmania.

Lock, A. (1987), 'Integrating group judgements in subjective forecasts', in G. Wright and P. Ayton (eds.), *Judgmental forecasting*, Chichester: Wiley, pp. 109–27.

Lorie, J.H. and Savage, L.J. (1955). 'Three problems in rationing capital', *Journal of Business* 28: 229–39.

Louviere, J.J., Hensher, D.A. and Swait, J.D. (2000), *Stated Choice Methods: Analysis and Applications*, Cambridge: Cambridge University Press.

Madridrakos, S., Wheelwright, S.C. and McGee, V.E. (1983), *Forecasting Methods and Applications*, 2nd edn, Chichester: Wiley.

Madura, J. (1995), *International Financial Management*, 4th edn, St Paul, Minn.: West Publishing Company.

Metcalfe, M. (1995). *Forecasting Profit*, Boston: Kluwer Academic Publishers.

Middlemiss, P. and Knowles, L. (1996), *AEM Agroforestry Estate Model, User Guide for v. 4.0*, Rotorua: New Zealand Forest Research Institute.

Miles, M E., Haney, R.L. and Berens, G. (1996), *Real Estate Development – Principles and Practices*, 2nd edn, Washington: Urban Land Institute.

Miller, M.H. and Upton, C.W. (1976), 'Leasing, buying and the cost of capital Services', *Journal of Finance* 31: 761–86.

Mills, T.C. (1993), *The Econometric Modelling of Financial Time Series*, Cambridge: Cambridge University Press.

Moyer, R., McGuigan, J. and Kretlow, W. (2001), *Contemporary Financial Management*, 8th edn, Cincinnati: South-Western College Publishing.

Mueller, G. (1997), 'Cycle theories', *Property Australia* 11(5): 10–13 & 11(6): 8–9.

Naylor, T.H., Banintfy, J.L., Burdick D.S. and Chu, K. (1966), *Computer Simulation Techniques*, New York: Wiley.

Nourse, H.O. (1990), *Managerial Real Estate*, Englewood Cliffs: Prentice-Hall.

Parente, F.J., Anderson, J.K., Myers, P. and O'Brien, T. (1984), 'An examination of factors contributing to Delphi accuracy', *Journal of Forecasting* 3: 173–82.

Pyhrr, S.A., Cooper, J.R., Wofford, L.E., Kapplin, P.K. and Lapides, S.D. (1989), *Real Estate Investment Strategy Analysis Decisions*, 2nd edn, New York: Wiley.

Reinhardt, U. (1973), 'Break-even analysis for Lockheed's TriStar: an application of financial theory', *Journal of Finance* 28: 821–38.

Robichek, A. and Myers, S. (1966), 'Conceptual problems in the use of risk-adjusted discount rates', *Journal of Finance* 21: 727–30.

Rowe, G. and Wright, G. (1999), 'The Delphi technique as a forecasting tool: issues and analysis', *International Journal of Forecasting* 15: 353–75.

Rowland, P.J. (1997), *Property Investments and Their Financing*, 2nd edn, Sydney: LBC Information Services.

Royal Institution of Chartered Surveyors (1994), *Understanding the Property Cycle*, London: Royal Institution of Chartered Surveyors.

Russell, J.S., Cameron, D.M., Whan, I.F., Beech, D.F., Prestwidge, D.B. and Rance, S.J. (1993), 'Rainforest trees as a new crop for Australia', *Forest Ecology and Management* 60: 41–58.

Schoemaker, P.J.H. (1991), 'When and how to use scenario planning: a heuristic approach with illustration', *Journal of Forecasting* 10: 549–64.

Shannon, R.E. (1975), *Systems Simulation: the Art and the Science*, Englewood Cliffs: Prentice-Hall.

Shapiro, A. (1996), *Multinational Financial Management*, 5th edn, Englewood Cliffs: Prentice-Hall.

Thompson, D. (2001), Personal communication, CARE Pty Ltd., Armidale.

Vlek, C. and Otten, W. (1987), 'Judgmental handling of energy scenarios', in G. Wright and P. Ayton (eds.), *Judgmental Forecasting*, Wiley Chichester: 267–89.

Weingartner, H.M. (1977), 'Capital rationing: *n* authors in search of plot', *Journal of Finance* 32: 1403–32.

Whigham, D. (1998), *Quantitative Business Methods Using Excel*, New York: Oxford University Press.

Wright, G. and Ayton, P. (1987), 'The psychology of forecasting', in G. Wright and P. Ayton (eds.), *Judgmental Forecasting*, Chichester: Wiley, pp. 83–104.

Index

Lightning Source UK Ltd.
Milton Keynes UK
14 August 2010

158380UK00001B/9/A